HIZBULLAH

In The Name Of God, The Merciful, The Compassionate

Naim Qassem

HIZBULLAH

The Story from Within

Translated from the Arabic by
Dalia Khalil

SAQI

ISBN: 978-0-86356-699-8

First published in hardback by Saqi in 2005
Reprinted in 2007 and 2023

This updated paperback edition published by Saqi in 2010

A full CIP record for this book is available from the British Library.
A full CIP record for this book is available from the Library of Congress.

Printed and bound by CPI Group (UK) Ltd, Croydon, CR0 4YY

SAQI
26 Westbourne Grove, London W2 5RH, UK
2398 Doswell Avenue, Saint Paul, Minnesota, 55108, USA
Verdun, Beirut, Lebanon
www.saqibooks.com

Contents

Maps

Preface

At a time when the Islamic banner was perceived as an unattractive, inadequate source of persuasion in the face of confrontation against Israeli occupation and international pressure, Hizbullah emerged as a distinct party *because* of its very adoption of this Islamic banner, as well as of its conduct as a resistance force. Islamic resistance operations were of such unique success that they earned the praise of supporters of liberation and adherents of justice, as well as the wonder and disbelief of the occupiers. Enemy aggression was thwarted many times, and the occupiers' dominant position shaken. Hizbullah's importance rose further with actual victory, achieved on May 25, 2000, when Israeli troops were forced to withdraw from Lebanon as a result of Hizbullah operations – an unprecedented achievement in fifty years of struggle with the Israeli enemy.

Many questions surrounded Hizbullah: about the Party's reasons for its inception, its goals, vision and values, about the time-frame it has set as an objective ... Is Hizbullah a temporary faction playing a definite role, it has been asked, or does it have the potential for continuity?

Equally, many answers, analyses and assumptions were put forward. Numerous published writings blemished the Party's image, with shreds of facts gathered mostly in presumptuous fashion. Gradually, the truth emerged through Hizbullah's open and declared mode of work, through its field operations, the expressions of its leaders and the practical implementation by its partisans and institutions. Where, then, is the truth amidst this amalgam of facts and suppositions?

Since the circumstances surrounding the Party's inception forced the deployment of all recruits directly in the field of operational resistance, little time was left for Party leaders to draw up frameworks and articulate visions or write manifestos, *raisons d'être* and manuals. Although such guiding beliefs were quite clear to Party leaders, they had yet to be laid in a format that addressed the queries of intellectuals, academics and concerned groups.

Many attempts were made to write about Hizbullah, by close Party supporters, the non-aligned and challengers alike. The Party itself had gathered and published many speeches, declarations, interviews and records of activist work, in order to create an asset base to aid in the Party's overall direction. A number of researchers conducted special interviews with Party leaders and activists, the better to present their direct and personal opinions. However, given the Party's level of recognition, presence and achievement – all realized within a short and critical time-span in the midst of a blazing region that is set for many more developments – whatever has been written thus far is insufficient to document and analyze this robust experience.

I found myself facing the responsibility of contributing to such documentation, so I embarked on this self-set mission despite my time constraints and the effort required. This work expresses my understanding of the Hizbullah order and its experience and future plans as gathered through my direct involvement with the Party since its inception and in various capacities.

Speaking of the 'order' is imperative, for it delineates the vision and goals of this Party that have sprung from a profound belief in Islam: *The religion before Allah is Islam [surrender to God's will and guidance].*[1] Hizbullah's framing of all issues emanates from such belief, and the Party's practical path is interconnected with the principles of faith it carries. It is not possible to generalize as to what 'Islamic' experiences concern, for many rationalizations exist and factions differ in their direction. The necessity to specify and scrutinize details thus emerges. The Islamic Resistance found a place in the hearts of many Middle Eastern populations, and the core reason for achieving such stature has to do with the order it followed: that order which reveals the foundations of the experience.

The 'experience' in this book reveals a resistance project characterized by a bountiful *jihad (holy war)* offering. The approach to Party organization and public action, and the more important milestones in Hizbullah's history, are laid out. The Party's stance with respect to the Palestinian cause, liberating the land from occupation, participation in a non-Islamic governmental system, issues of concern to the populace, and relationships with various parties and factions whether local or regional are all laid out. A summarized chronicle of the Party's key milestones is provided, along with its viewpoints and approach, and the circumstances surrounding these major issues.

As for the future, this outlook is based on our perception of historical divine intercession and of the state of nations and what governs their actions. As such, we were able to envisage a number of possibilities, all of which are worth consideration. Irrespective of the extent to which international players dominate our world, their influence cannot determine the fate of nations and

---

1. The Qur'an, surah no. 3, *al-'Imran*, verse 19.

peoples. *Such days (of varying fortunes) We give to men and men by turns.*[1] I could only find it appropriate to relay my personal view of the future.

This book can be used to draw an outline for further academic work on Hizbullah, which could fill volumes. I have sought brevity, and the provision of a general overview that can answer many key questions, and describe the approach adopted by this Party and its general direction. This is a book for those who would like to know or increase their knowledge, for those who would like to remember or document their memories, or for those who would like to research or benefit from material for their subjects.

While first outlining this book, I was under the impression that my library of information and documents would suffice as a research tool. The need for more soon became obvious. Many fellow partisans provided actual recollections and details, and research was extended to cover Hizbullah Council decisions and reports, issues of *Al-'Ahd* (*Al-Intiqad*) newspaper since its inception in 1948 and many other documents that served towards creating this book. References were quoted where the source was a clear document (book, newspaper or circular); recollections and analysis were used where sources were unavailable. I would hereby like to thank all of those who have assisted in attaining this work and in making it available to readers.

As a Hizbullah insider, I hope that I have successfully managed to communicate the facts and to inform the reader, with whom the final judgement rests.

To God I owe any success. Peace be upon you.

Naim Qassem

---

1. Surah no. 3, *al-'Imran*, verse 140.

Introduction to the Third English Edition

Praise be to God, the guide, protector and benefactor; prayers and peace be upon the great Prophet Muhammad (PBUH), the leader and exemplar; on the Imams (PBUT), the protectors of the faith and the custodians of the message; on the martyrs who have lit the way for humankind; and upon you and the mercy of God and his blessings.

The Middle East has been subjected to successive waves of imperialist exploitation over the years, which have shaped its current realities and territorial boundaries. The Sykes-Picot Treaty in 1916 and the Balfour Declaration in 1917 created the Israeli entity, leading to recurrent challenges that continue to impact upon the region. High-handed attempts by the United States have subsequently been made to control the region and establish a secure and powerful Israel, whether by occupying Afghanistan and Iraq, making repeated threats against Syria, preventing Iran from developing nuclear energy for peaceful purposes or attacking resistance movements such as Hizbullah, Hamas and Islamic Jihad at every opportunity.

How can the Middle East achieve stability and lasting peace, given the challenges it faces? Is it possible to find reasonable solutions to the problems of the region while two issues contrary to the interests of its peoples persist? These are, namely: the American project for a new Middle East that will allow the US to dominate the area and divide it geopolitically according to its interests, and an ambitious Israel that continues to occupy, expand and settle territory at the expense of Palestinian people and forms the pole around which the countries of the region orbit as economic and political dependents.

Although there are vague proposals that advocate sovereignty and independence for countries in the region, the US and the international community shamelessly intervene to impose conditions and resort to force if they encounter resistance – as happened in the case of the US invasion and occupation of Iraq as well as the Israeli aggression against Lebanon in July 2006. While the major powers pay lip-service to notions of democracy and popular choice, they support repressive authoritarian regimes and reject the outcome of popular elections such as the one that brought Hamas to power. Where is the democracy in that?

There is talk about human rights, but such slogans are selectively applied. Israel is said to be acting in legitimate self-defence when it kills and injures Palestinians, but the wounding of one Israeli is regarded as an act of aggression that must be condemned. The massacres carried out by Israel in Qana and elsewhere during the 2006 war against Lebanon have also gone unpunished.

Iraq under US Occupation

When George W. Bush assumed the presidency of the US in 2001, he commissioned a group of advisors, headed by Richard N. Haass, to formulate a working programme on the US role in the Middle East. Among its conclusions was a proposal that the US should distract the region by concentrating on Iraq, taking advantage of the fact that the Arab world had been in conflict since Saddam Hussein's invasion of Kuwait. Haass counselled against trying to find an ultimate solution to the Palestine–Israel question, as the key issues dividing the two sides were unlikely to be resolved. As he put it: 'The best way to deal with conflicts that are not yet nearing a solution is to lessen interference.' Iraq, on the other hand, was 'a special case when compared with Israel. It represents a threat to the neighbouring countries, while Israel faces a terrorist threat from within.'[1] In addition, the case of Palestine united Arabs against Israel, while the case of Iraq was contentious and divided them – thereby making it easier for the US to gain control in the region.

The events in New York of September 11, 2001 directed the US's attention away from the Middle East to Afghanistan, where al-Qaʻida, the group held responsible for the attacks, was based. The war against Afghanistan took precedence; Iraq was relegated to the second stage of the campaign rather than the first, as Haass and his group had originally suggested.

Though an international team of inspectors had failed to find any evidence of 'weapons of mass destruction' in Iraq, the Bush administration launched its invasion and occupation of that country on the pretext of the existence of such weapons. US politicians, along with military and security officials, bombarded the world and the American people with fictitious and mendacious evidence that, although quickly shown to be false, nevertheless became the accepted version of events in the media. However, the lack of sufficient and compelling evidence meant that the invasion failed to obtain the backing of the United Nations Security Council,

---

1. Article by Richard N. Haass in *al-Sharq al-Awsat*, September 4, 2001; see also the article by the same author in *al-Hayat*, September 30, 2002.

and countries such as France, Russia and Germany withheld their support. The US remained determined to proceed with its plans and the invasion eventually took place in March 2003. The US invasion of Iraq had three main objectives:

1. To gain control of Iraq's immense oil reserves, the second largest in the world, thereby enabling the US to control the oil market and guarantee its own oil requirements.

2. To allay Israeli concerns about Iraq's growing military power. Backed by various international sources and openly funded by the Gulf States, Iraq had obtained an arsenal of heavy and sophisticated weaponry as a result of Saddam's war against the Islamic Republic of Iran (1980–8) and now had the strongest army in the region after Israel. Israel, like its US sponsor, believes that the only way to guarantee its dominant position in the region is by ensuring that it is militarily superior to its neighbours.

3. To strengthen political control of the wider Arab region, using Iraq as a gateway. Iraq enjoys a significant geopolitical location, surrounded by the Gulf States, Iran – with which it shares the longest land border of any country in the region – and Syria. Control of Iraq, therefore, is a key factor in shaping the Middle East.

Although the occupation has lasted for more than five years to date, the US will not leave the country until it has concluded a political security treaty[1] that will make Iraq a US protectorate,

---

1. 'The ten-point US–Iraqi security agreement will transform Iraq into a US

stripped of decision-making power at regional and international levels, and which will allow the US to control the country's politics, security, oil and culture. It is in US interests for the contagious sectarian civil war to continue, as it provides an excuse for it to remain in the country on the pretext of maintaining security. However, the situation has got partly out of control.

Parliamentary and presidential elections are not enough to provide for popular choice and independence, because they are conducted under occupation and are therefore subject to control by the occupying power. Ministers are unable to take decisions or carry out activities without first receiving the consent of the US representative in charge of the ministry.

Hizbullah considers that the continued US occupation of Iraq is unacceptable on whatever pretext, and that the Security Council has the power to help Iraq by bringing in a limited and targeted international force to replace US rule and provide international cover. It also believes that the Iraqi resistance has the right to act to expel the occupiers. Hizbullah condemns every bombing and attack on civilians and Iraqis in general, and regards such attacks as completely unjustified. It rejects all forms of factional strife, and believes that Iraqis themselves

---

military base and strip it of its decision-making powers and sovereignty. The agreement gives US forces the right to establish military bases; to own and operate its own prisons, businesses, roads and land to which no one else has access; to capture anyone who threatens its security and peace without permission from the Iraqi government; and to use Iraqi land, water and airspace to attack any country that threatens international peace and security. In addition, the agreement extends immunity to US forces, civilian contractors and security companies belonging to them, and denies the Iraqi government and the Iraqi legal system the right to hold US forces and companies accountable for their actions.' See *al-Hayat*, June 15, 2008, and www.babil.info.

have the capability and competence to maintain their territorial integrity in the face of US occupation and to make political, security, economic, legal and future decisions that will benefit their country.

The US has failed both to impose its authority on Iraq and to drag Iraq's neighbours into the problem because it is in the position of occupier. Despite statements from officials that the political process is moving forward, and that conditions in the country are improving, Haass – in an article about the new Middle East – described the situation in Iraq after three years of occupation as follows: 'Iraq, traditionally a center of Arab power, will remain messy for years to come, with a weak central government, a divided society, and regular sectarian violence. At worst, it will become a failed state wracked by an all-out civil war that will draw in its neighbors.'[1]

The peoples of the region will not put up with a return to colonialism, mandates or high commissioners any longer. Other countries in the region, particularly Iran and Syria, have realized the magnitude of the damage inflicted by the occupation and are working to weaken the US position in Iraq in order to protect their own interests and security. The only solution now is for the US to withdraw from Iraq, to stop tearing it apart and using it as a base from which to tear the region itself apart. Perhaps what has taken place in Iraq will make Americans as well as the rest of the world realize that stability can only be achieved through the establishment of a properly thought-out political process within Iraq and between the countries in the region. Such a solution would respect the interests of Iraq and take into account the interests of the region as well. It is no longer possible to use

---

1. *As-Safir*, November 11, 2006; translated from *Foreign Affairs*.

international military or political might to impose a solution by force against the wishes of the people, who have become more conscious of what is appropriate for them in a changing and complex world.

The Iran–Syria Axis

With the collapse of the Soviet Union, a new, unipolar world order came into existence, dominated by a US intent on promoting its own policies and securing its interests. Given its vital significance, the Middle East was at the top of the US agenda. The US was not new to the area. It already had, as allies, Israel as well as a large number of Arab countries classified as 'moderate' because their policies were in line with US interests.

The Islamic Republic of Iran, which was brought into being by Imam Khomeini (May God sanctify his secret) on February 11, 1979, has refused to submit to US demands and has pursued a policy of non-alignment since its inception. It regards autonomy and political independence as the best way of serving its interests, and has rejected attempts to keep it as a base for the US as it had been during the time of the Shah. Iran has consistently espoused the cause of Palestinian resistance. It opened the first Palestinian embassy, and has continued to support Palestinian aspirations for an autonomous state with the right to defend its territory. Angered by this stance, and fearing that it was losing control of the country, the US instigated a boycott and a campaign of oppression that has continued to the present. It incited Iraq to launch an eight-year war against Iran, supported groups opposed to the regime and attempted to bring about regime change from within. Recently it has raised the issue of Iran's 'nuclear power' at the UN Security Council and urged the international community to stop Iran from acquiring a nuclear capability on the pretext that it will be used for military rather than peaceful means.

Syria, as the only state not to have accepted a humiliating treaty with Israel, has played a distinctive role in the region following the signing of the Camp David Accords between Egypt and Israel and the Wadi Araba Treaty between Israel and Jordan. It remains determined to regain all its territory in the Golan Heights, though it is unable to ignore the fact that the balance of military power is weighted in favour of Israel; it fears that it will be exposed to a debilitating embargo, which will end its role in the region and destabilize its regime.

Syria believes that supporting the Palestinian resistance will not only help the Palestinians liberate their land but also establish a new balance of power in the area more suited to Syrian stability than the constant threat of Israeli expansion. Similarly, it has supported the Hizbullah-led resistance in Lebanon, believing that a strong and resistant Lebanon able to withstand Israeli pressure will strengthen its own position, while a vulnerable one will only damage it.

The political map has been redrawn, and the region is now polarized between those who accept US plans for it and those who oppose them. The US has effectively created two axes – one that complies with American policy (an essential component of which is unequivocal support for Israel) and an opposition axis consisting of bodies that reject it, namely Iran, Syria, the Palestinian resistance led by Hamas and Islamic Jihad and the Lebanese resistance led by Hizbullah.

Since its inception, the Islamic Republic of Iran has adopted policies in keeping with its principles and vision. It has supported the Lebanese and Palestinian resistance movements against Israel, and now rejects the US occupation of Iraq, which it regards as contrary to Iraqi as well as Iranian interests. It believes that the US presence in a neighbouring country, as well as American plans for a Greater Middle East, pose a threat to its own security. It has forged a fundamental and important alliance with Syria based on Islamic solidarity and the need for a united front against US aggression that will enable both countries to survive and maintain their roles in the region.

Syria has been involved in the struggle against the Israeli entity since its establishment. It has backed resistance movements in Lebanon and in occupied Palestine, not only for reasons of geographical proximity but also because the existence of strong resistance movements in both countries strengthens its own position. It has obtained a strong regional ally and actor through its relationship with Iran; Iran, for its part, has obtained a means of communicating and interacting with Arab countries with which it shares common concerns.

The resistance movements in Palestine and Lebanon stem from the same root. Both parties are defending their land against occupation and the continuing dangers posed by Israel's expansionism. By cooperating, they are able to continue their struggle against Israel and prevent it from gaining power and achieving its objectives at the expense of the peoples of Palestine, Lebanon and the region as a whole. Such resistance requires support. If such support exists unconditionally and complies with the interests of the recipients and providers alike, there is no reason not to be clear and open about it. The Lebanese and Palestinian resistance movements are proud to acknowledge the help they receive from Iran and Syria, as it is compatible with their aspirations and is given freely and without any political strings attached. Is it reasonable to deny the resistance the right to seek support while Israel receives US$3 billion in aid every year, in addition to arms and others forms of assistance? If other Arab or Islamic countries were to offer unconditional support to the resistance, they would accept it as they have accepted Iran's and Syria's support.

The Iran–Syria axis that has developed in opposition to the US–Israel axis is a defensive alliance that stands counter to subordination and occupation, the imposition of US hegemony and the legalization of the Israeli entity at the expense of the peoples of occupied Palestine and the region. The struggle between the two blocs has impacted upon the region as a whole, as countries have been drawn into the crisis brought about by the Israeli and US occupiers and their expansionist aims.

Palestine is a Central Issue

The proposed solutions to the Palestinian issue have always been based on giving Israel the territory and stability it wants and depriving the Palestinians of the simplest sustenance, preventing the return of refugees and refusing to recognize the most sacred nature of Jerusalem. This course will not bring about a solution, but will only generate more problems.

The decision to use excessive force against Palestinians has deepened the crisis, made a solution more difficult and made the Palestinians more determined to resist. American and Israeli strategies, which have included fomenting sedition among

Palestinians, creating dissension between the Fatah and Hamas authorities and besieging Hamas in Gaza in order to bring about its downfall, achieve nothing. Such moves are clearly aimed at destroying the ability of the Palestinian people and their representatives to choose freely, and forcing them to come to the negotiating table not as equal partners in dialogue but as supplicants to whom the Israelis will dictate a solution. The pursuit of such actions by Israel and its sponsors, starting with Madrid and Oslo and followed over the years by the 'Road Map' and most recently the Annapolis conference, has only led to more complications.

The Bush proposal for a Palestinian–Israeli state amounts to nothing but a useless slogan. Experience has shown that its only purpose is to demonstrate US interest in the Palestinian issue. The administration has merely put a muddled framework for a solution in place and made no serious effort to put pressure on Israel, provide justice for Palestinians or draw up practical steps or a timetable that would shape the substance of the solution.

The US realizes that in order to secure support from influential Arab countries for its plans for a new Middle East, it must demonstrate its interest in finding a solution to the Palestinian issue. These regimes can then justify their subordination to US policy by pretending they are lobbying on behalf of the Palestinians.

We believe that agreement on a solution is deadlocked. Israel wants nominal negotiations that do not come close to obtaining a final solution and do not answer difficult questions such as the status of Jerusalem, the issue of refugees and the nature of the Palestinian state. It wants a say in the form of the Palestinian Authority with which it negotiates and refuses to recognize the choices made by the Palestinian people, who have voted for a legislative assembly in which Hamas commands a majority.

Palestinian National Authority President Mahmoud Abbas is not able to give the security guarantees that Israel is looking for, nor does he possess the legal authority that qualifies him to speak on behalf of all Palestinians. He and his movement in the West Bank are subject to Israeli restrictions as well as Arab and international pressures, which make him ineffectual. His position is further undermined by Israeli statements about his weakness, and their mistrust in his ability to bring about any progress.

Hamas, along with other Palestinian resistance factions and the Palestinian people as a whole – most notably in Gaza – believes that resistance is the only means of guaranteeing the continuance of the Palestinian project and ensuring that a solution is not simply imposed on the people for which future generations will have to pay. What is proposed is humiliating and unacceptable; however, shored up by its ideological beliefs, Hamas is prepared for sacrifice, martyrdom and patience. The brutal attacks on Gaza and the killing of women, children and the elderly in an effort to bring down Hamas will not benefit anyone; rather, such aggression will increase Palestinian commitment to the cause. Resistance offers the possibility of cherished hope, while submission only leads to certain loss.

It is impossible for Bush to fulfil his promise to find a solution before the end of his presidency in 2009. Any action undertaken by the US under this administration has been, like those in Israel, no more than a way of gaining time while waiting for fundamental changes in the region.

Lebanon in the Eye of the Storm

The Bush administration has made many efforts to eradicate Hizbullah in Lebanon. It believes that the resistance poses an obstacle to its new Middle Eastern strategy and also stands in the way of Israeli plans for resettling Palestinians in Lebanon and for securing its northern front in the same way it has secured its other Arab fronts, in order to isolate the Palestinians and restrict their options.

Israel, like the US, has persistently attempted to eliminate Hizbullah; to this end, it launched a major offensive against the resistance in July 1993, followed by an even larger offensive in April 1996 – but in both cases it failed to meet its objective. Exhausted by the military campaign waged by the resistance, Israel was forced to withdraw its troops from Lebanon on July 25, 2000, though it continues to occupy land near the border including the Shebaa Farms and Kfar Shouba Hills, which has justified the need for continued resistance. Hizbullah remained extremely cautious about the Israeli withdrawal from Lebanon, and believed it was necessary to be prepared for the onset of a new Israeli war.

On September 2, 2004, at the joint request of the US and France, the Security Council issued Resolution 1559. This marked the beginning of the dangerous political stalemate that has persisted in Lebanon ever since, and was the first serious expression of the US's determination to take control of the Lebanese dossier from Syria. It was also the beginning of regional and international confrontation over how to influence the choices of Lebanon. Resolution 1559 states that the Security Council:

1. Reaffirms its call for strict respect for the sovereignty, territorial integrity, unity and political independence of Lebanon under the sole and exclusive authority of the Government of Lebanon throughout Lebanon.

2. Calls upon all remaining foreign forces to withdraw from Lebanon.

3. Calls for the disbanding and disarmament of all Lebanese and non-Lebanese militias.

4. Supports the extension of the control of the Government of Lebanon to all Lebanese territories.

5. Declares its support for a free and fair electoral process in Lebanon's upcoming presidential election, conducted according to Lebanese constitutional rules devised without foreign interference or influence.[1]

Four points in the resolution proved particularly contentious. First was the call for the withdrawal of the Syrian army from Lebanon referred to in articles 1 and 2; second was the call for the disarming of Hizbullah and the elimination of its resistance wing, implied by the phrase, 'all the Lebanese militias' in article 3; third, also in article 3, was the call for the disarming of Palestinian camps in a manner that did not form part of an overall solution to the Palestinian question in the region, implied by the phrase 'non-Lebanese'; fourth was interference in the choice of a new president, by preventing the extension of Emile Lahhoud's

---

1. *An-Nahar*, September 4, 2004.

mandate for a further three years after it came to an end on November 24, 2004, implied in article 5.

In order to put pressure on the Lebanese Chamber of Deputies not to renew President Lahhoud's mandate, on the basis of article 5 of the resolution, the Security Council rushed through publication of Resolution 1559 one day ahead of the sitting on September 3, in which deputies were due to vote on extending the presidential term of office. However, in accordance with authorized Lebanese constitutional mechanisms, the Chamber of Deputies approved a constitutional amendment that would allow the president to stay in office for a further one-off period of three years, with 96 out of the 128 deputies voting in favour – representing 75 per cent of the total number of deputies.[1] An international campaign to not recognize the outcome of the presidential election was begun, which lasted for a further three years characterized by turbulence, insecurity and political instability.

The assassination of Prime Minister Rafiq al-Hariri on February 14, 2005 marked a distinct and dangerous development in Lebanese affairs and provided an excuse for further international interference. The US believed that the withdrawal of Syrian troops from Lebanon, which took place on April 30, would weaken Hizbullah and put the question of 'Hizbullah's disarmament' on the negotiating table in accordance with Resolution 1559. However, the so-called Quartet Agreement – the electoral alliance concluded ahead of the May 29, 2005 elections between Hizbullah, the Amal Movement, the Future Movement (headed by Saad al-Hariri) and the Progressive Socialist Movement (headed by Walid Jumblatt) – eased pressure on Hizbullah.

---

1. *Ad-Diyar*, September 4, 2004.

Under the agreement, the four parties pledged the following: to form an alliance in the parliamentary elections in different regions in Lebanon; to use every means in their power to uncover the perpetrators of al-Hariri's assassination; and to commit to the view, held by the late prime minister, that the resistance should hold onto its weapons until the remaining Lebanese territory was liberated and until it could be seen whether developments in the region would lead to a settlement. The agreement gave the Future Movement and the Progressive Socialist Party a majority of deputies in the Chamber of Deputies in return for an assurance that they would not touch the resistance or its weapons.

The Party Participates in Government

On April 18, 2005, a minister accountable to Hizbullah joined Prime Minister Najib Mikati's cabinet. This was the first time since its inception that the Party had participated in government, and the decision to do so came about after a series of important events – the most significant of which were the adoption of Resolution 1559, the assassination of al-Hariri and the start of discussions on the withdrawal of Syrian troops from Lebanon, which took place on April 3. It was based on the following rationales:

1. That the government would be responsible for the transition period leading up to the holding of parliamentary elections on May 29, and for establishing the role of the incoming government. Unlike governments formed under the Syrians' presence in Lebanon, the new government would play an active role in delivering policy rather than refusing this role

as it had done in the past. It was this responsibility that would make the government's role so essential.

2. That Hizbullah expected the US and the international community to continue to intervene in Lebanese affairs in order to force the country to pursue policies that would benefit Israel and harm Lebanese interests – despite the continuing threat posed by Israel, its occupation of the Shebaa Farms, the Lebanese prisoners under its control and its daily violations of Lebanese airspace. Hizbullah believed that by having representatives in government, joining with allies to protect the resistance and discussing this position with other forces in the government, it could bring about a shift in the balance of power that would help get policies adopted that were consistent with its vision. It also believed representation could provide it with a suitable means to defend its political programme and facilitate its adoption by the government.

The number of ministerial positions held by a party would not be its only means of influencing political, economic and social decisions within the government. Its public presence would also have a bearing on the formulation of policy, as would the popularity of its political allies and the nature of its alliances. The ministerial statement would be of fundamental importance in charting the way forward for the government as it interacted with influential countries in the region on matters requiring decisions. The government would exercise an active role in determining the direction of the country, rather than merely acting in an executive capacity as it had done in the past.

For the above reasons, the Party played an even more active

role in the government that followed, which was formed by Prime Minister Fouad Siniora on July 19, after parliamentary elections were held. This time, the cabinet included a minister from Hizbullah, another who was close to the Party and a third who was selected in agreement with the Amal Movement. Following a prolonged debate on the resistance, a statement was issued in the interests of continuity and support. It referred to the resistance in two paragraphs, declaring 'support for our brave resistance' in the first, and calling for 'quiet dialogue on the options available to us all within the framework of the Arab struggle against Israel and its occupation and ambitions, and the need to fortify Lebanon at the same time'.

The second paragraph was more explicit: 'The government considers that the Lebanese resistance is a true and natural expression of the national right of the Lebanese people to liberate their land and to defend their honour in the face of Israeli aggression and threats and ambitions, and believes that it is working for the complete liberation of Lebanese territory.'[1]

In the second half of November 2005, about seven months after it had been set up, Progressive Socialist Party leader Walid Jumblatt declared that the Quartet Agreement was dead. 'The Quartet Agreement never existed and will never exist,'[2] he said, giving Hizbullah's stance on Syria and its unnecessary retention of its weapons as his reasons for leaving. In a parallel development, ministers from the Amal Movement and Hizbullah suspended their participation in the cabinet on December 12. This followed the assassination of the journalist Gebran Tueni and the subsequent decision by the government, taken at a rapidly

---

1. *As-Safir,* July 26, 2005.
2. *Al-Mustaqbal,* December 30, 2005.

convened session held on the same day, to call for the setting up of an international tribunal to look into the assassination of al-Hariri without studying or discussing its status or powers. The ministers concerned believed this contradicted the spirit of the Quartet Agreement and the national partnership government.

A short while later, deputy Saad al-Hariri announced he was leaving the Quartet Agreement and no longer considered himself bound by obligations to it. This, in turn, precipitated an announcement by the Secretary General of Hizbullah, His Eminence Hassan Nasrallah, that the Quartet Agreement no longer existed. When the ministers of Hizbullah and the Amal Movement returned to government seven weeks later, he said: 'Today we are once again returning to government. The first political outcome is the ending of the Quartet Agreement. A member of the Quartet has ignored it and denied its origin and existence.'[1]

The Memorandum of Joint Understanding

Hizbullah and the Free Patriotic Movement headed by General Michel Aoun reached an understanding during this period that marked a significant development in Lebanese politics. Officially titled 'The Memorandum of Joint Understanding between Hizbullah and the Free Patriotic Movement', the agreement was reached after several months of negotiations and announced on February 6, 2006 at a joint meeting at the Church of St Michael, which was attended by Secretary General Nasrallah and General Aoun. The understanding had an undeniable impact

---

1. Ibid, February 4, 2006.

on the Lebanese political scene, creating an effective bridge of communication between the Shi'ite and Christian religious blocs, in which Hizbullah and the Free Patriotic Movement enjoyed broad representation, respectively. It strengthened the position of both parties domestically and laid the essential foundations for what later came to be known as the Lebanese opposition. The understanding also identified a mechanism for dealing with the weapons of the resistance as part of an overall national defence strategy. Such a strategy should be based on dialogue about the role of the resistance and its weapons rather than calls for its disarmament as outlined in Resolution 1559. This was made clear in item 10 of the document.[1]

Protecting Lebanon

The protection of Lebanon and the preservation of its independence and sovereignty are national responsibilities and duties, guaranteed by international charters and the Universal Declaration of Human Rights – particularly in confronting any threats or dangers that may harm them, irrespective of where these dangers come from. Therefore, carrying arms is not an objective in itself, but a noble and sacred means that is exercised by any group whose land is occupied, as political resistance. In this context, the question of Hizbullah's arms must be addressed as part of a comprehensive approach that falls within two parameters: first, retaining these arms relies on justifications reflecting national consensus and constituting sources of strength for Lebanon. Second, conditions must be

---

1. Document published in the Lebanese press, February 7, 2005.

objectively defined that would eliminate the justifications for keeping these weapons.

Since Israel occupies the Shebaa Farms, imprisons Lebanese resistance fighters and threatens Lebanon, the Lebanese people must assume their responsibilities and share the burden of protecting their country, safeguarding its existence and security and preserving its independence by:

1. Liberating the Shebaa Farms from Israeli occupation.
2. Liberating Lebanese prisoners from Israeli jails.
3. Protecting Lebanon from the dangers posed by Israel by formulating a national defence strategy to which the Lebanese agree and in which they are involved by assuming its burdens and benefiting from its outcomes.

Lebanese Dialogue

The period following the dissolution of the Quartet Agreement witnessed changes in the Lebanese political line-up as the various parties regrouped; the Future Movement and Progressive Socialist Party adopted opposing positions to Hizbullah and the Amal Movement, and Hizbullah and the Free Patriotic Movement concluded the Memorandum of Joint Understanding – even though the latter had been part of what was later to be called the March 14 Coalition (named after the popular rally organized to mark the four-week anniversary of Prime Minister al-Hariri's assassination). Political disagreements threatened to further complicate an already turbulent situation. The Speaker of Parliament, Nabih Berri, invited representatives from all parties with members in the Chamber of Deputies to take part in a round-table discussion. Everyone agreed, and the talks were scheduled to start in the Chamber on March 2, 2006. Fourteen leaders, representing the various political forces, attended together with their assistants; the agenda included the following points:[1]

1. The investigation into Prime Minister al-Hariri's assassination.
2. The situation in the Palestinian camps with particular reference to weapons.
3. Syrian-Lebanese relations.
4. Lebanese claims to the Shebaa Farms.
5. The position of President of the Republic.
6. The resistance and its weapons.

Several discussions were held, which led to agreement on the first four items; however, the fifth proved more difficult. The Future Movement, the Progressive Socialist Party and the Christian Qornet Shehwan coalition took the decision to bring down President Émile Lahhoud before his legal mandate expired on November 24, 2007, arguing that Resolution 1559 had 'declared its support for a free and fair electoral process in the coming presidential elections' and that President Lahhoud had been elected for a further three years as a result of Syrian pressure; they called for his mandate to be terminated and for new elections to be held, a move rejected by the opposition (comprising Hizbullah, the Amal Movement, the Free Patriotic Movement, various leading authorities including Sunni former Prime Minister Omar Karami, Dr Fathi Yakan, former Druze minister Talal Arslan,

1. *As-Safir*, article on the 2006 dialogue, December 30, 2006.

former minister Wiam Wahhab, and former MP Faisal Daoud, as well as members of other secular, popular and nationalist parties).

Delegates were unable to agree on the presidency, and it was decided to defer talks on the subject and discuss the question of the resistance and its weapons instead. At a meeting on May 16, 2006, it was concurred that the problem needed to be addressed through dialogue and agreement rather than by force or foreign interference, and that a defensive strategy should be drawn up by Lebanon itself; but the discussion was not concluded.

Israel's War against Lebanon

On July 12, 2006, Hizbullah captured two Israeli soldiers on the Lebanese Palestine border in the hope that the Party could exchange them for Lebanese prisoners being held by Israel despite attempts to gain their release through political channels. Using the liberation of its soldiers as a pretext, Israel launched an all-out war on Hizbullah, which it subsequently called 'The Second Lebanese War'. The thirty-four-day-long conflict was called 'The True Promise' by Hizbullah.

The Party did not expect the capture of the soldiers to result in a full-scale war, though it had been prepared for possible Israeli reprisals on Lebanon before or after the incident. Nevertheless, it had readied itself for some form of attack; the liberation of Lebanon on May 25, 2000 convinced the Party that Israel would renew hostilities against the country at some point in the future in order to minimize Hizbullah's offensive capability and prevent it from opposing Israeli expansionist plans in the region.

The decision to go to war was taken by the US and implemented by Israel. American and Israeli statements, informed press reports and the Israeli-commissioned Winograd Report enquiring into the 2006 war have subsequently made clear that the US put pressure on Israel to rush into war even though at least another two or three months were required to get ready. (Reports also indicate that Israel had intended to launch a war on Hizbullah between September and October that same year.) This meant that Israel was under-prepared, lacking an overall understanding of what was required if it was to achieve its desired ends.

Why did the US take such a step?

There are several reasons. The US had failed to secure Hizbullah's disarmament politically through Resolution 1559; rather than being weakened by the Syrian exit from Lebanon, the Party had consolidated its position. It participated in government and a ministerial statement was issued supporting the resistance and ensuring its political protection; Hizbullah was enjoying increased popularity, especially after concluding the Memorandum with the Free Patriotic Movement. The US also realized that any hopes it had of pitting the Lebanese army against the resistance were doomed to failure given the sectarian composition of the army and its anti-Israeli stance, formed according to the political reality in Lebanon. Furthermore, the March 14 Coalition had been unable to commit itself to a timetable that would address the existence of the Party's weapons despite international pressure – particularly from the US. It was later revealed that key figures from the Coalition had told Vice President Dick Cheney,

Secretary of State Condoleezza Rice and other US officials that, as they were unable to do anything and time was against them, the only remaining option was for Israel to launch a war against the Party and disarm it by striking at its power base.

The July 2006 attack was the start of a global war against Hizbullah and its supporters, carried out by Israel with the backing of many leading countries, the Security Council, some Arab states and the March 14 Coalition in Lebanon. The latter parties attempted to justify the Israeli aggression; they claimed that Hizbullah was responsible for the war and its consequences, and urged it to end its armed presence in Lebanon.

It is impossible to describe the brutality of the Israeli attacks and the widespread killing of Lebanese people that took place during the conflict. About 1,000 people were martyred and 3,000 people wounded; houses and buildings, particularly in the south and the southern suburbs of Beirut and the Bekaa, were destroyed. Israel dropped more than 4 million cluster bombs.[1] But the resistance wing of Hizbullah survived; not only did it prevent an Israeli advance on land, but its equipment and soldiers also inflicted heavy losses on the enemy, perhaps most prominently on August 12 when more than thirty-nine tanks and bulldozers were destroyed, killing more than twenty Israeli officers and soldiers and wounding more than 110 in what was described as a 'tank incineration'[2] in the region of Wadi al-Hajir, in southern

---

1. A spokeswoman for the office that coordinates the disposal of mines and cluster bombs in southern Lebanon said that 970 sites had been contaminated by cluster bombs in an area spanning 39 million square metres. She added that since August 2006, 256 civilians had been killed or wounded, including fifty-one people employed with the disposal programme. See *Al-Sharq*, June 5, 2008.

2. *As-Safir*, August 13, 2006.

Lebanon. By the time the ceasefire came into effect, at 8 AM on August 14 (as a result of Security Council Resolution 1701), Israel had suffered a heavy defeat both morally and militarily, instead of the victory it had hoped to achieve. Its failure was further compounded by the fact that it was unable to enter villages or outposts on the border such as Bint Jubail, Aita al-Shaab and al-Khayam.

Lebanon was united in the face of Israeli aggression; the Lebanese army came out in support of the resistance, and many of its soldiers died as martyrs or were wounded; people in the target areas, who bore the brunt of the war and were exposed to displacement and suffering, expressed their support for the resistance under the most difficult circumstances, as did people in other areas who sympathized with the displaced, and who gave them shelter and aid no matter where they came from or which sect they belonged to. Although some politicians did attempt to place the blame for the war on the resistance, this suggestion had little impact on the wave of national solidarity that greeted the Israeli aggression.

Hizbullah successfully prevented Israel from achieving the two main objectives of its second war against Lebanon, namely: 'the return of Israeli soldiers, and the implementation of Resolution 1559, including the disarming of Hizbullah',[1] which Prime Minister Ehud Olmert set out before the Israeli Knesset on the sixth day of the war as conditions for a ceasefire. Defence Minister Amir Peretz, who 'threatened to invade Lebanon',[2] failed to realize his dream; and any hopes Chief of Staff Dan Halutz had had of 'eliminating the missiles and stopping the people from

---

1. *An-Nasr al-Mokhaddab*, p.74, published by *as-Safir*, 1st edn, 2006.
2. Ibid, p.84.

launching them' were dashed as the Party continued to launch as many missiles as previously, right up to the moment when the 'ceasefire' came into effect, after the implementation of UN Resolution 1701. Secretary of State Rice, who had rejected calls for a ceasefire on the ninth day of the war, justifying the vicious attacks on Lebanon as 'the birth pangs of a new Middle East in Lebanon',[1] was also disappointed, as this 'new Middle East' failed to materialize. Since this notable strategic victory, the first of its kind in the history of the Arab–Israeli struggle, the Party has become an inspirational force for the peoples of the region.

Hizbullah's success in foiling Israeli military objectives and defeating the Israeli entity had far-reaching consequences within Israel. A large number of army leaders resigned, most prominent among them Chief of Staff Halutz. Defence Minister Peretz failed in his re-election bid as president of the Labour Party, and the Winograd Commission investigating the conduct of the war enumerated the many failures and shortcomings in the political and military systems as well as in the management of the home front.

Israel's thirty-four-day war had a severe impact on the Lebanese economy and on the country's infrastructure; 104,000 housing units were damaged and 16,000 completely destroyed, at an estimated total cost, according to the Lebanese government, of between $1–3 billion.[2] In addition, economic institutions as well as crops, livestock, poultry and machinery to an estimated value of $580,000 were also destroyed, according to the Consultation Centre for Studies and Documentation[3] – and this figure does

---

1. Ibid, p. 86.
2. *Al-Immar wal-Iktissad* magazine, August 3, 2007.
3. *Al-Anwar*, February 16, 2007; see also www.dirasat.net.

not take into account the large number of workers who lost their jobs. In a report to the Paris 3 Summit, the Lebanese government estimated that losses incurred during the 2006 aggression totalled $2.8 billion, 'which includes the cost of reconstruction, restoration and rebuilding of private and public infrastructure, replacement of destroyed plants, and compensation for private housing which constitutes the bulk of losses'.[1] (Hizbullah's own statistics indicate that costs were nearer the $2 billion mark.)

Hizbullah was quick to tackle the social impact of the war. It guaranteed financial aid to all those affected, and rented and furnished temporary housing to the value of $168 million while repairs or building work took place on property destroyed by Israel. It commissioned the Jihad Construction Company, which belongs to the Party, to repair communal sections of houses in the southern suburbs of Beirut, and met the costs of repair to homes in the Bekaa, the south, the suburbs and elsewhere in Lebanon to a total value of $188 million. In addition, it established the Wa'ad architectural firm to draw up plans for the rebuilding of the southern suburbs, in which 274 apartment blocks containing 6,000 housing units had been completely destroyed by the Israelis. It put the projects out to tender to major companies specializing in this field. Those who were hoping that the crisis would adversely affect relations between the people and the Party were disappointed, and observers and those hostile to the Party were taken by surprise.

There was no let-up for Hizbullah after August 14, when 'hostilities' came to an end. It studied the war and its outcome, and made use of the positive and negative lessons it had learned. In addition, it repaired and consolidated its position, helped by a

---

1. *Al-Immar wal-Iktissad*, August 3, 2007.

surge of popular sympathy, a rise in the number of young people joining the Party and broad and effective cooperation with the Lebanese opposition parties.

The Political Conflict Intensifies

Following the failure of the Israeli military aggression on Lebanon, the US renewed its campaign of political aggression against the country, thereby compounding the political crisis. After the war, the Lebanese leadership rejected calls for the formation of a government of national unity that would include General Aoun's Free Patriotic Movement. In addition, it agreed to the setting up of an international tribunal without first discussing the matter with Hizbullah and the Amal Movement, both of whom were part of the government. This time and on November 11, 2006, the ministers from both parties left the cabinet. They demanded that the government resign, and called for the formation of a national unity government that would be more representative and include members of the Free Patriotic Movement. In such a government, the opposition would have a blocking minority – that is, a third of the total number of cabinet positions plus at least one more – and would have the power to veto fundamental political decisions regarding Lebanese sovereignty and the role of the resistance as, according to the Lebanese constitution, 'fundamental issues require the agreement of two thirds of the members of the government'. Given that the opposition made up 45 per cent of the Chamber of Deputies versus the ruling bloc's 55 per cent, its members considered their request logical and normal. They believed that the nature of the Chamber, with its sectarian composition, required consensus between the various factions, and that a coalition government of national unity was the only way of finding a solution to political instability, insecurity and intractable economic problems, which the government had failed to address. However, supporters of the ruling bloc, backed by the US, refused to compromise and give the opposition seats totalling a third-plus-one, thereby plunging the country into a complex crisis. Opposition members refused to recognize the government and called on it to resign, while loyalists insisted that it remain in power, ignoring the fact that six ministers had already resigned, including all five representing the Shi'ite faction, and that the government was further weakened by the absence of any members of the Free Patriotic Movement, which represented a great number of Christians.

The opposition organized the largest demonstration ever held in Lebanon on December 10, 2006, calling for the overthrow of the government; when it failed to bring this about on the same day, it called on demonstrators to occupy the commercial centre of Beirut. The sit-in lasted for 538 days, but there was no let-up in the government crisis and the country was completely paralyzed. To make matters worse, the presidency was also in deep trouble. Government loyalists refused to deal with the president according to his constitutional powers, and behaved as if he wasn't there, although his mandate did not expire for another year.

When President Lahhoud's mandate came to an end on November 24, 2007, the Chamber of Deputies was unable to agree on a new president. As a result of the ruling bloc's continuing refusal to form a properly representative government of national unity, the opposition blocked the election by refusing to provide the necessary two-thirds quorum in Parliament.

The publicly declared US position was that the country should continue without a president, and that Prime Minister Siniora should run the government; this was to prevent the election of a president from within the political equation who would legitimize the resistance and give a role to the effective opposition in Lebanon.

On February 12, 2008, Israel assassinated the great *jihadi* leader of Hizbullah, Imad Mughniyeh (Hajj Radwan) in Syria, setting off a bomb as he was about to enter his car. Aware of the role he had played in the July 2006 victory and in building up and managing Hizbullah's military capability, it hoped that targeting him would weaken Hizbullah's resistance work. However, the Party quickly addressed any problems caused by the assassination and made a series of appointments that ensured its continuing strength and effectiveness, demonstrating that it had become a cohesive apparatus that could pursue its course with energy and skill in a precise, professional and prompt manner.

The Bush administration continued to intervene to prevent Hizbullah and the opposition from becoming a natural part of Lebanese political life, using Hizbullah's resistance as an excuse. A US-sponsored line-up of countries accused Iran and Syria of being responsible for the situation in Lebanon – a stand also adopted by government loyalists, who spread rumours that the crisis had come about because of Iranian–Syrian support for the opposition. But such accusations ignore reality. The resistance retains its right to carry arms because Israel poses an imminent and continuing danger to Lebanon. It occupies the Shebaa Farms and Kfar Shouba Hills, and its planes carry out several spy missions a day over different parts of Lebanese territory in order to photograph and compile a database of military targets.

In a briefing on the situation in the Middle East presented to the Security Council on April 23, 2008, Angela Kane, UN Assistant Secretary-General for Political Affairs, stated in paragraph 35: 'UNIFIL recorded a marked escalation in the number of Israeli air violations committed daily, which rose from 282 in February 2008 to 692 in March, and amounted to 476 during the first half of April. Such sorties constitute a breach of Lebanese sovereignty and the Blue Line, and continue to reduce the credibility of UNIFIL and the Lebanese armed forces.'[1] Hizbullah believes that the Lebanese have the right to express their rejection of foreign tutelage; to cooperate with each other, as Lebanese; to establish an independent state; to reject the continued occupation of any part of their land; and to retrieve their prisoners held by Israel.

The Communications Network Crisis

The political crisis remained unresolved and the situation, which had its origins in the adoption of Resolution 1559 three years earlier, grew ever more complicated. The post of president had remained vacant for almost six months, and investigations into the assassinations had proved inconclusive. Arab, Iranian–Saudi and French initiatives had failed to come up with a solution. The 'unconstitutional' Siniora government had assumed presidential powers and was making decisions without being sanctioned to do so – a development that was to have surprising consequences. On May 5, 2008, the cabinet met in the evening and remained in session for more than ten hours, until 4.30 AM, emerging

---

1. See http://domino.un.org/unispal.nsf.

with a resolution that Hizbullah regarded as dangerous and confrontational. The resolution stated the following:

> In view of the fact that the communications network, which Hizbullah has established in the Lebanese territories, is illegal and unlawful, and constitutes an assault on the sovereignty of the state and public property, [the government] will start criminal prosecutions against all those found to be involved in the action as individuals, parties, associations or companies.
>
> [The government] rejects the claim that Hizbullah's protection merits the setting up of such a network, or that it is an integral part of the party's weaponry, and also rejects statements linking it to jamming carried out by Israel, Syria or international parties, which the government has and continues to condemn and is constantly working to stop.
>
> [The government] has provided the Arab League and international organizations with details of this new attack on the rule of law in Lebanon, and exposed the role played, and being played, by Iranian organizations in this field.
>
> [The government] entrusts the relevant departments and the security forces to follow up and address the existing anomaly, given that this network belongs by law to the State of Lebanon, which has the right to remove it.[1]

The Party rejected the resolution and called on the government to withdraw it. Secretary General Nasrallah announced the

---

1. *Al-Anwar*, May 8, 2008.

Party's position explicitly at a press conference on May 8,[1] which contained the following points:

> III: The purpose of this resolution is to disarm the most important element [of the resistance's security apparatus], which protects its leadership, cadres and underlying infrastructure, and is intended to expose the resistance to assassination, murder and the destruction of its infrastructure. It follows, therefore, that those who are responsible for the resolution are complicit in any killing or assassination that results, by allowing them to happen if not carrying them out directly.

> IV: The purpose of this resolution is to set the national army and Lebanese security forces against the Lebanese resistance.

During the press conference, the Secretary General also made the following statement:

> After the black decisions taken by the government, we consider that a war has been launched against us, and that it is our duty to defend ourselves and our weapons; he who warns is excused. All red lines have been crossed; we will be lenient with no one, whosoever they may be. We have information that getting rid of the communications network is only the first step in stripping the resistance of its capabilities.

The situation deteriorated very quickly; armed militia groups belonging to the Future Movement and the Progressive Socialist Party moved into Beirut on May 7 and held up, at gunpoint, a demonstration called by the General Labour Union; the following

---

1. *Al-Intiqad al-Ousbouiya*, published by Hizbullah, May 9, 2008.

day, the groups took control of some streets in the capital and began firing at offices and at young men belonging to the opposition. This move, taken in conjunction with the government's decision to prosecute the communications network, appears to have had the following objectives:

1. To force the army and security forces to intervene on the side of the ruling party; this would, in turn, result in clashes between members of the resistance and their supporters and the army and security forces.

2. To tie down the resistance in an armed, internal conflict, forcing Hizbullah to use its weapons against other militias rather than keeping them for use against Israel.

Hizbullah believed that allowing itself to become embroiled in either of the preceding scenarios would only serve the government's interests and lead to further measures against the resistance; it decided instead, along with other opposition parties, to take limited and swift defensive action that would put a stop to the fighting. It confronted the gunmen deployed in the streets and offices in different parts of the capital, the overwhelming majority of whom had been brought from the north and the Bekaa; some of them surrendered, and others fled. Following these events, which took place on May 8, the Party quickly handed back the offices of the armed militias to the Lebanese army and its armed men withdrew from the streets. The Lebanese army took back overall responsibility for the security of the capital, and calm returned. On May 5, the Progressive Socialist Party killed two members of Hizbullah, but an agreement was reached several hours later that put an end to the incidents. The Lebanese army resumed responsibility for security in Mount Lebanon as well as in the offices and arsenals belonging to the Progressive Socialist Party. Parallel to these events, supporters of the Future Movement carried out several unprovoked attacks in the north, the Bekaa and on the international road into southern Lebanon. Several roads leading to the border were cut, and a massacre occurred in the town of Halba in Akkar, northern Lebanon, in which members of the opposition Syrian Social Nationalist Party were killed.

Hizbullah believed that its actions in Beirut and the mountains were necessary to defend the resistance, which was being targeted both by the government's resolution and by the movement of armed militia groups belonging to the ruling party. It did what was required to defend itself but limited its actions to areas that had been attacked. It did not leave an armed presence on the streets, nor did it consider imposing its authority on any part of Lebanon, but handed all areas back to the Lebanese army immediately. This limited defensive objective was clearly visible in the solution, which subsequently resulted in the Doha agreement (see below). The opposition did not try to benefit from what had happened; it was a direct result of the government's resolution on the communications network.

Given the generally held desire not to plunge the country into civil war, and the opposition's determination to continue the campaign of civil disobedience – announced on May 8 – until the government rescinded its resolution, there was a swift and favourable response to proposals put forward by the Arab League delegation headed by the Prime Minister of Qatar, Sheikh Hamad bin Jassem bin Jabr Al Thani, that the country return to the situation prior to the events caused by the cabinet's actions on May 5. Once the government reversed its decision regarding the resistance's communications network and the sacking of the head of the airport's security service, Brigadier General Wafik Shukair, the way was clear for an agreement. It was decided to convene a conference of national dialogue in Doha, Qatar. The head of the Arab League delegation announced the agreement[1] at the Phoenicia Hotel in Beirut, in the presence of representatives of the opposition and those loyal to the government.

The Doha Agreement

The conference in Doha was convened on May 16, 2008. Agreement was reached on the three main points[2] that had been the subject of controversy for the previous year and a half following the opposition ministers' resignation from the government. Hizbullah made the same demands at Doha that it had been making for the last year and a half. The parties agreed on the following:

1. The Speaker of the Lebanese Parliament, based on the rules in effect, should invite Parliament to convene within twenty-four hours to elect the consensus candidate, General Michel Sleiman, as President of the Republic.

2. A national unity government should be formed, composed of thirty ministers distributed among the majority (sixteen

---

1. *Al-Mustaqbal*, May 16, 2008.
2. *As-Safir*, May 22, 2008.

ministers), the opposition (eleven ministers, i.e. one-third-plus-one) and the President (three ministers), and by virtue of this agreement, all parties would be committed to not resigning or obstructing the government's actions.

3. The adoption of the *caza* (administrative district) as an electoral constituency in conformity with the 1960 law (using the majority system).

The Doha agreement was concluded against a backdrop of regional and international concern that the situation in Lebanon was getting out of control and could have damaging repercussions for the region at a time when calm was needed by all sides. Influential Arab parties were particularly concerned by the following: overall instability in the region, caused by the approaching end of the Bush administration and Bush's many failures in the Middle East; a possible change in the balance of power in Lebanon should the situation be allowed to develop any further; the dangerous and unforeseen events, precipitated by the May 5 decision; and the inability of the loyalists to apply pressure to the resistance despite the use of government resolutions, armed militias and official security forces.

The Doha agreement put the country on a new path. It revitalized Lebanese constitutional institutions by allowing the election of General Sleiman as president on May 25, 2008, and also paved the way for the holding of new parliamentary elections in June 2009, which will restore legitimacy to the country; in addition, it put the question of Hizbullah's weapons into the framework of discussions on a national defence strategy. These will be led by the President of the Republic and will address Lebanon's defence requirements in the light of threats posed by Israel to its territory, waters and airspace.

It is impossible to turn the clock back; continuing to ignore the preference of the Lebanese people for a strong country will not lead to a stable solution. If decisions were based on strictly applied laws and popular will, then the region as a whole would reject this disregard of national will and free choice. US policies in the region, as pursued by the Bush administration, have only prolonged the crisis and made it more complicated. There should be a different approach, based on the legal rights of citizens to their homeland and their right to liberate that land; respect for people's choices and the laws of their countries; an end to political interference by foreign countries, which favour one group's interests over another's; a recognition of the degree of Islamic awakening taking place across the Islamic world, and the extent of rejection and resistance among those who wish to solve the region's problems; an end to international alignment with Israel; confiscation of Israel's nuclear arsenal; fair and equitable treatment of the Palestinian people by giving them their rights, restoring their land, lifting the siege and stopping aggression; a serious effort to end the US occupation of Iraq; letting Iran possess nuclear energy for peaceful means, which is its natural right; and the return of occupied Syrian and Lebanese territories to their rightful owners.

The Vision of Hizbullah

Hizbullah believes that it owes its success in the divine victory of July 2006 to God and to the soundness of its programme and the political and *jihadi* management of the Islamic resistance.

It was comprehensive and far-reaching, much more than just a military victory. It was a victory for the frontline forces, for the broad mass of people who flocked to the resistance and for those who wish for liberation and independence.

The resistance wing of Hizbullah is part of an integrated philosophical and political vision of *jihad*, which aims to build a strong, stable and independent country in Lebanon. The Party gives expression to it through legitimate means; it receives popular approval and support, and is based on divine and tolerant teachings and the human right to justice, freedom, dignity and humanity. It has two main objectives: to liberate the land from occupation and to defend Lebanon against the threat posed by Israel.

Hizbullah is clear in its vision. The resistance is not merely an armed group that wishes to liberate a piece of land, nor is it a circumstantial tool whose role will end when the pretext for using it comes to an end. It is a vision and approach, not only a military reaction. Hizbullah believes in the need to build a resistance society in Lebanon in order to strengthen the country and reinforce its independence and sovereignty in light of Israel's expansionist project. The alternative is a weak state that will be dictated to by Israel. The resistance programme Hizbullah proposes is sustainable. It must be discussed with the Lebanese people so that agreement can be reached on the steps forward that should be taken.

Hizbullah's vision of a resistance society is one in which resistance takes place at all levels, be they military, cultural, political or media; it is resistance by the people and the fighters, by the rulers and the nation; it is resistance with a free conscience. We consistently advocate building a resistance society, and do not believe in resistance groups. A resistance society implies continuity, while resistance groups only have a circumstantial use.[1]

You may ask whether Lebanon can bear the cost of resistance. I ask instead whether Lebanon can bear the cost and consequences of occupation, for this is not a debate about the resistance and its weapons, but about the kind of Lebanon we want. If we want a free, independent and sovereign Lebanon, then it must be able to defend itself. Since we have a resistance with an organized defence capability, let us work to strengthen the Lebanese army, to put a defence strategy in place that will allow it to benefit from the ample elements of force available and to organize it in a manner that will enable it to achieve its goals. Since we agree we must build a powerful and just state, it would be wrong to abandon the very thing that makes us strong. There is no conflict between state and resistance; the resistance's objectives, to defend the land and to confront the occupation, serve the interests of the state's interests in a very fundamental way. The resistance should be considered an instrument of the state and not in competition with it. The resistance should be regarded as a support for the state and not a substitute for it.[2]

Not surprisingly, there has been a growing desire among intellectuals, journalists, academics and the general public to learn more about Hizbullah's vision, methodology, experiences and aspirations for the future. To this end, we decided to publish *Hizbullah: al-munhaju, al-tajribah, al-mustaqbal* in English in November 2002, as it provided a rich source of material for researchers. We did not modify it in the present edition, as its

---

1. See *Mujtama'a al-Muqawama*, by the author, p. 8; 2nd edn, published by Dar al-Ma'arif al-Hikmaya, Beirut, March 2008.

2 Ibid, pp. 16–17.

fundamental perspective on the Party's programme, history, vision and outlook for the future has remained constant and true. We have added a new introduction, which provides a brief chronology of events that have occurred since 2004, beginning with UN Security Council Resolution 1559 on Lebanon (passed on September 2, 2004) and ending with the incidents of May 2008, along with the Party's reaction to them. Thus we can look at the most significant developments, though we recognize that a new book would be required to fully record and analyse this historic, sensitive and important stage in Lebanon's history and the role Hizbullah has played in it.

I hope this book will provide the reader with an opportunity to learn from Hizbullah's contemporary experience, which has been such an inspiration to the peoples of the Middle East and to the resistance movement, and that this book can serve as a fundamental tool for all those who wish to be liberated from occupation, by pursuing a conscious and genuine *jihadi* political model.

Naim Qassem, 2008

ONE

Vision and Goals

Hizbullah's Foundation

The early 1960s in Lebanon witnessed the beginnings of an active clerical movement that served to re-invigorate Islam's key principles. Initiated by a number of Islamic clerics just back from the holy schools of religion in Najaf in Iraq, the clerical teachings, speeches and cultural dialogue that ensued prompted many concerns and queries about Islam's proposed role in life. Until then, neither the cultural nor political scene – both preoccupied with various core concerns – had lent any attention to the Islamic direction or foreseen a role for it.

Activity was initially limited to leading the faithful at mosque prayers and teaching religion at village schools and nearby environs. Gradually, cultural events proliferated across the various Lebanese districts, albeit within tight and limited circles. A number of young men with a serious interest in Islam attended, and then so did whole congregations. They all soon followed the clerics, forming small groups of individuals to watch over communities and playing educational and community service roles, always hinging on the cleric who oversaw and supported all efforts.

University students were rare at these gatherings, while highly motivated men actively participated in community work and gathered around the cleric and his activities. Female presence was scarce and underwhelming, and children who attended mosque prayers at the time were seen as the promising hope of the future. Indeed, this phase witnessed the Islamic condition's humble, embryonic beginnings.

Soon, three of the active clerics drew the spotlight. Their ideological visions were comprehensive; their cultural capabilities were high and they shared a belief in the necessity of taking action to trigger a change in then-prevalent living conditions. Each had his approach, practical logic and plan of action. They met in many gatherings with peer clerics and engaged in crucial discussions over the requirements for Islamic activity in Lebanon. Each had his personal agenda, and at the practical level their approaches were independent and different, solidifying later depending on the chosen course. While core groups gathered around each cleric and were considered to be his followers, an important number of those faithful attendants participated in the various activities of all three. These clerics are:

1. *Imam*[1] *Mussa al-Sadr.* The majority of his religious schooling was accomplished in sacred Qum in Iran and later resumed in holy Najaf. His activity started in the Lebanese city of Tyre, particularly through the 'Charity and Philanthropy Association'. Soon, a regional outreach was reflected in all of his activities, which expanded at the cultural level to cover all of Lebanon. He carried obvious weight on the local scene, with many a speech given at various cultural

---

1. The word *imam* indicates the leading religious figure who pilots the prayers in front of a group. It is permanently associated with the name of a religious person when he is chosen to be *imam* by his community.

and educational forums and a number presented inside churches. Prominent figures as well-cultured individuals from diverse backgrounds gathered around him.

His attractive personality, which was easily capable of drawing favourable public opinion, was complemented with solid, substantiated logic. His concern for the socio-political movement was early, and culminated in 1967 in the creation of the Highest Islamic Shi'ite Council as an official religious institution set up to support and see to the concerns of the Shi'ite congregation in tandem with peer institutions of other congregations in Lebanon. While this achievement came in spite of the disagreement and plain opposition he faced from prominent Shi'i politicians, he nevertheless believed that the role of this Council was to group the eminent members of the Shi'ite congregation, and is thus a specific role. The need to found a framework that bears the concerns and issues of the masses had posed itself.

In response, Imam al-Sadr founded the 'Movement of the Oppressed', a socio-political group with the primary mission of alleviating poverty, especially as represented by the hardship befalling South Lebanon, the Eastern Bekaa district and the so-called 'boroughs of misery' around the capital, Beirut (resulting from mass urbanization). Both religious as well as other types of groups joined, many simply drawn to the personality of the Imam and his ability to set the movement on its right path irrespective of the variety of individual ideologies present in its ranks. Imam al-Sadr held large-scale events in the name of the movement, rallying to drive his political statements home in the face of a neglectful and derelict government.

Imam al-Sadr also founded 'The Ranks of Lebanese Resistance [Amal]' – the military arm of the Movement of the Oppressed whose mission was to resist Israeli occupation. The movement was openly declared in 1974 following a bombing incident at a training camp,[1] one that clearly exposed the ongoing military training and necessitated its declaration.

Author of the famous slogan 'Israel is an utter evil', Imam al-Sadr never ceased to call for waging war on Israel and freeing the land from its occupation. At the time, the Palestinian Liberation Organization had supervised the majority of resistance activity against occupation in South Lebanon, and Amal's participation in a number of confrontations with Israel was recorded.

But the Imam's mission was, alas, discontinued. He was kidnapped in Libya following an invitation received from Libyan President Muammar al-Qaddafi to attend the annual September national celebrations. The date was August 31, 1978. To date, Imam al-Sadr's fate remains unknown.

2. *Ayatullah*[2] *Muhammad Mahdi Shamseddine.* Starting his activity in East Beirut, Shamseddine led prayers at the Dekwaneh mosque and looked after the social and cultural aspects of that congregation. He later moved to Beirut's southern suburb of Chiyah, where he chaired the Cultural and Charity Association, which worked to

---

1. The camp in question is Ain El-Binnieh, located in the Nabi Sheeth area of Bekaa (East Lebanon). Amal fighters were receiving military training from the Fatah movement when the camp was bombed.

2. The word *ayatullah* is a religious title awarded to clerics of high standing who experience deep religious revelations.

produce and distribute the set of 'Cultural Direction' educational booklets. The association was also active at the forum and discussion levels, later expanding its scope of activity to include a number of auxiliary institutions, the most significant of which was the Islamic Institution of the Arts.

He was notable for his intellectual capacity – a remarkable capability to shape words into well-founded expressions of depth and precision. He gave many lectures, held conferences for intellectuals throughout the Arab world and wrote many books. His prominence and distinguished cultural presence in many an intellectual forum was palpable.

Shamseddine's participation in public life was initially weak, despite his qualifications, according to many, for the post of Deputy Head of the Highest Islamic Shiʿite Council. During the tenure of Imam al-Sadr, his involvement was not proactive at the level of the Council, especially given his intellectual orientation. He was thus not part of any existing organizational frameworks, opting to 'remain at an equal distance from all' – as he famously chose to put it. Indeed, such a stance summarized his view of the Council's role: that of taking all of the Shiʿite congregation's divergent influences under its wing.

In the context of freedom from Israeli occupation, the Ayatullah's attempts to establish some form of large-scale civil resistance did not bear fruit, given the scope of the structure suggested by the concept. Though he was clear in his call to fight Israel and achieve liberation, his longing – as he had so many times expressed – was for assigning the larger portion of his efforts to intellectual work.

3. *Ayatullah al-Sayyed[1] Muhammad Hussein Fadlallah.* East Beirut also saw the beginnings of a third cleric's activity. Al-Sayyed Muhammad Hussein Fadlallah founded the Brotherhood Association in Naba'a, where a cultural centre was built grouping together a mosque, house of worship, school of religion and dispensary. His dedication to mosque activity was apparent, and he adopted a messenger role, continuously preaching across various Lebanese regions and holding regular weekly classes in many Beirut neighbourhoods and suburbs. Relocating to Beirut's southern suburbs, he led mosque prayers at the Imam al-Rida mosque, which later became an icon of Islamic work in Lebanon.

Cultural work, lectures and education were his primary concerns, in addition to the publication of many books. The messenger role dominated his activities, with political speeches emerging only after the Israeli invasion.

He founded the Association of Philanthropic Organizations, which groups together a large number of educational, religious and social institutions. It was a framework directly falling under his supervision and encompassing the variety of institutional activity that formed part of his concerns.

During the early years of the Party, the name of Ayatullah al-Sayyed Muhammad Hussein Fadlallah was closely associated with its own. He was a symbol of many ideological concepts within the Party, guiding Hizbullah through a mature vision of Islam and of the Islamic movement, supporting the Islamic revolution's leader in Iran, Ayatullah Khomeini. This prompted many to nominate him for a

---

1. 'Al-Sayyed' is a title pertaining to the descendants of the Prophet (PBUH).

leading position in this nascent faction. But al-Sayyed Fadlallah refused any participation in organized factional activity, opting to remain a cleric, overseeing all fields from his vantage point and supporting those Party directives that he deemed harmonious with his views.

On a broad spectrum of issues, al-Sayyed Fadlallah's views and propositions were harmonious with those of the Party, a fact demonstrated through his speeches in the majority of the Party's chief forums and conferences. In those early days prior to Hizbullah's formal declaration through the Open Letter (see Chapter Three), the absence of Party leaders, especially at the media and political level, led both local and international media as well as the bulk of political leaderships to consider al-Sayyed Fadlallah as Hizbullah's spiritual leader, the guiding figure in the arena of active Islamic groups. This impression came in spite of repeated denials by both the Party and al-Sayyed Fadlallah of any such relationship. This prevalent perception altered only of late, following the emergence of a clear Hizbullah leadership, most notably at the level of the Secretary General, as well as a number of independent activities which clarified the real context of the relationship.

Lebanese Islamists divided their allegiance among Amal, the range of Islamic committees, the missionary faction and the independents. The theoretical cultural foundation for all of these courses was subject to the influence of all or some of the three leading clerics, as well as to clerical activity in general. Given that Amal was the only political movement at the time, it attracted some activists either as a result of conviction in the organization's ideology or out of a belief that this was a transitory phase while awaiting alternatives. Others participated in the work of the various Islamic committees – essentially groups of local young men volunteering in areas such as education or mosque service; speaking in the name of the faithful youth; concentrating on providing religious education to communities; and following spiritual and cultural mobilization programmes in terms of organizing such religious events as the commemoration of Ashura[1] and Ramadan night rituals. A student movement under the name of 'The Lebanese Muslim Students' Association', concerned mainly with students' problems, found harmony with Amal, and worked to organize lectures and education sessions targeting youth. At the time, general political matters were not part of Amal's concerns.

During this time, in 1979, the Iranian Revolution led by Ayatullah Khomeini saw victory, drawing the faithful closer to Islam. Massive support was evident in demonstrations organized under the banner of 'Supportive Committees to the Islamic Revolution in Iran', a movement which eventually led to communication with the pillars of the young Islamic government in Iran, at the head of which was the religious leader of the Islamic *umma*, the Jurist-Theologian (*al-wali al-faqih*), Ayatullah Khomeini.

Prior to this development, there had been no connection with the Iranian Revolution, as such matters were in the realm of clerical issues. Such is the practice of the Shi'ite congregation, where 'interpretative judgment'[2] is possible, and where subjects are

---

1. The remembrance of the fateful killing of Prophet Muhammad's grandson, Imam al-Hussein (PBUH), in Karbala (Iraq).
2. Known in Arabic as *ijtihad*, this is a high level of clerical knowledge attained by religious clerics allowing them to hand down judgements based on

required to follow the religious interpretation of the more learned among the living clerics. Given that the majority of Lebanese clerics completed their disciplinary studies at Najaf in Iraq, thus did their summons concentrate on a relationship with the references and clerics of Najaf, and so was the call for imitating Imam al-Kho'i, and, on a tighter scale, the martyr al-Sayyed Muhammad Baqr al-Sadr. As soon as the Iranian Revolution was declared victorious, Ayatullah Khomeini was designated the leading religious authority, and the inquisition began into the appropriate means of liaising with the Islamic Revolution's leadership.

Thirst for an Islamic revolution came in tandem with a rising and insistent need for political revitalization in a country like Lebanon, a need that was not fulfilled by practical Islamic activity at the time of the Revolution. Perhaps the circumstances surrounding the Najaf clerical teachings in Lebanon and the nature of their concerns, together with the rise of youth activity, resulted in a dominance of intellectual and cultural aspects. Such was markedly different from the teachings and concerns of Qum clerics, who were inspired by an effective and influential political experience that culminated in the creation of a modern Islamic state in Iran.

Within their circles, Islamists discussed the issue of their own resurgence, the requirements of the then-prevailing political phase in Lebanon and the possibilities of benefiting from new insights brought about by the Iranian experience. They found that the organizational frameworks within which they operated did not serve their goals and aspirations, as they were unable to change and develop and could not be forged together if each

---

interpretations concerning the rights and obligations of Muslims, derived from a combination of Qur'anic revelations, the Prophet's Noble Mores (*Sunnah*) and logic.

was to preserve its particularity; such a formula would be simply a mere 'grouping', not a solid, united organization, and would therefore be unable to fulfil objectives.

Such discussions were taking place at a time when communication with the new pillars of the Iranian state increased, the objective being to remain informed of achievements there. At the same time, Israel invaded Lebanon. Groups of faithful men participated in confrontations at the outskirts of Beirut, collaborating with the Syrian army and a few Palestinian and Lebanese resistance fighters. Their efforts resulted in crippling Israel's advancement towards Beirut. However, none of the Islamic factional frameworks had been prepared for this grand mission. The concern for and need to found a united Islamic organization surfaced. Such an organization was to rest on three pivotal objectives:

1. Islam is the comprehensive, complete and appropriate programme for a better life. It is the intellectual, religious, ideological and practical foundation for the proposed organization.

2. Resistance against Israeli occupation, which is a danger to both the present and future, receives ultimate confrontation priority given the anticipated effects of such occupation on Lebanon and the region. This necessitates the creation of a *jihad* structure that should further this obligation, and in favour of which all capabilities are to be employed.

3. The legitimate leadership is designated to the Jurist-Theologian who is considered to be the successor to the

Prophet and the Imams (PBUT).[1] The Jurist-Theologian draws the general guiding direction for the nation of Islam. His commands and proscriptions are enforceable.

To achieve these ends, a number of representatives of the main Islamic groups launched many discussions regarding their perception of Islamic activity in Lebanon. Results were summarized in a final document, following which nine representatives were elected to speak for the convening parties: three stood for the clerical congregation of the Bekaa (East Lebanon); three represented the various Islamic committees; and three spoke for the Islamic Movement, Amal.[2] The document thus became known as the 'Manifesto of the Nine', which upheld the objectives mentioned above and was presented to Ayatullah Khomeini – who granted his approval, thereby bestowing the custodianship of the Jurist-Theologian.

Various Islamic groups then adopted the manifesto, dissolving their existing organizations in favour of one new framework, which later came to be known as 'Hizbullah'.[3] Its founding leadership was chosen following much deliberation, and the

---

1. The Twelve Imams are descendants of Prophet Muhammad (PBUT), and are intensely revered figures for Shi'is.

2. The Islamic Movement, Amal, led by its Deputy President Hussein al-Moussawi, seceded from the original Amal movement ('Amal' is an acronym [which also means 'hope'] for 'The Ranks of the Lebanese Resistance') – led by Nabih Berri – following a divergence of political views after the Israeli invasion. The split followed the creation of the Salvation Corps in which Berri was member, alongside Lebanese Forces leader Bashir al-Gemayyel, National Movement leader Walid Jumblatt and Prime Minister Chafic al-Wazzan. The Corps held its first meeting, chaired by President Elias Sarkis, on June 20, 1982, fourteen days after the Israeli invasion. The secession arose in objection to the participation of Amal (through Berri) in the Salvation Corps.

3. 'The Party of God'.

first steps towards capitalizing on the Party's potential were taken. Membership programmes were roughly drafted, and effective mobilization activity was launched with clerics summoning members to join military training and work towards the resistance of Israeli occupation. All of this took place within the Islamic framework guided by the Jurist-Theologian.

These developments occurred at a time of Iranian solidarity with Lebanon and Syria. Ayatullah Khomeini ordered the Iranian Revolutionary Guard to support Lebanon's confrontation with Israel, primarily through military training and the provision of the necessary infrastructure. A delegation of high-ranking Iranian military officials visited Syria for coordination. Syria agreed to the passage of the Iranian Revolutionary Guard into Lebanon, and training camps were set up in the Western Bekaa district. An advanced system of training, religious practice and personal as well as moral cultivation was devised, and large numbers of young men joined these camps. Hizbullah's participation was marked, and the Party had by then attracted many more believers in its goals.

The time lapse between training and execution of military activity in the occupied areas of the South and Western Bekaa was not considerable. A number of trained youth who had benefited from the experience provided through Palestinian resistance had already started their confrontations. Though their means were limited, their dedication was fervent, and so was their willingness to sacrifice. These developments rolled consecutively in the months following the Israeli invasion.

The Three Pillars of Hizbullah

In order to clearly present Hizbullah's intellectual background, we dedicate the rest of this chapter to the three objectives that represent the primary pillar on which Hizbullah is based.

First: Belief in Islam

Islam is the last and most comprehensive of heavenly messages. As God Almighty states in the Holy Qur'an:

> *This is in the former scrolls, the Books of Abraham and Moses[1] ... This day have I perfected your religion for you and completed My favour unto you, and have chosen for you as religion al-Islam.[2]*

It is a conviction, and code of law. The conviction speaks to the mind, calling on it to believe in one God, the Creator of this universe. For it is unthinkable that the sky and what is in it, the land and what lurks beneath it and lives on it, life with all its diversity and continuity as represented by the sum of creatures and the interrelationships between all of these subjects within such an accurate system, could have been the work of less than a powerful and mighty Creator.

He sent His messengers with miracles in order to alert humankind to its role on this earth, and to the good it has been created for, the most prominent of those messengers being those decisive five: Noah, Abraham, Moses, Jesus and Muhammad (PBUT). They dispensed their messages, and left us with heavenly

---

1. Surah no. 87, *al-A'la*, verses 18–19.
2. Surah no. 5, *al-Ma'ida*, verse 3.

books of religion, the last of which is the Holy Qur'an – that miracle book of which not a letter has been altered since the Lord gave it in its entirety to Muhammad through the Angel Gabriel. The Prophet's message and enlightenment continued through the infallible Imams, sons of Imam Ali (PBUT).

God has not created life in vain (*Deemed ye then that We had created you for naught, and that ye would not be returned unto Us?*[1]). His justice rewards the faithful – those who properly abide by God's principles – with Paradise, and punishes the blasphemous, divergent, and wrong-doers with Hell; on the Day of Resurrection, all creation will be assembled for punishment and reward. All Heavenly messages have concurred on the belief in a Day of Resurrection and on the importance of preparing oneself for it through rectitude and good deeds.

As for the code of law, it covers all of humankind's needs, both individual and social, and touches on all aspects of life through its provision of overall guidelines as well as small details. Both the Holy Qur'an and the Prophet's Noble Mores (*Sunnah*) have clarified these issues.

Islam as a Comprehensive Religion

In order to provide a thorough overview of Islam's comprehensive nature, we hereby use examples of a number of domains it encompasses:

1. *Belief in God Almighty.* Compliance with one's religion and avoidance of what it prohibits is attested in God's words:

---

1. Surah no. 23, *al-Mu'minun*, verse 115.

*And verily We have raised in every nation a messenger
[proclaiming]: Serve Allah and shun false gods. Then
some of them [there were] whom Allah guided, and some
of them [there were] upon whom error had just hold. Do
but travel in the land and see the nature of the consequence
for the deniers!*[1]

Settlement and consideration on the Day of Resurrection
shall be on the basis of such compliance, and on not wasting
one's time on earth in pursuit of life's pleasures; for as God
said:

*Every soul will taste of death. And ye will be paid on
the Day of Resurrection only that which ye have fairly
earned. Whoso is removed from the Fire and is made to
enter Paradise, he indeed is triumphant. The life of this
world is but comfort of illusion.*[2]

Henceforth, consent between the Lord and His servant is
mutual pending the results, for as God Almighty said:

And the first to lead the way, of the muhajirin[3] *and the
ansar*[4] *and those who followed them in goodness, Allah
is well pleased with them and they are well pleased
with Him and He hath made ready for them gardens
underneath which rivers flow, wherein they will abide
for ever. That is the supreme triumph.*[5]

---

1. Surah no. 16, *al-Nahl*, verse 36.
2. Surah no. 3, *al-'Imran*, verse 185.
3. Companions of the Prophet (PBUT) during his migration from Mecca to
   Madina.
4. The citizens of Madina who aided *al-muhajirin*.
5. Surah no. 9, *al-Taubah*, verse 100.

2. *Worship.* This is the means by which the believer cultivates his personality in terms of his relationship with his Lord. Worship is requested in such actions as prayer, fasting, pilgrimage and charity.[1] God's words in this context are clear:

> *And the believers, men and women, are protecting friends one of another; they enjoin the right and forbid the wrong, and they establish worship and they pay the poor-due, and they obey Allah and His messenger. As for these, Allah will have mercy on them. Allah is mighty, wise.*[2]

From the same perspective[3] the Prophet Muhammad (PBUH) clarified the pillars of Islam in these words:

> *Islam was built on ten pillars:*
> a. *Testimony that there is no other god but Allah – and that is the creed;*
> b. *Prayer, which is an obligation;*
> c. *Fasting, which is the shield;*
> d. *Charity – and that is purity;*
> e. *Pilgrimage,[4] which is the code of law (Shariʿa);[5]*
> f. *Jihad, the struggle;*
> g. *Ordinance, to do what is kind and right – and that is fidelity;*
> h. *Forbiddance of the prohibited – and that is the proof;*

---

1. Through the Islamic Alms Tax, known as *zakat*.
2. Surah no. 9, *al-Taubah*, verse 71.
3. Source: Zarara, as told through Abu Jaafar.
4. The *Hajj* pilgrimage to Mecca.
5. *Shariʿa* is the body of Islamic law encompassing all the rights and obligations of individuals in Islamic society.

    i. *The Group, representing affinity and
      harmony;*
    j. *Infallibility, which is obedience.*[1]

3. *Self-Discipline.* This is subject to man's direction and requires daily follow-up given its susceptibility to evil. God said:

> *... by the soul and its moulding and inspiration [with conscience of] what is wrong for it and [what is] right for it ... He is indeed successful who causeth it to grow, And he is indeed a failure who stunteth it.*[2]

The victor is one who succeeds in controlling the self, preventing it from disobedience and indulgence of whims. God Almighty has explained:

> *But as for him who feared to stand before his Lord and restrained his soul from lust, lo! The Garden will be his home.*[3]

In Imam al-Sadeq's interpretation of God's words, *But for him who feareth the standing before his Lord there are two gardens,*[4] we read 'He who knows that God sees him, hears his words, knows his good and bad deeds, and then seals himself from wrong-doing, is one who has feared God's standing and forbade himself from whims.'[5]

4. *Concern for Politics.* In the context of concern for the issues

---

1. Sheikh Suddouk, *al-Khisal*, p. 447.
2. Surah no. 91, *ash-Shams*, verses 7–10.
3. Surah no. 79, *al-Naazia't*, verses 40–1.
4. Surah no. 55, *ar-Rahman*, verse 46.
5. Al-Kallini, *al-Kafi*, vol. 2, p. 70.

of Islam, the Prophet (PBUH) said: that 'he who ceases to be concerned with issues of fellow Muslims ceases to be Muslim.'[1] In terms of mistrusting tyrants, God clarifies:

> *So tread thou the straight path as thou art commanded, and those who turn (unto Allah) with thee, and transgress not. He is Seer of what ye do. And incline not toward those who do wrong lest the Fire touch you, and ye have no protecting friends against Allah, and afterward ye would not be helped.*[2]

5. Jihad *in the Name of God. Jihad* is to be carried out even using the dearest of man's belongings of soul and wealth without hesitation and whenever obliged to. God Almighty's words on this were: *Go forth, light armed and heavy armed, and strive with your wealth and your lives in the way of Allah! That is best for you if ye but knew.*[3]

6. *Economics.* Islam calls for executing trading operations on the basis of sale and not through interest-bearing transactions. As God said: *Allah permitteth trading and forbiddeth usury.*[4]

   Islam has also directed rulers to the appropriate taxation methods intended to increase wealth. The focus here is on re-investment for development as a basis for drawing taxes, not the reverse. Commander of the Faithful[5] Imam Ali (PBUH) said in this context:

---

1. Al-Hurr al-Aamili, *Wasael al-Shi'a* (Means of the Shi'is), vol. 16, p. 336.
2. Surah no. 11, *Hud*, verses 112–3.
3. Surah no.9, *al-Taubah*, verse 41.
4. Surah no. 2, *al-Baqara*, verse 275.
5. This title was awarded to the Prophet's successors, or Caliphs – the fourth

And let your foresight for development be wiser than your aim of collecting tax, for tax could only be achieved through development. That who seeks to tax without development is but ruining the land and oppressing its people. His reign shall endure only shortly. And if they complain of burden, an ailment, lack of water or production, or land retirement resulting from floods or a drought, do reduce their liability so as to improve their stance. Do not be burdened by that with which you ease their burden, for it is only a saving which will return as development of your country and flourish of your rule, in addition to summoning their praise of you.[1]

7. *Joint Social Responsibility.* This is invoked through distribution of charity (*zakat*) funds among society's needy and in favour of God, who said:

> *The alms are only for the poor and the needy, and those who collect them, and those whose hearts are to be reconciled, and to free the captives and the debtors, and for the cause of Allah, and [for] the wayfarers; a duty imposed by Allah. Allah is knower, wise.*[2]

On the other hand, whoever rebuffs the orphan and does not strive to feed the needy is perceived to be in practical denial of the Day of Resurrection, as God Almighty said: *Hast thou observed him who belieth religion? That is he*

---

and last of whom was Imam Ali bin Abi Taleb (PBUH).

1. Imam Ali bin Abi Taleb (PBUH), *Nahj al-Balagha*, letter no. 53, sent to Malek al-Ashtar upon his assignment to rule Egypt.
2. Surah no. 9, *al-Taubah*, verse 60.

who repelleth the orphan, And urgeth not the feeding of the needy.[1]

8. *Using reason and refusing subordination.* This is the call for proof to be the basis for belief or disbelief:

> *Is not He (best), Who produceth creation, then reproduceth it, and Who provideth for you from the heaven and the earth? Is there any God beside Allah? Say: Bring your proof, if ye are truthful!*[2]

Following straying parents and family is thus wrong, despite the factors of birth and social status. In this context God said:

> *And when it is said unto them: Follow that which Allah hath revealed, they say: We follow that wherein we found our fathers. What! Even though their fathers were wholly unintelligent and had no guidance?*[3]

9. *Communication.* There is no need for pressure and tension: *There is no compulsion in religion. The right direction is henceforth distinct from error.*[4] One's ideas and convictions must be presented in an appropriate manner, as one is not responsible for others' convictions, and everyone's final return is to the Creator, as the Holy Qur'an puts it:

> *Call unto the way of thy Lord with wisdom and fair exhortation, and reason with them in the better way. Thy*

---

1. Surah no. 107, *al-Ma'un*, verses 1–3.
2. Surah no. 27, *al-Naml*, verse 64.
3. Surah no. 2, *al-Baqara*, verse 170.
4. Surah no. 2, *al-Baqara*, verse 256.

Lord is best aware of him who strayeth from His way, and
He is best aware of those who go aright.[1]

10. *Justice.* This is the adopted basis for every action. Its
controlling factor is being on God's straight path, shunning
whatever is loathed, immoral, oppressive or represents
straying from the right path. As God said:

Allah enjoineth justice, kindness and giving to kinsfolk,
and forbiddeth lewdness and abomination and wickedness.
He exhorteth you in order that ye may take heed.[2]

11. *Piety.* A person's value is not determined by race, gender,
colour or beauty, but by the level of devotion to religion – by
piety. God Almighty said:

O mankind! We have created you male and female, and
have made you nations and tribes that ye may know one
another. The noblest of you, in the sight of Allah, is the
best in conduct.[3]

In the Prophet's words: 'There is no preference for an Arab
over a non-Arab, or for a non-Arab over an Arab, or for a
black man over a red, or for a red man over a black, except
in devotion.'[4]

Based on the above, Islam is both worship and a policy applicable
for both life and the afterlife, relevant to the individual and

---

1. Surah no. 16, *al-Nahl*, verse 125.
2. Surah no. 16, *al-Nahl*, verse 90.
3. Surah no. 49, *al-Hujurat*, verse 13.
4. *Musnad Ahmad*, vol. 5, p. 114.

society, the mosque and the ruling authority, calling for mercy and firmness, *jihad* and peace. It is thus that the Prophet (PBUH) was a ruler, leader, politician and worshipper, portraying man at his best. By holding Islam's banner, we worship God in every position or situation, for our prayers are worship, and so is our *jihad*, our justice and our service of society. It becomes difficult to distinguish that which is done for the sake of God from that which is to please the ruler, or even to please humankind, for all at the end is for God: *He knoweth all that is before them and all that is behind them, and unto Allah all things are returned.*[1] In other words, in everything he does, man is concerned with looking after God's orders and forbiddances, for there is no circle to which God has not entered and which is solely left for the individual to shape. Even that space which was left by the Creator to man is also within the realm of the organized circle of life, and is governed by the fixed general rules of the sacred *Shari'a*.

As such, an individual has no right to remain isolated in the name of worship, or to detach oneself from society, confining it to the mosque. He is responsible both as an individual and as part of the nation. One cannot get closer to God by moving further from the realm of this world: *But seek the abode of the Hereafter in that which Allah hath given thee and neglect not thy portion of the world.*[2]

Three faithful men decided to abstain from life's permitted pleasures, each in his manner. One decided to devote all his nights to prayer and obedience of God. Another decided to fast every day of his life, while the third took a vow of chastity. When the Prophet (PBUH) learned of this, his retort was: 'What is the

---

1. Surah no. 22, *al-Hajj*, verse 76.
2. Surah no. 28, *al-Qasas*, verse 77.

matter with those who have vowed so and so? Here I am, praying then sleeping, fasting then breaking fast, and marrying women. He who has preferred another custom than mine is not of me.'[1]

Islam and Modern Society

But can Islam keep pace with present ways of life? The religion's comprehensiveness could have served well at the time of its dispense, but after 1,400 years of change, is it logical to implement what was fit for the past in today's day and age?

The answer becomes easy when we distinguish the fixed from the changing in Islam. The religion has rested on a number of permanent basics and verdicts related to the creation of man and the nature of his disposition, and these are harmonious with epochal changes. Prayer, for instance, is a form of worship destined to the cultivation and refinement of the human spirit, in whatever era the spirit may be existent. Fasting is a challenge to the willpower, providing it with strength for the sake of achieving that level of fidelity that leads to piety and directness. Marriage is needed for feeding the instinct and building the world's existence, based on permanent rules that protect progeny and family ties. Oppression is refused, whether its originator is a king, an emperor, a tribal chief or an elected representative of the people. And justice is required of the individual and society, while respect for high morals is a foundation for social stability.

The observer of Islamic verdicts and permanent policies, whether general or specific, notes their applicability to the individual and his interests irrespective of time and place.

This being said, what is considered to be 'varying' as opposed

---

1. Al-Muttaqi al-Hindi, *Kanz al-Ommal*, vol. 3, p.31.

to permanent is, indeed, quite a lot. Open interpretations of *Shari'a*, the body of Islamic law addressing all societal concerns, discuss all the requirements of modernity and answer to current events and arising queries, reconsidering previous interpretations and taking new circumstances into consideration. This creates the space needed to develop and keep pace with change.

Islam has set guidelines for the 'good' governor or leader while leaving the choice of government framework up to that leader. As such, electing a president could be through direct popular vote or through a parliament. So is the question of forming a government left free of strict rules; the existence of any form of government, its membership, role assignment, or authority are all issues left to choice. Likewise, there is no interference with the chosen method for electing representative members, whether these are individuals or groups or in any other form. Islam thus permits the creation of what is deemed to be an appropriate set-up for each epoch.

Islam has also drawn the basics of educational organization in terms of the obligations of the student and the teacher and the responsibility of family and society in cultivating generations. Nevertheless, the religion is open on the issues of coordination, organization and management as the time and age deem fit. Thus, whether education is provided under the tree, in the mosque, at school or in mobile buildings, and whether it is dispensed through a book, multi-media tools, the computer or the Internet, is a matter falling within the realm of allowable choice.

Islam urges cleanliness; as the Prophet (PBUH) said: 'Cleanliness is a form of belief.'[1] The Prophet (PBUH) concentrated on the importance of water as a means for achieving desired

---

1. Al-Sayyed al-Kho'i, *Kitab al-Tahara* (Book of Purity), vol. 1, p. 46.

purity, and also defined the specifics of using water in order to achieve the cleanliness needed to complete certain forms of worship. Having said that, he left the possibilities open as to the methods to be followed for achieving general cleanliness and safety of the environment, be that through the use of water or other alternative cleaning means, and be it applied to houses, streets, agricultural pastures, seas or rivers.

Rules that appropriately serve the human condition have thus been set by Islam and were deemed permanent for all time, akin to man's permanent need for them. In contrast, a wide margin was left to accommodate change, and keep pace with any place and age. Such space is what Martyr Muhammad Baqr al-Sadr termed 'the gap' in his discussion of the economic perspective in Islam:

> The economic point of view in Islam has two aspects. One has been completely filled by religion and is deemed invariably permanent, and the other represents a gap left to the governing bodies or custodians of the state to fill according to Islam's objectives and their requirements at any time. When we mention this 'gap', we thus refer to the reality present in Islam's Shari'a or doctrinal writings, and not to Islam's applicable reality in its early days. The Prophet (PBUH) had amply filled this gap based on the objectives of the doctrine in what concerns economic subject matters and in light of Islamic society's circumstances at the time. He filled this gap not as a prophet (PBUH) whose duty is to convey God's permanent message, thus expressing fixed doctrinal practices, but rather as a custodian of the people, charged by doctrine to fill this gap based on time and circumstance.[1]

---

1. Muhammad Baqr al-Sadr, *Our Economy*, p. 365.

What applies to economics in terms of an open space permitting change is also true of Islam's other doctrinal disciplines. As such, response to contemporary needs hinges on human choice, which in turn excels when man realizes the multiple facets of such needs and becomes proficient at implementing the appropriate rules for every situation.

But whatever man's capabilities, they will not achieve the level of God's exemplary system. If we undertake but a preliminary and general comparison between a legislation that God had decided for His servants, He being the All-knower, and one that is constantly amended by powerless humankind, thereby subjecting humanity to dire and painful experiments ranging from slavery to repression to capitalism, then communism, of which the world emerges exhausted if only from the dangerous aftermaths that affect life – despite a number of positive enlightenments here and there – the obvious result would be in favour of Heavenly legislation. Such is what Islam portrays in its all-encompassing message covering all previous Heavenly religions. It is therefore imperative for us to listen to, become acquainted with and understand this true religion before refuting it for religious, ethnic or constituency reasons. We are similarly obliged not to burden it with the errors of those who have borne the religion erroneously, nor with the responsibility for those conspiracies woven by Islam's prejudiced enemies whose purpose is to tarnish the religion's image.

Establishing an Islamic State

Do these arguments represent a prologue to the call for establishing an Islamic state? Such a project is the natural expression of allegiance for any committed Muslim holding on to Islamic conviction and persuaded by its code. It represents the ultimate justice to which man aspires. However, we seek here to detail the difference between the intellectual vision and its practical manifestation: in the first we summon the creation of an Islamic state and encourage others to adopt it as the supreme representation of human happiness; while on the second, practical level, we recognize that such development requires a proper foundation that accommodates the creation of the state.

Such a foundation is the represented by the populace to whom the freedom to choose a ruling body has been provided in Qur'an's holy words:

> *There is no compulsion in religion. The right direction is henceforth distinct from error. And he who rejects false deities and believeth in Allah hath grasped a firm handhold which will never break. Allah is Hearer, Knower.*[1]

The creation of an Islamic state is thus not a function of adoption by one group or branch and a subsequent imposition on other groups. Such a path is refused for both this project and others, irrespective of who its originators are.

The first official expression in this context was issued through the Open Letter declared by Hizbullah in 1985, through which it was stated: 'We confirm our conviction in Islam as a tenet and system, both intellectual and legislative, calling on all to learn of it and abide by its code. And we summon the people to adopt it and commit to its instructions, at the individual, political and social levels. Where the freedom of choosing a governing system

---

1. Surah no. 2, *al-Baqara*, verse 256.

is attributed to our people in Lebanon, they will not find a better alternative to Islam. Hence, we call for the implementation of the Islamic system based on a direct and free choice of the people, and not through forceful imposition as may be assumed by some.'[1]

The message is clear, and beckons the creation of an Islamic state based on free public choice. We are hence in perfect harmony with our convictions and with the practical, objective circumstances surrounding us. As long as such circumstances are not in support of the project, either due to people's diverging opinions or for any other reasons, we would consider ourselves forgivable in the sense that we have conveyed the message and declared our stance, thereby leaving it up to the people to choose their governing system and bear the responsibility for such choice: *And if thy Lord willed, all who are on the earth would have believed together. Wouldst thou [Muhammad] compel men until they are believers?*[2]

We strive to project our convictions in the context of the social work in which we participate, hoping to diminish those negative effects of distancing from God's code. We believe that our political experience in Lebanon has proved a pattern that is harmonious with an Islamic vision within a mixed society – a country not following the Islamic mode of thinking, neither in public administration nor through an overall vision or fundamental belief in Islam as a governing system. As such, we can state that our belief is in harmony with Islamic thought, which no one has a right to obliterate, create a new design that refutes any of its content or correct interpretation or object to

---

1. The Open Letter, drafted by Hizbullah in 1985 to the oppressed in Lebanon and the rest of the world, pp. 19–20.
2. Surah no. 10, *Yunus*, verse 99.

such conviction which is tied to belief in the righteous claim for God's system over any other. But practical accomplishment has its foundations and objective circumstances. Our duty is thus to summon to God's religion through wisdom and reasonable advice: *Call unto the way of thy Lord with wisdom and fair exhortation, and reason with them in the better way.*[1]

An Ideological or Sectarian Party?

Following Islam requires a detailed understanding and adoption of a context for interpretation. Given the number of Islamic schools of thought, patterns chosen by their originators to express their views of the appropriate means for achieving abidance by Islamic *Shari'a*, one is prompted to follow a specific path. The Party thus chose to follow that of the Prophet's descendants; such is the general direction of faith adopted by the Shi'is. These teachings, to which the Party's followers are utterly committed, comprise a number of various founding rules that stand for the whole of Hizbullah's intellectual and doctrinal background and the basis of its understanding of Islam.

It might be asked: 'Why not draw your choice from the realm of all Islamic faiths, finding some doctrinal common ground between all? For then you would have confronted the challenge of creating a practical scheme for unifying all Muslims.' Our response would be that it is our great aspiration to be in a position to unify Islam's various schools of thought. But this is a complicated issue at which religious jurisprudents have not succeeded over hundreds of years. It is one that requires specialized religious committees of high intellectual calibre undertaking objective

---

1. Surah no.16, *al-Nahl*, verse 125.

and bold research on all issues while recognizing the possibility that success is not a sure result, let alone the prospect of creating yet another faith or school of thought.

This is notwithstanding the fact that such an issue is not confined to Islam's branches of faith, as there are differences of interpretation within the same branch, which is only the result of research, knowledge accumulation and interpretative judgement (*ijtihad*) – matters that may not be simply ruled out. In lieu of diving into a sea of hopes and dreams, creating conflict or obstacles out of our differences, let us instead strive for strengthening the common ground at the practical level. This should eventually lead to unison at the various cultural, political, holy struggle or other levels. While such unison may not be completely achieved, the inter-relation of issues should likewise not be complicated, for there are many issues on which consensus exists among Islam's clerics and organizations, and which could represent introductory steps towards further unity. The requirement is for us to be together in the confrontation of challenges, and not to dissipate time trying to determine the gender of angels while our land is being robbed and our future is under the menace of world hegemony. We would then otherwise be taken unexpectedly, as has happened many times over throughout our history, when we targeted the wrong battle in the midst of challenges. Given that the owner of choice is responsible towards God Almighty, let him thus do as God would be pleased and as one's principles dictate, the final judgment being up to the Lord, to whom is ascribed all superiority and might.

Based on the above, there is quite a difference between a sectarian, confessional confederacy and a systematic, doctrinal one. The first draws its disciples based on the influences of birth and belonging irrespective of substance, while the second is founded on conviction and commitment, and harbours a set of guidelines as to moral and practical execution. We should also distinguish between compulsory allegiance to a particular denomination, which is assigned to an individual at birth, and a free-will allegiance to an all-embracing vision of the world, humankind and life. Whoever confounds the two is either deluded, which therefore necessitates learning, knowledge and awareness of distinctions, or one who intends to confuse and deceive, heaving accusations which would exempt him from objective discussion, or yet one who has been confused but refuses calm, objective discussion from which positive or negative resolution of his decisions would result.

As the Party's choice of Islamic teachings was based on the principles followed by the Prophet's descendants, it thus naturally followed that a coterie of believers adopted the Party's main objectives and related to them. Such groups form the organization's asset of supportive and devoted members. It was also natural for the Shi'is (as a congregation) to represent the majority of those members who responded to the choice adopted by the Party, given the few obstacles and complications that would deter them from the faith. This does not mean that any other groups or individuals would be denied commitment to the objectives and organizational set-up of the Party, nor allegiance to its trajectory. This is so given that the participation of some Shi'is in Hizbullah was the result of doctrinal and not confessional allegiance, as many other Party members do not follow the sectarian element – thus rendering the common ground doctrinal as opposed to confessional.

The essence is to be found in the effects of the system. The

Party executes a nationwide role based on its Islamic background, while adhering at the same time to internal national unity. It works with all branches in the political field to achieve a synergy of roles destined to serve all of society, and struggles to free the land from Zionist occupation. When such actions assure the Party an Islamic and Arab stature, and principles are put forth through the political means available to all others, the flow of criticism that is applicable to all national and political parties is eased, notwithstanding a few exceptions. It is impossible to cluster all people under one banner; there is always a need to define a particular vision, to which some would adhere and which others would refute. Such is the mode of life.

Similarly, no one can appoint oneself as the ultimate judge with regards to what is open for discussion and what is not. Just as every branch or party or organization carries a set of convictions for which it seeks supporters, so does Hizbullah. And there is no 'forbidden' unless it is a representation of oppression, aggression or forceful imposition. The social and political reality is capable of discontinuing any unilateral pattern that compellingly annuls the will of others.

Second: Jihad

Jihad, or Holy War, has its root in the verb 'to struggle' or 'to strive'. It signifies endeavouring and making every effort to battle against the enemy. In its Islamic context, the word has a broader reach than military combat, embracing as well the struggle against man's internal foes as represented by the soul's insinuations and temptations to evil or satanic calls to falsehood, and all that leads to straying and corruption.

The Prophet (PBUH) expressed this meaning upon his reception of a group of Muslims just back from combat: 'Welcome to a troop that has fulfilled that smaller *jihad* (battle) and whom the bigger *jihad* still awaits.' When asked of that bigger challenge, the Prophet (PBUH) answered: '*Jihad* with the soul'.[1]

Jihad thus bears a great influence on the trajectory of a Muslim's life. It is an integral part of one's true belief, without which God's acceptance of such belief is not granted. *Jihad* is a complete, not a partial, fulfilment, for which complete readiness is required. For as God Almighty said in the Holy Qur'an:

> *And strive for Allah with the endeavour which is His right. He hath chosen you and hath not laid upon you in religion any hardship; the faith of your father Abraham [is yours]. He hath named you Muslims of old time and in this [Scripture], that the messenger may be a witness against you, and that ye may be witnesses against mankind. So establish worship, pay the poor due, and hold fast to Allah. He is your Protecting Friend, a blessed Patron and a blessed Helper!*[2]

The renowned cleric al-Tabtabai mentioned in his interpretation of the Qur'an: 'The essence of the strife required by God is in the broader sense. The meaning of striving for Allah with the endeavour which is His right is that man should be well-versed in the meaning of *jihad*, which should be purely for the sake of God and not for any other.'[3]

---

1. Al-Suddook, *al-Amali*, p. 355.
2. Surah no. 22, *al-Hajj*, verse 78.
3. Al-Tabtabai, *Tafsir al-Mizan*, vol. 14, p. 114.

View of the World

Such guidance towards *jihad* is closely associated with Islam's vision of life. This world is a perishable home, a departing pleasure and temporary life. It is a place of test and tribulation for man, the outcome of whose actions determines his fate on the Day of Resurrection when God revives all Creation, committing the disbelievers to Hell and the believers to Heaven. Testing is usually coupled with difficulties, pain and weariness. For as God said: *We verily have created man into toil and struggle,*[1] and thus man has to prepare himself for tolerating and confronting challenges in search of success: *Thou, verily, o man, art working toward thy Lord a work which thou wilt meet [in His presence].*[2]

No one can avert life's difficulties, for this capability is beyond man's control and the natural code of life. And if some believe that through blasphemy, disobedience or straying they would deter such difficulties, then they are simply mistaken; for sterner difficulties await them as a result of harmful conduct, while their chance of positive toil during their living days is forgone, and lead to punishment in the hereafter.[3] It is thus worthier for suffering to be for the benefit of righteousness and goodness in order for one to win both the present and the hereafter. As such, we all endure, for we are all in the circle of examination, the difference between us resting in the final result.

The principal dispute is between two sets of logic: the first is that adopted by those materialist devotees to life who practically believe that the world is the end of all existence and who thus

---

1. Surah no. 90, *al-Balad*, verse 4, translated by Yusuf Ali.
2. Surah no. 84, *al-Inshiqaq*, verse 6.
3. The world to come after the Day of Resurrection.

place in life all their efforts, resorting to any and all means, irrespective of the evil repercussions of such means. Their basic vision is confined to personal interests and aspirations from life, even where such ambitions may lead to corruption, individual or community diversion from the correct path, oppression, killing or violation of other individuals' rights. Such in their view is legitimate as long as life is the end in itself, and the yardstick.

The second is the logic of the believers in God who go through life as a trail leading to the hereafter. To these, life is not the eternal abode, and should they suffer loss as a result of adhering to their obligations and being indifferent to whims, then they are promised reward on the Day of Resurrection. There is therefore no need for oppression, tyranny and aggression, for these only bear temporary results. It is the duty of believers to refuse and confront oppression, and to struggle with their inner selves towards the victory of virtue, justice, human rights and uprightness. They are also not free to marginalize their roles or remain observers, giving up their choices and conceding to their tormenters. God Almighty said: *And incline not toward those who do wrong lest the Fire touch you, and ye have no protecting friends against Allah, and afterward ye would not be helped.*[1]

The logic of the believers is positive and optimistic whatever the sacrifice, for to them, God Almighty never fails to reward. The prize could be victory and success on earth or a postponed recompense earned in the hereafter. What matters is dedication to the path of uprightness, that which is represented by those ordained and comprehensive rights and obligations the objective is goodness, not pleasure; justice, not domination and supremacy; consent and submission to what God's recompense will be after the

---

1. Surah no. 11, *Hud*, verse 113.

effort is proven, and not resorting to the path of abominable deeds, of repression or antagonism. The vision should be for freeing the land and man whatever the cost may be, not for acquiescence and submission to an abject life or for resignation from life's influential and virtuous roles.

The Foundations of Jihad

Islam considers *jihad* to be a basic behaviour in a Muslim's life, be that a *jihad* with one's soul or a struggle against the enemy. The second form of struggle is the more difficult practical evidence of the concept and comes only after fulfilment of the first, after man shuns his wants and prepares himself for practical confrontation with oppressors and occupants. *Jihad* with the soul is the larger of the two challenges, as it is a daily and permanent struggle, present in any conflict between virtue and vice, between obedience to God and to the soul's impulses. Struggle and battle with the enemy is the lesser test, for it is called upon during specific occasions of one's life as part of rising to the triumph of principles, morals, righteousness and the victory of the nation, when the nation is subject to oppression, occupation or humiliation.

Islam has built *jihad* on a number of objective pillars, of which four are most prominent:

1. *Tribulation and misfortune.* Life is a continuum of ordeals and hardship. Not a day passes when man is free from facing difficulties either with oneself, society, or any partaker of this world. In lieu of inquiring about the reasons for such misfortunes which represent an integral part of our creation, and on which we have no influence, let us work towards

using our God-given powers in order to win over our internal weaknesses and external enemies, and achieve such triumph through exertion. Let us be patient and enduring, for the results are well warranted. God Almighty said:

> And verily We shall try you until We know those of you who strive hard [for the cause of Allah] and the steadfast, and until We test your record[1] ... Or deemed ye that ye would enter Paradise while yet Allah knoweth not those of you who really strive, nor knoweth those [of you] who are steadfast?[2]

2. *The path towards God. Jihad* for the sake of God is the objective. Thus, he who abstains from wrongdoing is on the path towards God, and he who fights for the sake of exalting God's word above all else and executing His ordinance is on the path to God. But he who fights for pay or material remuneration is but fighting for the sake of that, and so is he who fights for the sake of a predisposition or fanaticism. We have not been ordained to *jihad* out of nothing, or for the objective of suffering, but rather to be on the road towards God with his instructions as our guide and model.

This does not mean that God needs us to struggle on His behalf or for His sake, for He could replace us with others and we would be of no harm to Him. But He is seeking our uprightness, and where He accepts and chooses us to be on the path of belief, such would be the blessing that He bestows upon us. 'For the sake of God' or 'towards God'

---

1. Surah no. 47, *Muhammad*, verse 31.
2. Surah no. 3, *al-'Imran*, verse 142.

are expressions chosen by man from the realm of available choices:

> *O ye who believe! Whoso of you becometh a renegade from his religion, (know that in his stead) Allah will bring a people whom He loveth and who love Him, humble towards believers, stern toward disbelievers, striving in the way of Allah and fearing not the blame of any blamer. Such is the grace of Allah which He giveth unto whom He will. Allah is All-embracing, All-knowing.*[1]

Dedication to the right choice requires courage and audacity. It is thus not possible to trust in the two inhibitions of firm will and resolve that are borne by other disciplines. The essence lies in exerting the utmost, trusting and having faith in the task, come what may. Commander of the Faithful Imam Ali (PBUH) said: '… Strive for Allah with the endeavour which is His right, and do not be taken by the reproach of a blamer.'[2]

3. *Man's interests.* When you succeed at uprooting your enemy from your land, then that is in your interest. Where you succeed at your *jihad* against your demons, then that too is in your interest. When you defeat evil and work to see goodness predominate among people, then that is in your interest. And when you struggle, working to render your innermost self civil, peace can settle there, and that is also in your interest. In God Almighty's words:

> *And whosoever striveth, striveth only for himself, for*

---

1. Surah no. 5, *al-Ma'ida*, verse 54.
2. Imam Ali bin Abi Taleb, *Nahj al-Balagha*, letter no. 31.

Allah is altogether independent of [His] creatures¹ ...
Whosoever doeth right it is for his soul, and whosoever
doeth wrong it is against it. And thy Lord is not at all a
tyrant to His slaves.²

Jihad is a rewarding anguish in favour of humankind,
whereas pursuit of whims, sin and disapproved deeds results
in suffering to the individual and society. Let judgement
be not based on the quick realization of events, but rather
on the nature of results. A pleasure is in its moment very
tempting and attractive, but could be destructive by result
and consequence. Dominance and command might be
appealing and a source of exhilaration, but bear painful
social repercussions and future ramifications.

4. *Illumination. Jihad* is a conduct the results of which are
only fully perceived when the rewards are counted. It opens
wide the door for prosperity and achieving illumination,
and is not confined to man's limited calculations. For man is
incapable of understanding the secrets of this universe, the
world of the unseen, and what God Almighty has appraised
and evaluated in life: *As for those who strive in Us, We surely
guide them to Our paths, and Allah is with the good.*³

Jihad is a door towards life, not death. For uprightness is a
concern of life, as are pride, freeing the land and overcoming
oneself. Even martyrdom is life, in the sense that it is the
triumph of spending one's eternal afterlife in Paradise; and
so are the verve, pride and victory of a nation influenced by

---

1. Surah no. 29, *al-'Ankabut*, verse 6.

2. Surah no. 41, *Fussilat*, verse 46.

3. Surah no. 29, *al-Ankabut*, verse 69.

the blood of its martyrs. Such is what opens the doors wide for all that is good and virtuous in the life of an individual and humanity.

Military Jihad

Since military *jihad*, as represented by fighting the enemy, is an integral part of this book, we shall concentrate our research on it. Religious clerics split military *jihad* into two parts:

1. *Groundwork* jihad. This is the confrontation of the Muslims with others and the entry into others' lands for reasons not tied to the reclamation of land or the fighting of aggression. It is an ordainment by the Prophet (PBUH) or one of the Infallible Imams (PBUT),[1] and is therefore not considered applicable in our present day, given the as-yet non-appearance of Imam al-Mahdi (PBUH), may his emergence be soon.

2. *Defensive* jihad. This is the defence by Muslims of their land, their people or their own selves upon facing aggression or occupation. This is considered not only legitimate, but a duty. In the words of Ayatullah Khomeini: 'If an enemy comes to pass the land of Islam or its borders, one from whom there is a threat to Islam's existence and societies, then such societies are obliged to defend the land in any possible way, dedicating wealth and souls.'[2]

---

1. As per the majority of clerics. Very few exceptions to this rule exist.
2. Imam Khomeini, *Tahrir al-Wasilah*, vol. 1, p. 485.

But the *jihad* decision is tied to the Jurist-Theologian, upon whom rests the duty of diagnosing the situation and categorizing it as falling under the banner of defensive *jihad* or not. He is entrusted with defining the fundamentals and guidelines of confrontation. The responsibility for blood is great, and fighters should not be consigned into any battle without identifying that which is in harmony with the duty and objectives of *jihad*.

Though clerical opinion may differ from that of the Jurist-Theologian, the latter's verdict is supreme and binding, for he is the primary defender and the person voted for by the people. Risky consequences accompany such overtures, as betting on consensus is not possible given the natural possibility of disagreement. Being within the Jurist-Theologian's authority, such a decision is to be taken only by him and is binding on all Muslims.

Where the call for *jihad* by the Jurist-Theologian is not embraced by other clerics who, to many, could represent spiritual authority of last resort, the question of whose opinion is supreme was clearly answered by Imam Khamenei: 'It is a duty to obey the orders of the custodian of all Muslims on all general matters, of which defending Islam and Muslims against aggressors, tyrants and the blasphemous is one.'[1] Such is also the opinion of other expert clerics.

The *jihad* decision may well lead to conquering aggression and achieving liberation, but it may also not do so in the foreseeable future. Should *jihad* therefore hinge on certain and definite victory, and is it linked to any limits of sacrifice?

It is doubtless that the assurance of victory is a goal sought by all, one that reduces any uncertainty surrounding the *jihad*

---

1. Imam Khamenei, *Ajwibat al-Istifta't*, vol. 1, p. 21.

decision. However, variations in people's material capabilities, the possibility of tremendous sacrifice as well as the uncertainty of achieving quick results, are all issues that raise the level of discussion around the gains from *jihad*. Assessment of these issues is up to the Jurist-Theologian. To him is referred the task of evaluating the objective circumstances, weighing the advantages and hardships and exercising the *jihad* option.

Jihad may be required for the sake of affirming rights and laying their proper foundations without foreseeing immediate practical results. It could thus be a resurrection movement aimed at mobilizing the nation, raising its strengths to the surface, encouraging it to believe in its position and stature and in God's blessing of it. It could thus be a long-term plan during which the levels of sacrifice differ, amassing from one phase to another until victory is achieved.

This does not mean that capabilities and circumstances are not factors in the *jihad* decision. On the contrary, they are integral parts of the decision's limitations and guidelines. As we do not possess the full picture of checks and balances, it is not possible to evaluate the Jurist-Theologian's judgement given the limits of our analysis. He may thus explain to the nation the full set of factors and reasons that led to his resolution, or may only reveal some, guarding others as part of the battle's ammunition.

Jihad is founded on material and physical sacrifice, of money and soul, for which all available and appropriate means should be dedicated. Going to battle is not a haphazard decision, and the aspiration for martyrdom does not justify any squandering of the battle's resources. However, death, injury and captivity are but natural consequences of the defence decision, not representing a deliberate intention for mortality. The results of *jihad* cannot be attained without the offers of martyrs, the wounded and the captive, for the enemy's aggression is by default founded on inflicting pain to achieve desperation, spread fear and impose surrender. *Jihad* is a defence aimed at conquering those objectives through paying the necessary price, whatever it may be. It succeeds where administration of the *jihad* process is virtuous and responsible, and where objectives are clear and legitimate.

Jihad's *Status*

Islam has awarded *jihad* a distinguished status, considering it the path for receiving the faithful and the individual's course of uprightness. God Almighty has provided a detailed and definite comparison of man's daily and direct needs and relationships as opposed to *jihad* on the path of God and the Prophet (PBUH). In these verses, He has provided a choice between the two:

> *Say: If your fathers, and your sons, and your brethren, and your wives, and your tribe, and the wealth ye have acquired, and merchandise for which ye fear that there will be no sale, and dwellings ye desire are dearer to you than Allah and His messenger and striving in His way: then wait until Allah bringeth His command to pass. Allah guideth not wrongdoing folk.*[1]

Priority is thus for the love of God, His Prophet (PBUH) and *jihad*. This is distinct from and paramount over love of one's family, relations and material pleasures. Such priority is clearly evident during times of conflict where if money is denied *jihad*

---

1. Surah no. 9, *al-Taubah*, verse 24.

for fear of loss, or a son is spared battle for fear of bereavement, this is considered deviation from obedience to God. In contrast, with sacrifice for the sake of God Almighty, the love of wealth and sons becomes one with the love of God, His Prophet (PBUH) and *jihad*. As such, there is no conflict between the two objects of love, for the eight matters mentioned in the verse would then form part of the path towards God, earning legitimacy from being driven according to God's will. These matters no longer become life-related issues straying one from his religious commandment, but factors in support of such duty or commandment.

Jihad and its freedom fighters carry a high status in Islam, for as the Holy Qur'an clearly states: *But the messenger and those who believe with him strive with their wealth and their lives. Such are they for whom are the good things. Such are they who are the successful.*[1] The Prophet (PBUH) also said, in his Noble Traditions (*Hadith*): 'Paradise has a gate called the Gate of the *Mujahideen* (freedom fighters), which when they approach they will find open, their swords they will bear and all shall stand to receive them, and the angels shall welcome them.'[2]

Commander of the Faithful Imam Ali (PBUH) also said in this context: '*Jihad* is one of the gates of Heaven which God has opened for the preferred among his devotees, for it is the adornment of piety, God's shielding armour and His formidable Paradise.'[3] And, further: 'Belief has four pillars: patience, certitude, justice and *jihad*.'[4] Imam al-Sadek elevated the issue of *jihad* to being 'the paramount occurrence after the [main Islamic] ordainments.'[5]

1. Surah no. 9, *al-Taubah*, verse 88.
2. Al-Kalini, *al-Kafi*, vol. 5, p. 2.
3. Imam Ali bin Abi Taleb, *Nahj al-Balagha*, speech no. 27.
4. Imam Ali bin Abi Taleb, *Nahj al-Balagha*, p. 31.
5. Al-Kalini, *al-Kafi*, vol. 5, p. 4.

Jihad is a pivotal pillar of Islam, bearing an imperative preparation for sacrifice of soul and belongings wholly and not partially, despite their being the two possessions of utmost importance to man. *Jihad* is a contractual obligation with and a pledge of allegiance to God Almighty for the sake of achieving Paradise in return for sacrifice:

> *Allah hath bought from the believers their lives and their wealth because the Garden will be theirs: they shall fight in the way of Allah and shall slay and be slain. It is a promise which is binding on Him in the Torah and the Gospel and the Qur'an. Who fulfilleth His covenant better than Allah? Rejoice then in your bargain that ye have made, for that is the supreme triumph.*[1]

It is thus not a surprise that believers flock towards martyrdom, for this is part of commitment, religious recruitment and mobilization, as well as an expression of obedience to God through practical implementation of *jihad* following order. It is a fulfilment of the religious commandment that is cast as the believer's responsibility for defending land and rights.

To the extent that *jihad* achieves honour and freedom, so does its abandonment lead to disgrace, loss, demise and crumbling of the individual and the nation. In the *Hadith* it is stated: 'He who abandons *jihad*, God will dress his soul with disgrace, his living with misery, and his religion with a fate of eradication. God has graced my nation with a pride drawn from the hooves of its horses and the targets of its spears.'[2] He who abandons *jihad* thus lives in a personal disgrace that is the outcome of defeat, powerlessness and subjugation to the enemy's will. He also lives

---

1. Surah no. 9, *al-Taubah*, verse 111.
2. Al-Suddouk, *al-Amali*, p. 673.

in poverty, as his land's wealth, his life and national fortunes all fall under the enemy's rule. Gradually, he loses his religion, the strength of which is a function of commitment to *jihad*.

Where a believer is not capable of performing the duty of *jihad* for any objective reasons, he should at least live the *jihad* atmosphere and the aspiration for it, even if this is simply represented by private meditation on his desire for *jihad*. The Prophet (PBUH) said: 'He who dies without conquest, and does not even speak to his soul of it, has died on a basis of falseness.'[1] It is thus another form of appraising life: death with surrender and shame versus a life of *jihad* ending with martyrdom for the sake of virtue's victory and national pride. In this context, Commander of the Faithful Imam Ali (PBUH) said: 'Death shall defeat you in life, and you shall defeat life through death.'[2]

Recruiting Young Men with Imam Hussein (PBUH) as Role Model

Islam carries tremendous recruiting potential for its followers. Concentration on the spiritual aspects of life, abandonment of those bodily and soul pleasures in favour of the more virtuous goals, the promise of Paradise and of the Almighty's blessing, all empower the Muslim in his quest for achieving true belief and defending his thesis. But we do find a considerable difference among Muslims. Some are content with simply practising the basic duties of Islam and detaching themselves from the nation's issues and problems. Some stop short of sacrifice, but recognize its importance. Others shun all those who do not form part of their group, denomination or sect, and spend their days contemplating

---

1. *Mizan al-Hikmah*, vol. 2, p. 125.
2. Imam Ali bin Abi Taleb, *Nahj al-Balagha*, speech no. 15.

internal conflicts in lieu of facing the nation's enemy or the symbols of dominion. Yet others link their commitment according to various yardsticks, especially when it comes to blood sacrifice. These are committed to the path of God whatever the sacrifices and whenever ordained to do so by the Jurist-Theologian. As such, there are numerous ways for understanding and implementing Islam, and this is very much a result of the direction, cultivation and teachings of the leading clerics and what they deem to be an interpretation of Islam's content. Based on such differences, we observe the variety of movements, factions and individual behaviours in society.

What Hizbullah has contributed is a representation of Islamic cultivation in general, not that of a particular faction. Where the nation is not living up to the spirit of martyrdom or laying proper grounds for it, such would only be due to its lack of awareness or to a deficiency in its commitment to the ordained Commandment. Hizbullah succeeded at recruitment and mobilization efforts because the Party was harmonious with Islam's teachings. The existence of the Jurist-Theologian Imam Khomeini and his instructions and teachings, as well as those of his successor Imam Khamenei, have laid the foundations for an exemplary dispensing of *jihad*'s willpower in a realistic, effective and practicable manner.

The West was astonished at the level of sacrifice demonstrated among Hizbullah's ranks and resorted to such invalid explanations as the submission of youth to the influence of chemicals, their subjugation to peculiar ways of life or complicated psychological training or, alternatively, their enticement through material reward in compensation for their deprivation and in encouragement of martyrdom. Western thinking sanctifies life and attempts to affix the individual to it at all costs. It was therefore only natural for the West to grasp the meaning of martyrdom by resorting to a material explanation for these fighters' religious attachment. Westerners have every right not to understand the spiritual and developmental results of following the Islamic order, since such understanding is not confined to mental comprehension of the facts but requires actual contextual existence, and calls for a working observation of those freedom fighters' lives and of the overall conditions of Islamic society. Even then, only partial knowledge of how the *jihad* spirit is formed could be attained. Westerners who have accepted the fact of *jihad* have done so only due to the impossibility of negating it, but partial explanations still reign and the core reasons for *jihad* are still misunderstood.

The essence – that which springs from commitment to religion – lies in launching towards martyrdom and not escaping it. We thus notice that a large number of martyrdom seekers hope to be assigned a martyrdom mission as part of their aim to please God and win His acceptance of their obedience. This is only a result of spiritual cultivation, a product of active religious worship. Martyrdom is therefore not a concept solely destined for winning conviction among the masses; it is a choice requiring religious belief, laborious effort and *jihad* with the soul.

But does the desire for martyrdom mean a renunciation of the desire for victory? By no means, for there are two fruits to the act of *jihad*: martyrdom *and* victory. The martyr wins martyrdom, while the nation and its freedom fighters win victory. The Qur'an has expressed these two aspects as 'the two rewarding attributes':

> *Say: Can ye await for us aught save one of two good things [death or victory in Allah's way], while we await for you*

*that Allah will afflict you with a doom from Him or at
our hands. Await then! Lo! we are awaiting with you.*[1]

When a man is cultivated to seek victory, making it the sole
purpose of his actions, his quest ceases as soon as the possibility
of victory seems vague or difficult to achieve. But when brought
to learn of *jihad* and martyrdom, his sacrifice would be of the
highest order, his actions effective, his martyrdom a fulfilment
of desire, and thus victory would be but a worldly blessing and
reward for his efforts. Cultivating victory does not assure it,
and may weaken the strengths of a nation, while cultivation of
martyrdom invests all resources to achieve either martyrdom
or victory or both, opening the horizon to all possibilities and
carrying the hope for victory. Cultivation of victory requires
reliance on material capabilities, while martyrdom bears on
human morale and on an individual's relationship with God, and
therefore requires few resources.

When cultivating martyrdom, the adoption of a strong role
model increases the effectiveness of influence and conviction.
One of the greatest events in history took place in Karbala,
where Imam al-Hussein[2] (PBUH) and seventy of his followers
– the finest of his family – faced martyrdom in defence of the
nation. 'I have come out seeking to mend my grandfather's
nation,' Imam al-Hussein said. His quest was to abolish the rule
of Yazid, the oppressing deviant governor, 'killer of venerated
souls, promulgator of lechery and wantonness. He who is of
my kind cannot elect his kind.' Knowing that his stance would
lead to martyrdom, Imam al-Hussein declared: 'God to whom

---

1. Surah no. 9, *al-Taubah*, verse 52.
2. Grandson of the Prophet, son of Imam Ali bin Abi Taleb (PBUT).

belongs all might and majesty has willed to see me die, killed and slaughtered, in cruelty and aggression.'[1]

A society nurtured with the exemplary story of Imam al-Hussein (PBUH) and his followers is enriched and reinforced by their conduct. Man deems his sacrifices little as compared to theirs, and understands the importance of confrontation even with no hope for victory, realizing that grand objectives require high levels of sacrifice without anticipation of compensation.

Since the meagre number of devotees in the Husseini *jihad* was never an obstacle to Imam al-Hussein (PBUH), and since the modest battle resources available did not deter them from going to battle, and since the choice that was limited to either victory or defeat, combat or martyrdom, was sealed in favour of martyrdom, what then could be a possible justification for his nation's present-day succumbing to oppression and submission to tyranny?

We have learned through Imam al-Hussein that the love of martyrdom is part of the love for God. We have learned to glorify *jihad* for the sake of Islam. Generations after al-Hussein's resurgence in Karbala, we still learn from the magnificent accomplishments that materialized through his martyrdom. His vision was not momentary or restricted to the battle: it was directed at the future of Islam and of Muslims.

It has been observed that when society experiences martyrdom, the cultivation power of this form of sacrifice is multiplied many times over. Speaking of martyrdom is one thing, but directly interacting with those who are willing to

---

1. Reference can be made to *Ashura': madad(un) wa hayat* by the same author, where the first chapter recounts the life and words of Imam al-Hussein (PBUH), citing sources.

offer it, such distinguished givers, is quite another. Even if we were to intensively teach the importance of these people and of martyrdom to the masses, and to make of the issue our motto and cultural banner, and even if we were to spend years in this direction, we would only achieve but an insignificant portion of the increasing numbers of today's youth that are a direct result of martyrs' sacrifices.

The martyrs influenced everyone, and the spirit of martyrdom became present at all levels. People interacted strongly with the notion, to the extent that some felt discontent upon being incapable to provide a family member for this endeavour. Children carried the spirit of freedom fighters until their aspirations for martyrdom became a common and widespread phenomenon. Despite the non-existence of any political or practical privileges assigned to these groups at the national level, the number of freedom fighters grew. And even though the wind of circumstance was blowing against the course of martyrdom, the influence of martyrs' blood was stronger, a fact which proves that martyrdom carries a vitalizing and lively power which is capable of spreading across the nation without hindrance, its movement taking lead with remarkable speed in preparation for investing the nation's potentials.

A woman bears the greater share in the recruitment and cultivation role, and this through her various functions as mother, spouse, sister and daughter. Many a mother has raised her child to believe in religion when young, and then sent him to battle when he became of age. Many a wife has supported her husband, bearing with him the sacrifices of *jihad*. Such is the cultivation and family education that elevates woman to the highest levels of giving and sacrifice.

This has been clearly felt within the families of fighters and martyrs. Some women went as far as requesting permission to carry weapons and go to battle. But religious commandment does not require this form of sacrifice from women given the sufficient number of men, which renders female participation in combat unnecessary. The woman's role in this context is in the back ranks, through support and recruitment. This is deemed more befitting of a woman's physical capabilities and of the sharing of responsibilities between her and man. Her Godly reward is thus not diminished, for reward is linked to religious commandment, which she fulfils from her own position.

Martyrdom versus Suicide

The culture of martyrdom reinforces one's readiness for death for the sake of God, as the founding logic is based on the religious conception that there is life after death, in which man lives happily and realizes all of his dreams. This goes alongside the benefit reaped on earth by the nation as a result of the martyr's action. Martyrdom for the sake of liberation goes beyond its material aspect, representing a form of obedience to God's ordained duty of defending the land. It is thus a death for the sake of God.

Martyrdom is a voluntary act undertaken by a person who has all the reasons to live, love life, and cling to it, and also possesses the means for living. It is thus an act of one who does not suffer from any reasons compelling him to commit suicide. It is an accomplishment by men at the early stages of their lives, young and full of vitality and hopes for the future. But it is also an act of those who are attached to a religious and spiritual cultivation based on altruism and manifested through preferring the hereafter to life, the nation to the individual, and sacrifice to small, contemptible gains.

Martyrdom is thus the supreme manifestation of self-giving, a form of confrontation with the enemy within clear, legitimate *Shari'a* guidelines. As such, if hurting the enemy and causing the highest possible amount of loss in its ranks, or achieving victory over it, hinges on the death or martyrdom of some freedom fighters, then martyrdom would be a legitimate endeavour.

Martyrdom is therefore different from suicide, which is an expression of despair, hopelessness, frustration and defeat, all of which lead to a loss of meaning in existence and push a desperate man towards ending his life. This is usually an act committed by a non-believer. By contrast, the believer expects an eternal Godly reward, knows that his patience will be repaid, realizes that he may not end his life in desperation as and when he wishes, whatever the anguish he may be going through, for Hell would await him. He understands that he does not have the right to terminate this existence that God has endowed on him in such a manner, for he is custodian of this God-given gift and is not free to dispose of it whichever way he wishes.

As such, we notice that individuals who commit suicide for economic, social, family or political reasons do so upon reaching a dead end on the path towards their objectives. They are also those who face the pressure of trials and tribulations.

Understanding the notion of martyrdom and its acceptance are not subject to international conventions, the politics of the intimidators or the appraisal of the enemy. It is only normal for these to launch an organized and intensive assault destined to condemn martyrdom, describing it in various notorious ways. For the notion is a weapon that is primarily beyond their control and, secondarily, one that cannot be defeated. Thus, he who is marching towards martyrdom is a religious individual who has sold his soul and body to the Lord, against whom nothing is a threat. He is one who has built his stance on the foundation of offering his life to the cause. The enemy only possesses the weapon of inflicting danger on life, and such weapon is only effective with those who seek life. It is consequently futile to combat those who believe in martyrdom.

When not endowed with equivalent material and military resources, what could those who hold a legitimate right do in the face of aggressors? What can the Palestinians, legitimate owners of the occupied Palestinian land, do to confront the Israeli occupier who possesses the strongest and most modern military machine and benefits from international support for his aggression and occupation?

Many calls for diplomacy and resort to political means continue to be launched. Even these are not balanced or proportionate. International bias is clearly in favour of Israel, and there has been no international resolution to save our region and restore our lands as of yet. The predominating pragmatic approach is also unacceptable, for it speaks of mighty and grave circumstances that require flexibility and submission to the status quo, a pause while awaiting some vague future changes, or a change in international convictions leading to an imbalance against Israel, or yet an increase in our military power that would eventually settle the conflict. Such logic only breeds surrender. It ends with an abandonment of responsibilities towards recovering land and rights.

What if the majority chooses to desert the duty of defence? This by no means justifies following suit, as the believer is responsible, and upon him rests the duty and fulfilment of the commandment. He should work with whatever minimal means are available to resurrect the nation, for he is not excused from duty should others desist from it. And where there is no equivalence in terms of strength and capabilities, other methods that recompense for the weakness should be sought in order to inflict loss on the enemy until such time as the equation is changed and achievements are realized.

All that the enemy is capable of is implanting the fear of death in us. When we halt this fear, we render the power of death with which he menaces us futile. We walk forward, reinforcing morale and marking gains on the path of victory, and we accumulate these positive achievements across time while waiting for the sought change to take place: *Victory cometh only from Allah, the mighty, the wise.*[1]

The weapon of martyrdom is the main and pivotal weapon on which we can rely, one that has proven its effectiveness and that prompts the enemy to reconsider its objectives. The enemy understands that military might and international-conspirator support do not produce stability, for the youth of martyrs bears belief that is strengthened through religion, and that is more effective than armies of occupiers and aggressors.

Practical Achievements in Lebanon

Martyrdom and *jihad* operations conducted by the Islamic Resistance in Lebanon have marked many objectives and achievements, the most prominent of which are the following:

---

1. Surah no. 3, *al-'Imran*, verse 126.

1. *Compensation for military imbalance and infliction of painful losses on enemy ranks.* This was realized through simple and humble technologies that, on the one hand, shook the Israeli army's ability to defend itself, and on the other unsettled its ability to retaliate. The Israeli army withdrew in 1985 from over half of the occupied territories in South Lebanon in order to reduce its spread and susceptibility to attack by the Resistance. The enemy could not tolerate many attacks like that from the pioneer of all martyr attacks, Sheikh Ahmad Kassir, who (on November 11, 1982) drove a car trapped with explosives right into the headquarters of the Israeli commander in the city of Tyre, wounding and killing 141 Israeli officers, a further ten declared missing.[1] The enemy was forced into defeat and withdrawal from the majority of Lebanese territories on May 24, 2000, marking the largest and first liberation of its kind in the region resulting from resistance operations.

2. *The Israeli command's reconsideration of its military approach in Lebanon.* The decision to invade was no longer easy, and aggression was not possible at any time for fear of retaliation. Menacing those who aspire to martyrdom with the notion of death was a futile threat.

   Enemy command admitted to the effectiveness of the martyrdom weapon. In the words of one northern region commander: 'The war with Lebanon did not achieve any success. Divergent views existed for its reasons and objectives. We have miscalculated the effect of those ravagers [the Resistance], and went astray in our evaluation of

---

1. *Al-Kifah al-Arabi*, November 10, 2001.

time and place. We have underestimated the extent and complication of confessional interlacing in Lebanon. We miscalculated people's reactions. We were wrong on many counts. Rather, we were wrong on all counts.'[1]

Knesset member Yossi Beilin said in the same context: 'The members of Hizbullah do not only drive our army mad, but leave the whole of Israel insane. Everyone is concerned with this issue.'[2]

3. *The surge of patriotic fervour across the region, the outbreak of the Palestinian Intifadah[3] and the restoration of hope for a comprehensive liberation.* Such zeal accompanied the mood of enrolment that appeared in several states and regions, especially in the Palestinian territories, where martyrdom operations became the primary effective means of facing Israel.

4. The exposure of the Israeli soldier as one who hides in the safety of his military machines, afraid of direct military conflict. This was manifested through many occurrences of army desertion and the desire of many to return home with the least delay possible. They were worn out, and lost hope of achieving anything out of their presence in Lebanon.

Martyrdom alone does not achieve victory or tip the existing balance, and all other possible means should be used in conflict. However, martyr operations fill a significant gap in the imbalance

---

1. *Davar*, June 7, 1985.
2. Interview, Channel 1 (Israeli television), February 3, 1984.
3. The term used to describe the Palestinian uprising, launched with the most modest of means against the might of the Israeli occupier.

of powers. Attempting to defeat the enemy with the minimum possibility of bloodshed is a duty. Martyrdom calls for breaking the balance of power, and this should be sought through other means, as the soul is precious and is only to be given up after all else fails. If, for instance, it were possible to target and inflict casualty on the enemy by way of a grenade, then exposing oneself to death would not be a permissible alternative. This is why it was always intended for such martyr operations to inflict the highest number of casualties and losses on the enemy, to carry a good probability of assuring objectives, and to be well designed in advance at all planning, accuracy, follow-up and accountability levels.

Third: Jurisdiction of the Jurist-Theologian (al-Wali al-Faqih)

The Prophet (PBUH) is the messenger, the bearer of the holy doctrine of *Shari'a*, who has been inspired to see to its execution and to define the nation's path towards its fulfilment. Following the Prophet in referential supremacy are the infallible Imams (PBUT), starting with Commander of the Faithful Imam Ali bin Abi Taleb and ending with Imam al-Mahdi. Their role is to interpret and clarify the various aspects of the Message, and monitor its proper execution. In the absence of the infallible, the nation needs to master both knowledge of the commandment to which it is assigned, and implementation of *Shari'a* in public and private life.

The masses would find this knowledge difficult to grasp were it not for the labour of experts and clerics who work to derive legislative and doctrinal judgments, in order to clarify what falls under the realm of duty and what it denies, what is admired and allowed and what is abhorred. They are the ones who place the greatest effort towards understanding *Shari'a* jurisprudence, and are distinguished by their diligence, justice, deep piety and a general lack of devotion to life. Imam al-Sadek (PBUH), for example, is 'among the jurists who preserves himself and his religion and denies his whims in obedience of his Lord's order should be followed by the masses.'[1] Among the many clerics, he who is most knowledgeable naturally emerges and gains the approval of the discipline's experts. He thus becomes charged with revealing *Shari'a* verdicts and judgments, becoming the spiritual authority of last resort. To him, all those charged with a religious commandment are imitators, following his words and thus absolving themselves from the possibility of straying from Islam's teachings.

Of the manner in which man is directed to his religious arbitrator and related to him, the martyred clerical authority al-Sayyed Muhammad Baqr al-Sadr wrote:

> The Prophet (PBUH) and the imam are assigned and named by God Almighty, while the spiritual authority is assigned qualitatively. Islam thus defined the general qualifications of a religious arbitrator, leaving the tasks of confirming qualification to the nation itself. From here, following the path of the arbitrator was a Godly decision, while the choice of the arbitrator is a physical manifestation of such a decision, one undertaken by the nation.
>
> One's religious attachment to the Prophet (PBUH) and resort to his teachings when receiving God Almighty's

---

1. Al-Tabarsi, *al-Ihtijaj*, vol. 2, p. 262.

> judgments makes of one a believer in the Prophet. By the
> same token, the same relationship with the *imam* makes
> of one a believer in that *imam*, while one's connection
> with the spiritual authority makes of one an imitator of
> that authority.[1]

Implementation can take one of two forms: one is individual and linked to forms of worship, treatment of others and all that is related to personal and daily life. The other is general, pertinent to the nation as a whole – its interests, its wars, peace, and overall direction.

As such, in the first stage of implementation the charged individual is in need of a religious arbitrator in order to be aware of the guidelines and verdicts of jurisprudence, while in the second, he is in need of a leader, as represented by the Jurist-Theologian, who defines the general politics of a nation's life – the practical role of the charged in executing holy judgments. The spiritual authority and the Jurist-Theologian may be one and the same person.[2]

Within the realm of duty, it is not directly possible to distinguish religious from political obligations. Likewise, it is not possible to separate the masses into religious devotees and life-seekers. Imam Khomeini said:

> If you were able to understand the essence of religion
> in this Islamic culture of ours, you would clearly see no
> distinction between religious and political leadership,
> and moreover, it would become apparent that political

---

1. *Man's Succession and the Testimony of the Prophets*, p. 26.
2. Such was the case of Imam Khomeini upon the victory of the Islamic revolution in Iran. It was also true of Imam Khamenei, who held both titles shortly after he was elected to rule.

strife is an integral part of religious duty. Leading such political strife and steering it in the right direction is thus an element of the religious leader's functional responsibilities.[1]

The characteristic interrelation of Islam's verdicts places the individual at the centre of all responsibility, to which he should respond to the best of his abilities according to his situation and capability. Should distinction among people be applied, then that would only be in response to differences in capability, situation or the objective circumstances surrounding individuals.

Guardianship by the Jurist-Theologian is imperative for the preservation and implementation of Islam. It is not possible to achieve Islam's large-scale project through individual initiatives or detached programmes. There is a need for one clear path that practically brings the nation together. Through his guardianship and custodianship, the Jurist-Theologian achieves these very ends.

In the words of Imam Khamenei:

> The purpose of such absolute custodianship by the Jurist-Theologian, who fulfils all qualifications, is that Islam, this true religion – the end of all heavenly religions and one that shall remain until the Day of Resurrection – is the religion of ultimate verdict and societal organization. As such, Islamic society needs a curator, a jurist and leader who would guard the nation of Islam and Muslims against enemies, protect the nation's structure and ensure justice among its constituents, deterring the might of the strong from

---

1. Imam Khomeini, *Manhajiat al-Thawra al-Islamiah*, p. 138.

the weak, securing the means for cultural, political and social development and prosperity for all.

Such a principle may be against the aspirations, liberties and interests of some. It is up to the ruler, upon his execution of leadership functions in light of Islamic jurisprudence (*fiqh*), to implement the necessary measures as and when he deems fit.[1]

The Jurist-Theologian's authority thus represents a continuation of that of the Prophet and the infallible Imams (PBUT) insofar as its role is concerned. This by no means signifies a personal resemblance between the Jurist-Theologian and the Prophet or any infallible Imam, nor a similarity in God's chosen stature for them. Rather, the Jurist-Theologian is the Imam's secondary, one who carries out the Imam's doctrinal and jurisprudence functions as required.

The Jurist-Theologian's Authority

As Imam Khomeini put it:

> The illusion that the Prophet's leadership authority was higher than that of Commander of the Faithful, or that the latter's authority was higher than that of the Jurist-Theologian, is but a delusion. It is doubtless that the Prophet's virtues are more numerous than those of all people, but the sum of moral virtues does not increase one's ruling authority. Those same mandates awarded to the Prophet and the Imams (PBUT) in terms of mobilizing soldiers, assigning rulers and governors, collecting taxes and redistributing wealth among

---

1. Imam Khamenei, *Ajwibat al-Istiftat*, p. 24.

Muslims have also been provided by God Almighty
to the governments of today. More than one person
was chosen by God and assigned this authority. The
assignment was rather bestowed on he who symbolizes
knowledge and justice.[1]

The degree of authority awarded to the Jurist-Theologian is
obviously high, for he is entrusted with implementing Islamic
jurisprudence, guarding the Islamic structure, undertaking
political decisions of considerable weight and bearing on the
nation's overall interest. He has the authority to decide on
issues of war and peace, is accountable to all, through verdicts
and implementation, for their personal security and safety of
wealth, and preservation of personal honour. He is also custodian
of the nation's wealth as collected through *zakat* and *khums*[2]
and other sources. He sets the guidelines for any Islamic state
upon its inception, directing it towards abidance by doctrinal
jurisprudence and to preservation of its constituents' interests
in accordance with Islam.

Such a load may not be entirely and directly undertaken by
one person, which therefore calls for delegation of authority and
assignment of individuals and responsibilities to a number of
high-level, foundational offices. The Jurist-Theologian is faced
with alternative modes of action, from which he chooses those
that are considered to be in best accordance with Islam.

This authority is not distinct from the qualifications that
should be present in the Jurist-Theologian himself, those that
require doctrinal knowledge at the *ijtihad* (interpretative-

---

1. Imam Khomeini, *al-Hukuma al-Islamiah*, p. 86.
2. Whereby a Muslim is obliged to pay one-fifth of his annual earnings, later
   redistributed among the needy or as deemed fit by the ruler.

judgment) level enabling the inference of *Shari'a* verdicts. Requirements also include political capability and practicality in what serves a proper administration and accompaniment of societal needs, alongside personal qualities such as justice and religious devotion of the level that instils strong internal defences in terms of one's relationship with God and the preservation of *Shari'a* limits.

The issue is thus not limited to Islamic jurisprudence (*fiqh*) and interpretation. In this context Imam Khomeini explained: 'The interpretations taught in religious schools are never sufficient, for even if the teacher in these gatherings is of the highest educational order, he may still be incapable of modeling the needs of society or signifying the virtuous from the wicked. Such a person would generally lack proper judgment on societal or political matters, and may also have a deficit in terms of decision-making. As such, he would not be a fit jurist in governmental or social issues and may not a good manager of society.'[1]

Custodianship by the Jurist-Theologian is not a new issue. It has been mentioned over time by the leading clerics such as al-Sheikh al-Mufid and the Shi'ite congregation's prominent Sheikh al-Tusi, followed by al-Muhaqqiq al-Helli in his book *Islam's Codes*; al-Muhaqqiq al-Karaki, the sage al-Helli, the second Amili martyr, Najaf Sheikh, author of *al-Jawaher*, narrators al-Sayyed al-Burujerdi; and al-Sayyed al-Kalbaykani, in addition to the martyred al-Sayyed Muhammad Baqr al-Sadr and Imam Khomeini, among many others.[2]

But the issue surfaced at this level only with Imam Khomeini, for two reasons. First, the level of importance he attached to it

---

1. Imam Khomeini, *Manhajiyat al-Thawra al-Islamiah*, p. 163.
2. Sheikh Malik Wehbe, *al-Faqih wal Sulta wal Umma*, pp. 428–42.

was evident through his exile conferences in sacred Najaf, where the details of his vision were presented, later to be compiled in his book *The Islamic Government*. The second source of importance came with practical implementation resulting from the fall of the Shah of Iran and the rise of an Islamic state there, following which a constitution based on commitment to clerical custodianship was adopted as one of the basic pillars of governance.

Previously, circumstances surrounding Muslims and their clerics were not in favour of expressing such an issue at the practical level, nor in contexts narrower than that of creating an Islamic state. Power was either not in their hands, or the circumstances surrounding such governance were not available. The issue does not rest simply on the existence of a qualified cleric but also of believers and devotees who commit to executing the cleric's orders and forbiddances in their daily lives.

Since the days of the infallible Imams (PBUT) there has never been a similar stature for the religious head as that of Imam Khomeini. He has achieved such stature through merit, juristic and political competence, and fulfilment of the required qualifications. Simply assuming the role of Commander of the Faithful, Caliph or Jurist-Theologian does not qualify one for it, as the custodian of Islamic *Shari'a* is not he who executes it as he sees fit, but rather he who is of adequate knowledge and leadership to do so.

The Party's Relationship with the Jurist-Theologian

The Jurist-Theologian's native land has no relation to the scope of his dominion. The same is true of the spiritual authority and the geographical scope of such authority. He could be Iranian or

Iraqi, Lebanese or Kuwaiti, or any other. His nationality is thus not related to his qualifications, for he carries the toll of Islam and works for this religion that is merciful on all beings: *We sent thee not but as a mercy for all creatures.*[1] The limits of authority are defined by the response of those responsible individuals.

As guardian of Muslims, Imam Khomeini governed the Islamic state in Iran as a guide, leader and supervisor of the Islamic system on that territory, but defined the general political commandments for all Muslims anywhere they lived in the context of preservation of the resources of Muslim states; enmity towards hegemony; protection of independence from domination and subjugation; work towards unity, especially on fateful and common issues; confrontation of the cancer implanted forcefully in Palestine as represented by the Israeli entity; refusal of all forms of oppression and deflection; caring for the needy and repressed; and strengthening of the practice of joint responsibility amongst people. His successor, Imam Khamenei, assumes the same role and authorities.

Connection with this guardianship is thus an obligation and commitment that encompasses all those charged, even if one's spiritual authority is not represented by the Jurist-Theologian himself, for the ultimate command in this Islamic path emanates from the Jurist-Theologian.

Discrepancies among people's living circumstances are not a source of concern, for the limits set by the Jurist-Theologian take two issues into consideration: first, undisputable implementation of the doctrinal *Shari'a* principles, and second: the objective and specific conditions of every group or country which falls within and affects the circle of responsibility and concern.

---

1. Surah no. 21, *al-Anbiaya'*, verse 107.

Hizbullah's commitment to such jurisprudence is a link in this chain. It is work within the sphere of Islam's implementation, a behavioural given that is an integral part of the directives and rules drawn by the Jurist-Theologian. Following this main category come the tasks of administration and oversight of details and particulars; implementing procedures; daily political, social and cultural work; and *jihad* against the Israeli invader, in all senses. Such responsibility is assumed through Party members elected according to the internally adopted consultation system, and is headed by the Party's Secretary-General. The set-up earns its legitimacy through the Jurist-Theologian, and thus receives the authority and accreditation necessary for it to perform its duties with a margin of manoeuvring room left to the Party's leaders and consultations enabling them to decide and evaluate what is applicable and appropriate in their fields.

Such authority is reflected as substantial independence at the practical level, not necessitating direct and daily supervision by the Jurist-Theologian. Where Party leadership is confronted with essential issues or overtures that might affect any of the working principles or requiring knowledge of legislative jurisprudence, the Party would then take the initiative of inquiry or of requesting clerical permission that should provide the legal *Shari'a* grounds for executing or ceasing a certain action.

Such commitment to the Jurist-Theologian and his jurisprudence does not limit the scope of internal work at the level of forging relations with the various powers and constituents of Lebanon. It further does not limit the sphere of regional and international cooperation with groups with whom the Party's strategic direction or concerns meet.

Given that working within a particular country is connected

to a given set of circumstances and individuality, it is so that Hizbullah's work concords the Islamic order with the Lebanese national background. It is a Lebanese faction by all means, from its framework to its members. The Party is concerned with all that takes place on its turf, be it political, cultural, social or *jihad* work, and harbours Islam, which accommodates it and is open to accommodating the world. Concern for the Islamic world's issues and those of the oppressed does not conflict with interest and concern for national issues that fall within the realm of refuting occupation and oppression, struggling for justice and preserving interests and national priorities.

There is no party or group in the world that does not have its internal and external delimitations, based on its vision of its own interests, and in harmony with the convictions it holds. Such points are not considered negative except where they are a source of subordination which hampers free choice, of a clear conspiracy with the enemy, or of an action which results in domination and annulment of others' rights. Should Lebanon be in accord and agreement with its surroundings while striving to achieve its aims, and should it receive the support and backing of other nations in its quest for resistance and liberty, then these are only normal legitimate requests. Attenuation occurs when we are forced to deal with our own issues in seclusion and are denied support. Wisdom is in forging those relationships that assist in achieving our rights while coinciding positively with the aims of others.

When Hizbullah benefits from the support of the Islamic Republic of Iran, just as the Republic of Lebanon would benefit, it is in harmony with Iran's conviction of Hizbullah's soundness of path, right in *jihad* and resistance, and Lebanon's rights to reclaim lost land (which is also the Palestinians' right). It is also in harmony with Hizbullah's conviction of the soundness of the Islamic Republic of Iran's approach and practice, in the change it brought to the region's map through independence from subordination to the West and adoption of a promising Islamic vision. Iran's commitment to the Jurist-Theologian's commands eased the identification of common ground with Hizbullah's vision for the region and liberation objectives. There is no connection between the internal administration of the Iranian state and Hizbullah's administration. These are two separate issues, each having its particularities and bodies of administration despite the commitment of both to the commands and directions of the Jurist-Theologian, who is custodian of the entire nation of Islam and whose power of command is not confined to any circle within it.

The Party's commitment to Islam translates as an obligation to all that is ordained and forbidden by God. The Party has thus pledged not to swerve from these Godly instructions. For these reasons, commitment to a doctrinal instruction or opinion is not considered to be a point of view open to change. However, where an issue falls in the circle of allowable choice, re-evaluation of any opinion becomes possible based on evidence, general interest and such other relevant considerations. Occupation is thus considered a sin, and this represents a juristic verdict that is irreversible, irrespective of conditions. However, the mode of confrontation enters into the realm of choice, which in turn is a function of circumstance.

TWO

Organization and Public Work

Hizbullah, or The Nation of the Party of God

Research started into the practical implementation of those objectives endorsed by Imam Khomeini in the Manifesto of the Nine. Wide-ranging discussions ensued at the Party leadership level, particularly in what relates to the ideal organizational set-up and directorial framework, and as to how the Party's merits could serve for magnetizing and bringing the nation together. There was a need to answer the question that reflects the overall direction to be adopted: should the party be called 'Hizbullah' or the 'Nation (*umma*) of Hizbullah'?

A danger inherent in the structure of parties is that of restricting size to members, thus leading to the exclusion of 'others'. Whatever the organization's scope or capacity, a party is still limited in terms of rank and functions. This fact could easily translate into a forfeit of human potentials and a possible rise of partisanship spirit, one that shuns non-members and individuals whose goals are not in line with the party's objectives.

On the other hand, the concept of the nation or body politic rests on a platform that recognizes all, whatever their allegiances, obligations or preparation for participation, but does not lack in implementation hurdles. It is founded on the existence of a leadership that issues instructions to mosques, community clerics and committees. Direction is provided in a general context and on particular occasions, to which the nation reacts and responds. However, in a diverse society like Lebanon such direction does not answer to the challenge of convening the nation's potential and organizing its roles and capabilities; variety of opinion; individual obligations; discrepancies across intellectual levels and practical experience; decision-making process; and inter-factional ties.

A hierarchical pyramid structure was finally adopted as the Party's organizational formula, and was designed within guidelines that exclude the disadvantages of both aforementioned propositions, thus taking the following shape:

1. Entitlement to Party membership was conferred upon those who adopted the Party's goals in their entirety, committed to Party organizational directives, agreed to the time limit projected for the Party to undertake its functions, and possessed general personal, religious belief, behavioural and *jihad* credentials which qualified them for entering the system and for growing within it while undertaking their obligations.

2. No membership tokens were distributed, as affiliates were not the only individuals contributing to the Party's goals. The definition of affiliation to the Party was not tied to a Party identification card.

3. Individuals were required to observe and comply with their assigned Party functions, the most important of which was resistance activity. Making available the appropriate job-description framework was another Party priority,

alongside the distribution of functional responsibilities and authority boundaries needed for effective goal execution and the facilitation of coordination among the Party's various units.

4. A broad recruitment process was launched across the various districts and villages, one encompassing all those interested in joining the Party. The hierarchical management of these recruits was based on district demographics and geographic distribution. Participation was a function of individual circumstances and time availability. All affiliates took part in military and cultural training, combat and post guardianship, as well as any general functions required by the Party.

5. Women's societies were created, and roles distributed throughout mosques and districts. The objective was to achieve cultural and societal recruitment to the end of securing participation in the activities and general call of the Party.

6. Youth recruitment and cultivation was channelled through founding the Imam al-Mahdi Scouts, where alongside general participation in the Party's broad undertakings, activities that were in harmony with the young generation's needs were planned.

7. Independently-run organizations in the educational, cultural, health, media, agricultural, construction and other domains were created, which complied with the Party's general goals

and objectives. A margin of discretion was awarded to these entities in terms of membership selection, while observing minimum Party guidelines for political and cultural direction as well as monitoring security-breach regulations.

8. Cultural recruitment targeting students and secondary-school and university teachers was activated. Events in line with the educational sector were planned, and the scope of membership encompassed all those interested in participating within the pre-defined Party policies and declared objectives.

9. Participation in the creation of various societies and circles – be they professional, syndicated or specialized – is another Party goal. Here, a wider margin for selection is possible whereby direct Party participation rules were not applicable, but where observation of minimum compliance with the general goals and policies of the Party was a necessary condition for participation. The programmes and activities of such circles were limited to the members' professional spheres of specialization.

10. Continuous cooperation with clerics, associations and the various created organizations was required and should be in harmony with the general objectives of Hizbullah.

11. All those who participate in the rallies, activities and concerns of Hizbullah as well as those who support the Party's ideology were considered as supporters of Hizbullah.

This organizational framework thus encompassed those segments comprising fundamental believers in the Party's goals while honouring and maintaining inter-segment differences. It thus avoided the pitfall of excluding 'others'. However, the search continues for means to enlarge the circle and benefit from further supporters and Party admirers, means that would widen the scope of societal membership and the utilization of available potential. Further, there is a steadfast effort to dilute any extremist partisanship spirit that is a natural byproduct of any congress or assembly. The fostering or waning of such spirit is a function of overall Party guidance as directed by the body of responsible supervisors. The aim is thus to limit such partisanship to an acceptable minimum that falls in line with Party formation requirements.

As such, the problem was no more deemed to lie in the name assigned to the Party, as this is of little bearing on the reality of Hizbullah's activities. The choice was made to become 'Hizbullah', or the Party of God. The Party covers and includes all of the nation's segments as outlined above and observes a complete readiness for amendment of internal policies when the need for scope enlargement or stature change arises.

The Council and the Organizational Framework

The choice was in favour of group as opposed to individual leadership, the title of which was to be *al-Shura* – the Council. Membership was to result from deliberation among the Party's primary figures of authority. The number of elected delegates differed between one Council and another, and there was initially no single head or general secretariat. This organizational set-up lasted for seven years, until the declaration of the Open Letter in 1985 necessitated the creation of a post for Official Spokesman. The declaration was as a response to the need for an official political appearance and expression of the Party's position.

As work progressed, the need for amending the Council's organizational set-up, and membership criteria surfaced. An internal regulation was adopted whereby the number of Council members would be limited to nine individuals elected for a period of one year. Such election was to be made by the principal cadres who occupy a post of Section Head and above. Thereupon, the Council would elect a Secretary General from among its members and assign responsibilities as per the authority outlined in its internal policies. The first such elected Council – which was the fourth in sequence – elected Sheikh Subhi al-Tufaili as Secretary General on November 11, 1989. A six-month extension to this Council's term was granted given the impossibility of holding the annual Party conference (hostility between Amal and Hizbullah at the time had forced a siege on the Iqlim al-Tuffah area where the conference was to be held).

Thereafter, some policy amendments were made. Yet another reduction in the number of Council members was decided, the total brought down to seven, which was more in accordance with assigned responsibilities, and the Council's term was decided to be two years. The Deputy Secretary General position was also created. In May 1991, the Council elected as Secretary General al-Sayyed Abbas al-Moussawi, who was martyred on February 16, 1992. The Council then elected as successor al-Sayyed Hassan Nasrallah, who came to effectively assume its term activities.

The election of al-Sayyed Hassan Nasrallah occurred in mid-May of 1993, and was to recur in the election rounds since then, inclusive of the seventh round of August 2003. Two amendments to the Council's policies were passed over the period, the first of which was to extend its term to three years, while the second provided the Secretary General with the possibility of candidacy even following success in two consecutive elections.

On the general organizational set-up level, several amendments were made in an effort to conform to Hizbullah's functional requirements. Five boards or council assemblies were finally created, these being: the *Jihad* Assembly; the Political Assembly; the Executive Assembly; the Parliamentary Assembly; and the Judicial Assembly. Leadership of each of these was to be assigned to one Council member.

The Political Assembly groups those responsible for political portfolios as well as members of the Analysis Committee. Its scope involves providing the Council with political analysis while continuously working on fostering relationships with the various political powers and parties in the country.

The *Jihad* Assembly comprises those in charge of resistance activity, be that in terms of oversight, recruitment, training, equipment, security or any other resistance-related endeavours.

The Parliamentary Assembly groups the Party's Members of Parliament and oversees the functions of the Allegiance to the Resistance coalition. In addition, the Assembly is concerned with studying proposed legislation brought before Parliament, and follows up on the needs of citizens as well as the Party's relationship with the government and its various bodies. It adheres to the Party's political stance and expresses it through the Party's MPs at various functions.

The Executive Assembly groups the unit heads in charge

of cultural, education, social, professional and various other groups. It is thus in charge of activities and procedures related to the formation of the Party. It is also in charge of overseeing the activities of various Party organizations that are managed through a board of directors.

The Judicial Assembly groups the judicial representatives in different areas who work together with Hizbullah members on conflict resolution, verdicts related to abidance within *Shari'a* limits, and the reinstatement of rights.

Every assembly member is considered to be a Unit Head overseeing a committee of Section Heads, to whom responsibilities are delegated. The organizational set-up at the sub-unit levels then interconnects at either the *jihad*, recruitment or support ranks.

The Council is considered to be at the top of the strategic objectives pyramid, in charge of drawing the overall vision and policies, overseeing the general strategies for the Party's functions, and taking political decisions. The Secretary General is charged with supervisory, administrative and guidance responsibilities, coordination between the members of the Council and the various Assembly Heads, as well as expression of the Party's official leadership stance.

Attracting Membership

Interest in Hizbullah membership increased following clear demonstration of achievements on the resistance-to-occupation front. To some, direct involvement in the Party's framework was an obstacle, as not all of those who believe in the righteousness of Hizbullah's resistance could abide by and conform to its

Islamic ideology. Similarly, those who believe in the Party's political movement may not be compliant with the worship and behavioural rules of Islam, or may be interested in such compliance while guarding a personal margin that could conflict with the Party's goals and membership requirements. Further, the Party's ability to accommodate individuals and assign them to particular functions may not be in line with those individuals' perceptions of what is appropriate for their careers or personal paths.

Leadership formally requested a number of assemblies to discuss modes of attracting membership from these special groups, and the following suggestions were made:

1. *The creation of a new Party framework that reduces the specifications and objectives adopted by Hizbullah.* Given an indisputable priority to resistance activity, it was suggested that conferences and meetings would be held to discuss the existing framework and its objectives with the aim of achieving the best possible formula for the accommodation of new members.

   Here, a number of pivotal questions surfaced: would this new framework replace Hizbullah and thus mean that all current Party members would become, by default, part of the new setup? Or would it be an alternative to the Party that only some would join, leaving others within the original framework?

   Creation of a new party with lesser requirements and objectives than those of Hizbullah would simply mean a renunciation of those visions and objectives in which the Party believes, a fact that is ultimately in conflict with

Hizbullah's ideology and values. Further, such a split would trap the Party in a functional dualism whereby the very potential that it seeks to cultivate and benefit from would be compromised and threatened in a context of divisions and dispersions.

Further, would Hizbullah decide the new party's policies and assume a supervisory role? If so, then what use is there in creating a new independent set-up and wasting resources running more than one organizational framework? Alternatively, would this new party take its decisions independently? If so, how would Hizbullah be related to it, and would there be any assurances of compliance with Hizbullah's practical path? Would this be a party, a group or an assembly? Given the numerous controversies, this option was ruled out.

2. *The creation of independent groups and circles, or participation in their creation.* These groups must comply with some Party objectives and observe a number of specifications and guidelines. In principle, there is no objection to this concept, which essentially requires agreement between Hizbullah and individuals or groups who are interested in forming a framework of some sort. Where the minimum guidelines for Hizbullah membership are observed, any new set-up may be related to the overall framework akin to the various existing groups and professional structures that harbour an organizational relationship with the Party. A set-up would thus have rights, observe obligations, and harbour a directorial system tied to the Party in accordance

with pre-defined responsibilities, objectives, policies and scope of authority.

3. *Peripheral membership.* Where the new set-up does not conform to the minimum Party membership requirements, it could still be entirely independent and take on individual characteristics, choose for itself or in conjunction with Party cadres whatever objectives and functions it may deem appropriate, and become a formation that is supportive of Hizbullah but which does not form part of its integral organization.

Variation among people is a natural human condition linked to culture, upbringing, inclinations and interests, and as such cannot be dealt with within a single unifying frame. The responsibility of choice is left to individuals according to their own convictions. The Party was launched with specific objectives, and is supported by organizational mechanisms for functioning. Those who agree to and are in harmony with such objectives are on the track of affiliation or membership, while those who are not remain at a distance from the Party just as the Party accommodates or excludes applicants on the basis of individual and group rules.

Such is the mode of life, and there is no need to succumb to the pressure of accountability where the alternative is either adhering to objectives or attracting membership, for objectives come first and membership follows on that basis. Invitation to membership in a manner that jeopardizes one objective after another is a weak link that would disintegrate with any imminent change of course.

Islamic Resistance

The Beginnings

Israel's invasion of Lebanon in 1982 was the sixth in a series of Arab-Israeli wars:

1. The Israeli occupation of Palestinian territories in 1948, covering 20,770 of the 27,027 square kilometres comprising Palestinian land. These have been termed 'The Occupied Territories' since then.

2. The trio aggression against Egypt in 1956, marked by the alliance of France, Britain and Israel.

3. In 1967, Israeli aggression occupied the remainder of Palestinian territories (now termed 'The '67 Territories'), in addition to the Egyptian Sinai, Syrian Golan Heights and Jordan's Arabah Valley.

4. The October 1973 war by Egypt and Syria against Israel was marked by the reclamation of some lost land by these two countries.

5. In 1978, Israeli aggression resulted in the occupation of a large portion of South Lebanon and in the creation of a 'security zone' in which a number of Lebanese collaborators headed by Saad Haddad remained.

Initiation of five wars is attributed to the Zionists, while on one count the Arabs were the first to enter combat. These wars had the effect of enlarging the geographical control of Israel to include land beyond Palestine and into the nearby Arab territories of Egypt, Lebanon, Syria and Jordan. Israeli military might, supported by international political means – led by the United States – created sufficient pressure to impose concessions and legitimize the fait accompli that the occupation had become.

The Zionists considered that the invasion of Lebanon would cripple the infrastructure of the Palestinian military resistance and alienate Palestinian fighters from Lebanon, thus breaking their future ability to continue their quest for land reclamation. This was thought to facilitate the political steps aiming at strengthening and confirming the existence of the Israeli entity within boundaries that would ensure its survival and security from its Arab surroundings.

Given a generally lax and submissive Arab environment, in addition to a demonstrated readiness by Palestinian and Arab leaders to reach a compromise on the Palestinian issue – one protected by the Arabs and leading to a closure of the Palestinian cause as per dictated Israeli rules – Israel could have easily achieved its objectives.

However, as Palestine is an Arab and Muslim occupied land, and it is the duty of every Muslim to work for its liberation, and given that other areas of Arab land are similarly occupied (including Lebanon) and to which the Islamic duty of liberation is also applicable, the Jurist-Theologian Imam Khomeini declared: 'Israel is a cancerous gland.' As such, Hizbullah rose to this target and launched Islamic resistance operations against Israel with whatever limited numbers of individuals and capabilities were available. This was a step on the path towards achieving a more comprehensive and all-encompassing resistance movement that does not compromise land and that refuses the enemy's exploitation of the Arab world's weaknesses and those of Palestine.

Priority was therefore awarded to confrontation, which called for employment of all resources towards this end. The training camps set up in the Bekaa area and supervised by the Iranian Islamic Revolutionary Guard constituted the primary source of resistance fighters – or *mujahideen* – for the 'Islamic Resistance'. These camps were also the source of inspiration for cultural, spiritual, behavioural and *jihad* qualities, all of which were essential traits in the personalities of Revolutionary Guard members. Many Hizbullah members participated in such training irrespective of their functional posts in the Party or their assigned tasks, as training is a pre-requisite for Party membership. The martyred former Secretary General, al-Sayyed Abbas al-Moussawi, was among the first to go through such training, which he achieved towards the end of 1982.

At that time, the capital city and its immediate suburbs as well as the South, the Western Bekaa and parts of Mount Lebanon were under Israeli military occupation. Resistance fighters worked in secret circles without any political or media appearances. Parallel to this was a general recruitment and cultural movement, which also took place without any formal organizational framework.

Resistance fighters quickly accumulated military experience. In addition to what was learned from the Palestinian experience in Lebanon and what was accumulated through training camps, especially those in the Bekaa, focus was awarded to directing individuals towards specializing in exploration, engineering, artillery, and other military areas. Tasks were distributed hierarchically in a manner conforming to the requirements of field battle and back-up support.

Youth and Effectiveness

Resistance work was not limited to those fully dedicated individuals, but rather extended into general enrolment of volunteers for field operations and garrisons over limited recurring periods, all while taking into account the individual circumstances of each affiliate. Participants conducted their daily lives in a normal manner, at work or university, in any private sector field be it engineering, office employment or otherwise. The number of young men attracted, and the scope of their power, were considerable; there was never any shortage of affiliates or members for the resistance movement. Participation was always abundant and only increased with time, and with the sacrifices of martyrs. Despite the confrontations experienced during the two Israeli invasions of 1993 and 1996, not many resistance fighters were allowed on the front lines in South Lebanon and the Western Bekaa, as the nature of the conflict required a mode of performance that did not call for direct participation except by a limited number of individuals – those with professional specializations or those assigned along the length of the front.

With an increasing presence of educated and cultured members, it became possible to employ resources and benefits to the largest extent possible from modern computer, communications and various engineering technologies. The *mujahideen* succeeded at inflicting pain to the enemy's weakest military positions while working on improvement of their own feeble areas detected through field battle performance.

A noticeable military advancement was that associated with the accuracy of hitting targets. The engineering and artillery arms units achieved strides in this regard: hitting the enemy right in the centre of the target area; mastering the geographic technicalities of launching Katyusha rockets; understanding the weak points of both the classic and advanced Merkava tanks which became a graveyard for whoever was in them;[1] mastering the preparation of bombs in their various forms; developing expertise in bomb direction during battle; acquiring proficiency in exploration strategies allowing resistance fighters to reach enemy and collaborator posts; mounting round-the-clock surveillance of enemy posts directly or through night or day field glasses; and employing trap tactics, martyrdom operations and many other strategies.

Such levels of military work cannot be perceived in isolation from the fighter's belief in the cause, the fighter's cultivation, courage and fearlessness of martyrdom. This is the real essence of the Islamic Resistance's success. Experience has proven that spiritual mobilization is a foundation for additional power that comes to aid at the time of battle irrespective of the modesty of military equipment available, and any military might may fall prey to self-defeat and dejection during enemy confrontations. No field desertion has ever been recorded in resistance ranks, and no objection to the battle's extension was voiced. On the contrary, steadfast desire for highly dangerous activities and for martyrdom was common, although many such expressions went unapproved for the sake of adhering to confrontation tactics and requirements.

---

1. A deal to sell advanced Merkava tanks to Turkey was called off following the first resistance operation targeting such tanks. The operation served to expose the Merkava's inability to endure attacks by those who understand its mode of confrontation.

The individual's personality is the core of resistance configuration. For this reason, the applicant's file is studied in depth prior to granting approval for membership in the Resistance. Under focus is the individual's belief in Hizbullah, his preparedness for further developing this belief, his cultural and military capabilities, and the non-existence of any security or questionable doubts around him. The individual is closely followed up and appraised throughout his functional training and development in order to determine the benefit that he could bring to the Party.

Operations and Military Combat Methods

Secrecy was the key to success on the *jihad* battlefield. Surprising the enemy achieved the best results with the fewest possible losses. The enemy worked through spies and agents to uncover targets and operations, benefiting from aerial exploration and various military surveillance means in order to detect signals of preparation for possible attack. As such, secrecy was important for rendering such surveillance and investigation futile. A limited circle of individuals was aware of resistance operations. Only those directly involved with planning and execution within the tactics set by the military command formed part of this circle. In addition, Hizbullah participants were selected with extreme accuracy. Taken together, these are the reasons behind the enemy's inability to discover any operation before its execution or during its preparation. All this is what made resistance operations so surprising and successful.

Combat equipment was easily carried, transported and hidden. There was no need for tanks or heavy fixed artillery that could easily be targeted by aerial bombardment and which was not in harmony with the Resistance's weapons plan. Appropriate means of combat were sought from different sources among which were the arms dealers on the various Lebanese fronts. The Resistance, even when short on weapons, always managed with whatever was available, making considerable effort to fill in any gaps. The wisdom employed in the management of scarce military resources led to use of weaponry only at the appropriate time and place. Wisdom was no less important than the resources themselves.

Practical procedures were taken to build a resistance movement that is different from a formal army organization. The Resistance usually acted within secretive circles, even on the battlefield. This allowed for flexibility and permitted members to resume their normal daily lives across the various towns and villages, whether these were situated on the front or back lines. There was no need for any military exposure, which could only turn into a futile show of force not admired by many and would have posed risks as outward exposure was only a clear declaration of targets for the enemy. Training camps also fell under this scope of concern and were thus mobile and camouflaged in order to avoid bombardment by the Israeli warplanes continuously flying across Lebanese skies.

The Resistance did not require fixed posts except in particular mountainous and tree-covered areas[1] given their topographic particularity, remoteness from populated villages, and strategic coverage of all occupied lands (such posts existed within enemy-occupied territory). The need for a number of operation-launching posts was necessary, but none were along

---

1. This was the case in Iqlim al-Tuffah, where presence was essentially in Mlita, Jabal Safi and Sujud – mountainous areas with no civilian population.

front-line villages, despite the favourable geographic terrain. Based on this line of attack, there was no need for weaponry and military posts to be visible along the back lines (in the villages and main cities such as Beirut, Sidon and others).

As such, it was not expected of the Resistance to occupy any of the liberated lands, as was the case with the liberation of the Sujud, Aramta and Dabshe posts as well as many others that saw the planting of the Hizbullah flag and the brief presence of resistance fighters before Israeli planes arrived for intense bombardment. A successful resistance operation was considered one that achieved the wounding, death or expulsion of the post's occupiers, and not necessarily one that resulted in reclamation of the target post.

It was also not expected of the Resistance to concentrate its equipment and resources on the front lines and go through a classic war with the enemy, for this was an army role and required sufficient numbers, equipment and military capabilities. Resistance work was essentially 'hit and run', leaving the enemy surprised without any visible retaliation target.

Such intensity, diversity and extension of operations helped achieve several objectives:

1. Confusing the enemy and obliging its command to call for a constant state of alert, eventually leading to the exhaustion and decline in power.

2. Spreading panic among enemy troops; the fear of death persisted after every successful or possible resistance attack. This served to shake enemy morale and subsequently affected troop performance.

3. Forbidding further expansionist goals from being realized, given the pressure exerted in already occupied areas.

4. Liberating the land as a final and ultimate objective; this occurred in stages, and through many confrontations. Examples include Israeli withdrawal from Toumat Niha and other Western Bekaa areas, retreat from many areas surrounding Jezzine in the south and then from Jezzine itself, and the final wide-range and first-time victory in five decades represented by the liberation of the larger part of South Lebanon and the Western Bekaa on May 24, 2000.

The choice of time and place was of high importance for the success of any of the operations, but the main strategy was one of continuous operations (depending on field circumstances), avoiding any futile and ineffective fire opening, and working independently of any developments taking place on the political scene. Such a comprehensive plan for operational launch helped achieve, first and foremost, field objectives, and had natural repercussions on the political front.

Between Liberation and Negotiation

The Resistance had always defined its *jihad* operations as aiming for land liberation and not bearing any political character. Liberation operations are planned and executed on the field without resorting to any political developments or hinging on the needs and interests of politicians for succumbing to or exerting pressure. Political operations, on the other hand, call for an effort to improve the conditions for political negotiation with the enemy, to provide it with grace periods, and to link the fate of field operations altogether with the nature and course of such political negotiations or even to the pressures that the management of such politics may result in.

Hizbullah was not convinced of those compromise scenarios brought to the table. These only allow the enemy further investment of the occupational fact, and bar any constructive role for the counter parties given of course the power imbalance and the small margin of negotiation available at the political level. Hizbullah thus saw no positive consequence to political negotiation. Besides bloodshed, it leads to sacrifices that do not fall in line with its expected results. The practical, legitimate and objective solution is therefore represented by resistance operations that prompt, as a clear effect, retreat of the enemy and reconsideration of political agendas and methods. It is not possible to isolate any *jihad* movement from its political repercussions, and it is only wise to take some practical steps in the wake of an important change of political course. But there is a great difference between politicized operations aimed at soliciting negotiation bids with a narrow margin of manoeuvre and liberation operations that reinstate rights and refute enforced standards, achieving political results on the road towards freedom.

The Party drew general guidelines for resistance activity, both before and after the liberation, and the effort continues in the still-occupied Shebaa Farms. The Resistance does not act mechanically towards executing such guidelines, but leaves room for concealment and manoeuvre that are only part of war tactics. Perhaps the most notable event of this nature was that which took place on February 8, 2000, when the Israeli army executed focused bombardment targeting the electricity plants of Baalbeck and Jamhour, completely demolishing them and leaving Beirut and its suburbs, Mount Lebanon and Baalbeck in the dark and wounding a number of individuals. The operation's objective was to entice the Resistance to respond, thus creating an excuse for a widespread military operation termed by the Israeli Cabinet as the 'Cascading Operation'. The Resistance did not respond, thereby collapsing the enemy's pre-requisites for launching the operation at the time planned.[1]

Resistance is perceived to be the only available solution for confronting the power imbalance between the Israeli occupiers and the rightful owners of the land. Field tactics are directly linked to the land's natural topology, the extent of enemy proliferation, prevailing circumstances in their various forms, the stance of the country's political body, and available means of combat. As such, the performance of a resistance movement varies from one country to another. Circumstances in Lebanon differ from those in Palestine, and have their effect on the nature of field activity. The common denominator between these two countries is the existence of the same occupier, which allows for a better understanding of the enemy's strengths and weaknesses. As the only solution for occupation is deemed to be military resistance, one combatant's

---

1. Note that the atypical Blat operation in the south, where the Resistance bombed an Israeli patrol on February 6, 2000, led to the death or injury of the patrol's nine soldiers. This operation was broadcast in the media in the wake of the incident. The Israeli inner cabinet's decision is thought to have been directly linked to this operation. Hizbullah was informed of the Cascading Operation through party sources, and decided not to retaliate in order to collapse the Israeli plan. A few days later, the Israeli media exposed the plan, quoting the Israeli prime minister's confusion and discontent at not being able to understand Hizbullah's plans or strategy. See print media sources.

experience can be transferred in essence, objectives, development and procedures from one country to benefit another. The founding block on which all tactics depend is represented in one's perception of what constitutes a plausible solution: resistance or negotiation? Both modes have clearly demonstrated their results. There is no land reinstatement following negotiations, and occupation cannot sustain the pressure of resistance.

Dependence and subordination to regimes trap resistance activity in a realm of obligations and system requirements, and compromise the freedom and efficacy that usually characterize such activity. Suffice it to coordinate with the movement's supporters and benefit from their espousal without falling into their sphere of obligations and requirements; for otherwise, coordination and support would be futile.

The Target Sphere

The resources available to a resistance movement are, by default, weaker than the occupier's means. What buttresses such weakness is the appropriate selection of damaging combat methods, of the type that would force the occupiers to succumb to the bitterness of their occupational feat, obliging them to realize the difficulty of sustaining it any further. The Resistance recognized that security is the pivotal weak point of the Israeli enemy. Field operations thus concentrated on inflicting the highest number of casualties, and the particularities of the Lebanese topography served as an added value towards this aim.

When the enemy persisted in exceeding his bounds during combat through continuous bombardment of civilian targets, the Resistance resorted to aiming Katyusha rockets at the northern

Israeli settlements. The formula of hurting the enemy through direct targeting of Israeli soldiers was proving insufficient to deter Israeli targeting of Lebanese civilian targets. As such, direct bombardment of Israeli civilian areas was a reaction, a reciprocal to what was initiated by the Israeli army. These measures helped achieve the July 1993 Accord and thereafter the April 1996 Accord, in both of which it was agreed that civilian areas should fall within a sphere of neutrality, a fact that is only appropriate and harmonious with the objectives and approach of the Resistance. On the one hand, the Resistance protected its national extension of inhabitants. On another, it concentrated on inflicting casualties on the Israeli army given the *mujahideen*'s resolve, quest for martyrdom and demonstrated excellence during confrontations. The capability of those freedom fighters to shake the Israeli soldiers' sense of security was an important stride forward, one that only served to boost morale and elevate spirits, a sure point of strength in favour of those fighters.

The Resistance considered it futile to target Israelis around the world. Confrontation within the circumference of occupied lands is not only righteous but also fruitful, convincing, and could draw tremendous support for the movement. Land liberation is an objective and substantiated aim, and make the direct occupiers bear the consequences of their actions. Despite the fact that external support can foster a widespread confrontation, increasing the scope in this manner was thought to be controversial and a waste of effort. Limiting the target sphere to occupied lands serves to break the enemy's security, stability and self-protection. It has a cumulative effect and does not bear any negative consequences or side effects to the Resistance. This vision is not separate from the doctrinal aspect of determining the rules and guidelines for confrontation.

The power imbalance could only be equalized through martyrdom. As such, the Resistance focused on hitting the enemy hard, given all means available to the Resistance, irrespective of the enemy's security levels, and this through making use of traps, mortars, bombs or any other methods.

Where it is possible to inflict losses on the enemy without martyrs, such would be indisputable, for the foundation rule is to breach the enemy's security with a priority awarded to bombing as opposed to a *jihad* operation or the falling of martyrs. Next in priority, and where an important military target calls for it, comes the martyrdom operation, conducted either individually or through participation by a *jihad* group.

Given that the resistance fighter, whether in garrison or at the front, is essentially set on the path of martyrdom (harmonious with his Islamic belief and *jihad* obligations), and in view of the high possibility of his death given the magnitude of the danger faced, a martyrdom operation rises in priority where the target is of such importance that it could be achieved only through such an operation. Choice may sometimes be limited to a specific type of operations given the lack of alternatives. The objective is to keep the pace and frequency of field operations at the appropriate level required.

Resistance activity is a cumulative effort that cannot be achieved through a limited number of rounds, for it is the persistence of such activity that achieves future results. Further, victory is not only bound up with military activity. Many factors come into play in the achievement of victory, including effective performance and high morale as well as local, regional, and international circumstances:

> *For had it not been for Allah's repelling some men by means of others, cloisters and churches and oratories and mosques wherein the name of Allah is oft mentioned would assuredly have been pulled down. Verily Allah helpeth one who helpeth Him. Lo! Allah is strong, Almighty.*[1]

Martyrdom operations emerged as an approach adopted by the Resistance. Despite the fact that only twelve such operations executed with car bombs were recorded, those dangerous resistance undertakings where the possibility of martyrdom was high are of incalculable value. Many *mujahideen* were martyred through atypical operations where death was an expected result. Martyrdom renders the military power threatening death ineffective, for such a menace acts only upon those who fear it, and is powerless in front of those who seek it. The spirit of martyrdom spread largely due to religious abidance, which is an integral part of the Islamic order.

This detailed understanding of resistance and martyrdom is not only a product of occupation, for otherwise it would have been applicable in many spheres. We do not attempt here to allude to any lack of commonality between the Islamic Resistance's work and that of other resistance fighters, or any incapacity for sacrifice in other resistance fields. However, it could only be as thorough as described above within an Islamic context. Liberation and refusal of occupation are forms of obedience to God. Martyrdom for the sake of triumphing in God Almighty's heaven and attainment of His blessing, and cultivated worship

---

1. Surah no. 22, *al-Hajj*, verse 40.

and conduct based on spreading this belief and carrying out one's duties without aiming for direct victory as a result, are all expressions of the Islamic order.

Islamic Nomenclature

The name Hizbullah – or 'Party of God' – derives from the Qur'an:

> *Your friend can be only Allah, and His messenger and those who believe, who establish worship and pay the poor due, and bow down [in prayer]. And whosoever taketh Allah and His messenger and those who believe for friends [will know that], Lo! The party of Allah, they are the victorious.*[1]

It is also present in God's words:

> *Thou wilt not find folk who believe in Allah and the Last Day loving those who oppose Allah and His messenger: Even though they be their fathers or their sons or their brethren or their clan. As for such, He hath written faith upon their hearts and hath strengthened them with a Spirit from Him, and He will bring them into Gardens underneath which rivers flow, wherein they will abide. Allah is well pleased with them, and they are well pleased with Him. They are Allah's party. Lo! is it not Allah's party who are the successful?*[2]

Freedom fighters benefited from the title 'Hizbullah' prior to its formal adoption by Party leadership. The Committee of the Nine had suggested an alternative ('The Islamic Movement of

---

1. Surah no. 5, *al-Ma'ida*, verse 56.
2. Surah no. 58, *al-Mujadala*, verse 22.

Lebanon'), which had already been adopted by another Islamic group in the country. The choice was excluded and no alternative was sought for some time, except for the common term used to denote *jihad* activity, namely the 'Islamic Resistance'. The Council finally decided to adopt the name 'Hizbullah' shortly before the Open Letter declaration.

The term 'Islamic Resistance' came as an expression of an Islamic character representing firm belief in the heavenly doctrine:

> *And strive for Allah with the endeavour which is His right. He hath chosen you and hath not laid upon you in religion any hardship; the faith of your father Abraham [is yours]. He hath named you Muslims of old time and in this [Scripture], that the messenger may be a witness against you, and that ye may be witnesses against mankind. So establish worship, pay the poor due, and hold fast to Allah. He is your protecting Friend. A blessed patron and a blessed helper!*[1]

In the wake of the inauguration of activities and for many years thereafter, a wave of criticism targeted this Islamic nomenclature, and had one of three possible reasons at its roots, or all three simultaneously:

1. There was the possible fear of embarking on an Islamic path, given incidents of wrongdoing and contemptible behaviour by some Muslims. The negative effects of propaganda and misinformation aimed at disgracing the image and teachings of Islam could have served in this direction.

---

1. Surah no. 22, *al-Hajj*, verse 78.

2. There was a prevalent consideration among religious sects that the establishment of any military power of significance would create an imbalance among the various Lebanese sects, and would thus benefit one at the expense of another, charging the whole country with the consequences of that military group's actions.

3. The name 'National Resistance' had already been in use by many national factions that cooperated with the Palestinian Liberation Organization, and these groups sought exclusivity over any terms denoting 'resistance operations'. Such exclusivity was not coupled with a clear definition of objectives, even where these groups spoke on behalf of resistance in general, undertaking combat activity as they deemed fit.

The Resistance was familiar with these issues, but did not find them impartial. The first was deemed inapplicable to Hizbullah, given that Islamic movements are quite diverse, not bearing any unified vision in terms of either approach or procedure. Each had its vision and understanding of the Resistance, and Hizbullah was only accountable for its own. Experience is the best proof of practical success or failure, and as such, condemnation of Hizbullah's ideology through deficient comparisons is not suitable.

It is well known that claims against Islam from both the Western capitalist camp and the Eastern socialist bloc were widespread, owing to either ideological convictions or power interests. Fear is deeply entrenched where ignorance of the truth breeds and where submission to rival propaganda is rampant.

The second issue originates from Lebanon's various sectarian interests, which were so extensive it was difficult for one to distinguish among them. However, where military power is only and exclusively employed to combat the enemy, aiming at liberating the land irrespective of geography, and when Lebanon is chained to a set of balances which would render thinking of defeating the 'other' futile or a source of unity for belligerent foes, and where the military supremacy of one sect over others leads to internal strife in which all are losers, then would a serious resistance mission gain natural legitimacy. Any other form of military mission would quickly be exposed and lose its objectives. Hizbullah has always made it clear that resistance weaponry will only be aimed at Israeli occupation, and that any use of weapons for internal civil combat is but futile strife.

The third issue was one that various resistance parties on the ground were evading, each attempting to differentiate through affixing extra names to the term 'National Resistance'. As such, the only benefit from a common name was simply the name's grouping character. But this is already present in the term 'Resistance', under which all factions operated in their quest for liberation.

Why is it that the various resistance factions did not convene to decide on one name and other such details, rather resorting to announcing titles and leaving others to follow? Each group's final objective was not clearly declared in order for a unified label or designation to be adopted. Whether resistance was part of the political choice of negotiation or simply a liberation movement remained a question. Similarly, was resistance a temporary endeavour, or was it to be weighed, at some point during the development of confrontations, against the internal situation?

The Resistance was startled when some of its operations were declared under different banners, a fact which compromised credibility and was in conflict with the grandeur of the final objective. This is despite the fact that the Resistance only announced its operations a full year and nine months following their initial launch, which was primarily due to security considerations as well as for the purpose of confusing the enemy as to the identity of the faction undertaking operations. The first declaration came on April 12, 1984 with the announcement of the martyrdom of Ali Safieddine[1] and following a stretch of resistance activity. Declaration of operations became a drawing power for new recruits, a proof of the movement's effectiveness and sound direction. Declaration became a battleground necessity.

In all cases, nomenclature is merely an identification of that group which is responsible for a certain endeavour, and it is up to that group to benefit from the positive repercussions on fighter morale, recruitment and preparation of interested recruits for combat and its ensuing results. This is but a natural right for all resistance factions. It is therefore futile to conceal the identity of fighters and waste their efforts, for resistance is an honour that warrants competition within the nation for sacrifice. It forms part of everyone's duty – an issue about which all non-participants are questioned and accountable.

Whatever the name adopted, practical execution will expose the nature of a resistance group's objectives. Whether attributed

---

1. Prior to this operation was that executed by the martyred Ahmad Kassir against the Israeli military command post in Tyre on November 11, 1982. Another martyr, who did not identify himself, also executed a car bomb operation targeting Israeli forces at al-Shajrah School in Tyre on October 4, 1983. These were part of a range of operations, which were not of a martyrdom nature, executed in the occupied areas of Beirut, the Jieh Boulevard, the Mount Lebanon highway, South Lebanon and the Western Bekaa.

to the nation, the masses or Islam, a name would not change the fundamental nature of those objectives. It is therefore preferred for a name to clearly and truthfully express objectives from the start, as this would set the movement's progression on a sound track. Hizbullah chose its name to reflect the visions and goals harmonious with its beliefs.

Practical experience proved that the name was not a predicament; it was positively perceived and easily absorbed. Further, the number of titles did not affect the reality of resistance, for that which counts most resides in operational reality and results, not in nomenclature.

Resistance and Public Work

Resistance and Political Work

It could be said that the early 1990s witnessed Hizbullah's broad openness to politicians and public figures as well as other factions. Such a delay between foundation and the launch of political interactions was due to the following main reasons:

1. The foundation period had concentrated on military build-up as a main priority given the primary objective of resisting occupation.

2. Secrecy was a main characteristic of the foundation period. Resistance work requires underground preparation as part of the crucial security needed to ensure the persistence of confrontations, especially in light of the initial scarcity of

individuals and resources. Given that Lebanese airspace was open to the enemy, while collaborators were spread out and ready to execute assassinations and bomb targets, secrecy was vital to avoid any expected losses that could potentially be inflicted by the enemy on the fighting brigades. Political work requires pronouncement, which was not appropriate at the time.

3. Since 1975, the Lebanese terrain had been the domain of complicated circumstances generated by a civil war that hauled the majority of powers into a harsh internal conflict at both the military and political levels. Interest was thus directed internally. This was coupled with the expulsion of the Palestinian Liberation Organization from Lebanon. The power imbalance that ensued included the launch of a number of secondary military conflicts stemming from the Lebanese war; Israel's invasion of Lebanon; and the halt of any interconnection between East and West Beirut due to the set-up of two practically independent states, a condition which endured until the dismissal of General Aoun in the wake of the Taif Accord.

4. Initial concern for the preservation of the Resistance required unequivocal attention, one that postponed involvement in the political scene. Political work could require certain relinquishments and considerations that could have consequences on the undertaking of resistance activity, a fact that politicizes the Resistance movement within a sphere of interactions and demands. When the Resistance came of age, proved itself and its weight of presence, such

concerns were diluted. Focus was then directed towards the formulation of a definition for Hizbullah, one that is indisputably clear and that determined, once and for all, the relationship between the politician and the *jihad* combatant: 'Hizbullah is a *jihad* movement having as a primary mission to undertake *jihad* against the Israeli occupier'; and 'intelligent and wise political effort could and should be a pivotal support for such a *jihad* movement.'

5. The Party's house had to first be put in order. Issues of concern included stabilizing its identity and individuality; clarifying its theoretical and practical objectives; resolving some internal discussions over a number of matters such as the Party's thoughts on the Lebanese government, especially after the Taif Accord; defining the general policy approach towards relationships with the various political powers; and, finally, participation in parliamentary elections.

6. It is no secret that this nascent party absorbed the experiences of its early members, benefiting greatly throughout its foundation year. Appraisals were undertaken on various milestones, the outcome of which was to resolve the Party's stance, verbal communication approach and practical measures. The Party went through a growth and development phase whereby its plans and methods crystallized, and its position on various issues was more clearly determined.

7. At the level of its relationship with the populace, the Party's distinctive move forward was realized with the decision to take part in parliamentary elections. In the years prior to

this development, young men had primarily been concerned with military activity, and were somewhat at a distance from direct and widespread contact with societal segments in cities and villages. The decision to participate in elections created a set of new responsibilities and relationships. Plans and general policies were drawn up, individuals were charged with seeing to the achievement of objectives, and focused guidance of all brothers was aimed at fostering stronger ties with the populace, understanding civilians' needs and pains and cooperating with the inhabitants of various towns and villages to resolve their concerns.

Another distinctive step in tandem with the above-described decision was the experience of working with the ruling body of government and parliamentarians, raising people's concerns and internal issues to the public level; following up on proposed legislation; and executing the representation function in Parliament in accordance with the underlying reasons for such participation. The nature of the relationship with the ruling body and its basic pillars crystallized as an opposition voice that was preceded by abstentions during the first Hariri government.

Relationships with the various political powers and factions had in fact started before then, but spread out considerably and increased in importance along with the Party's stance in political life.

Relationship with National Figures and Power Forces

The Party's approach to political work with national figures and societal powers was based on a practical methodology expressed as tolerance preferred to hostility; cooperation preferred to contempt; the call to God preferred to blasphemy; unity of powers preferred to dispersion; and confronting occupation as more important than internal differences.

This approach accommodated all divisions under the realm of Hizbullah's political interaction except those harbouring direct relations with Israel. Ideology was never a reason for conflict; rather, it was the role and nature of resistance activity. Political reality calls for concentrated effort in order to group resources for defiance of the occupiers which, if neglected in favour of resolving strategic or ideological conflicts, would result in many a discord, hauling everyone into a discussion of inflexible fundamentals and drawing all into debates on secondary issues and internal contests instead of concentration on the main battle. Everyone would lose.

By assigning the priority to resistance for the sake of liberation, and thus postponing debates about the future and strategies in anticipation of the fruits of confrontation with the Israeli enemy, all concerned would have a chance to participate in the struggle against the Zionist project, each from their respective positions and within the boundaries of their convictions and capabilities.

Many factions, movements and organizations formed in our Arab region have only reaped loss when they diverted attention towards minor details, mobilizing their resources towards inconsequential issues and losing track of the fundamental causes. No objectives were achieved, and these entities are to date incapable of participation in issues of relevance to self-determination and their own future.

Based on this viewpoint of relationships with other groups, many important conferences, committees, and inter-party meetings were recorded. It was Hizbullah that called for the convention of all Lebanese factions which took place on August 18, 1997 at Le Bristol Hotel, fifteen years after the collapse of the National Movement. The majority of partisans were thereby grouped together, be they right-wing or leftist; religious or secular; Muslims or Christians; or any of the many other groups which had never been part of the National Movement. The objective was to 'revive the political movement in Lebanon, develop it, and rally support for the Resistance activity taking place in South Lebanon in defiance of the Zionist plan.'[1] Twenty-seven political parties, represented by the general secretariat or presidents, edited the Bristol manuscript, and this inter-party conference still takes place today, issuing declarations on ongoing developments, supporting the Resistance, and undertaking joint public activities.

Hizbullah also actively participated in the Arab National Conference and the Islamic National Conference, bringing closer the views of Arab nationalists and Islamists in preparation for facing those prevailing political necessities at the pinnacle of which is opposing the Zionist plan.

Hizbullah did not spare any effort at conducting bilateral meetings with spiritual leaderships, figures of power and factions in the country, whether these were simply aimed at keeping channels of communication open or revolved around particular discussions intended to converge viewpoints, or even to decide on modes of cooperation between parties.

Social Services

Hizbullah paid particular attention to social work. Not one aspect of aiding the poor was neglected as the Party worked

1. As stated in Hizbullah's declaration of August 17, 1997.

towards achieving joint social responsibility, answering to urgent needs and introducing beneficial programmes. Such work was simply considered a Party duty, and concentrated effort towards raising funds and making available social service resources served towards achieving these goals. The Party worked to the best of its capabilities, cooperating with official public institutions to respond to societal needs.

Along these lines, Hizbullah founded the Jihad al-Binaa Association (for construction and development) less than three years after the Party's creation. The institution's first task was to restore buildings damaged by the Bir al-Abed bombing of 1985.[1] Next, it undertook in 1987 to restore damage caused by torrential streams in the northern Bekaa, working in the same year on refurbishing homes in the southern Lebanese villages of Kafra and Yater, which had been targets of Israeli aggression. Every home damaged by Israeli raids since 1991 was restored by this institution, and this is true of other homes across Lebanese regions, especially in the South and Western Bekaa, bringing the total of refurbished buildings to 17,212 homes, shops and public utility structures.[2]

Between 1988 and 1991, the Party worked to remove all waste accumulation in Beirut's southern suburbs, where more than half a million residents live. Waste collection running at an average of 65 tons per day solved the problem of government neglect of that area and contributed to environmental preservation.

---

1. The bombing aimed to assassinate Ayatullah al-Sayyed Muhammad Hussein Fadlallah.
2. This includes homes damaged as a result of the July 1993 Israeli aggression, totalling 4,873, as well as those impaired by the April 1996 Israeli bombardment of Lebanon, totalling 6,714. The institution always mobilized its home restoration activities the day after any Israeli bombardment, and covered all Lebanese regions. See www.jihadbinaa.org for official figures.

No financial remuneration was requested of residents, and the service continued to be provided free of charge as part of the Party's humanitarian efforts.

With 110 water tanks distributed across Beirut's southern suburbs, the Party makes drinking water available to areas not endowed with such a public service. Three hundred thousand litres of water, available daily via mobile cisterns, reach 15,000 families. This service has been running free of charge as of March 1990 until the present day.

Hizbullah also concerned itself with agricultural activities, including the observation of annual agricultural cycles, distribution of saplings, field visits, provision of agricultural credit, distribution of tractors, fertilization, herbicide spraying, transfer of knowledge for honey production and other cultivation, and set-up of guidance and piloting centres. Attention was also directed at vocational training, providing villages with water, electricity and sewage utilities, working towards the creation of health centres and infirmaries, construction and restoration of educational institutions, cultural clubs, mosques and homes for needy families or martyrs' relations.

Focusing on health, the Party founded the Islamic Health Organization (IHO)[1] managing nine health centres, sixteen fixed and three mobile infirmaries catering to fifty-one villages. These centres have treated 111,077 cases since 2001, provided free medication and free health services to eighty-eight schools, and continue to provide regular vaccination rounds, in addition to launching promotions against smoking and disease-prevention awareness campaigns. The IHO has also been concerned with

1. See the IHO's media announcement of 2002.

civil defence, executed through the ten centres created for this purpose.

The Party was attentive to the educational requirements of the needy, subsidizing these through 'educational mobilization', which has provided educational support to 16,679 students[1] (part of which was in the form of books and stationery provided to 2,300 students), in addition to assisting with the school fees of some 6,355 students. Scholarships or grants ranging in value from 25 per cent to 100 per cent of school fees were awarded to 8,024 students. Further, the Paramount Martyr stationery fairs were launched, featuring discounted prices that facilitate access to learning for the population.

A special set-up, the Institution for the Wounded,[2] follows up on the physical state of the wounded and has taken care of 3,150 injured individuals – of whom 2,307 were resistance fighters, the balance being civilians injured during the war or as a result of stepping on land mines planted in the south of Lebanon. Care involves provision of monthly allowances, medical treatment, and rehabilitation for the handicapped in preparation for their re-integration into society. The Institution has created four treatment, rehabilitation and recreational centres distributed between Beirut, South Lebanon and the Bekaa.

Alongside the Party, the Philanthropic and Social Martyrs' Institution[3] works independently at the financial, operational and managerial levels. It is concerned with taking care of 1,284

---

1. Figures are drawn from a press conference held by Central Education Administrator Dr Bilal Naim on November 18, 1999.
2. Information on this institution is available in brochures titled *The Institution for the Wounded*.
3. See the publication issued by the Institution under the title *Continuous Giving to Preserve Custody*.

families of martyrs who had given their lives in the Resistance. It attends to 684 spouses, 1,215 children and 1,596 parents. A programme of joint social responsibility ensures the availability of housing, education, clothing, health services and various other social needs, in addition to active participation in job placement once children complete their education. The Institution also monitored and assisted, at one time, the families of 276 war prisoners. It founded the Greatest Prophet Hospital as well as the al-Shahed Educational Forum, alongside many other services.

Imdad – The Islamic Philanthropic Committee[1] – is another financially, managerially and operationally independent institution. It fills an important gap at the social level through its provision of aid to orphans, the destitute, the handicapped and the displaced, as well as to elderly persons. In 1998, the Committee followed up on 4,160 families, of which 3,519 (encompassing 9,722 individuals and 3,529 orphans) were assisted on a monthly basis. Facilities provided were in the form of financial support in marriage, residence, food and education. It also supervised four free schools and three centres for incapacitated children, alongside other activities.

The above-mentioned is only part of what is being provided in the sphere of joint social responsibility or assisting the needy and incapable for sustenance of self and family. Added to this is the work undertaken by the Social Unit of the Party, which involves the provision of support and services through international, local and official organizations, as well as through the allocation of Islamic funds (distributed according to *Shari'a* principles). Further, the work of Party parliamentarians is also aimed at provision of service and support to individuals. Many other

---

1. Ibid. The Committee's scope of work has developed since then.

Islamic social institutions have been set up independently to fill an important gap in terms of reaching the greatest possible number of orphans and deprived individuals. Were it not for such concentrated social work, large-scale social crises affecting tens of thousands of people would have come to pass. This exposes the extent of government negligence and deficiency in the fulfilment of many important and fundamental duties.

Such social work, which has evolved alongside resistance activity, served to relieve the Resistance of a considerable burden by assisting the populace in their endurance of Israeli aggression and of the remnants of occupation. It also fostered a humane and social environment of joint responsibility, thus shielding the Resistance from social catastrophes – those from which the government simply alienated itself.

Westerners have suspected that Hizbullah's social work was essentially aimed at recruitment, even where this was a natural consequence of the Party's social activities. They have also suspected that people gathered around Hizbullah mainly in order to benefit from these services. While such services do have a considerable effect on the populace, the essence of participation ultimately resides in belief in the overall path. Social work serves to enrich supporters' confidence in the viability of the Party's cause and course, as it cooperates, collaborates and joins forces to remain strong and tenacious in its political and resistance roles.

THREE

Key Milestones in the History of Hizbullah

From Invasion until the First Withdrawal

The core objective of Israel's 1982 invasion of Lebanon was to annihilate the military structure of the Palestine Liberation Organization (PLO) – a fact that was thought to guarantee the end of resistance activity, thus bringing security to the northern borders of occupied Palestine. The Lebanese were not perceived to represent a great threat, as Israel believed their resistance to be only an addendum to the Palestinian one, its financial, military and political powers merely annexed to the Palestinian resistance. As such, Israel was of the opinion that striking one resistance automatically meant breaking the other. Further, a tense social atmosphere had prevailed in Lebanon as a result of the Palestinians' manner of conduct, especially in South Lebanon. Hostile Palestinian military presence in towns and cities, and interference in people's daily lives, resulted in clashes and an attitude of aversion. The Israeli enemy was therefore at ease and assumed that armed resistance would be minimal, not supported by a civilian movement. This, it was thought, would facilitate capitalizing on the reality of occupation to the extent of Israeli interests.

A motive for the invasion had to be created, which would make the assault appear as a reaction to some Palestinian deed instead of straightforward aggression. A flimsy pretext was chosen: on July 3, 1982, Shlomo Argov, the Israeli ambassador to the United Kingdom, was the object of an armed attack in front of London's Dorchester Hotel. He was severely injured, but escaped death. On July 4, Israel announced that this attack constituted a breach of the ceasefire accord concluded with the PLO in 1981 and achieved under US auspices. Based on this claim, it launched air raids on Palestinian targets in Beirut, to which the PLO responded by blasting missiles and mortars on the northern areas of occupied Palestine.

On July 6, 1982, the Israeli army invaded Lebanon as part of its wider 'Peace of the Galilee' operation, the declared objective of which was to distance the inhabitants of the Northern Galilee from the so-called 'terrorist' attacks emanating from Lebanon. Informing US President Ronald Reagan of his intentions, Israel's Prime Minister Menachem Begin ordered the Israeli army to expel the Palestinians beyond a distance of 40 kilometres from the internationally recognized border, thus to the outskirts of the Awwali area near Sidon in South Lebanon.

Resistance was limited and ineffective, the PLO attributing this to the element of surprise and a general lack of capabilities. Resistance fighters were ordered to barricade the back lines, following news that Israel would not advance any further than the Awwali River. As a reaction to the hostility towards Palestinians that had engulfed some inhabitants of South Lebanon for the above-described reasons, the invaders were welcomed with trilling cries of joy and the spraying of rice – a sad and hurtful sight foreseen by the Israeli plan.

Israel's declared invasion limit was not adhered to. The invaders continued towards Beirut, reaching its outskirts at the town of Khaldeh where they clashed with the Resistance. The latter was composed of a number of young believers and supported by youth from the Amal movement, some Palestinian fighters, National Lebanese Front members, and the Syrian army overseeing the Aramoun area. Creeping forward no more, the invading army barricaded in that area for two weeks. This same scene was repeated on the outskirts of the Lebanese University's Faculty of Science in Hadath, where thirteen resistance fighters who had contributed to stalling the aggressor's advance went missing.[1] Israeli forces stayed put in the Science Faculty, advancing no more towards al-Laylaki. Similarly, confrontations led by Palestinian as well as compatriot Lebanese forces occurred in a number of areas, especially following the invasion of the capital.

Beirut lived its toughest, most gruelling days under destructive Israeli aerial bombardment. The capital's numerous points of entry fell under siege, supplies grew scarce; life came to a halt; a great number of people were displaced, died or were injured, and many a building came down on those in it.

A US-led agreement between Israel and the PLO called for the departure of all Palestinian fighters from Beirut, at the head of whom was Yasser Arafat, along with various other Palestinian leaders. They were allowed to carry some of their private weapons. It was thought that this alienation of leadership would serve the Israeli objective of breaking the PLO infrastructure and would free Israel's northern borders of danger.

Multinational forces led by US, French, British and Italian

---

1. The fate of these young men remains unknown. They are considered among the missing individuals whose destiny Hizbullah still demands Israel reveal.

troops arrived in Lebanon on August 12, 1982 to oversee the execution of this agreement. Bashir al-Gemayyel was elected Lebanese President on August 23, in an election that occurred under the supervision of Israeli tanks and troops. Following this, Palestinian leader Yasser Arafat departed from Beirut on August 30, 1982.

On September 14, Bashir al-Gemayyel was assassinated by a bomb placed in the offices of the Phalangist movement in Achrafieh. The Israeli army entered Beirut thereafter, taking the Sabra and Shatila Palestinian camps under siege and coordinating with the Lebanese forces[1] to enter the camps on September 16. Horrifying massacres ensued; the death toll reached 1,500 Lebanese and Palestinian individuals.[2]

Amine al-Gemayyel was elected president on September 23, 1982, succeeding his late brother. Israeli forces withdrew from Beirut on September 28.

During those rapid and successive events, resistance groups had started formation, executing more than one military operation against the occupation forces in Beirut,[3] the coastal boulevard and the Western Bekaa, operations which were crowned by the first martyrdom attack executed by Ahmad Kassir on November

---

1. The Lebanese forces were one of the armed militias existing in Lebanon during the civil war period.
2. This is the figure quoted by Palestinian sources. Lebanese civil defence sources estimated around 1,239 dead and missing, the majority of whom were Palestinian women, children and old men.
3. Among these resistance operations executed in Beirut and its suburbs was an ambush in the Msaitbeh area; confrontation with an infantry patrol in the Parliament area; operations along the road leading to Saadiyat and the old Saida Boulevard in Beirut; and widespread activity in the south of Lebanon. These operations are well documented by the Resistance, and include records with specific dates and the names of those involved.

11, 1982 and targeting the headquarters of the Israeli command in Tyre, South Lebanon. This operation shook Israel like a tremor. The Resistance refrained from announcing responsibility or declaring the name of the martyr, given the subjection of his native village – Deir Kanoun al-Nahr – to occupation. Even the procedures adopted to execute the operation were not announced, and Israel remained baffled at what really took place. The Resistance declared the details of the operation and the identity of its executor only after the Israeli withdrawal of 1985. Video recordings of the operation's details were broadcast in the martyr's village during a crowded celebration in late April of that year.

The May 17 Accord

The security measures undertaken on Israel's borders are ultimately those that guarantee its security. Israel benefited from its military superiority and the expulsion of the PLO from Lebanon, as well as US and international support, and on September 28, 1982 entered into negotiations with Lebanon – a country still suffering under the Israeli bayonet. Thirty-five negotiation rounds between Lebanon and Israel ensued, all held under the auspices of the US and finally culminating in the May 17 Accord (1983).

The drafting of the May 17 Accord and its subsequent security annexes represented a complete fulfilment of Israeli conditions, posting Lebanon as the police officer in charge of the occupier's security, an assignment that was to be executed as per a set of Israeli-dictated details and controls. A brief run-through the Accord's details easily reveals this fact.

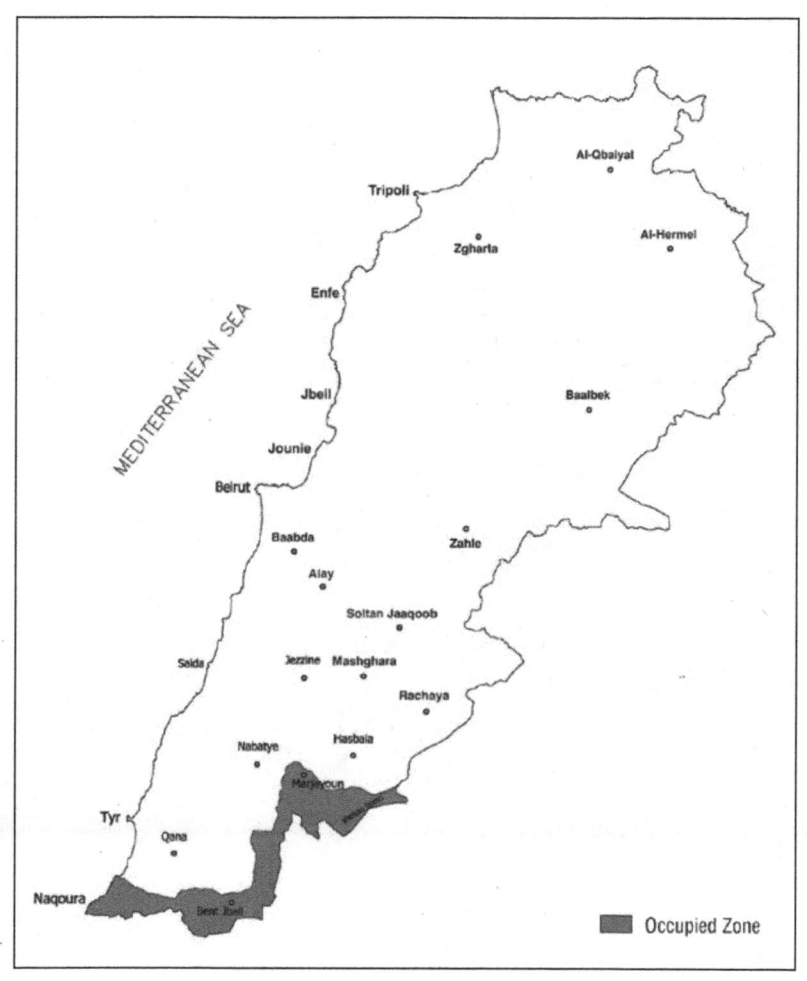

1. The Occupied Zone of 1978: 500 square kilometres covering 61 towns and villages.

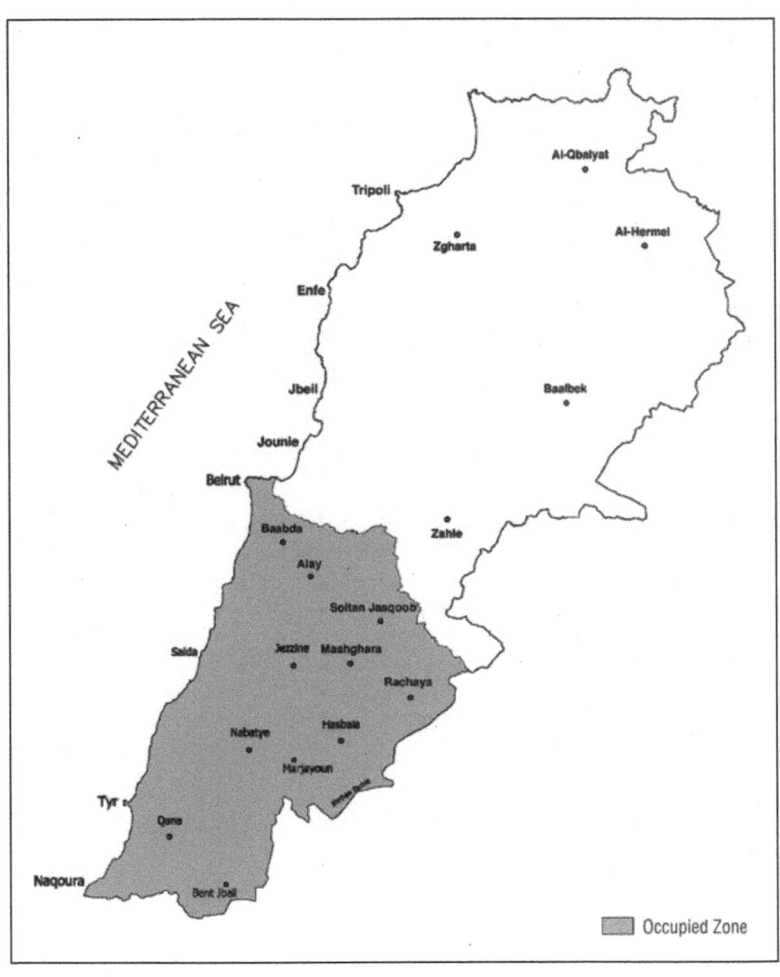

2. The 1982 Invasion: 3,560 kilometres of land, representing one third of Lebanon and covering 801 towns and villages.

Article 1, paragraph 2 of the Accord reads: 'The Parties confirm that the state of war between Israel and Lebanon has been terminated and no longer exists.' This meant the complete removal of Lebanon from the sphere of confrontation with Israel.

In Article 3, 'the Parties agree to establish and implement security arrangements including the creation of a Security Region'. Such a region was determined as running from the international borders north towards the al-Awwali River near Sidon, therefore entirely within Lebanese territory. Given its capability of directly attacking Lebanon as and when it deemed fit, and with US and international blessing, nothing would oblige Israel to comply with such security measures. Lebanon was left cuffed within its own territory, responsible at its own expense to guarantee the stability of the occupier's borders.

The issue transcended security to enter the realm of culture and enrolment. Paragraph 5 of the Accord stipulated: 'Consistent with the termination of the state of war and within the framework of their constitutional provisions the Parties will abstain from any form of hostile propaganda against each other.'

Further, the Lebanese government was liable for supervising follow-up, as clearly stated in the Security Arrangements Annex: 'The Lebanese authorities will enforce special security measures aimed at detecting and preventing hostile activities as well as the introduction into or movement through the Security Region of unauthorized armed men or military equipment.'

However, this provision did not entitle the Lebanese government to full authority at the level of military preparedness, for as item (i) of the Annex stipulated: 'The forces, weapons and military equipment that may be stationed, stocked, introduced into or transported through the Security Region are only those mentioned in this Annex and its Appendix.'

The upper allowable limit for the Lebanese army was defined as being two brigades, each having a limited number of tanks, armoured vehicles, infantry transportation trucks, anti-armour weaponry, air defence weapons, and signal apparatus. As such, the count was detailed as forty tanks, twelve 120-millimetre mortars, 112 RPGs, etc. In addition, no offshore or on-land rockets could be erected. A total of 4,341 individuals was allowed to form the Lebanese army, of which 323 were commanders and the balance of 4,118 officers and infantry whose functions and ranks were also clearly defined.[1]

Opposition to this humiliating accord was clearly voiced, but effective action was represented by one call for protest issued by an assembly of Muslim clerics, called to take place in Beirut's southern suburb of Bir al-Abed, inside the Imam al-Rida Mosque, and on the day of signature. The youth of Hizbullah participated in this demonstration of opposition, although the Party had not called for it given that its organizational set-up was yet to be officially declared. Regrettably, a Lebanese army unit used shooting signals in order to disperse the demonstrators, killing young Muhammad Najdeh as a result. The government's oppressive measures continued throughout the era of Amine al-Gemayyel who used the army on several fronts, ordering the destructive bombardment of Beirut's southern suburbs in early February 1984. Confrontations with the Lebanese army developed into what became known as the February 6 uprising (1984), which took place in West Beirut where Hizbullah forces,

---

1. Refer to *May 17*, a book published by the Centre for Islamic Unity (1988).

headed by Amal and the Progressive Socialist Party, penetrated into the Lebanese army barracks. The army's image was shaken and its capability to maintain control was compromised. West Beirut and its southern suburbs started to break away from Amine al-Gemayyel's authority.

Practically, the May 17 Accord never saw the light. The Lebanese Council of Ministers declared its cancellation on March 5, 1984, at the time when Israel was still occupying a large portion of Lebanon.

This was not a solitary development. On another front, the multinational forces that had greatly assisted Israel in the implementation of Israeli conditions came under attack on October 23, 1983, when the US marines and French paratroopers' bases were both bombarded at one time. The Islamic Jihad Organization declared responsibility for the bombings, which led to the death of 241 Americans and 58 French people. Multinational forces thus withdrew from Lebanon on April 31, 1984.[1]

International and political cover for the Israeli occupation did not help Israel achieve its aspirations for harvesting the fruits of invasion. The May 17 Accord was annulled, multinational forces departed from Lebanon. Bashir al-Gemayyel was assassinated, and Amine al-Gemayyel lost control over the situation.

Prologue to the First Withdrawal

The occupation turned attention towards the role of clerics in the drawing and cultivation of the populace against Israel. The most prominent of clerics was Sheikh Ragheb Harb, who had

---

1. Centre for Islamic Unity, *May 17*, p. 111.

returned to his village of Jibsheet following a conference in Tehran in the wake of the Israeli invasion of South Lebanon. The *sheikh* had started an activist mobilization movement against Israel, which prompted the occupying power to exert pressure on him. An Israeli commander visited him at his premises; the *sheikh* refused to shake hands, famously declaring: 'Our stance is armament, and a handshake would be admission.' Israel captured him on March 8, 1983.

Civilians marched from various villages and towns in the south towards Jibsheet in a show of support for the *sheikh*, forcing the occupation to release him seventeen days into this concentrated civilian pressure movement. Coming out of prison, the *sheikh* was received as a conqueror. He continued his activity, circles of education and prayer – especially those heavily attended Friday mosque prayers which became a routine weekly meeting of congregations at the Jibsheet mosque and which took place in spite of all Israeli measures. The *sheikh* had visited Beirut occasionally. Following his last trip to Tehran to attend the 'Crimes of Saddam' conference that took place in January of 1984, he returned to his hometown to find fate awaiting him. On the night of February 16, 1984, following his complete reading of *The Supplication of Kumail*, the *sheikh* convened with a number of believers at a nearby house. Upon his return home late that night, he was assassinated at the hands of Israel's collaborators, becoming the first cleric to be assassinated by Israel after the 1982 invasion. Sheikh Abdullatif al-Amine, murdered on November 15, 1984, was the next targeted cleric.

Following the removal of a number of clerics from South Lebanon, Israel began focusing on the sudden Islamic state that had grown in its hatred of Israel and which was moving in two concurrent directions: one marked by clerical mobilization, and the other represented by military training in the Bekaa camps. The enemy discovered it was confronting a new force that only grew by the day.

Israel's concern was not limited to resistance on the Lebanese front, but extended into a growing fear of transferring this experience to the Palestinian mainland. This came following many *jihad* operations undertaken by Palestinian fighters in Qalqilia, Jerusalem and Gaza. Minister of Defence Yitzhak Rabin declared his concern that so-called 'terrorist' tactics employed by Lebanese revolutionaries might be transferred across the border to the Gaza Strip and West Bank.[1]

The following was reported in the Israeli newspaper *Davar*:

> The success of military operations against Israeli forces in Lebanon had an uplifting effect on the Arab inhabitants of the occupied Gaza strip, especially on the youth. There is no doubt that the strikes suffered by the Israeli army were a source of joy and celebration for the inhabitants of those areas. The seeds of rebellion are planted, although these people had more than a reason to rebel given that the pressure of the occupation's might can never be considered to represent a normal and natural life under any circumstances.[2]

Knesset member Mordechai Bar-On was quoted in *al-Hamishmar* newspaper as saying:

> The tremendous audacity demonstrated during the

---

1. *Al-'Ahd*, May 16, 1985, p. 11. (*Al-'Ahd* has since been renamed *al-Intiqad*.)
2. *Al-'Ahd*, May 23, 1985, p. 8.

> Shi'ite guerrilla warfare of South Lebanon, or rather
> the significant extent of its success over the past few
> months, has instigated in the minds of [Israeli] so-
> ciety a comparison between Lebanese terrorism and
> Palestinian terrorism. There are those who believe that
> the escalation of aggression in Palestinian-inhabited
> [Israeli-occupied] areas over the past few months has
> its source in the Shi'ite success up north.[1]

During this period, resistance operations built up significantly
with the collaboration of the Islamic Resistance, the National
Resistance and Amal. Caught off guard by such heightened
intensity and coming under the continuous pressure of resistance
fire, Israel decided to shrink its military presence in Lebanon.
The Israeli cabinet met on January 14, 1985 and approved a
withdrawal plan of three steps, launched on February 16 and
ending on April 30. Withdrawal from Sidon, Tyre, Nabatieh,
some Western Bekaa villages and other areas left 1,100 square
kilometres of land representing 55 per cent of South Lebanon
and 11 per cent of the country's total area of 10,452 square
kilometres under Israeli occupation.

---

1. Ibid.

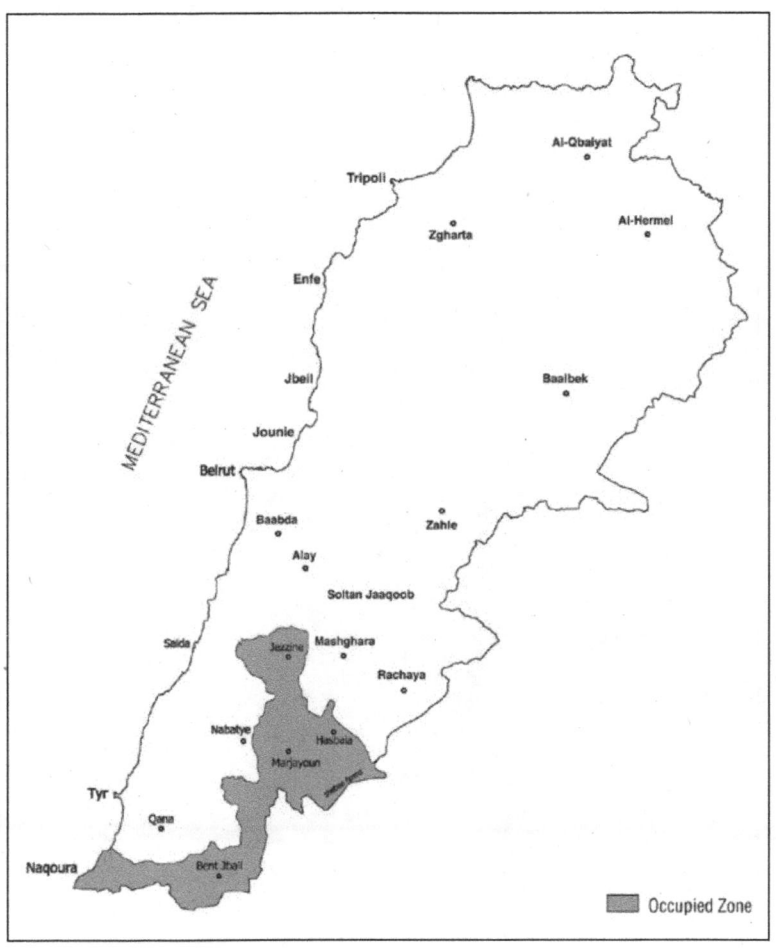

Labels on map: Al-Qbaiyat, Tripoli, Al-Hermel, Zgharta, Enfe, Baalbek, Jbeil, Jounie, Belrut, Baabda, Zahle, Alay, Soltan Jaaqoob, Saida, Jezzine, Mashghara, Rachaya, Nabatye, Hasbaia, Marjayoun, Tyr, Qana, Naqoura, Bent Jbail

MEDITERRANEAN SEA

■ Occupied Zone

3. The 1985 Occupied Zone: 1,100 square kilometres representing almost half of the South Lebanon and Nabatieh Districts (2,034 square kilometres), covering 168 towns and villages.

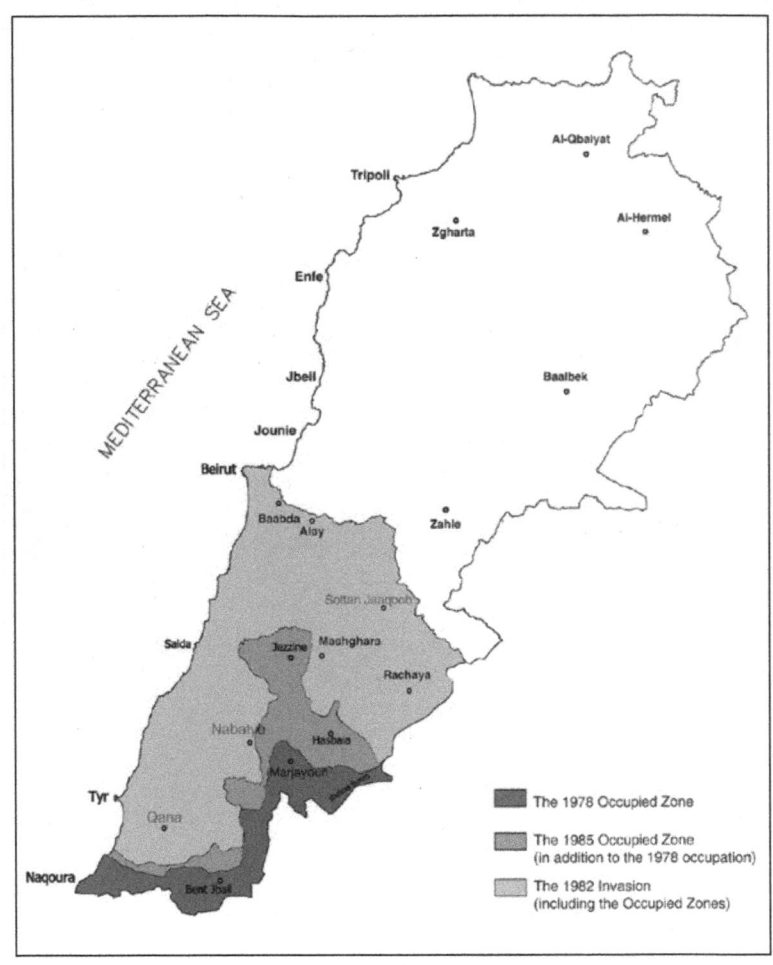

Al-Qbaiyat

Tripoli

Zgharta

Al-Hermel

Enfe

MEDITERRANEAN SEA

Jbeil

Baalbek

Jounie

Beirut

Baabda
Alay

Zahle

Soltan Jaqoob

Saida

Juzzine

Mashghara

Rachaya

Nabatiyb

Hasbaia

Marjayoun

Tyr

Qana

Naqoura

Bent Jbail

The 1978 Occupied Zone

The 1985 Occupied Zone
(in addition to the 1978 occupation)

The 1982 Invasion
(including the Occupied Zones)

4. The Occupied Zones from 1978–85

The Open Letter

Hizbullah's two and a half foundation years were sufficient to shape an effective *jihad* operation as represented by the Islamic Resistance forcing Israel's partial flight from Lebanon in 1985. It was also enough time for the crystallization of a political vision, the facets of which were harmonious with faith in Islam as a solution. A working agenda defining and expressing the entity called 'Hizbullah' could thus be formulated and used as a point of entry into the Lebanese scene. The Party thus declared its ideological, *jihad*, political and social visions, as well as the launch of its political movement, when it issued the Open Letter, on the day of the first commemoration of Sheikh Ragheb Harb's assassination. The Open Letter was orated on February 16, 1985 by the official Party spokesman, al-Sayyed Ibrahim Amine al-Sayyed.

With this declaration Hizbullah entered a new phase, shifting the Party from secret resistance activity that ran free from political or media interactions into public political work. On the one hand, such work is coupled to resistance as a main and fundamental priority. On another, it is an expression of the Party's vision and directive, as no *jihad* movement could separate itself from complementary political work that builds on the fruits of resistance and draws the objectives nearer. The Party's accomplishments are also not limited to the resistance of occupation as an exclusive objective. Even where resistance is the ultimate form of expression, the movement receiving highest priority, the Party would still form a comprehensive scheme emanating from the Islamic view of work on the Lebanese scene. The breadth of scope includes regional issues inasmuch as these are related to what takes place in Lebanon, and what repercussions such issues may have on the Party either due to its beliefs or given doctrinal *Shari'a* responsibilities.

Hizbullah continued its mobilization efforts, focusing on resisting the occupation. The three-year period following the 1985 withdrawal saw an escalation of distinguished resistance operations, the most notable of which was called 'The Two Captives'.[1] Other operations included the destruction of the enemy post in Huqban; the incursion on enemy and collaborator bases in Sujud, Bir Kallab, Toumat Niha, Barasheet, Tallat Ali Altaher, Alaman al-Shomariya, Saidoon, and Rimat; the Great Badr operation (which deterred the enemy from advancing towards Loueize in Iqlim al-Tuffah); and many others. Occurring at a time of clear contraction of National Resistance operations, these far-reaching events marked an ever-widening target scope that ran along the entire borderline of the occupation's forces in the South and Western Bekaa. Alongside those atypical and effectual operations, minor routine skirmishes by way of hand grenades, ambushes, sniping and various other confrontation methods used by the Resistance persisted on a daily basis.

The Assassination Attempt against al-Sayyed Fadlallah

Assassination through the use of car bombs was a standard style overtly employed by Israel and its collaborators, aimed at spreading confusion within the local arena and keeping alive the internal strife of Lebanese civil war. The novelty, however, was represented by direct US involvement in these assassinations, staged in cooperation with Lebanese army intelligence units

---

1. Details later in this chapter. See page 246.

during Amine al-Gemayyel's presidency and in coordination with the faction that operated under the banner 'Lebanese Forces'. US involvement was clear in the attempt to assassinate al-Sayyed Fadlallah on March 8, 1985. The attack was executed through a car bomb placed near the cleric's home in Bir al-Abed, and the target's survival was miraculous. The plotters had, in fact, suspected another vehicle approaching the house after the Friday prayers. The massacre's toll was eighty martyrs, mostly young girls and women, in addition to 256 wounded, and heavy destruction of buildings and assets.

Shortly thereafter, *The Washington Post* revealed through highly-placed sources:

> President Reagan has approved towards the end of last year [in 1984] a secret plan allowing the CIA to train and support a number of counter-terrorism units, the objective of which was to strike against potential terrorists before these become capable of launching attacks against US targets in the Middle East. Sources indicated that four months later, one of these units, composed of Lebanese intelligence service members and other foreigners, carried out an independent operation by way of which some Lebanese individuals were paid off to blast a car heavily loaded with bombs just outside the home of a leading Shi'ite combatant thought to be behind the terrorist attacks aimed at American establishments.

In truth, the Lebanese army had indeed established the 'Foreign Work and Analysis Unit' under the leadership of Major Adonis Nehme, who was in charge of Colonel Simon Kassis's office. The major had set the assassination of al-Sayyed Fadlallah at the top of his agenda. Hizbullah party segments monitoring such security issues had uncovered traces of the attempt, which resulted in the detention of a number of individuals directly involved with the largest assassination network in Lebanon. Death sentences were passed on eleven of these collaborators, who had all confessed.[1]

Tracking down this network took a full year of relentless work. The group's involvement in various other bomb attacks was proven, and the target list was found to include such national and political figures as Prime Minister Salim al-Hoss and the minister Walid Jumblatt, in addition to a number of congested locales such as the Cinema Salwa; the Druze Centre; the Egyptian embassy; the al-Rafidein Bank; the Raouche Market; Sabra Street; the Abu Nawwas restaurant; and others. The total casualty toll resulting from the network's bombing attacks amounted to 277 dead and 1,111 injured. The diversity of targeted areas and public figures reveals this group's intention to make the most out of the various conflicts and contradictions, thus leading to confusion as to the identity of those responsible and igniting further internal strife.

War in the Camps

Against a background of opposition to Arafat's control over the Palestinian camps in Beirut and of the subsequent disarmament of camp combatants, the middle of 1985 saw the launch of the Palestinian camps war. Hizbullah remained at a distance from

---

1. *Al-'Ahd* published a special issue in March 1986, detailing the course of interrogations, the complete confessions, the names and photographs of those involved and the identification of those who backed them.

this friction, working closely with the belligerent parties to bring it to an end. Credit is also due to the Islamic Republic of Iran for striving to end the conflict. Hizbullah suffered the discontent of its family of supporters as a result of tense relations between Palestinians and Shi'is existing prior to the Israeli invasion. Pressure groups insisted that Hizbullah participate in the war against Palestinians in the camps. However, the basic priority on which the Party was founded was that of combating Israel. Any internal strife, whatever its justifications, was simply refused. Thus did Hizbullah work on abating the fire of the Palestinian camp wars. However, the Arab world's perception of the conflict did not differentiate among those involved, and some extremist circles contributed to tarnishing the *mujahideen*'s image, as did Israel. The camps war ended through direct Syrian sponsorship. An organizational setup was created for Palestinian work within the camps on the condition that no Lebanese security or defence forces enter those camps and that armaments therein be limited to individual and regular middle-range weapons. Furthermore, while awaiting the results of development of the Palestinian cause on which expectations for the camps were clearly hinged, the camps were not to be used as a political ticket from within Beirut.

Amal and Hizbullah

Working on one front, partisans of the Amal and Hizbullah factions interacted as one family, the sharing of experience becoming the bread and butter between these brothers of the same household and sons of the same village. Mobilization and recruitment efforts by either party did, however, create a competitive atmosphere, occasionally expressed through a few negative incidents at the individual level. This was also coupled with a divergence in opinion over major political issues such as UN Resolution 425, which was criticized by Hizbullah for the ambiguity surrounding security measures with Israel and for recognizing Israel as a nation. Added to this was the breach of trust between the two parties resulting from the interpretation of major issues on various political stances, and a conflict ensued leading to a tragic series of clashes, a black page in history. Both parties paid dearly to finally overlook these painful incidents, which lasted for two and a half years and bred only wound and suffering.

Suffice it to mention here only a number of key episodes, and this in order not to overlook this sensitive point in the history of Hizbullah. Analysis, justifications and categorization of the two parties' positions will not be dealt with.

At first, limited skirmishes started in a number of South Lebanon villages, escalating by the day through incidents of beating, armed confrontations and a general tense atmosphere across villages. The problem took a dangerous turn on April 5, 1988 at the Harouf checkpoint, which was erected by Amal to disarm Hizbullah fighters given Amal's conviction that the Party had exceeded its bounds. Following clashes in Nabatieh and Ghazieh, the fighting was likely to have spread, had it not been for Hizbullah's high command decision to refuse fighting, ordering all combatants to stop the bloodshed even if this should mean complete disarmament of Hizbullah in the south. The Party was banking on communication channels opened with the clerics and politicians of the South, hoping that these would revert matters to their previous status. The result was, however, the disarmament of Hizbullah, with the channels yielding no results.

The situation escalated, spreading to the southern suburbs of Beirut. Clashes started on May 6, 1988, at which time the Hizbullah leadership labelled it a fight for existence and ordered the resumption of warfare. Contributing to the decision was uncertainty of what a political approach would yield. The result was the withdrawal of Amal from its southern suburb positions following intense fighting, and the reinstatement of Hizbullah's control of that area.

This view of events remained constant following similar transfer of control over the Iqlim al-Tuffah villages back to Hizbullah towards the end of 1988, adding to those areas already under the Party's control in Loueizeh and Jabal Safi. In Bekaa and the Western Bekaa towns, power was primarily in the hands of Hizbullah and no clashes were recorded between the two parties there.

The situation became more and more difficult with the political developments that accompanied the Taif Accord, where it was assumed that secure implementation of the accord would require Hizbullah to be dissolved, especially in the South. The first ceasefire agreed between Amal and Hizbullah in February, 1989 was not effective. The Iqlim wars followed in July, 1990, and a tight siege of Party combatants ensued, lasting for more than 100 days and ending towards the beginning of Iraq's invasion of Kuwait[1] and the looming Gulf War.

The need to close this chapter rose to the surface in preparation for the response to the new developments storming the region. Steadfast efforts and concentrated meetings by the Syrian foreign minister Farouk al-Shara and his Iranian counterpart Ali Akbar Wilayati took place, attended by Nabih Berri, leader of the Amal movement and Hizbullah Secretary General Subhi al-Tufaili.

---

1. Iraq invaded Kuwait on August 1, 1990, occupying it in four hours.

These efforts were crowned by the Amal-Hizbullah agreement of November 9, 1990, which concentrated on dissolving hostilities between the two parties, a programme for reconciliation, and Hizbullah's return to the South. The accord ended that painful episode and laid the foundations for a relationship of mutual understanding between the Party and Amal, alienating the spectre of strife in favour of cooperation and coordination. The Lebanese army planned to become the custodian of security in South Lebanon, such that no independent party would have military control in the area. Actual deployment of army troops began in early February, 1991.

Resistance activity weakened during that period, given that the main battlefield – South Lebanon – was largely out of the scope of activity except for the areas of Loueizeh, Jabal Safi and the Western Bekaa. Although the number of operations was limited, this did not deter the Resistance from preparing for martyrdom attacks inside the occupied zone. Three grand martyrdom operations were executed using car bombs.

First went martyr Haitham Dbouk, who executed his operation in Tal al-Nahhas of the Deir Mimas area in the Marjeyoun District on August 19, 1988. Thirty Israeli soldiers fell dead or wounded. (The Israeli army declared only one dead and three wounded.)

Second, Abdallah Atwi gave his life on October 19, 1988 in Kfar Kila, near what is known as the Fatima Gate in the Marjeyoun District. Forty-three Israeli soldiers were killed or wounded; enemy sources confessed to only eight dead and eight wounded.

The third operation was conducted by Sheikh Asaad Berro on August 9, 1989, at the entrance of Quleya'a in the Marjeyoun

District. The toll was twenty soldiers; Israeli sources declared only one general dead and five soldiers wounded.

The Taif Accord

The internal Lebanese environment was not in any better state than the battlefront. Civil war and the Israeli invasion had taken their toll on the population, fragmenting and segregating East from West Beirut – or, in broader terms, Muslims from Christians, as per the prevailing sectarian and geographic distribution. On September 23, 1988, President Amine al-Gemayyel commissioned Major General Michel Aoun to form a government, thereby breaching the conventional practice of commissioning a Sunni Muslim to head the cabinet. Further, the country was not sufficiently ready for presidential elections by the end of Amine al-Gemayyel's term, a fact that only served to increase internal conflict and accentuated the impossibility of convening under the auspices of any sort of government, especially given the pressure of an entrenched sectarian reality. Considering the president's action unconstitutional, Salim al-Hoss continued to assume the role of prime minister in West Beirut, and the country thus had two governments at one point in time.

Efforts at the Taif meetings in Saudi Arabia focused on constitutional amendments tackling the political organizational set-up, the authority of the three main heads of state, and alterations to the constitution that had a bearing on sectarian specifics. It laid the foundation for putting an end to the Lebanese war and its repercussions within the framework of a political agreement accommodating the minimum acceptable requirements of all existing divisions along with their respective concessions. Parliamentarians came up with the Taif Accord, which was achieved under the custodianship of Syria and Saudi Arabia, blessed by the US, and agreed to by all religious and political leaders of the various Lebanese sects.

The Taif Accord was announced on October 22, 1989, and thereafter adopted as a constitutional pact during the parliamentary session held in Lebanon on November 5, 1989, at which time Rene Mouawad was elected President. He was assassinated one week later on November 22, following which Elias al-Hrawi was elected President on November 24. Major General Aoun rebelled against these developments, holding on to his position as prime minister. The al-Hoss government, led by President al-Hrawi, took a decision to oust the general through a military operation to be undertaken by the Lebanese army. The decisive military battle, which resulted in the defeat of the general on October 13, 1990, was launched with the participation of Syrian forces in Lebanon.

To Hizbullah, the Taif Accord was not convincing and below the minimum required. The Party made do with a political expression of discontent, communicating the necessity of developing and improving this formula into one that would, at the least, result in the abolishment of political sectarianism. However, some resorted to linking the Amal-Hizbullah conflict in the South, which still raged after the accord, to Hizbullah's attempt at rupturing the Taif Accord and using the situation in the South as a pretext. This was entirely untrue and not even conceivable to the Party. The subsequent Amal-Hizbullah agreement proved the Party's true intentions, which concentrated on securing a presence for the Resistance in the South without any consideration to the internal politics that would bear on the balance of powers among various divisions. The approach chosen by Hizbullah in its objection to the nature and structure of the confessional regime in Lebanon, was the correct political approach in expressing political positions.

Testing the Army's Custodianship of Security

Was the health of Lebanon really back on track after the Taif Accord, the discharge of Major General Aoun and the agreement between Amal and Hizbullah? Did the Lebanese army have a change of heart, shifting from rival to supporter of the Resistance? Was it possible to accept the army's entry into Beirut's southern suburbs and thereafter to the South? Could one be sure that the experience of bombarding the southern suburbs, as was the case under President Amine al-Gemayyel, would not be repeated?

Difficult questions faced Hizbullah with the creation of the Taif government. Given the Party's priority for resistance activity, the non-intervention guarantees received through Syria, the changed political direction and of the army's function, and Syrian guidance over these developments, Hizbullah decided to respond positively to the 'Greater Beirut' project whereby the army would take custody of security over the capital and its suburbs. This was not an easy decision for the youth who had grown accustomed to bearing weapons, having lived under the pressure of assassination and aggression for some time. Many concentrated meetings with the Party's cadres and members followed to explain the necessity for such an action and the fact that it would not represent danger to the cause and its progression. The success of this disarmament and its exemplary implementation are credited to the accurate implementation and abidance by the agreement demonstrated by both the army and the Party, in spite of many expectations that clashes would result.

This development originated in the Party's vision of refusing a government-within-a-government. It was also an element of the Party's methodical frame of mind to forbid the use of weapons by Party members for any internal balance or control purposes under the umbrella of an existing government, otherwise such use would only lead to antagonism and internal dissension. Given that the requirement was to preserve the Party's resistance function, there was no need for maintaining armaments outside the sphere of confrontation in the occupied zones and their immediate vicinity, especially given a political atmosphere supportive of the Resistance and of protection to its back ranks. As for the continuing danger facing the leaders of the Resistance wherever they were, this was dealt with in cooperation with the relevant security organizations, through providing them with arms-bearing licences within the limits of use for personal protection against any Israeli breach of security.

The army's arrival in the South during February 1991 came as a result of acknowledgment by the Lebanese government of its natural position as the country's administrator after the Taif Accord. It was also a result of the Amal-Hizbullah agreement, a recognition that security should be in the hands of the army and none other. It was, however, a difficult compromise, given concerns that the army's entry into the South might only be a prelude to barring the Resistance from its activities, and to excluding the South from the equation of struggle with Israel despite the persistence of Israeli occupation in the Western Bekaa and South Lebanon.

However, the Resistance's approach to field activity was not based on established, declared bases or public displays of armament across villages. Further, confrontation was limited to those areas where Israeli soldiers and their collaborators, headed by Antoine Lahd, existed. Moreover, a political decision was undertaken by the Lebanese government not to interfere with resistance activity within the described scope. For all of these reasons, Hizbullah was excluded from the government's decision to disarm militias, for the 'militia' label was not applicable here, given that the Party did not enter the crux of Lebanese civil war, nor did it cling to armed presence in those liberated or internal areas. The Party had also refrained from using weapons to solve any political differences, which thus alienated it from the circle of pressure and demand for disarmament. Proven effectiveness was demonstrated through resistance activity at a time when Lebanon was in need of such success. Resistance was to be Lebanon's strength in the challenge against the Israeli project.

Harmony between the Government and the Resistance

With a growing capability to inflict pain on the Israeli occupier, a capacity that slowly returned to the South following the Amal-Hizbullah agreement, the pressure of international requests to disarm Hizbullah and halt resistance operations escalated. Key members of Lebanon's government were of the opinion that Hizbullah should succumb to the government's political decision. The famous catchphrase of the time, as coined by then-Minister of Foreign Affairs, Fares Boueiz, was 'imperative harmony between the government and the Resistance.' The basis for such a stance was that Lebanon was responsible to Israel and the international community for all actions undertaken within its boundaries. The notion was thus one of direct involvement by the government in the administration of resistance operations, or at least its having knowledge of their timing and a say in their level of intensity or abatement. Through such concord the government thought it possible to manage its political course in harmony with resistance activity, and thus be better prepared for internationally exerted pressures.

Hizbullah had a different view. The Party considered that where resistance falls under the willpower of government, it loses its capability to achieve liberation and is placed inside a sphere of political limitations. As such, when Lebanon was under international pressure and the Lebanese government became the organ responsible for administering the resistance, the latter might have been obliged to take steps that could have encumbered resistance activity. Similarly, the government would be responsible in front of the international community for the execution of decisions that might be prejudiced in favour of Israel, a fact that would defeat the Resistance's ability to manoeuvre, or simply incapacitate it.

On the other hand, a resistance movement that is free of any political obligations can operate without restraint, not charging government with responsibility for its actions. This could assist the Resistance in its capitalization on the liberation cause, and support the government's natural political communication and pressure-exertion, the objective of which were to demand and draw the international community's attention to that very danger which bred resistance. As such, the bottom line in the Lebanese government's approach was that there was no solution except for Israel to withdraw unconditionally from Lebanon.

Perhaps it was the notion of benefiting from the existence of the Resistance and using it as a ticket during political negotiation that prompted the discussion on 'harmony'. The government was, however, incapable of capitalizing on the Resistance given Israel's patronizing presence, Israel being a country prepared to engage in any horrific action merely in order to enforce its conditions, a country infringing all international laws and regional agreements while enjoying full US bias in its favour and unconditional sanctioning of its activities.

To avoid clashes between the government and the Resistance, Hizbullah proposed working along a dual path: the one of resistance and liberation without subjugation to the negotiation channel, and the other being the political path followed by the government in pursuit of the implementation of UN Resolution 425, which called for Israel's complete withdrawal from Lebanon. Such a call for retreat, the Party insisted, should always be bound to the word 'unconditional', and this in order to downplay those concerns surrounding security measures that the resolution might be interpreted as referring to. The race should thus be for liberation instead of competition over the nature of the proceedings. Although no formal agreement was drafted to this end, practical implementation imposed itself, especially in light of Syria's decision to adopt Lebanon's right of resistance, the effect of which was the creation of the political cover needed to avert any political clash that might have weakened both the Lebanese government and the Resistance.

The Martyrdom of al-Sayyed Abbas al-Moussawi

The Council elected al-Sayyed Abbas al-Moussawi for the Hizbullah Secretary General post in May, 1991. His Grace was distinguished by perseverance, relentless work and energetic fervour, as marked by his continuous daily trips across the Bekaa, the South and Beirut regions – long distances travelled during any one day to ensure participation in a variety of activities.

Resistance fighters prized him for his devotion to living amongst the people and accompanying them in their days. Such was also his determination before receiving the Secretary General post. He never missed an opportunity to meet with fighters in their borderline crevices, preaching to them and gracing them with his farewell blessings before they went off to their *jihad* missions. His concern for strengthening the resistance effort against the occupation was paramount. People loved him for his genial disposition and jovial spirits, for his refined perception and attentive ear to societal needs.

After setting the Amal-Hizbullah accord on the right implementation track and following the return of the Resistance to the South, he turned his attention to the social cause, touring the homes of the displaced in West Beirut, particularly those in the Wadi Abu Jmil area, supporting them and adding their human-rights plight to his log of duties. He charged himself with founding the Panel for the Rehabilitation of Beirut's southern suburbs, the body that appealed for making social services available in this area and for tackling the problems of a significantly deficient infrastructure. He was present for fieldwork in the aftermath of those natural disasters hitting the Bekaa area – snowstorms that damaged roads and stranded civilians. His work was crowned with the final speech delivered on the day of his martyrdom from the podium of the Jibsheet mosque bearing the name of Sheikh Ragheb Harb. The speech focused on criticism of the government's negligence and lack of attention to subdued and deprived areas, proving the extent of such negligence with numbers, calling for carrying the social and subsistence cause on behalf of all, and vowing in front of God and the people that he would continue to 'resist occupation and resist negligence'.

His Grace's position was an expression of the path adopted by Hizbullah after the Taif Accord, which aimed at putting the internal state of affairs high on the priority agenda. He played a part in those preliminary discussions concerning the participation of Party members in parliamentary elections.

His work was not limited to internal Party functions or even to activity across Lebanon. His reach extended to support the Palestinian cause, and to him is attributed the unification of all ten Palestinian wings in Tehran. On a broader level, his concern for Islam and the issues of Muslims in the world was demonstrated through direct visits and involvement in many a conference, whether in Kashmir, Pakistan, Afghanistan or elsewhere.[1]

His term as Secretary General was, however, briefly limited to nine months. For after participating in the eighth commemoration ceremony of his late companion Sheikh Ragheb Harb on February 16, 1992, and after visiting the latter's family and the Jibsheet martyrs, his convoy departed from the town and as soon as it reached the village of Teffahta, was hit by Israeli warplanes. Al-Sayyed Abbas died instantly, a martyr, along with his wife and young child Hussein.

The following day, Hizbullah's Council convened to unanimously elect His Grace al-Sayyed Hassan Nasrallah as al-

---

1. Central Media Unit, Hizbullah, *The Prince of Memory*, pp. 54–5.

Sayed Abbas al-Moussawi's successor for the remainder of the term. This took place prior to the awe-inspiring escort of the paramount resistance martyr al-Moussawi to his final resting place in his village, Nabi Sheeth. The appointment of a successor was intentionally quick in order to confiscate the opportunity awaited by Israel to shake the Party's resolve at this sensitive milestone in Hizbullah's *jihad* history.

The assassination of the late Secretary General placed resistance activity at a crucial turning point. For the first time, the Resistance launched Katyusha rockets at the settlements in northern occupied Palestine in response to the assassination, thereby introducing the rockets as a new factor in the confrontation. Afterwards, Hizbullah clearly tied such action to reciprocity of the same suffered by Lebanese civilians at the hands of Israeli aggression, the latter not sparing an opportunity to target civilians of any town or village alongside civilian infrastructure.

Israel tried to seize the moment, and attempted land advancement along the Kafra-Yater axis in the South three days following the assassination of al-Sayyed Abbas. But the Resistance forced it back effectively. This took place in tandem with fierce confrontations along the length of the borderline with the enemy, which retreated without marking any gains, having discovered the tenacity and determination of the Resistance to persist with its *jihad* mission.

The July 1993 Aggression

The Resistance continued to exert effective pressure, raiding enemy bases and laying ambushes for their patrols, continuously inflicting casualties on enemy soldiers and their collaborators.

The enemy then launched another grand assault on the morning of July 25, 1993 that lasted for seven continuous days and ending on the night of July 31. The operation was labelled 'Accountability', and had a two-fold objective as declared by Israel's foreign minister Shimon Peres:

> To attack those who directly attack us, especially Hizbullah, and to alert the population of Lebanon and the concerned governments to the necessity of terminating the activity of Hizbullah.[1]

Israeli Chief of Staff Ehud Barak warned the Lebanese government that it should 'disarm Hizbullah or watch Israel do it'.[2] The objectives of the July 1993 aggression clearly revolved around:

1. Disarming Hizbullah and rendering it inactive by way of a fierce military offensive targeting the Party's infrastructure.

2. Breaking the Party's relationship with the populace, and providing the latter with a reason to exercise public pressure, thus building a civil cordon around the Party.

3. Exerting pressure on the Lebanese government, forcing it to take the necessary steps to impede resistance activity.

Israel used its air force, navy and land artillery during this mission of aggression, targeting the South, the Bekaa and Western Bekaa areas, al-Bared Palestinian camp in the north and the Nameh area

---

1. *Glorious Pages in the Nation's Book*, 1993, p. 67.
2. Ibid.

near Beirut. UN sources counted 1,224 air raids and more than 28,000 shells.[1] The Resistance stated through Secretary General al-Sayyed Hassan Nasrallah: 'We consider ourselves to be in a state of open warfare with this enemy. The measures we will take to defend our people in the South and Western Bekaa will not be bound by any red lines or limits imposed by the enemy. Only the [Islamic] resistance defines those limits.'[2]

In retaliation, rockets were launched in the direction of Israeli settlements in northern Palestine – a 'hell of shelling', as described by Agence France-Presse (July 25, 1993), 'lasting for ten continuous hours, a true state of horror. Such was the situation in the Galilee settlements when ambulance sirens were heard speeding across empty streets.'

The enemy's army intelligence estimated that Hizbullah possessed around 500 rockets that would be depleted in the span of a few days, following which military control would completely be in the hands of the Israeli army. Hizbullah would then succumb, according to these calculations, and gradually become incapacitated through a series of unremitting attacks. However, the enemy soon felt Hizbullah's serious readiness for a long war, and understood that annihilating the Resistance was not feasible. For in addition to the intensive bombardment of Zionist settlements in northern Palestine, the Resistance executed thirty military operations during the seven-day invasion, targeting Zionist and collaborators' bases on the length of South Lebanon's occupied borderline, hitting ten bases at a time, and

---

1. Ibid., p. 71.
2. Ibid., p. 36. Quoted from the press conference held by Hizbullah's Secretary General in Baalbeck on the eve of the aggression.

this in spite of continuous Israeli aerial raids covering the skies of the entire region.

Resorting to its supporter and mediator, the US, Israel sought a solution proposing that Katyusha bombing of its settlements halt in return for Israeli aggression ceasing in Lebanon. The Party informed Syria of its acceptance of this deal, which linked Katyusha attacks to the reciprocal aggression by Israel on civilian targets in Lebanon, for this was perceived as a buffer of safety for Lebanese civilians and was to limit Israel's ability to exert this kind of pressure, thereby confining Israel to a direct military confrontation with the Resistance. It was thus decided that Israel would halt its assault in return for the ceasing of Katyusha bombardment. And so on the evening of July 31, 1993, precisely at 6:00 PM, the agreement which later became known as the 'July Accord', was put into force, an expression of oral concord achieved through mediators without any formally written blueprint.

Israel's aggression resulted in the death of 140 civilians, including 13 members of the Resistance. Five hundred people were wounded, and around 200,000 inhabitants of 120 South Lebanon villages were displaced. Thousands of homes were completely or partially destroyed.[1] But the Resistance, and Lebanon, came out victorious. The enemy was unable to achieve its direct objectives.

The surprise came three days after the halting of enemy aggression. Internal rumours circulated by a number of Lebanese officials suggested that internal strife was brewing in South Lebanon between Hizbullah and 'other groups'. Such talk continued for a number of days, following which it was suggested that the

---

1. Jihad al-Bina accounted for the restoration of 4,873 of these, a figure thought to represent the approximate total of demolished or damaged homes.

Lebanese army be deployed in the South, take control of security and solve this 'problem'. Lebanese military sources declared that the army's presence in the South 'will not be under the auspices of any other Party, and will not be in concord with anyone. It will be absolute and for all. Possession and carrying of weapons will not be allowed.'[1] Thus, what the occupation failed to achieve by way of aggression was to be attained under a pretext of internal unrest. Army deployment along the length of the southern-occupied border was simply a deterrent to resistance combat and a guarantee for Israel's much-sought security needs.

These developments were directly related to the covert Oslo Agreement preparations between PLO chairman Yasser Arafat and Israeli Prime Minister Yitzhak Rabin. Representatives of both sides in the Norwegian capital came out with the infamous Oslo Agreement on September 13, 1993, which was declared under the banner of 'Gaza and Jericho First'. Designed to put an end to the first Palestinian uprising against Israeli occupation, this major step in Palestine was planned to synchronize with a similar one in Lebanon, both of which would relieve Israel of the pressure of resistance in preparation for tailored political solutions that would serve to sideline Syria as a solo player. However, the speed with which Syria reacted to this step, which represented a dangerous free gift to Israel, resulted in abandonment of the decision to deploy the Lebanese army in South Lebanon. Following discussions between Syria and Lebanese officials, the initially planned widespread propagation was replaced with a limited deployment in a number of villages, and did not threaten the existence of a resistance against occupation.

Confrontations with occupying forces continued. The Shiheen

---

1. *Glorious Pages in the Nation's Book*, p. 78.

operation, carried out inside the occupied zone, was atypical. On August 19, 1993, the Resistance succeeded in bombing a Zionist patrol following which the enemy confessed to seven dead and a number of wounded. In the wake of this operation, Israel's Prime Minister Rabin declared: 'I regret saying this, but Hizbullah has conquered us.'[1] Only twelve hours after the operation, an Israeli air raid was flying over the Borday, Jenta and Nabi Sheeth perimeter in Baalbeck, but no casualties were recorded. The enemy made do with this form of retaliation in order not to face the brunt of reprisal through Katyusha attacks.

The September 13 Massacre

When the Oslo Agreement was declared, and it was decided that both Israelis and Palestinians counterparts would be signing it on September 13, 1993, Hizbullah – in cooperation with the various Lebanese parties and Palestinian groups – called for a march of denunciation and censure of this agreement to convene in front of the Imam al-Mahdi mosque in Beirut's southern suburbs on the date of signature. Intense communication took place to forbid such a demonstration under the pretext of a Lebanese government decision banning such marches across all Lebanese areas for security reasons. President Elias al-Hrawi was ready to defend this ban, requesting Minister of the Interior Bechara Merhej[2] and Minister of Defence Mohsen Dalloul to urge the security forces to fulfil

---

1. *Al-'Ahd*, August 20, 1993.
2. Merhej actually refused to abide by the ban, and later declared his stance contradicting the government's decision.

their duties and execute the government's decision. At the time, Lebanon's prime minister was out of the country.

However, the organizers insisted on holding the march while observing the necessity of reaching an agreement over the issue with the Lebanese government. The event was briefly postponed until such time as coordination with Defence Minister Dalloul could be achieved. The route of the march was changed, and its duration was limited. In compliance with the objective of voicing an expression of discontent with the Oslo Agreement, Hizbullah accepted these amendments, and so the march was launched. But as soon as the procession advanced a few metres into Airport Boulevard as per the planned route, demonstrators were surprised by a Lebanese army shooting squad stationed at the Airport Boulevard bridge. Nine demonstrators were martyred, including two sisters, and tens were wounded. Instantly, the organizers issued orders to demonstrators to simply gather the wounded and not take any retaliatory action in order to avoid internal strife.

Hizbullah was astonished at what happened, especially given that the march was launched following coordination with the authorities. Clear aims to draw Hizbullah into internal confrontations were proven to exist. Even though all concerned parties denied any responsibility and linked the massacre to a communication mistake with the army, had there been any response by the demonstrators against the army the procession and its organizers would have been considered responsible for staging an attack against the Lebanese army, the latter only shooting back in response. This would have been a prelude to other measures leading to internal discord, pulling the Resistance into the maze and corridors of Oslo's repercussions. Despite the harshness of the Airport Boulevard massacre, that massacre which was for the renunciation of the Oslo Agreement which was christened by the blood of Lebanese *mujahideen*, Hizbullah's tolerance and the positive resoluteness of martyrs' families seized the opportunity from the hands of those who were aiming at distorting the Party's objectives, distracting it from the more worthy cause and towards internal issues.

For a year and eight months, tension continued between the Party and the ruling government as a result of the September demonstration and the government's responsibility for the bloodshed. But such tension persisted without any miscalculated moves on the part of Hizbullah, given the priority awarded to resistance activity. The case was finally closed in mid-1995 through the following declaration of the High Commission for Rescue, chaired by Prime Minister Rafik al-Hariri:

> The Commission considers the victims of the September 13 sorrowful incident to be amongst the convoy of martyrs paid by the Resistance and the nation of believers in the cause of defending the land, national soil and the sanctified, those who refuse partial and unilateral solutions and defend their stance with their dearest of capabilities.[1]

The Party replied with a statement that contained the following: 'Pausing to consider the political signals of this decision, we find it to be a favourable initiative on the path towards solving this issue in a manner which achieves the aims and aspirations of those righteous martyrs.'[2]

---

1. *Al-'Ahd*, May 19, 1995.
2. Ibid.

The April 1996 Aggression

The Sharm-El-Sheikh summit convened in Egypt on March 13, 1996 was assembled in support of Israel, under the banner 'Peacemakers'. The US grouped together the world's nations, including the majority of the Arab world, for the summit – the final proclamation of which contained the objective of 'forbidding the enemies of peace from destroying the true chances for peace'. The summit also called for bilateral arrangements to combat terrorism.[1]

The summit took place concurrently with four martyr attacks performed by the Hamas movement in Palestine between February 24 and March 14, 1996. It was also around the time when Hizbullah's retaliatory Katyusha attacks were being launched towards the northern Israeli settlements in response to Israel's aggression against civilians in Yater on March 30 and in Barasheet on April 9. The retaliation was preceded by a martyrdom operation executed by the martyr Ali Ashmar on February 20 in the Adaiseh-Rab Thalatheen triangle in South Lebanon.

Israel's April aggression started at dusk of Thursday April 11, 1996. An air raid was launched at 4:20 AM targeting Tallat al-Kayyal in the city of Baalbeck and was followed by raids later the same day aiming for a building in Ain Bosoir in the Iqlim al-Tuffah region. Thereafter, the Lebanese army base in the city of Tyre came under attack, followed by shelling of a building in Beirut's southern suburb of Haret Hreik, only a few metres away from Hizbullah Council headquarters. This was the first time

---

1. The Consultative Centre for Studies and Documentation, *The Eighth War*, Beirut.

that the southern suburbs had been directly shelled since the 1982 Israeli invasion. The aggression gradually enlarged in scope, for, as enemy leaders mentioned, the operation was cumulative and cascading, with the objective of exerting continuous pressure.

'Grapes of Wrath' was this operation's infamous label. It was tougher than the July 1993 aggression, for it covered a wider geographic scope and lasted for sixteen days. It was notorious for four massacres: Suhmor on Day 2; al-Mansouri ambulance on Day 3; Upper Nabatieh on Day 7; and the Qana massacre, also on the same day, when 118 martyred civilians and 127 injured were recorded. In total, 250 civilians died during Israel's April 1996 aggression, including four members of the Resistance. Hundreds of thousands were displaced in South Lebanon. Destruction was extensive, affecting social, economic and service infrastructure. About 7,000 homes were completely or partially destroyed.[1]

But the Resistance put up a show of resilience that stunned the enemy. Katyusha rockets were fired on a daily basis, and benefiting from previous experience, the *mujahideen* planned well for a new aerial invasion. Israel was incapable of directly targeting and hitting any *jihad* combatant, or of preventing one rocket pad from launching attacks. The dynamics of military resource distribution proved durable when back provision lines were cut off or during coverage of the skies by enemy raids. Suspected individuals were sent away from the battle domain in order to deprive the enemy of information provided by collaborators. Contrary to Zionist expectations, the intensity and scope of shelling did not deter the thrust of retaliation with Katyusha rockets until such time as a ceasefire was declared.

---

1. Jihad al-Binaa restored 6,714 homes damaged during the April aggression in the various Lebanese regions.

Israel's aggression aimed at:

1. Battering Hizbullah, putting an end to resistance operations, and preventing the drop of Katyusha rockets on Israeli settlements.

2. Exercising pressure on the Lebanese government for taking a decision regarding the Resistance and leading to the cessation of resistance operations.

3. Concentrated displacement of civilians and threatening peace in the villages, thus attempting to divide the populace from the Resistance.

4. Fulfilling the need of Shimon Peres to record a military victory that would assist his election campaign for prime minister, given his lack of a military background (contrary to other Israeli prime ministers).

5. Incapacitating Lebanon, and denying Syria the advantage of power-sharing with Lebanon, thus finally disconnecting the Syrian and Lebanese courses.

6. Capitalizing on the results of this aggression to amend the July Accord in a manner that would guarantee the halt of resistance activity from within the occupied zone.

Israel was sure of success. An important international political cover was provided for it in the Sharm-El-Sheikh summit, while military operations were well prepared. Added to this was the initiative of spreading horror through massacres and the escalation of assaults and displacements, in addition to gambling on the Party's inability to endure; the Israeli army considered all indicators of success to be present.

Hizbullah's dynamic military activity was accompanied by an effective political effort. Appearance on local and foreign media was necessary for exposing the reality of events and of Party responsibility. The Party was thus active on the political and media scene, conveying developments with successive statements and undertaking open discussions with various political powers. Hizbullah called, together with other Lebanese parties, for a broad national-level meeting[1] that was to be an expression of Lebanon's unity against this Israeli aggression. Hizbullah's Secretary General Nasrallah visited the Syrian leadership in Damascus together with his political assistant Hajj Hussein al-Khalil. Intensive meetings were held with Syria's foreign minister Farouk al-Shara, where information and suggestions were exchanged and the most minute of details were discussed, in order for political standpoints to be harmonious. Meetings with other figures visiting Syria at the time were also held, the most notable of which was the April 19 convention with Iran's foreign minister Ali Akbar Wilayati.

The Party also undertook a major effort at the social level, working together with public and social organizations for lodging the displaced, providing them with food, clothing and health care facilities, and securing their return to their homes following the ceasefire. The Party actively took the initiative of restoring homes damaged by the Israeli aggression.

---

1. The meeting was to be held at the Alexander Hotel in the Achrafieh area where the Israeli army leadership was headquartered during the 1982 invasion.

The Qana massacre came back to haunt the Israelis. Instead of horrifying Lebanese civilians and confusing combatants, it was transformed into an international condemnation of Israel. In spite of this, Israel continued to do its utmost in order to continue as planned, refusing to cease fire until a full nine days after the massacre, at which time Israeli impotence against the Resistance's effectiveness and the resilience of the populace had been clearly demonstrated, as was the effectiveness of cooperation with the Lebanese army and of harmony between the Resistance and the Lebanese government.

Through US Minister of Foreign Affairs Warren Christopher, Israel suggested a temporary ceasefire. The Lebanese cabinet almost adopted this suggestion unilaterally, but the Party refused it, demonstrating the dangers of keeping the initiative in the hands of Israel without the latter's abiding by a resolution to halt aggression. The Party assured all those concerned with the political horizon that it was ready to sustain further battles, to hurt Israel for a long time to come. The ceasefire offer thus failed, and discussions reverted to a more complete solution.

In the event of signing a ceasefire accord with Israel, the role of the Lebanese government became a debatable issue. To such problematic notions the Party replied through Secretary General Nasrallah: 'It is inconceivable for us to sign a written accord with the Israeli enemy, and we do not compete with anyone to be party to such written accords.'[1]

It was no secret that the Party was unconcerned about aggression, but about the internal political state of affairs within Lebanon; the worry was of being sold out or betrayed, of being

---

1. *The Eighth War*, p. 659.

weakened while challenging the grander and more worthy cause.

Syria succeeded through the personal follow-up of its late President Hafez al-Assad in directing a written agreement tailored to the requirements of the Resistance, or what became known as the 'April Accord'. The arrangement was delayed for a whole day due to disagreement on one particular word: 'launch'. While the American mediator had provided a text that referred to refraining from the use of civilian areas as launch bases for the Resistance, Hizbullah was about to accept a solution that only spoke of refraining from the use of civilian areas as launch pads for the *firing* of attacks. There is a significant difference between 'launching' and 'firing'.

With the phrase finally amended, combatants could launch their attacks from any bases that they would consider to be sufficiently safe and beyond the reach of Israel given that the latter is bound by agreements and understandings not to shell civilian areas or else face the wrath of Katyusha rockets on its northern settlements. As such, civilian areas constituted an area from where attacks could be launched, but not a base for firing rockets in the direction of Israel. This was in agreement with the policy of the Hizbullah resistance of directly targeting occupation soldiers as opposed to civilian areas.

Hizbullah thus successfully extracted this written April Accord, which saw the light with the declaration of a ceasefire at 6:00 PM on the evening of April 27, 1996. Being a written agreement, it differs from the July Accord, which was more of an understanding. The April Accord was supported by a follow-up entity, a five-member committee in charge of overseeing its execution. It also provided the Resistance with the legitimacy of defying occupation through the recognized right for self-defence. It spoke of the neutrality of civilian areas, insisting as in the July Accord that Israel should cease to bombard civilians and civilian targets in Lebanon and that in return, Katyusha rocket attacks on northern Israeli settlements would come to a halt.

Iran played an effective role in those Damascus negotiations through its foreign minister Wilayati, while Syria, Iran and the Resistance succeeded at ensuring the participation of France in the committee for overseeing the implementation of the accord. The committee grouped Syria, Lebanon, France, the US and Israel – a balanced five-member body.

The star achievement was represented by public support, both Muslim and Christian, for the Resistance. All partisan powers on the Lebanese front, along with the Lebanese government and its institutions, lent their full backing. Talk spread of 'national concurrence around the Resistance' – a slogan later used by many politicians – in its confrontation with the occupation and in its approach towards the exertion of pressure by international missions sent to Lebanon and aimed at ceasing resistance activity. Further, resilience and victory led to a new Arab-wide and Muslim-wide recognition which was felt at the regional level, both by the ruling regimes and by the populace. Hizbullah emerged out of this confrontation stronger than before, exposing Israeli impotence. The first fruit of this defiance was the defeat suffered by Peres, who was backed by US President Clinton, in the Israeli elections for prime minister on May 29, 1996.

The Ansaria Operation

Israel fell into the April Accord trap that denied it the possibility of using civilian bombardment as a pressure tactic against the Resistance. The accord confined Israel to confrontations only with Resistance combatants who possessed the drive, capability and determination to deal harmful blows and quickly disappear, without leaving a chance for vengeance. The Resistance thus continued to score more points, as Israel's ground intelligence services only grew weaker, failing time and again to expose Resistance operations or ambushes before their actual launch. It became increasingly difficult to take preventive measures and decrease the risks faced by Zionists and their Lahdist[1] co-conspirators.

The Israeli army then chose to lay ambushes in the rear areas within the occupied zone, succeeding, through a night commando mission, at planting a bomb in the Kfour area of Nabatieh, which later exploded amongst a number of *mujahideen* fighters.

Planning a repeat of the experience, an elite squad of the enemy's Shiyetet marine commandos infiltrated the environs of Ansaria in the South Lebanon district of Sidon on the night of September 5, 1997. Upon their arrival at the target destination, they fell into a tight ambush prepared by resistance *mujahideen*. All sorts of weapons were used, and following three hours of clashes the results were seventeen casualties on the Zionist side, their remnants spreading all over the combat zone. Despite intervention by the Israeli air force and efforts at clearing the

---

1. The Lahdist forces were led by Antoine Lahd, a former Lebanese army commander for South Lebanon who had switched allegiance to Israel in the early days of occupation.

place of any traces, *mujahideen* fighters succeeded in gathering bodily remains of hands and feet and the head of one of the infiltrators, which later proved an important asset in the exchange for detainees in Israeli prisons.

What the enemy did not know back then was that the Resistance was well aware of the planned operation, and that *mujahideen* combatants stood ready to receive the infiltrators, shadowing the Israeli forces from the moment of their landing on the shore to their passage into the fields, until their arrival at their destination point in Ansaria. Remote-controlled bombs were planted in all directions, and many *mujahideen* fighters were present with vital weaponry in the zone. This explains the intensity of the engagement, the types of weapons used, the extent of losses on the Israeli side and the necessity of Israeli air force intervention.

The Ansaria operation bewildered Israel, leading to a cancellation of its plan to retaliate to confrontations within the occupied zone with the laying of ambushes in the rear ranks of the Resistance. The April Accord came back to the forefront, and a new victory was added to the Resistance's record.

Martyrdom of the Secretary General's Son

Seven days following the Ansaria operation, on the afternoon of September 12, 1997, resistance fighters detected a movement by an Israeli patrol in the Jabal al-Rafi' area of Iqlim al-Tuffah. The patrol was heading in the direction of a target in Arabsalim. Orders were issued to many resistance groups to take action and set up ambushes. The Secretary General's eldest son, al-Sayyed

Hadi Nasrallah, was a member of one of these groups. His unit engaged in combat with an Israeli force, landing sure casualties on the Israeli side. The operation was completed without any losses in the ranks of the Resistance, and fighters took the trail back to rear lines. However, the abundance of mortar fire poured by the Israelis on the return track led to the martyrdom of three resistance fighters – the Secretary General's son, Ali Kawtharani and Haitham Mughnieh – while a fourth fighter managed to return unharmed. The enemy took possession of the three martyrs' corpses, as the operation took place within the occupied zone.

At the same time, anti-aircraft missiles were fired by the Lebanese army in the direction of Israeli military helicopters; the latter retaliated by bombarding Lebanese army bases. Six martyrs fell, among them First Lieutenant Jawad Azar, while eight others were wounded.

The martyrdom of al-Sayyed Hadi Nasrallah greatly empowered the Party's mission as the son of a leader who has devoted his entire life to the cause, and who provided him with the free choice of treading on this path or not. The martyr's efforts were not simply limited to adherence to the course. He took part in dangerous frontline confrontations, where the insignia of martyrs is planted. His endeavours were a representation of leadership's harmony with itself and with its own propositions, a practical implementation of those principles that Hizbullah carries and of the intention to go through the confrontation with all that one owns and holds dear. The martyrdom of al-Sayyed Hadi added a new emblem to the chest of the Secretary General, who demonstrated his commitment to the path chosen by Hizbullah, imperturbability and bold persistence despite all challenges and perils.

The following night, coincidentally, marked the fourth commemoration of the September 13 massacre. The event was to be held in the Council's open forum, and it had been previously decided that the Secretary General would speak on the occasion. I called him that afternoon, offering to speak on his behalf in view of the circumstances of his son's martyrdom, for the loss was great and fatherly emotions are only natural. He replied with a resolute determination to speak at the commemoration, that it would be inappropriate to offer any signals from which the enemy might benefit. He added that he saw no necessity to alter the plan. I cautiously repeated that I would be ready and standing by at any moment should he change his mind. The Secretary General took the podium to deliver an eloquent and profound martyrdom speech:

> The martyrdom of al-Sayyed Hadi is a grand title indicating that we, in the leadership of Hizbullah, do not spare our children and save them for the future. We pride ourselves when our sons reach the frontline, and stand, heads high, when they fall martyrs.[1]

Lebanon marched in its entirety to pay its respects and hail the martyrdom of the Jabal al-Rafi' heroes as led by al-Sayyed Hadi. This was a one-of-a-kind demonstration, a testament to the appreciation for Hizbullah and its leadership, and yet another source of pride enriching the course. Israel's record of aggression was gradually being transformed into victory for the Resistance.

---

1. The Central Media Unit, *The Book of Light: Lanterns Towards the Other Era*, p. 225.

Practical advancement was being recorded on a daily basis, and was on an exponential rise. Public support only grew, from the time of the first Israeli withdrawal in 1985 up until the 'Two Captives' operation of 1986; the martyrdom of former Secretary General al-Sayyed Abbas al-Moussawi, which accentuated the leadership's credibility; the July Accord and then the April Accord; all the way to the pioneering Ansaria operation and the subsequent martyrdom of the Secretary General's son. The extent of youth enthusiasm for the Resistance was becoming palpable, as was the increasingly elevated opinion of the Resistance by the Arab and Muslim world. The Party's ability to draw on the nation's human potential and forge a unity of power among the factions and resistance organizations confronting Israel was quite evident. The conviction of political powers, including the Lebanese government, in the effectiveness of the Resistance and its importance to Lebanon as a result was becoming apparent. Hizbullah had never praised itself for its capabilities. Victory only served to strengthen beliefs, confidence, dependence on God, and trust in the righteousness of this *jihad*.

The Lebanese Brigade for Resisting Occupation

A number of political figures and powers raised the issue of why resistance activity was exclusively in the hands of Hizbullah, charging the Party with the responsibility of initiating a practical measure that could draw from other available and willing participants. Given the topography of the occupied Southern and Western Bekaa zones as well as the prevailing political circumstances, any group could have engaged in resistance activity if it so wished. In spite of Hizbullah's concentrated attempts to coordinate with various Lebanese party powers and Palestinian groups, and to facilitate their participation in operations against Israel within the occupied Lebanese zone, this step was never successfully taken, and there were several reasons. Certain groups were interested in recording a resistance presence without actually bearing the brunt of battle repercussions, and even without offering the necessary manpower or morale during confrontations, settling for merely holding up the political banner of resistance. Others were interested in an exclusive geographic area to be agreed upon with Hizbullah for the set-up of permanent bases and specific presence. To Hizbullah this would have been a sure peril given the constant presence of Israeli warplanes in Lebanese skies. Furthermore, it was the nature of resistance activity to be undercover; an overt presence was unacceptable to civilians in the villages. The Party could not bear responsibility for such plans, for the terrain was open to all, and it was not proper to allocate parts of it, erecting borderlines between the various combatants on the ground. Moreover, no party or group was positioned to actually execute such a proposition.

In spite of this, coordination did succeed to a limited extent with some groups, albeit at a modest level. Other groups interested in resistance activity were operating independently and declaring their actions. However, Hizbullah's distinguished level of achievement and the priority it set for confrontation with Israel made of it the spearhead of prominent and effective resistance work.

On another track, the Party took an extraordinary step in its accommodation of those young individuals who aspired to resisting occupation but who were not firm believers in the Party's ideological and cultural background, despite their belief in Hizbullah's qualification to lead resistance activity. In this context, the Secretary General declared during the first memorial held on September 21 to commemorate the Jabal al-Rafi' martyrs that Hizbullah intended to devise a formula of participation for those interested in resistance activity without full-fledged membership in the Party. He was later to specify the framework for such a model during a press conference held on November 3, now called 'The Lebanese Brigade for Resisting Occupation'. This was to include Lebanese individuals who aspired to combat Israel regardless of their sect, convictions or political affiliations, the only conditions being the intactness of their security record in order to prevent any Israeli penetration, and their physical capacity to endure training and combat.

Upon declaration of the Brigade's formation, phones at the assigned centres rang off the hook, a signal of the thirst for such an initiative. Calmly and meticulously, work started on the training and preparation of these individuals. High states of alert were observed for fear of incursions. Analysis of the social and political constitution of this Brigade revealed the following:[1]

1. 75 per cent of the Brigade's resistance fighters were above twenty-five years of age, which indicated the clarity of their decision, firmness of their conviction, and physical and mental maturity.

2. 58.5 per cent of them held a secondary school degree or higher, and 5.9 per cent pursued postgraduate degrees.

---

1. The Lebanese Brigade, *Resistance of a Nation and Willpower of a People*, March 14, 1999, The Consultative Centre for Studies and Documentation, *Social and Political Structure and the Role's Horizon*, a study published in *Al-Anwar*, December 5, 1999.

The majority were students, a fact directly related to the concerns prevalent amongst this segment of society.

3. 51 per cent were former partisans, and 6.8 per cent still were partisans upon their application to join the Brigade. The balance of 42.2 per cent had never had any political experience. Percentages indicated the level of trust awarded by these individuals to the Party through such willingness to partake in Hizbullah's *jihad*.

4. 38 per cent were of the Sunni sect, 25 per cent were Shi'is, 20 per cent Druze and 17 per cent Christians. It was apparent through the overwhelming turnout of Muslims that their situation prepared them for enmity with Israel, notwithstanding of course the importance of the Christian percentage – especially when viewed in light of Lebanon's circumstances and the divergence of societal convictions, aspirations and sectarian interests.

Following all the necessary preparations, the first Brigade operation was launched on March 14, 1998. Until November 15, 1999, a total of 175 Brigade operations were recorded, although none had reached a dangerous level given the level of participants' capabilities. Some proposed including Brigade fighters in dangerous operations sure to result in martyrdom, in order to give Hizbullah tangible evidence of the Brigade's capabilities. But the Party refused this logic, for Hizbullah was not in the business of using Brigade fighters for political or media purposes. These fighters were carrying out national duties and Hizbullah was responsible, in front of God, to ensure their safety and make all proper circumstances available to them. Whoever was naturally martyred during a *jihad* operation would have reached his fate and the destiny of martyrdom to which he aspired, and it would not have been moral to stage results, whatever the size of political gains might have been.

The formation of the Brigade represented cooperation on one particular issue. It was a pioneering experience of gathering under a specific banner when it was not possible to pull all constituents towards one vision, or when the combat zone was in need of fighters to face the grand entitlement of opposing occupation, the expulsion of which calls for collaboration of all parties. It was always required to seek common ground, that which was a source of assembly and unity and where collaborative group work was a source of strength.

The Revolution of the Famished

Disagreement with the previous Hizbullah Secretary General, Sheikh Subhi al-Tufaili, was not spontaneous; it had taken various forms since mid-1991 following the election of former Secretary General al-Sayyed Abbas al-Moussawi. Sheikh Subhi had not practically borne the responsibility of a post despite his membership in the Council. He had opposed the Party's participation in parliamentary elections in 1992 and later abstained from candidacy to the Council. He had his particular opinions and positions, which were publicized often through the media, regarding the performance of the Party, the manner of addressing the Bekaa's social and developments needs, the form of Party leadership and various other political issues.

The Party considered these differences to lie within acceptable boundaries until the *sheikh* launched what he termed 'The Revolution of the Famished' – a banner for an independent movement with a particular claim. On May 4, 1997, he published a call for civil disobedience to take place in front of the Government House in Baalbeck on July 4, and thereafter for road blockades on October 26, without resorting to any coordination or even deliberations with Hizbullah.

Many efforts were made to discuss the priorities of resistance work with the *sheikh*, the necessity for social and developmental work, and the objective of voicing the people's concerns and exigencies without clashing with the government or instigating internal strife. A Party committee of mediators was formed in order to discuss sources of conflict with the *sheikh*, search for solutions and channels for coordination, and at least allocate roles without dissociation and disagreement. Deliberations came to no avail, and such was the result with the various other committees that were formed to this end across all discussion stages.

Hizbullah refuses dualism in its endeavours. The Revolution of the Famished was of a divisive and independent nature, while any field movement ought to have been bound by the Hizbullah Council decision. The *sheikh* did not cooperate and continued with his independent movement until open conflict came on World Jerusalem Day, which was announced by Imam Khomeini on the last Friday of Ramadan. The Party was accustomed to holding this special event in the Ras al-Ain Square of Baalbeck city, but Sheikh al-Tufaili announced the holding of this event with his own movement in that same customary place, repeating the Ashura Day experience of the previous year.

This announcement was a sufficient declaration of demarcation and led to Hizbullah's decision to dismiss the *sheikh* from the Party on January 24, 1998. A statement was issued in this regard, which stated:

> Sheikh al-Tufaili's insistence on carrying out events known to be part of Hizbullah's customary event schedule clearly reveals to all after several months of similar moves that the *sheikh*'s actions do not fall in the realm of a plight movement. They are but an attempt to divide the domain, partition it and impose himself on it with all his available means irrespective of the losses and damages foreseen ... After all that Sheikh Subhi al-Tufaili did to oppose our course of work yesterday and has done over the past several months, he is no longer a member of our continuous progression from which he has deliberately swayed and which he has openly opposed.[1]

This was not an easy decision. Long discussions were undertaken in the Council over the *sheikh*'s issue, and there had been every intention to reach a solution that would avert such a result. But actions necessitated this conclusion, and the Party's statement at the time clearly outlined all reasons that led to the adoption of the dismissal decision.

Lebanon First or Jezzine?

Successive Israeli prime ministers attempted a variety of political solutions that would block the Resistance's capability in Lebanon, confine it to a political position, and spare Israel that heavy

---

1. *Al-Safir*, January 26, 1998.

price it was enduring for its occupation of Lebanon. Yitzhak Rabin's famous proposal was one where Israel would reach an agreement with Lebanon to disarm Hizbullah and forbid any resistance activities for a period of six months, following which Israel vowed to withdraw from Lebanon but only after testing the Lebanese government's capability to fulfil its end of the obligation. Shimon Peres publicized the notion of partial withdrawal, for instance, withdrawal from the area of Jezzine and its vicinity, in return for guaranteeing that no resistance operations would be undertaken there. This was proposed as a testing phase to be gradually repeated in other occupied areas and eventually covering all of occupied Lebanon. The proposal was brought forward in 1996 before the April aggression. After assuming the post of prime minister, Benjamin Netanyahu followed with a similar scheme, but one carrying the banner 'Lebanon First'. This formed part of a comprehensive solution that would entirely remove Lebanon from the circle of confrontation with Israel, achieve Israel's security and end any convergence between the Lebanese and Syrians.

By then it was clear that Israel's power over Lebanon had been depleted and that its presence was turning into a burden of heavy human losses amidst its ranks. Israel had entered Lebanon in order to increase the advantage it held, widen its occupation and leave its choices open as to stabilizing its existence and secure its future. Given that occupation, aggression and successive wars could not subdue resistance and only served to increase its fervour, resorting to a political solution akin to the May 17 Accord or one of slightly amended resemblance was thought to represent an important political score for Israel. For this would remove Lebanon from the formula, alienate Syria and isolate the Palestinians completely.

The notion of 'Lebanon First' was comparable to Camp David's 'Egypt First' solution, which removed Egypt from the confrontation circle. It was also akin to the 'Gaza First and Jericho' plans, which came as part of the Oslo Agreement and isolated the Palestinian cause from all surrounding events or anything that would help strengthen it. It resembled the 'Wadi Araba' situation that officially set apart Jordan's position outside the conflict while charging it with the exceptional responsibility of securing Israeli borders from the concentrated Palestinian presence within. 'Lebanon First' was therefore a continuation of the fragmentation plan for dissociating Palestine from its surrounding neighbours. It was also aimed at isolating Syria, in addition to binding Lebanon to agreements and pledges that would deny it the ability to secure its own future through disarming it of its main point of strength: the Resistance, with all that could mean in terms of existence or political achievements or land gains.

Lebanon refused the so-called 'Lebanon First' proposition, counting on its successful resistance as well as Syrian support and considering the project's danger to Lebanon as prime justification. For the plan would only served to safeguard Israel's security and political exigencies without guaranteeing the unconditional liberation of Lebanon. Taking the top view of things, the internationally adopted decision represented by UN Resolution 425 required Israel to withdraw from Lebanese territory, and there was therefore no need for any bilateral agreements. Israel had simply to abide by it immediately. Even today, Lebanon still awaits the complete fulfilment of this UN decision.

At that point, the occupiers concentrated on the 'Jezzine First' proposition. The Jezzine area had the distinction of being under the control of Israel's co-conspirators led by the collaborator Antoine Lahd. No direct Israeli presence existed in Jezzine, as Israel hoped for an agreement between the Lahdists and the Lebanese government that would simply consecrate the legitimacy of the Lahdist group. The proposition called for a halt to all resistance activity in this area. The Israeli enemy exploited the fact that Jezzine was a Christian area, to stir inhabitants' apprehensions of 'what Hizbullah might do' if it were to ever enter Jezzine. The Lebanese government refused any agreement that would touch on security measures. Regrettably, some Christian figures worked through what became known as the Mar Roukoz Meeting, using an organized propaganda campaign to accentuate Israel's claims and spread the anxiety already stirred among Christians in that area. Intense political meetings attempted to induce international support for its aims.

Despite lasting as a proposal for three years, 'Jezzine First' did not sway the Lebanese government from its determination and refusal of any discussion over the subject. Should Israel or its collaborators have wished to withdraw from any occupied area in Lebanon, the Lebanese government would have then fulfilled its duties and closed any gaps without resorting to bilateral agreements with the enemy and its co-conspirators, and without outlining beforehand any political or security mechanisms that might be adopted – and this in order to thwart enemy plans for making gains during withdrawal.

The year 1999 was marked by intense resistance operations against Lahdist groups who deserted their posts by the numbers, horrified by the high number of casualties among their ranks and the direct targeting of their homes and posts. Lahd himself could no longer remain in Jezzine and its vicinity, given the dearth of supporters available for defence and on security patrols. To Israel, further involvement through soldier deployment in Jezzine was out of the question. Lahd was thus obliged to withdraw from Jezzine and its surroundings on the night of June 1, 1999, a move for which he obtained Israeli approval. Thus Jezzine was liberated, unconditionally.

The Mar Roukoz milieu was astonished by what happened after the Jezzine liberation. The young men of the Islamic Resistance did not enter the area, and none of its inhabitants were harmed whatsoever. Resistance operations against Israel continued from the Jezzine vicinity without any friction with civilians. Lebanese security forces took measures for the safety of the Jezzine population, but no full-fledged military deployment was planned, as this would only have served as a security guarantee for Israel. The Jezzine experience was a successful and luminous achievement in favour of the Resistance, one that proved the deceptive nature of those apprehensive claims associated with liberation. The citizens of Jezzine discovered the true burden of occupation and the blessing of liberation, and claims that collaborator presence was only for their protection proved false.

Victory

Had Hizbullah leadership been asked during the early years of the Resistance, or even a few years thereafter, about the possibility of actually realizing liberation in the South and Western Bekaa, of achieving freedom from Israeli occupation through the limited means available to the *mujahideen*, the answer would have simply been: 'We carry our duty and rely on God. Should we succeed in shaking the existence of this enemy and turn its occupation into a gridlock, this would be an important achievement. Victory, however, is affected by many factors at the pinnacle of which is divine levelling. We aspire to it, but realize that its possibility is known only to God Almighty.'

However, the possibility became much clearer only two years before the grand liberation. Hopes increased and ran high in the last year when the pledge to withdraw from Lebanon entered the political agendas of contestants for the Israeli prime ministerial post: Benjamin Netanyahu and Ehud Barak.

The Zionists tried through several mediators, American, European and international, and through various interest-generating and intimidation tactics, to execute a withdrawal from Lebanon preceded by a political agreement. Their attempts failed, for theirs was the weaker position, and Israeli society had grown tired of watching television images of soldiers killed in Lebanon during resistance operations. Lebanon was no longer a source of power or a channel for exerting pressure. Barak thus announced his intention to withdraw from Lebanon in July, 2000 as a fulfilment of his election promise, leaving the details vague and signalling more than once that withdrawal would be conditional upon achieving an agreement on security issues with Lebanon.

Despairing of reaching any agreement with Lebanon, Barak preferred to withdraw suddenly, thus avoiding *mujahideen* fire on his fleeing soldiers, as was the situation when the collaborators fled Jezzine. This debacle took place on May 24, 2000, marking the grandest and most important victory over Israel since it commenced its occupation fifty years before – a liberation that was achieved at the hands of the weakest of nations, of a resistance operating through the most modest of means, not at the hands of armies or powerful military arsenals.

The victory, in its manner of achievement and details, exceeded the Party's expectations, for the possible withdrawal scenarios available to Israel were limited to three:

1. *Withdrawal by the Israeli forces from the majority of occupied villages and towns, leaving the Lahdist group in these areas as a 'National Guard'.* The Lebanese army would remain within a border zone of specific depth, and provide logistical support to the collaborators whenever needed, thus leaving the Resistance in direct confrontation with collaborators and removing Israeli soldiers from the scope of direct targeting. Israel would then declare its first phase of withdrawals to have been fulfilled.

2. *An Israeli withdrawal from Shi'ite villages, leaving collaborators in other areas.* This would leave the latter stranded behind villagers, using them as shields during confrontations and leading to cries of sectarianism and targeting based on confessional lines.

3. *Leaving Lahdists within an occupied border zone tighter than the one actually occupied, thus requiring fewer Lahdist participants.* The Zionists would then withdraw, leaving behind a pure Lebanese-Lebanese conflict, one where the collaborators would seek refuge and safety in villages still under occupation.

But what actually took place was entirely outside the scope of expectations: Israel withdrew from Lebanon in one night, completely surprising its own collaborators. Upon entering the abandoned Lahdist posts, *mujahideen* fighters discovered fully prepared dinners, left untouched by the fleeing conspirators who had suddenly learned of Israel's withdrawal. Fighters captured forsaken artillery and weapons, which were later delivered to the Lebanese army, and seized detailed security-related documents and computer files containing the names of collaborators and their ranks and service details, as well as the assaults they engaged in. Important classified military information was also captured.

On the other side of this liberation front, civilian marches had started from the Ghandourieh village towards the just liberated town of Kantara, led by the Allegiance to the Resistance member, parliamentarian Nazih Mansour. At the time, Lahdist militias had withdrawn from the areas surrounding Kantara, and the march entered the centre of this town where coordination between resistance leadership, mobilized youth and citizens led to a decision to organize similar marches across the other villages. Resistance fighters would check for safety at the deserted posts, following which citizens would march forward. Collaborators fled their posts before the marches arrived, and some surrendered. Members of the Resistance escorted these marches in order to thwart any danger.

One by one, occupied villages fell out of enemy control. Israeli air raids targeted a number of roads in order to halt the processions, but the brave citizens were determined to achieve liberation. Collaborators were living their moments of defeat, while the Israeli army was preparing for withdrawal from the back lines which it still occupied. Liberation was accomplished over three days, marking the successive disintegration of collaborators and the final exit of the Israeli forces, and so it finally came on May 24, 2000. Families sought their loved ones in Khiam prison, breaking the siege of captives detained in that horrific place. Many collaborators surrendered and were handed over to the Lebanese army, while others fled with their families to the Occupied Territories in Palestine.

The victory was a divine blessing, an honour bestowed by God on the devoted and the oppressed. It was a victory for the Resistance and for all the political and factional powers that had participated in it; a victory for the people, the army and the government, for Arabs and Muslims. It was a victory for all those who esteemed the Resistance and a defeat for all those who loathed it. The victory led to an important turning point in our region, converting weakness into power; resignation into audacity; frustration into resolve; and languor into trust. It opened new doors that are bound to change the reality and future for all of us.

This victory drew its core value from the untarnished image of the Resistance. Liberation was not marked by any deliberate assassinations of Lahdist collaborators, or by finishing off the wounded or detained. Not even one incident of vengeance by citizens against collaborators was witnessed, contrary to what is customary in all revolutions and struggles around the world. Not one clash with the families of collaborators, who were present in the liberated regions, was recorded. This was stunning to observers. The morals of Hizbullah partisans and the level of discipline demonstrated by its *jihad* combatants were of a very high calibre.

It is no secret that some young combatants, as well as some of the region's citizens, had a desire for vengeance – especially those who were aware of what collaborators and their families had inflicted on the *mujahideen* and their next of kin across the occupied villages. Resistance leadership issued a strict warning forbidding any such action and vowing to discipline those who took it whatever the justifications.

The value of this victory also lay in the perception it painted of this Islamic party, which had borne many difficulties yet remained on its unswerving course; which extended a hand to all and did not use any politics of blasphemy or alienation against any individuals demonstrating a willingness to cooperate on the objective of liberation; which was exemplary in the use of limited means when confronting the powerful and well-equipped force of the Israeli army; and which blended a belief in God, trust in victory, eagerness for martyrdom and preparation for sacrifice. It was the combination of all of these factors that achieved victory.

The victory's worth also lay in its having been a challenge to Israel and not to any other party in our region, an aim for pure liberation without any bartering in the bazaar of cheap political values. It was a reality that has made its way into modern history, and has laid the foundations for a new era calling for a revision of principles, methods and modes of operation for all groups, factions and parties, all of which could now benefit from the Lebanese resistance experience.

This victory came to prove that the military arsenals of the Arab world do not represent a solution for the menace of the Israeli project, that negotiations do not achieve any tangible gains for the Palestinian cause and for other occupied Arab territories, and that international support for and persisting apprehension about Israeli might are but a scarecrow planted to defeat our spirits. We are indeed capable of changing this formula if we analyze our sources of strength and capitalize on them, analyze the enemy's weakness and work on confronting them.

Resolution 425 Has Not Been Implemented

Another chapter of confrontation with Israel started. The US worked together with the United Nations and the Western world to portray Israel's escape from Lebanon as an implementation of UN Resolution 425, a fact that would oblige Lebanon to deploy its army on the southern borders in order to avoid any attacks against Israel. As such, the security measures required by Israel would have been fulfilled without concluding any agreements and using the pretext of implementing Resolution 425.

Lebanon refuted this logic, and it was now in a more advantageous position. Israel's withdrawal came only following a long period of occupation, and an Israeli withdrawal was only a Lebanese right. It came as a result of resistance operations against Israel, and was not an Israeli initiative for the implementation of UN Resolution 425. Further, withdrawal did not cover all areas, for the Lebanese Shebaa Farms and a number of borderline zones are still under occupation.

The UN's denial of Shebaa's Lebanese identity was not effective. Moreover, altering the international borders and replacing them with the so-called Blue Line drawn by UN envoy Terry Larsen was unacceptable to Lebanon, for this Blue Line – which leaves the Shebaa Farms to Israel – is but a withdrawal demarcation line and not an alternative to the internationally recognized borders. Lebanon held fast to its claim for this and other zones from which Israel is yet to withdraw.

Pressure increased on Lebanon to accept the Blue Line, with UN Secretary General Kofi Annan declaring on June 16, 2000 that Israel had completed its withdrawal based on which Lebanon was demanded time and again to deploy its troops in the South and thus live up to its responsibilities. Several justifications were claimed for these demands: a pretext that Israel had actually completed its withdrawal; concern over internal strife inside the liberated areas given the security gap – strife that fell under the pretext of sectarian antagonism; concern over tension on the Lebanese-Israeli border based on the promise that UN peacekeeping forces would not be deployed in Lebanon if the latter did not acquiesce to and fulfil UN demands; and the consequential warning of a dangerous escalation of events in the South.

The first surprise to the US, Israel and their adherents was the non-existence of any internal strife between Muslims and Christians inside the liberated zone, a zone that was living some of its best days, where no citizen was harmed and no chaos or breach of security was recorded either during or after liberation.

The UN and those orchestrating its actions were concerned about apparent Lebanese indifference to any delay in deploying UN peacekeeping forces along the Blue Line. In view of the stability inside the liberated zone, which existed even in the absence of the Lebanese army, concerns surfaced that UN forces might lose their importance. The UN thus overstepped its own conditions and decided to deploy peacekeeping forces on July 28, 2001 in the liberated areas.

The second surprise came when Israeli and US attempts to capitalize on the withdrawal and force the latter to recognize that UN Resolution 425 had actually been implemented at a time when parts of Lebanese territory – mainly the Shebaa Farms – remained under occupation, proved futile.

Finally, surprise was the answer to all attempts at stranding the Lebanese army in a conflict with the resistance in the South. Israel's attempts to guarantee security through Lebanese army deployment in the South went unanswered by the Lebanese government.

Army Deployment in South Lebanon

The alleged reasons that some Lebanese have provided for deploying the army in the South were not convincing, inconsistent with the victory, and incapable of achieving their publicized goals.

Where the objective is to protect, guarantee the security of and thwart any attacks against the civilian population in the liberated zone, then Civil Defence forces could do the job appropriately. Their role in conflict resolution between individuals and in barring any aggression whatever its source has effectively been demonstrated. The government has indeed lived up to its responsibilities in this context, and it should not be in the Resistance's realm of concern despite its physical presence throughout the area. The Resistance could not be a substitute for government and never posed itself as such. Further, the Resistance refuses any governmental resignation of duties.

Where the objective is to secure borders against Israeli aggression – essentially an army role, the army being the palisade and protector of national boundaries – then it is public knowledge that the Lebanese army is much weaker than its Israeli counterpart, and an Israeli decision to invade Lebanon whether by land, sea or air would be faced by army retaliation of a limited effect that could not impede a wide-scale aggression, given the obvious imbalance in capabilities.

Two objectives for army deployment in the South remain, one sought by a Lebanese segment and the other needed by Israel. The first of these represents a desire to deploy the army in the South in order to forbid the Resistance and any other faction or force from undertaking operations against Israel, be they in the Shebaa Farms or otherwise. In our view, this would only serve to remove Lebanon from the circle of confrontation with the Israeli enemy whatever the results of such a resignation. The Shebaa issue would then be routed through diplomatic channels should its Lebanese identity be recognized in the first place. Thus the channel would be the same as that used for the issues of captives and detainees in Israeli prisons, the Palestinian presence in Lebanon, Israel's continuous infringement of Lebanese airspace, and any other pending or upcoming matters. As such, resistance work in Lebanon would totally cease, and the Lebanese army could seize all available weapons and take charge of controlling the borders.

This alternative expresses a political viewpoint that is different from what Hizbullah or a large portion of the Lebanese population, including current Lebanese president Emile Lahhoud, envision. They consider war with Israel to be ongoing, even if a chapter has indeed ended following the liberation of the larger part of the South and Western Bekaa. The occupation is still represented by the seizure of the Shebaa Farms, the capture of *mujahideen* and their imprisonment by Israel, the danger of nationalizing the Palestinians in Lebanon, and Israel's expansionist avarice for land and water. The peril of the Zionist aggression persists, especially when calculations reveal possible gains in favour of the Israelis. Indeed, who is capable of halting or even hindering Israel's voracity and criminal practices?

Experience has clearly shown that Resolution 425, diplomatic efforts and US promises did not liberate Lebanon from a twenty-two-year occupation. Lebanon was liberated through resistance and public support for such resistance. Since we are in possession of such effective means, why would we intentionally incapacitate them? What do we fear by maintaining them? And who could guarantee a deterrence of Israel should we lose them?

Perhaps such apprehensive groups harbour a fear of associating Lebanon with the Palestinian cause. But who was in charge of creating such a link in the first place? Did Israel not occupy Lebanon under the pretext of safeguarding its northern borders and in order to guarantee the political and security latitude for its project? Furthermore, is it practically possible to disconnect the issues in the region from one another in this day and age of globalization?

Had the Resistance not remained at a heightened state of alert after liberation, Israel would have launched many assaults against Lebanon using the Palestinian uprising or *Intifadah* as a pretext, along with such issues as Israel's security and the existence of safe havens for the *mujahideen*. Had resistance operations not continued to liberate the Shebaa Farms, the world would have forgotten the existence of an occupation in Lebanon. Were it not for the three Israeli captives seized in a resistance operation after liberation, the world would have forgotten our captives and detainees in Israeli prisons.

Who said that Lebanon is capable of remaining neutral? Lebanon's geographic and political positions impose two alternatives on the country: either an allegiance to Syria or an allegiance to Israel. It is only natural for us to choose the former. Furthermore, Lebanon's political stance could be either in support of the Palestinian cause or in defence of Israel. It is again, in this case, natural for us to choose Syria.

We do not consider ourselves isolated from the region's issues. We believe that Lebanon's aspirations cannot be realized in isolation from the influential powers in our region, at the head of which are Syria and the Palestinian *Intifadah*. We also consider the great victory that took place in Lebanon as being one of the fruits of such a realistic and comprehensive view.

The second objective, which is necessary for Israel, is represented by charging the Lebanese army with the responsibility of impeding any operations along the length of Lebanon's southern borders, as well as forcing the political authorities in Lebanon to exert the necessary pressure and channel communications to this end at the risk of being held liable in the eyes of the international community. In this way, Israel's security requirements would be transformed into security guarantees, while Lebanon's requirements would be bound to political channels and common diplomatic routes leading to future follow-ups, an approach that is known to fail in the case where conflict is with Israel.

The Lebanese government should not bear such burdens, deprive itself of power sources, or act as Israel's executive arm, for Israel possesses ample means of exerting pressure, whether political, military, or in the form of active international support.

Refusing to deploy the Lebanese army in the South is a wise decision that Hizbullah supports and regards as a point of strength in favour of the Lebanese government. Many years have passed since liberation and Israel has not yet been able to reap the fruits of its withdrawal, while Lebanon can rejoice with victory, safeguard its power sources and draw the attention of large nations to analysis of its requirements – all of this without suffering any consequential losses.

The various Lebanese groups and factions are called upon to accurately study their positions, for the political conditions surrounding our country could lead matters in any direction. Internal political standpoints cannot be formed in isolation from international repercussions. Even if the segments supporting such an alternative do wish it, claims for closing the southern front serve only Israel, and abandoning the fight for the Shebaa Farms would only lead to the loss of this zone and to the advantage of the occupier.

The Shebaa Farms Operations

The Shebaa Farms area carries a special importance that is related neither to its geographical position nor to its size of merely 50 square kilometres, but rather what it represents. When Hizbullah persisted in its resistance of Shebaa's occupation, the area's Lebanese identity was only further accentuated – proof that such resistance is a natural continuum of the fight against the Israeli occupation of Lebanon that existed prior to liberation. For it is not conceivable to waive land the size of even one hand span, irrespective of this land's location and significance. It is a question of principle; Israel's presumptions of stability should be blocked as long as land occupation unjustly persists.

Resistance cannot be held as an *a priori* reason for future possible developments; it is simply a reaction, a defence against occupation. Any repercussions that may ensue are the results of occupation and not the result of resistance activity. Further, the enemy always exerts pressure through military power and attempts to impose its conditions through such power. As such, challenging this force and rendering it ineffectual would stifle its ability to overstep boundaries and aspire to more.

Whatever the costs in terms of sacrifice, the fruits of resistance are always greater than the damage generated from resignation to occupation, succumbing to its blows and acquiescing to its conditions.

Some consider the Shebaa Farms to be a pretext for the continued existence of an armed resistance movement. If so, and should this be the only reason for occupation and its repercussions, then let pressure be directed towards Israel, and let claims be for withdrawal and subsequent annulment of this allegation.

Given the narrow topographic features of the Shebaa Farms and the few movements of the limited number of Israeli troops deployed in that area, and given that concentrated operations there might not result in inflicting much injury on the enemy, Hizbullah's leadership drew confrontation guidelines which it then left to the field command to implement.

This does not negate the fact that the Shebaa Farms area carries a political message of higher importance than that of other previously occupied areas. It is required that Shebaa expresses resolute resistance and refusal of occupation; that it forbid Israel from contemplating an aggression against Lebanon; that it publicize a readiness for resistance that is in line with the regional developments that bear on Lebanon; and that it represent a podium for sending messages of solidarity to Palestinians subjected to Israeli massacres and assaults, notably such aggression as 'Operation Defensive Shield' launched against Jenin, Nablus and other areas.[1]

Current resistance activity in the Farms, whether through the launching of anti-aircraft missiles against infringing Israeli warplanes or through carefully timed operations that directly target the occupation's patrols and bases, is thought to be the most effective method for achieving the Resistance's objectives.

Trying the Collaborators

Israel's first invasion of Lebanon started on March 14, 1978 with a military offensive known as the 'Litani' operation. The Israeli army advanced into some 1,000 square kilometres of Lebanese territory, withdrawing thereafter to settle within a 500-square kilometre zone covering sixty towns and villages[2] in the South Lebanon districts of Hasbaya, Marjeyoun, Bint Jbeil, and Tyre. UN Resolution 425 was issued then, calling on Israel to withdraw to internationally recognized borders. But Israel did not comply.

On April 18, 1979, and with Israeli blessing, Major Saad Haddad of the Lebanese army declared his creation of 'The Free Republic of Lebanon'[3] within the occupied zone, thereafter

---

1. During the Israeli 'Defensive Shield' operation, which started on March 29, 2003, the Resistance escalated its activities in the Shebaa Farms, increasing the frequency to a daily basis, between March 30, 2002 and April 13, 2002, sending a message of solidarity with the Palestinian people's uprising and pain.

2. Adnan al-Sayyed Hassan, *Israeli Occupation of Lebanon*, p. 21. The author puts the figure at fifty-six. The source of our citation (sixty towns and villages) is the Department of Geography of the Islamic Resistance.

3. Monther Mahmoud Jaber, *Lebanon's Occupied Zone*, The Institution of

declaring the 'The Free Army of Lebanon' on May 17, 1980. These declarations constituted an obstacle against the execution by the UN forces in Lebanon of Resolution 425. Israel thus used a Lebanese front to disavow its responsibility for abiding by the international resolution, turning its occupation into a purely Lebanese conflict. The declaration of 'The Free Republic of Lebanon' signalled a conflict between the army and the central Lebanese government. The occupied area became known as the 'Borderline Occupied Zone'.

This zone was to extend deeper into Lebanon after the 1982 invasion, ultimately settling in 1985, after the first Israeli withdrawal due to resistance attacks, over an area of 1,100 square kilometres covering 168 villages,[1] towns and farms. The army of collaborators changed its name on April 4, 1984 to the 'South Lebanon Army',[2] a title indicating exclusive concern with the South and its liberation. This title served to annul the concept of cessation from Lebanon's central government. Major General Antoine Lahd succeeded Saad Haddad following the latter's death. Lahd continued to head this army of collaborators until the day of his escape with his conspirators into Israel following the resistance victory in 2000.

Israel used the false banner of 'protecting the Christians' in the South from the alleged dangers posed by the National Movement and the Palestinians, whose intentions – it was claimed – were to isolate the Christians and eventually eliminate them. The occupied zone thus turned into a haven for those harbouring relations with Israel, including members of the Lebanese Forces and Cedars

Palestinian Studies, p. 237.

1. Ibid., p. 384.
2. Adnan al-Sayyed Hassan, *Israeli Occupation of Lebanon*, p. 14. The author puts the number of villages under collaborator control at 167.

Guard who fled East Beirut upon the return of the Lebanese government to power following the defeat of General Michel Aoun in 1990. However, the drafting of collaborators was not restricted to one sect or religious congregation. Despite the fact that elite leadership was essentially composed of Maronite Christians, a large number of Muslims and Christians of other sects formed part of the composition of this group.

Doubtless, these collaborators were supportive of the occupation, providing it with the capability to remain longer inside Lebanon. Through taking charge of frontline bases and the organization of road patrols, they diminished risk to the Israeli forces. Their control of villages was tight, executed through assaults and menace, and their practical execution of collaborator missions directly served the Israeli enemy. They were thus the sandbags behind which Zionist forces took cover.

But Israel did not succeed at painting an image of these collaborators as a Lebanese group at odds with the other Lebanese groups. Through politics, Israel also failed to justify its occupation as support for this particular group. Opinions were voiced in Lebanon in defence of the collaborators, suggesting that the links of these individuals with Israel were purely reasons of sustenance. Others claimed that the pressure of living under occupation was sufficient reason for such collaboration. Still others suggested the collaborators were fearful of living amongst other citizens. True patriotism, it was finally suggested, is what led these individuals to hold on to the villages from within in order for Israel not to take control, as was the case in Jezzine.

In targeting collaborators, the Resistance made no distinction between Muslim and Christian, considering them all to have rebelled against all sectarian and national values. Many were killed in resistance operations targeting their bases and units. Horror infiltrated into the collaborators' ranks, and members had almost reached total breakdown around the time of the liberation. This explains the rapid disintegration of their forces over a three-day period, with thousands[1] of them fleeing together with their families into the occupied Palestinian territories, while others laid down their arms and surrendered to the Lebanese security forces, thereby closing this terrible chapter of conspiracy with Israel.

The Resistance took a decision not to even the score with these collaborators after liberation, considering their trial and punishment to be the responsibility of the Lebanese judicial system. Thus, no revolutionary tribunals were to be held, and no field vengeance was to take place. Charging the traitors was to be done through the Lebanese government. However, the 1,550 court verdicts issued by the military tribunal until November 24, 2000 and covering the interrogation of 2,159 individuals, were all mild, hovering between one and ten years in prison with the vast majority receiving less than two years imprisonment.[2]

Hizbullah was unhappy with these verdicts and demanded sterner judgments in order to discourage working with Israel in future, especially given that a mild verdict and the great lure of cash might prompt individuals to pursue that track again. Social responsibility requires that a lesson be taught to others about the repercussions of traitorous involvement. Moreover, the families

---

1. Knowledgeable sources suggest that the number of collaborators who remained inside Israel in September 2002 was 3,000, in addition to their families. A number of defectors had surrendered to the Lebanese authorities during the time of liberation, and their families have returned to their villages in South Lebanon.

2. *An-Nahar*, November 27, 2000.

of those killed, detained or wounded should have been permitted to witness the just punishment of these aggressors.

However, officials in charge of collaborator files had two-fold justification for the mild sentences: First, there was the high number[1] of individuals involved in such conspiracy – too many for Lebanese prisons to handle. Long sentences were also thought to be socially detrimental to conspirators' families, especially where these resided in the liberated zone.

Second, a particular group that considered those individuals to have been compelled and obliged to collaborate with Israel raised political objections and called for pardon. Seeking a sterner verdict was subsequently classified as a form of sectarian targeting.

Even though the Party was not convinced of these justifications and openly declared its denunciation of such mild sentences, and despite the high pressure exerted by the families of casualties who suffered at the hands of these collaborators, and even given the Party's concern that incidents of vengeance tarnishing the image of liberation and contradicting the Party's vision might indeed occur, the Party resorted to simply declaring its position and taking the necessary steps to communicate and support it. No practical condemnation measures were taken, a stance aimed at protecting the victory, persisting with *jihad* as a paramount priority, and refusing the distraction of internal tensions. Great attention is still paid to evading any breach of the internal

---

1. A report prepared by the Coordination Committee of Hizbullah issued on January 10, 2001, stated – according to prominent sources at the military tribunal – that the number of individuals to be arrested was in the vicinity of 20,000. Based on the tribunal's records back then, the last case carried the number 6,640, while some cases covered tens of names at once. The total number of verdicts issued at that time was a little over 1,550.

domain by these collaborators. Follow-up of these individuals by security forces is still closely observed, as is the implementation of supplementary judicial verdicts that called for their temporary banishment from their villages.

Captives Detained in Israeli Prisons

Detainees were distributed amongst Israel's forty prisons and the al-Khiam prison in South Lebanon, the latter holding hundreds of prisoners, many of them female. Israel openly kept this prison in the hands of its conspirators, the so-called 'South Lebanon Army', in order for them to denounce any responsibility for the precarious forms of torture practised inside this prison which led to the martyrdom of a number of *mujahideen* fighters therein.

Hizbullah found that the issue of captives could only be solved through an exchange of war prisoners with Israel. The Resistance therefore focused on operations of capture, planning for a number of these and often concentrating its efforts. No declaration of such intentions was made, and some operations ended in clashes with Israeli patrols or at Israeli bases leading to death on the enemy side.

The 'Two Captives' operation, also known as the 'Kounin' operation, was the first such successful mission. Combatants planned for months, and the operation initially failed. Almost a month after the first attempt, on February 16, 1986 – the very day when Sheikh Ragheb Harb was martyred – the Resistance laid an ambush for an Israeli secret service patrol in the South Lebanon village of Kounin. *Mujahideen* fighters succeeded at capturing two squad members and fled with them. In the wake of this operation, Israel executed its six-day aggression and seventeen villages fell under enemy occupation. Resistance fighters continued with their confrontations until Israeli forces returned to their previous positions.

The two captives were used in two separate exchange deals, the first taking place in 1991 over three phases extending between September 11 and December 1. Designed as an exchange for information about the two captives' fate, ninety-one Lebanese individuals were liberated, one from inside Israel, the rest released from al-Khiam prison, including ten women and the remains of nine resistance fighters.

The second exchange took place on July 21, 1996. Traded for the bodies of the two captives, forty-five individuals were liberated from al-Khiam prison, including three women and the remains of 123 martyrs.

The Israelis ignored the fate of seventeen Lahdist collaborators held by the Resistance.[1] These individuals were then re-educated in captivity, leading to a change of principles for many, and after losing hope of using them in any exchange operation the Resistance set them free. They all opted to remain inside liberated zones.

The third exchange operation occurred on June 26, 1998. In return for the remains of Zionist soldiers who fell during the unusual 'Ansaria' operation of 1997, sixty captives were liberated among whom fifty were from al-Khiam and ten from Israeli prisons. The remains of forty martyrs were also returned.

To Israel, the capture of individuals from within the occupied zone was insufficient. The scope enlarged to include kidnapping from liberated villages, and two operations of high significance

---

1. Of whom three were held captive in the Lucy and Sariria areas of Western Bekaa and fourteen in the Tloussa area of the South.

were carried out in these areas. The first marked the kidnapping of Sheikh Abdelkarim Obeid from his house in Jibsheet on the night of July 28, 1989. Israeli commandos arrived by night in an airdrop operation on the outskirts of Jibsheet and continued by land into the town. The sheikh was the town's *imam*, leading its Friday prayers and all its gatherings. He was a cultural and social activist who insisted on remaining in Jibsheet despite the mutiny between Amal and Hizbullah, and lived up to this pledge later during the Israeli occupation following the martyrdom of Sheikh Ragheb Harb. The second significant operation was the kidnapping of Hajj Mustapha al-Dirani on the night of May 31, 1994 from his home in the Bekaa town of Kasr Nebba. Again, commandos were air-dropped into a nearby army shooting range that had been vacant for some time. Land infiltration followed through to eventual completion of the plan.

The Zionists justified these two operations as being a prelude for the exchange of the Israeli pilot Ron Arad whose plane had crashed in the Sidon region of South Lebanon while engaging in an air raid in 1986. Amal had taken him captive, following which he was handed over to Hajj Mustapha al-Dirani, who was Amal's officer in charge of central security. When al-Dirani broke away from Amal, he and a number of other dissidents founded the 'Believers' Resistance'. Al-Dirani took Arad with him to the Bekaa town of Nabi Sheeth, holding him in one of the town's houses with al-Dirani's followers providing guard. He then lost trace of the captive in vague circumstances.[1]

---

1. According to Hajj Mustapha al-Dirani, Ron Arad went missing from his house of detainment towards the end of April 1988, during the Israeli assault on Midoun in the Western Bekaa. The famous carnage that resulted from *mujahideen* confrontations with the enemy led some guards to leave the house in pursuit of battle news. Upon al-Dirani's return, the house was

Israelis charged Hizbullah with responsibility for Arad, given that the Believers' Resistance was associated with the Party. Israel's kidnapping of Sheikh Obeid, a core official for the Party in South Lebanon, was for exchange purposes, while al-Dirani was kidnapped for interrogation in an effort to unveil the fate of Arad and exchange him.

Hizbullah had no relationship or knowledge whatsoever of Ron Arad's fate. The Party did, however, pay great attention to this issue, considering the unveiling of Arad's fate to be a key towards a solution for all those held captive in Israeli prisons whether Lebanese, Palestinians or others. The Party pursued all methods and paths, working with all individuals who had any sort of connection with the issue or within the geographical radius where Arad could have been, investigating all possibilities but without results.

Liberation was achieved on May 24, 2000, and all those detained in al-Khiam prison were set free. But Israel still kept nineteen captives in its prisons, among them Sheikh Obeid and Hajj al-Dirani. The conviction settled in that nothing would serve to free these prisoners except the capture of a number of Zionists.

The Resistance planned a capture mission in the Shebaa Farms and designed it professionally. This was the first distinctive operation in the area following liberation. It took place on October 10, 2000 and led to the capture of three Israeli soldiers – the Israelis discovered this only half an hour later. The UN and the world's great nations immediately launched a pressure campaign, calling on Hizbullah to release the soldiers unconditionally.

---

empty and the pilot had fled. The circumstances of his disappearance remain a mystery.

On October 12, UN Secretary General Kofi Annan visited Beirut,[1] meeting with President Lahhoud and requesting a release of the three prisoners who, according to the Secretary General, were kidnapped from 'non-Lebanese land': the Shebaa Farms. He also accentuated an earlier request that resistance activity should cease since Israel had implemented Resolution 425. He brought proposals, and did not commit to anything with respect to the Lebanese detainees in Israeli prisons, considering this to be a separate issue and promising to work on what could be done in this regard. The meeting did not yield any practical results.

Only a few days later, al-Sayyed Nasrallah declared the detainment of another Israeli officer, a ranking colonel. Declaration came during his opening speech at the urgent round of the joint National Arab and National Islamic conferences held in Beirut on October 15, 2000. The Secretary General later revealed the name of this new captive as Elhanan Tenenbaum, who was gradually induced to come to Lebanon via Brussels and who carried a fake Belgian passport. Tenenbaum was not conscious of the fact that his Israeli nationality was well-known to his captors.

---

1. The UN Secretary General had visited Beirut on June 20, 2000, and had held a meeting with Hizbullah Secretary General al-Sayyed Hassan Nasrallah – thus breaching all internationally adopted conventions, for this was the first visit by a UN Secretary General to a political party leader at the latter's leadership premises. Annan had requested that Hizbullah accept the Blue Line, acknowledge that Israel had fully withdrawn from Lebanon and, based on this, end all resistance activity. Al-Sayyed Nasrallah requested a solution for the issue of captives and detainees in Israeli prisons, and Annan promised to look into the matter but had no proposed solution for this issue. The meeting availed nothing, but was a victory for Hizbullah in the sense that recognition of the Party had come through the highest representation of international states, indicating the stature and importance that the Party had achieved in the eyes of global powers.

The issue of captives in Israeli prisons surfaced due to the detainment of these four Israelis. All leading countries used their diplomatic influence, communicating through their ambassadors and envoys to end the matter. Efforts included exerting pressure for information on the detainees' fates, offering mediation services, forewarning of the repercussions of persistence with such action, carrying messages, or even plainly requesting some information that would improve some of these nations' relationship with Israel. The UN and the International Red Cross also exerted efforts, concentrating at first on unveiling the detainees' fates and securing visits in order to learn more about their conditions.

Hizbullah turned down all mediation efforts, insisting instead on a full-fledged exchange or, alternatively, on a partial exchange as the Party deemed fit. As such, there was to be a value for unveiling the fate of detainees, be that information partial or complete, and another for exchanging one or more of the detainees and so on ... Haste was never a choice, and neither was submission, for the Zionist detainees were seen as the only channel for the release of captives in Israeli prisons. The humanitarian aspect of the issue was to fully prevail and to be applicable to both parties; only a full exchange of all detainees was to be considered.

Freeing the Captives

The parties to the exchange – Hizbullah and Israel – agreed to the adoption of German mediation as the sole interceding channel between them. German mediation had proved its prowess during previous exchange efforts and gained the trust of both groups with respect to negotiation, the mechanisms of exchange and the accompanying assurances.

As such, German mediation effectively began; the mediator shuttled between the two parties, holding long meetings. He was not simply a messenger: he suggested alternatives, communicated proposals and discussed many solutions and ways out. Nevertheless, the arduous negotiations lasted for three years and were intermittent, with some months lapsing without any contact and others congested with meetings. The silent lapses were longer and during these periods, Hizbullah had no reason to take further initiative, for the Party's stance was clear to all and the initiative was requested from the Israeli side, whose responsibility it was to decide on an exchange that was costly to Israel and adequate to Hizbullah.

All the 'comprehensive exchange' proposals presented by Israel excluded a number of Lebanese individuals. Hizbullah refused all such proposals, insisting on all detainees including a number of other Arab and Palestinian captives. Israel agreed to only a number of Palestinians that was too modest for Hizbullah to accept. The German mediator finally arrived in August 2003 with Israel's acceptance to free all Lebanese detainees, 400 Palestinians and Arabs from Syria, Libya, Morocco and Sudan. The proposal included the remains of fifty-nine martyrs, the unveiling of the fate of twenty-four missing individuals, and the release of maps revealing the location of land mines planted by Israeli troops on boundary lands within Lebanese territory.

Hizbullah agreed to the exchange and received, in writing, the details from the German mediator regarding the exchange of detainees in Israeli prisons for the four Israelis held by Hizbullah. The Party regarded the inclusion of Arabs and Palestinians in the exchange as a considerable achievement, alongside the deal's general positive significance in terms of putting an end to the suffering of Lebanese detainees and their families and of realizing a true victory following many sacrifices over the three-year negotiation period.

Israeli Prime Minister Ariel Sharon leaked the details of Israel's offer to the press, hoping perhaps for a preview of general reactions to his decision. Reaction was indeed strong, a matter which prompted Sharon to depart from what had been promised to the German mediator. Sharon held a cabinet meeting where it was decided that the exchange would take place as agreed with the exception of the release of Samir al-Kuntar on the grounds that al-Kuntar had executed an operation inside Palestine. With this, Sharon bypassed the Ron Arad impasse and covered himself politically through satisfying his government with this exception. Hizbullah was surprised and irate at this last-minute recoil, and decided to stop the negotiations concerning the mechanisms of the actual exchange. That was during October 2003, on the eve of the holy month of Ramadan.

Nevertheless, the two parties agreed to continue negotiations through the German mediator. In search of a solution, the process was taken through secret channels away from media pressures and was given sufficient chance for success prior to any condemnations or declarations of collapse.

Three months of secret negotiations took place. On January 25, 2004, Secretary General Nasrallah declared that an agreement had finally been reached. His press conference declaration stated:

> We negotiated throughout the months of Ramadan, Shawwal and Zoul Ka'da, with the major obstacle being

the release of Samir al-Kuntar. This complication was a surprise to us, for we had obtained a written promise from the German mediator that Sharon had agreed to the release of all Lebanese detainees, a promise obtained since the early negotiation phases. There had never been a problem we know of with regard to 'Samir al-Kuntar'.

The Party reached one of two conclusions, with no other possibility: 'Either the entire exchange deal would remain in an interim phase, or a two-phase solution could be agreed to. Owing to our moral obligations, we opted for the second choice, despite the allusions to withdrawal that had been made during the negotiation struggle.'[1] This was the best option possible after the long negotiation process.

Ernst Uhrlau, the German official in charge of the mediation process, declared on January 24, 2004:

> We expect the deal to be implemented over the course of one week starting the day before yesterday. As per the exchange deal, Hizbullah shall release the Israeli businessman Elhanan Tannenbaum, who was abducted in October 2000, along with the bodies of three Israeli soldiers ... In return, Israel promised to release 400 Palestinians, 23 Lebanese captives, 5 Syrians, 3 Moroccans, 3 Sudanese, 1 Libyan and 1 German, as per a declaration made by the US embassy in Israel. Israel further undertook to deliver information on the fate of twenty-four missing individuals, and return the remains of fifty-nine fighters killed during Israel's occupation of South Lebanon.[2]

---

1. *As-Safir*, January 26, 2004.
2. *Al-Kifah al-Arabi*, January 26, 2004.

Direct exchange was the first component of the agreement, to be followed by a second phase comprising two steps: First was a 'document declared by the German mediator and agreed to by both parties and entailing the fact that Samir al-Kuntar will be released as soon as the current negotiations concerning his state are successfully concluded. All parties [Hizbullah, Israel and the German mediator] hope that this will be achieved during the course of the coming two to three months.'[1]

The second phase entailed the creation of two committees: the first was to consist of Hizbullah and German delegates whose mission was to investigate the whereabouts of the disappeared Israeli pilot Ron Arad using all data, methods and technical means available. The second committee was to group Israeli and German delegates with the aim of unveiling the fate of the four Iranian diplomats kidnapped in East Beirut's al-Barbara checkpoint during the Israeli invasion of 1982. Based on the outcome, a new exchange deal was to be negotiated, the main guidelines of which were set with the details postponed to an appropriate time.

The exchange deal was clearly affected by the political as well as personal circumstances affecting the Israeli prime ministers who escorted the process, Barak and Sharon. Barak had attempted to revive the process during his last days as prime minister in an attempt to reap higher electoral support, efforts that availed to nothing. Sharon, on the other hand, did not initially feel the need for the process, but lent it attention on several occasions and especially during the last days preceding the actual exchange. It is not possible to credit the achievement of the exchange deal to only one factor; for one, Israel would like to put the impasse to rest in order to reduce the number of justifications for resistance force

---

1. Ibid.

in Lebanon. Furthermore, the personal relationships with the family of Elhanan Tannenbaum, the pressure exerted by captives' families, the religious considerations calling for the retrieval of corpses and their proper burial, the Israeli command's concern for army morale and the need to abate the negative psychological implications connected to the prolongation of this impasse are all factors that served towards its conclusion. It is therefore not possible to judge one factor as being all-important in this deal, which has proven to be costly and painful to Israel, but which the Israeli viewed as less harmful than the status quo.

In retrospect, Hizbullah successfully and patiently managed the deal while making good use of three factors:

1. Three years of resolute determination with which Hizbullah held onto the four Israeli captives despite all internationally exerted pressures and in spite of the ranks of delegates and volunteers who came with conciliatory as well as menacing messages;

2. The level of understanding and support expressed by captives' families, who placed faith in Hizbullah and refrained from exerting pressure on the Party despite Israel's efforts at instigating such pressure through the psychological warfare waged via enemy media;

3. Acknowledgment by the Israelis that captives held by Hizbullah were a source of power to the Party, one that it was not about to relinquish easily. On the contrary, Hizbullah was prepared to take more hostages and further confuse its enemy.

Negotiations were restricted to the humanitarian aspect, and were limited to a dialogue over actual exchange procedures. No political issues were raised throughout the process, as neither party took the initiative to raise them. Furthermore, no direct contact was made, and all issues were communicated through the German mediator. As such, Hizbullah held onto its Party principle of refusing political negotiation with the Israeli enemy, and ensured that the mechanism of mediation served to achieve the humanitarian target through an exchange of information and facts as opposed to direct negotiation.

Results of the Exchange Deal

The historical exchange brought a sense of triumph to Lebanon. Captives and detainees in Israeli prisons were freed on January 29, 2004, and the remains of martyrs were handed over the following day. Official reception of the liberated at Beirut International Airport was hosted by representatives from all sectors of Lebanese society and by the entire Lebanese government cadre, headed by Lebanese President Emile Lahhoud, Parliament Spokesman Nabih Berri and Prime Minister Rafik al-Hariri, alongside a Hizbullah delegation led by Secretary General Nasrallah and, of course, the families of the captives. Roads surrounding the airport overflowed with people, and a large number took part in the celebration held by Hizbullah in the Beirut suburb of Hayy al-Abyad, where the Secretary General welcomed the liberated. In Palestine there were scenes of jubilation for the liberation of the 400 captives, as they were released and greeted by their families and compatriots.

The remains of martyrs were received on January 30, 2004 in Naqura, on the southern Lebanese border with Palestine. The hand-over was witnessed by representatives of the three aforementioned Lebanese heads of state, Hizbullah's Deputy Secretary General Sheikh Naim Qassem and political and civilian authorities.

The scene was imbued with a sense of victory, a second conquest won after the land liberation of May 2000. This so-called 'Second Victory' had many repercussions, the most notable of which were:

1. Hizbullah achieved more than a direct gain limited to Party ranks. The achievement touched many segments of Arab society. Of the 435 individuals liberated, only eleven were Hizbullah partisans, the rest being mainly Palestinians. Of the fifty-nine martyrs, twelve were Hizbullah partisans while the rest had formed part of Fateh, Amal, al-Saiiqa, the Democratic Front, the Nidal Front and the Lebanese Communist Party. The Party did not only consider its partisans in this exchange, but benefited from the means made available to increase its circle of concern and include the resistance fighters and civilians of Palestine. This served to elevate Hizbullah's standing in both Lebanon and the region.

2. The exchange process played a pivotal role in gathering Lebanese support around the Resistance. In an opinion poll initiated by the Beirut Research and Information Centre[1] between January 31 and February 4, 2004, and covering a sample of 1,200 individuals categorised by region and by religious sect,

---

1. These poll results were published in *As-Safir*, February 6, 2004.

it was revealed that 70 per cent of the Lebanese population supported continued resistance for the sake of liberating the Shebaa Farms. A noticeable improvement in the level of support was observed following the liberation of captives. This translated into an additional 14 percentage points in support of the Resistance (as compared with a poll taken prior to the exchange), and a loss of 8 percentage points (composed of previous supporters) due to a shift in opinion regarding the continued need for it. The balance change was thus 6 per cent in additional supporters in favour of the Resistance. Such a step forward was of prime importance when facing mounting pressures exerted on the Resistance and its supporters. It represented a form of additional fortification in the quest for confronting the continuously growing Israeli danger.

3. Wielding pressure tactics proved beneficial in targeting the enemy's weak points and forcing it to pay dearly no matter how high the price. Land liberation came without any liberation of captives, and this issue only surfaced after Hizbullah succeeded at capturing three Zionist soldiers followed by Elhanan Tannenbaum. Steadfast efforts by the Resistance during its *jihad* against Israel were rewarded. Were it not for the successive and painful military operations against the Israeli army and its collaborators, Israel would still be occupying Lebanon today. For not once has Israel respected international resolutions, and the clear and forthright Resolution 425 issued by the UN in 1978 and calling on Israel to withdraw from Lebanon went unacknowledged for a long time. On the other hand, we witnessed international attention to Israel's concerns, and international protection

of Israel's operations irrespective of individuals' rights. Only force, the steadfast adherence to it, sacrifice and patience could bear any fruit in a world where diplomacy has become a tool in the service of the oppressors.

4. In a region where sour events took their toll on the populace, the exchange deal served to lift crushed spirits. Difficulty and complication prevailed as of the September 11, 2001 events in the US, which were followed by the occupation of Afghanistan and subsequently of Iraq; the daily unceasing attacks against Palestinians in occupied Palestine, and the continued menacing remarks by the US and Israel targeting Lebanon, Syria, Iran and other countries in the region, also added to the peril. The liberation of captives came as a bright step amidst the challenges and successive obligations that predominated.

On the Israeli side, the scene was of sulking faces. The retired Major Elhanan Tannenbaum was immediately taken into custody for interrogation. A deluge of media and political accusations targeting the Israeli government followed, and some background facts emerged to further scandalize Israel's shortfall: Sharon was accused of having a commercial relationship with the major's mother; the major himself was accused of possibly divulging information during captivity, and his credibility during interrogation came into question.

FOUR

The Palestinian Cause

The Zionist Project: Foundation Steps

Modern twentieth-century history has not witnessed a situation comparable to the Palestinian situation. Zionists from around the world arrived in Palestine to occupy its land and force the exodus of the majority of its populace, achieving this under the custodianship of the international community. The Zionist occupation of Palestine became an internationally claimed right, while Palestinian claims for reinstatement of their rightful land were perceived as unacceptable aggression. The United Nations Security Council acted only in favour and in support of this distorted view. It is incorrect to classify this cause simply as strife or rivalry, for it is a great crime against humanity, the attributes and facets of which have been partially demonstrated over a whole century in a manner that warrants putting an end to this looming danger.

The first World Zionist Conference was held August 19–31, 1897 in Basel, Switzerland, under the chairmanship of Theodore Herzl. The conference called for 'a homeland for the Jews in Palestine' through 'the promotion by appropriate means of their settlement in Palestine [...], the organization and uniting of the whole of Jewry by means of appropriate institutions, both local and international [and] the strengthening and fostering of Jewish national sentiment and national consciousness.'[1]

Many other conferences serving to implement the political, financial and practical plans for fostering the successful creation of the Jewish state were held in the years that followed. The religious and national sentiment motives behind the creation of this entity became intertwined. Some sought explanation in the Torah promises that 'God's Chosen People' shall achieve control over Palestine, while others considered the presence of Jews in one specific geographic location to be a solution for the suffering they had been subjected to in a great number of European and Russian lands. Given that the magnetism of national sentiment was insufficient for drawing Jews from all corners of the world, the two streams (one religious and the other based on secular nationalism) concurred on the importance of religion as the main founding springboard. As such, the Zionist project was formed with a focus on religious fanaticism and Semitic prejudice, using the most dreadful of methods to achieve the project's aims.

It was not strange that voracity for occupation increased by the day, first starting as seizure of land and villages and followed by gangster wars waged against the Palestinians (all achieved under the auspices of Britain during the British Mandate), thereafter culminating in the declaration of the Jewish state on occupied Palestinian land in 1948. Subsequently, the whole of Palestine was occupied along with those parts of neighbouring countries (Syria, Jordan and Egypt) seized in 1967. The Israeli entity thus continued in its occupational expansion and legitimacy claims, for the basic foundation of the racially prejudiced Zionist movement

---

1. Palestinian National Liberation Movement (Fatah), Nicholas Ziade (ed.), *Diary of Jerusalem*, 1981, p. 208.

is expansion, an aim supported by religious foundations drawn from the Torah.

According to the Torah, Palestine is an inheritance for the people of Israel whose lives will not stabilize except through the expulsion of Palestine's original inhabitants. In the Torah's *Book of Numbers* it is stated:

> *And the Lord spoke unto Moses in the plains of Moab by the Jordan at Jericho, saying: 'Speak unto the children of Israel, and say unto them: "When ye pass over the Jordan into the land of Canaan then ye shall drive out all the inhabitants of the land from before you, and destroy all their figured stones, and destroy all their molten images, and demolish all their high places.*
>
> *"And ye shall drive out the inhabitants of the land, and dwell therein; for unto you have I given the land to possess it. And ye shall inherit the land by lot according to your families – to the more ye shall give the more inheritance, and to the fewer thou shalt give the less inheritance; wheresoever the lot falleth to any man, that shall be his; according to the tribes of your fathers shall ye inherit.*
>
> *"But if ye will not drive out the inhabitants of the land from before you, then shall those that ye let remain of them be as thorns in your eyes, and as pricks in your sides, and they shall harass you in the land wherein ye dwell."*[1]

And in another chapter:

> *And the Lord spoke unto Moses saying, 'Command the children of Israel, and say unto them: "When ye come into the land of Canaan, this shall be the land that shall*

---

1. The Torah, *Numbers*, Chapter 33, verses 51–5.

> *fall unto you for an inheritance, even the land of Canaan according to the borders thereof.*"[1]

The boundaries of Israel, as they are stated in *Deuteronomy*, are from the Euphrates to the Nile:

> *Then will the Lord drive out all these nations from before you, and ye shall dispossess nations greater and mightier than yourselves. Every place whereon the sole of your foot shall tread shall be yours: from the wilderness, and Lebanon, from the river, the river Euphrates, even unto the hinder sea shall be your border. There shall no man be able to stand against you: the Lord your God shall lay the fear of you and the dread of you upon all the land that ye shall tread upon, as He hath spoken unto you.*[2]

The British recognized the creation of the Zionist entity, working to ensure that Palestine was within the scope of their colonial mandate as based on the Sykes-Picot agreement of 1916 between France and Britain, two victors of the First World War. The British government thereafter issued the Balfour Declaration on November 2, 1917, a letter written by the then British Foreign Minister Arthur James Balfour and addressed to Lord Rothschild. The declaration stated:

> His Majesty's Government view with favour the establishment in Palestine of a national home for the Jewish people, and will use their best endeavours to facilitate the achievement of this object.

When the League of Nations convened on June 24, 1922 to

---

1. The Torah, *Numbers*, Chapter 34, verse 2.
2. The Torah, *Deuteronomy*, Chapter 11, verses 23–5.

adopt an official resolution regarding the British Mandate, the Balfour Declaration was incorporated therein and supported with practical measures embracing the set-up of a Jewish agency in charge of taking command of those requisite lands, drawing on the support of Jews around the world, facilitating inbound migration for all those who sought it, providing new migrants with Palestinian nationality and creating a national Jewish homeland. This was clearly evident in the first seven articles of the subsequently issued resolution:

The Council of the League of Nations:

Whereas the Principal Allied Powers have agreed, for the purpose of giving effect to the provisions of Article 22 of the Covenant of the League of Nations, to entrust to a Mandatory selected by the said Powers the administration of the territory of Palestine, which formerly belonged to the Turkish Empire, within such boundaries as may be fixed by them; and

Whereas the Principal Allied Powers have also agreed that the Mandatory should be responsible for putting into effect the declaration originally made on November 2, 1917, by the Government of His Britannic Majesty, and adopted by the said Powers, in favour of the establishment in Palestine of a national home for the Jewish people, it being clearly understood that nothing should be done which might prejudice the civil and religious rights of existing non-Jewish communities in Palestine, or the rights and political status enjoyed by Jews in any other country; and

Whereas recognition has thereby been given to the historical connection of the Jewish people with Palestine and to the grounds for reconstituting their national home in that country; and

Whereas the Principal Allied Powers have selected His Britannic Majesty as the Mandatory for Palestine; and

Whereas the mandate in respect of Palestine has been formulated in the following terms and submitted to the Council of the League for approval; and

Whereas His Britannic Majesty has accepted the mandate in respect of Palestine and undertaken to exercise it on behalf of the League of Nations in conformity with the following provisions; and

Whereas by the aforementioned Article 22 (paragraph 8), it is provided that the degree of authority, control or administration to be exercised by the Mandatory, not having been previously agreed upon by the Members of the League, shall be explicitly defined by the Council of the League of Nations;

Confirming the said Mandate, defines its terms as follows:

Article 1: The Mandatory shall have full powers of legislation and of administration, save as they may be limited by the terms of this mandate.

Article 2: The Mandatory shall be responsible for placing the country under such political, administrative and economic conditions as will secure the establishment of the Jewish national home, as laid down in the preamble, and the development of self-governing institutions, and also for safeguarding the civil and religious rights of all the inhabitants of Palestine, irrespective of race and religion.

Article 3: The Mandatory shall, so far as circumstances permit, encourage local autonomy.

Article 4: An appropriate Jewish agency shall be recognized as a public body for the purpose of advising and cooperating with the Administration of Palestine in such economic, social and other matters as may affect the establishment of the Jewish national home and the interests of the Jewish population in Palestine, and, subject always to the control of the Administration, to assist and take part in the development of the country.

The Zionist Organization, so long as its organization and constitution are in the opinion of the Mandatory appropriate, shall be recognized as such agency. It shall take steps in consultation with His Britannic Majesty's Government to secure the cooperation of all Jews who are willing to assist in the establishment of the Jewish national home.

Article 5: The Mandatory shall be responsible for seeing that no Palestine territory shall be ceded or leased to, or in any way placed under the control of, the Government of any foreign Power.

Article 6: The Administration of Palestine, while ensuring that the rights and position of other sections of the population are not prejudiced, shall facilitate Jewish immigration under suitable conditions and shall encourage, in co-operation with the Jewish agency referred to in Article 4, close settlement by Jews on the land, including State lands and waste lands not required for public purposes.

Article 7: The Administration of Palestine shall be responsible for enacting a nationality law. There shall be included in this law provisions framed so as to facilitate the acquisition of Palestinian citizenship by Jews who take up their permanent residence in Palestine.

Great Britain expended every effort to make available the circumstances that would guarantee Jewish jurisdiction over Palestinian territories and ensure the set-up of settlements, possession of military power, and control over crucial ports, turning a blind eye to terrorizing Zionist massacres of Palestinians – all in preparation for founding a Zionist entity. As such, United Nations Resolution 181 of November 29, 1947 emerged to recommend the partitioning of Palestine, a move to which the US and the USSR lent their full support. In its preamble, the resolution states that the United Nations:

> Takes note of the declaration by the mandatory Power that it plans to complete its evacuation of Palestine by 1 August 1948 and Recommends to the United Kingdom, as the mandatory Power for Palestine, and to all other Members of the United Nations the adoption and implementation, with regard to the future Government of Palestine, of the Plan of Partition with Economic Union ...

The plan set out for this partitioning was outlined in Articles 2 and 3 of Resolution 181:

Article 2:

[...] The mandatory Power shall use its best endeavours to ensure that an area situated in the territory of the Jewish State, including a seaport and hinterland adequate to provide facilities for a substantial immigration, shall be evacuated at the earliest possible date and in any event not later than 1 February 1948.

Article 3:

Independent Arab and Jewish States and the Special International Regime for the City of Jerusalem, set forth in Part III of this Plan, shall come into existence in Palestine two months after the evacuation of the armed forces of the mandatory Power has been completed but in any case not later than 1 October 1948. The boundaries of the Arab State, the Jewish State, and the City of Jerusalem shall be as described in Parts II and III below.

With such partitioning, the Zionist entity was to receive an approximate 54 per cent of Palestine.

As soon as practical implementation of this arrangement was set on track, British forces withdrew and the Jews took control on May 15, 1948, by way of an inequitable war and of land exceeding the partition plan, part of which covered West Jerusalem. Outside the scope of occupation remained East Jerusalem, the West Bank and the Gaza Strip. Given that Palestine's total area amounts to 27,027 square kilometres, the lands annexed by the emerging Zionist occupation in 1948 and amounting to 20,770 square kilometres actually represented 77 per cent of Palestine.

In lieu of lending attention to the fact of occupation, the United Nations turned its focus to the social problems represented by the exodus of the displaced, as international support for the Zionist entity was already on track and part of a continuous plan. UN Resolution 194, issued on December 11, 1948, was programmed around providing the Palestinians with a choice of exercising their 'right of return'. In reality, it came to lay the foundations for the displacement of Palestinians. This resolution states that the United Nations:

> Resolves that the refugees wishing to return to their homes and live at peace with their neighbours should be permitted to do so at the earliest practicable date, and that compensation should be paid for the property of those choosing not to return and for loss of or damage to property which, under principles of international law or in equity, should be made good by the Governments or authorities responsible.

US Support for Israel

The US was demonstrating increasing support for Israel and a continuation of what British colonialism had laid the grounds for – that colonialist power on which, back then, the sun never set. The Jewish lobby played an important role in terms of capitalizing on US capabilities and international posture, drawing on it to the extent of the Zionist entity's interests.

As communicated through his government's representative, President Franklin D. Roosevelt was in opposition to the British White Paper issued on May 17, 1939. On March 6, 1944, the representative declared the importance of opening the doors to Jewish immigration into Palestine. Thereafter, Roosevelt issued a direct statement in this regard: 'We favour the opening of Palestine to unrestricted Jewish immigration and colonization, and such a policy as to result in the establishment there of a free and democratic Jewish commonwealth.'

Then came the era of President Harry S. Truman (1945–48), whose first official initiatives included exerting pressure on the British government to allow 100,000 Jewish immigrants into Palestine, followed by an equal number in 1946. Truman raced to recognize the 'State of Israel' only eleven minutes after announcement of the UN declaration ending the British Mandate in Palestine on the night of May 14–15, 1948. Excluding later President Dwight D. Eisenhower, who had his particular views of US priorities and who had worked to reinstate the situation back to its status quo following the triple aggression against Egypt in 1956, what followed in terms of US policy was only in support of Israel both politically and militarily. This was evidenced throughout the 1967 aggression, the pressure on Syria and Egypt after the 1973 victory, and the assaults on Lebanon in March 1978, July 1993 and April 1996. President Bill Clinton's programme came to clearly express the US course in its support of Israel: 'The United States has a fundamental interest not only in the security of Israel but also in our two nations' strategic cooperation in the region.' Before President Clinton, President Ronald Reagan had declared in the wake of the Islamic Revolution's success in Iran in 1979 and the fall of the Shah – an ally of the US – that the fall of Iran exposed the fact that Israel was the only strategic ally on which the US could capitalize and rely.[1]

---

1. See *US-Zionist Relations* by Amine Mustapha for an overview of US support for Israel.

The final toll of US support to Israel has exceeded that of a superpower's backing for an entity implanted in the Middle East, turning into a bilateral interest, a permanent political fact for both Republicans and Democrats. The pro-Israel lobby exerts strong influence at key political and strategic junctions in the US, and the US now sees Israel as a point of entry into the countries and endowments of the Middle East, as an entity that should be provided with all the reasons for existence and power, one that should be turned into a military might that cannot be surpassed by all Arab forces combined, one that enjoys international political custodianship and protection, in favour of which the right of veto is used time and again in the UN in order not to delay or impede Zionist plans for moving forward. US support of Israel is expressed through making available all those circumstances that serve to exercise aggression on the Palestinian people in order to draw Israel's geographic and political outlines, ensure Palestinian acquiescence and secure a Palestinian signature that would only serve to legitimize the Israeli entity and abate its fears for its existence.

The Aggression Expands

Then came the 1967 invasion whereby the scope of occupation expanded to cover the remainder of Palestine, including Jerusalem, in addition to parts of Syrian, Jordanian and Lebanese territories. The UN Security Council issued Resolution 242 on November 22, 1967, five and a half months after the aggression, ensuring in Article 1 that the UN:

> Affirms that the fulfilment of Charter principles

requires the establishment of a just and lasting peace in
the Middle East which should include the application
of both the following principles:

Withdrawal of Israeli armed forces from territories[1]
occupied in the recent conflict;

Termination of all claims or states of belligerence and
respect for and acknowledgement of the sovereignty,
territorial integrity and political independence of every
State in the area and their right to live in peace within
secure and recognized boundaries free from threats
or acts of force.

The Resolution thus laid the foundations for securing Israel's 1948
occupation of Palestinian lands and allowed for the discussion of a
compromise vaguely termed 'just and lasting peace in the Middle
East', without drawing any specifications or laying a practical
mode of execution, with the exception of a few hollow words
which could be interpreted in any manner. The 1967 Occupied
Territories that were to form the subject of Israeli withdrawal
remained an oscillating issue.

Then came the October 1973 war where Syria and Egypt
fought side by side against Israel, redeeming part of their occupied
lands. Egypt then partially withdrew from these reclaimed lands,
obliging Syria to discontinue its military operations. The UN

---

1. Arab interpretation of the word 'territories' differs from the US-Israeli
understanding. To Arabs, proper understanding of the word should lead
to withdrawal from all land occupied in 1967, including East Jerusalem, the
West Bank and the Gaza Strip. Israel considered the word to mean only
part of those areas occupied in 1967, and thus implemented the resolution
partially through its withdrawal from Jordan, Egypt and some Palestinian
territories.

Security Council was quick to issue Resolution 338 of October 22, 1973, which stated in its first two articles that the Council:

1. Calls upon all parties to present fighting to cease all firing and terminate all military activity immediately, no later than 12 hours after the moment of the adoption of this decision, in the positions after the moment of the adoption of this decision, in the positions they now occupy;

2. Calls upon all parties concerned to start immediately after the cease-fire the implementation of Security Council Resolution 242 (1967) in all of its parts ...

The speed with which the decision was taken and the specification of a time delay for ceasefire implementation served to prevent the Arabs from realizing further gains in the war and protected Israel from further loss of occupied land, reverting the discussion to Resolution 242 with all of its ambiguities.

Aggression against Lebanon ensued in March 1978, whereby Israel occupied half of the South. A few days later, UN Resolution 425 was issued (March 19, 1978), its three articles stating that the UN:

1. Calls for strict respect for the territorial integrity, sovereignty and political independence of Lebanon within its internationally recognized boundaries;

2. Calls upon Israel immediately to cease its military action against Lebanese territorial integrity and withdraw forthwith its forces from all Lebanese territory;

3. Decides, in the light of the request of the Government of Lebanon, to establish immediately under its authority a United Nations interim force for southern Lebanon for the purpose of confirming the withdrawal of Israeli forces, restoring international peace and security and assisting the Government of Lebanon in ensuring the return of its effective authority in the area, the force to be composed of personnel drawn from States Members of the United Nations ...

This allusion to concern for the integrity of Lebanese soil was ambiguous. Israel was later to erect a security belt in the invaded area, leaving almost one quarter of South Lebanon under occupation, an area that was to be administered by its agents in Lebanon as led by Saad Haddad. UN peacekeeping forces were later to enter as a buffer force forbidding any military operations against the now-imposed fact of occupation. Israel did not recognize Resolution 425 either practically or publicly, considering the erected security zone to possess sufficient vigour to ensure the safety of its northern settlements against any PLO attacks. The UN Security Council did not take any action to ensure the implementation of Resolution 425.

US-Israeli efforts continued in the direction of disbanding any unified Arab stance, isolating each of the confrontational parties, including Palestine. The first such efforts bore fruit with the abstraction of Egypt from the Arab-Israeli conflict through the Camp David Accord of March 26, 1979, which was sponsored by US President Jimmy Carter and which marked the agreement of Egyptian President Anwar al-Sadat with Israeli Prime Minister Menachem Begin. The Egypt-Israel

Peace Treaty was signed on that same day, whereby Egypt was to redeem Sinai and take all the necessary actions and measures for guaranteeing Israel's security. The state of war between the two entities thus came to a halt, both parties agreeing to 'apply between them [...] the principles of international law governing relations among states in times of peace.' Furthermore, the two countries were to cooperate with Jordan and the representatives of the Palestinian people in the negotiations pertaining to resolving all aspects of the Palestinian problem.

Camp David was to result in disbanding the Arab stance and the loss of Egypt as a major power in the conflict with Israel. The agreement also made an *a priori* allowance for leaving Lebanon and Syria out of the Palestinian problem and its solutions, laying the foundations for the steps leading to eventual Palestinian self-rule, which were to be completely outlined later in the Palestinian-Israeli Oslo Agreement of 1993.

The 1982 Israeli invasion of Lebanon marked the first entry by the Zionist entity into an Arab capital city, the objective of which was to demolish PLO infrastructure and evict Palestinian resistance from Lebanon indefinitely. It was also a move towards abolishing any faculty of liberation or negotiation in the context of confrontation with Israel. And so the PLO was evicted, taking up in Tunisia after Israel expanded its previous occupation, retaining in 1985 an area equivalent to 11 per cent of Lebanese soil. The UN Security Council sufficed with issuing reminders for the implementation of Resolution 425.

As soon as the US and its allies waged the Gulf War against Iraq on January 16, 1991 following the latter's occupation of Kuwait in 1990, the Madrid Conference emerged as a war prize. Calling, on October 13, 1991, for a 'Land For Peace' principle, the conference based itself on the international Resolutions 242 and 338 in order to resolve the Palestinian problem and all issues linked to it. Benefiting from the show of force demonstrated during the Gulf War, the Madrid Conference was aiming for bilateral solutions that would only serve as a continuation of the plan for isolating the concerned countries one after another.

All efforts geared towards dealing with the confrontation as one portfolio went in vain. Thus, Yasser Arafat signed the Oslo Agreement on September 13, 1993, which was to isolate the Palestinian course from all others. Fourteen rounds of secret negotiations held in the Norwegian capital between Israeli and PLO delegates concluded with the achievement of an agreement that outlined the principal arrangements for transitory Palestinian self-rule, at the kernel of which was 'Gaza and Jericho First' – a proposition contained in the draft agreement of August 19, 1993. The agreement spoke of a conclusive settlement between the conflicting parties to be achieved over a five-year period and aiming at 'putting an end to decades of conflict and confrontations, aspiring for peaceful coexistence, mutual dignity and security, while recognizing their mutual legitimate and political rights; and reaffirming their desire to achieve a just, lasting and comprehensive peace settlement through the agreed political process.'[1]

The Oslo Agreement directly provided Israel with peace and security guarantees, while to the Palestinians it provided a first step on a long track of mysterious consequences, given their lack of any effective pressure capabilities. Management of negotiations was granted to Israel under US auspices thus opening the door wide for interpretations that would serve to evade the timely implementation of the agreement.

1. *Al-Safir*, September 1, 1993.

We shall only pause briefly on the Israeli-Jordanian Peace Accord, which was delayed until October 26, 1994 for particular Jordanian considerations. Jordan's situation does not allow for signature of an accord with the Israelis prior to other Arabs, and especially prior to the Palestinians, for the country had taken a neutral stance over a long period of time while secret Jordanian-Israeli negotiations were actively taking place.

Throughout all previous phases, Syria had tried to foster Arab-Palestinian bonding relationships within a unified and supportive framework. But US pressure succeeded at achieving the disintegration and isolation of the Arab parties in the conflict. Syria was thus disconnected from the rest, and chose the course of refusal of any temporary solutions, seeking a comprehensive agreement that answered to all concerns and solved all problems between Syria and Israel. Negotiations stalled more than once, and the achievement of an accord always hinged on pivotal questions, for instance the extent of Syrian exploitation of the Lake of Tabarayya, given the June 4 demarcation lines. Syria worked to benefit from its presence and role in Lebanon, turning this relationship into a point of strength for both countries. Israeli efforts have yet to succeed in overtaking the Syrian obstacle.

Lebanon, on the other hand, endured two massive aggressions on its territory after the Madrid Conference, in June 1993 and April 1996. On both counts, Lebanon emerged victorious over the Israeli plan to demolish Hizbullah's infrastructure, annihilate the military force of the Resistance and subsequently disband the Syrian-Lebanese alliance, thus segregating Lebanon to ensure Israel's security needs. Despite the enormous pressure exerted on Lebanon, Israel was forced to withdraw as a consequence of concentrated resistance operations against Israeli forces and their collaborators. Liberation came on May 24, 2000, with Israel failing to record any political or security gains.

From the above we conclude that:

1. The creation of a Zionist entity on the land of Palestine represents a manifest aggression on the peaceful Palestinian people, and replaces one population with another, dispersing the true owners of the land across the territories of the world, and puts them in confrontation with a unified group of world extortionists. This is not a conflict over borders between two neighbouring countries. It is an uprooting of a nation and a people, a substitution of a state by another.

2. The religious and historical justifications which date back 3,000 years and the nationalistic rationalization speaking of a desire for the creation of a Jewish state do not legitimize the right to the creation of such a state in Palestine, for the changes that have been brought about by history are facts of the past, and every nation in this world has a history that is different from its present. World peace can only stabilize if nations and populations are left to express their existence and reaffirm the liberty and independence of their people.

3. Absolute support for the creation of the Israeli entity was granted first by Britain and then by the superpowers – the US and the USSR – as well as by France (which had shared those First World War prizes with Great Britain). Were it not for this international conspiracy that persisted (and which in the case of the US still persists) either through

the United Nations or individually, Israel could not have
survived.

4. The Israeli plan continued to be expressed through military
expansion and forceful imposition of conditions until Israeli
occupation reached parts of those Arab countries that
neighbour on Palestine: Syria, Jordan, Egypt and Lebanon. International resolutions only represented interludes
wherein Israel would re-organize its occupational strategy
in preparation for new hegemony, additional conditions,
and another Security Council Resolution to serve as cover
for its occupation. Had the Zionists been able to control
Arab nations from the Gulf to the ocean in one stroke and
impose their domination, they would have done so without
a doubt. But experience called for gradual occupation and
legitimization, until such time as Israel could find stability
within a scope of borders, capabilities and provisions that
would allow for its political, cultural and economic domination of the Arab world, all based of course on military
might and on international support as led by the US.

Based on the above, the discussion does not end at the borders
of Israel, but transcends to include the project that bears on the
life of the entire Arab nation, a plan that is advancing quickly and
dangerously. With every phase, additional land is stripped away
and a new reality is created, at which the plot does not come to a
halt but only pauses. The countdown for this expansionist project
can only begin by refusing it through choosing the manner of
confrontation, be it a resistance, an *intifadah*, refusal, defence
or perseverance.

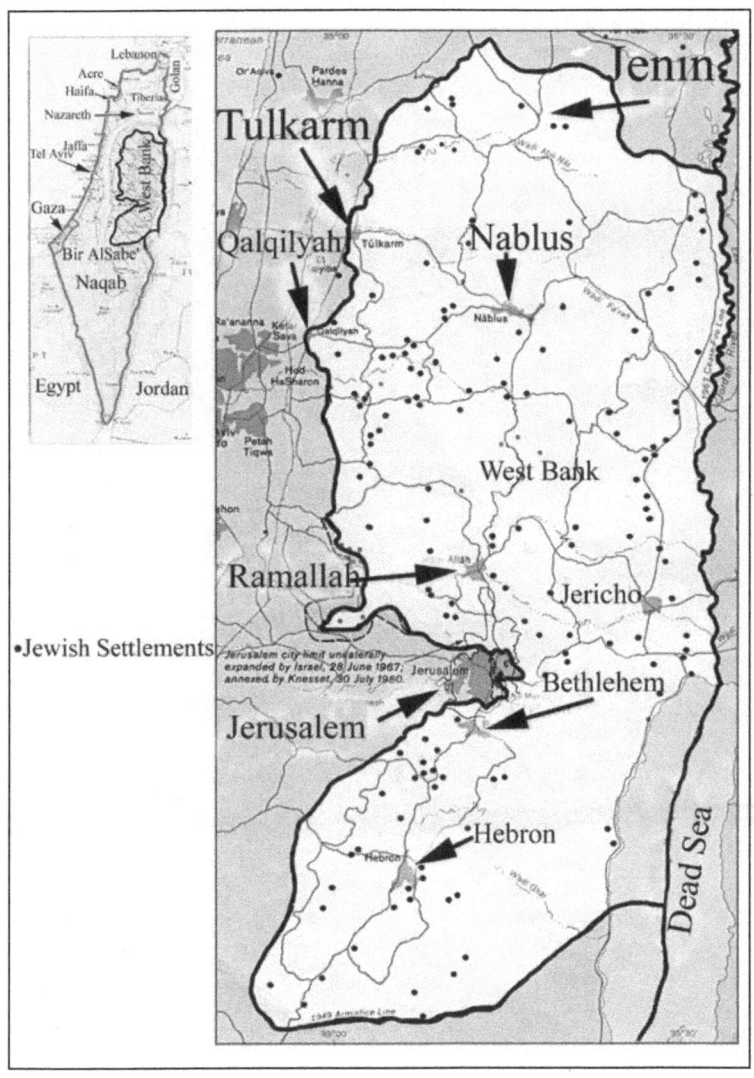

5. The West Bank and the Distribution of Jewish Settlements

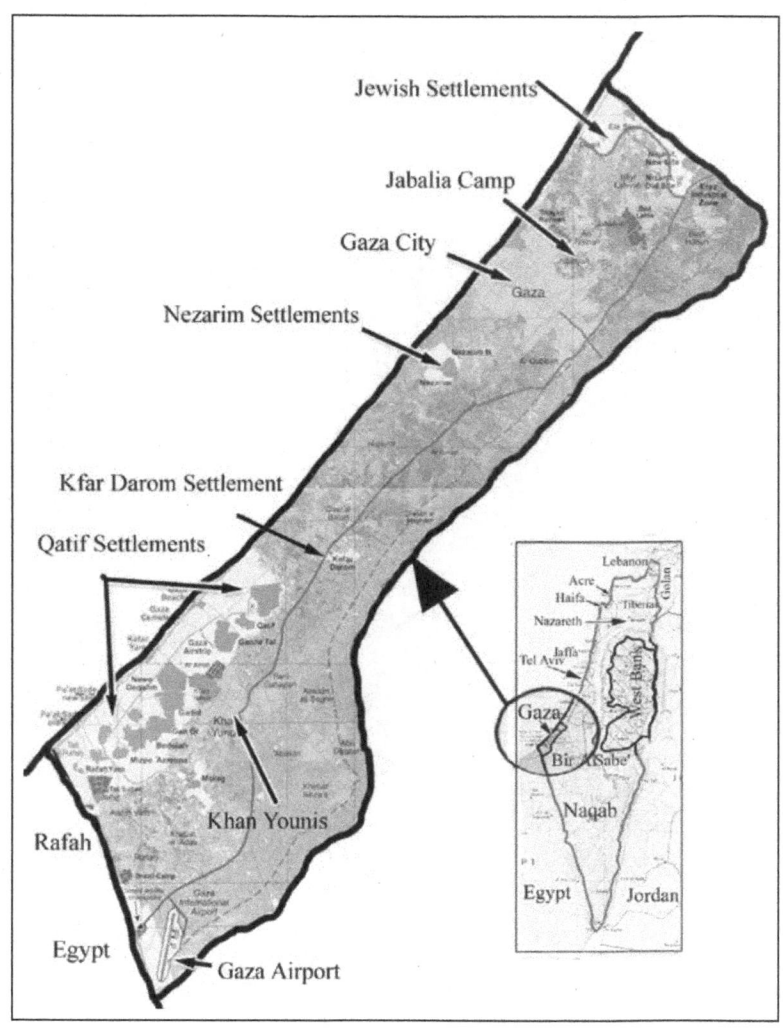

6. The Gaza Strip

The Choice of Compromise and the Language of Numbers

In retrospect, some propose the choice of compromise, considering it to be a feasible solution in light of the inevitabilities, requisites and challenge of facing international resolutions that are only tailored to Zionist requirements and only serve the interests of the world's dictating powers. Before taking a final decision on this alternative, it is important to specify the meaning of compromise, its foundations and the issues it entails.

The proposed compromise is in essence a guarantee for the existence of the 'State of Israel' within boundaries recognized by the Palestinians and by the international community, and under conditions providing Israel with eight-ninths of Palestinian land while limiting Palestinian presence to the remaining one-ninth of their legitimate right. This, as 'compromise' suggests, should take place in the frame of a Palestinian state that is closer to a nomenclature than an actual nation, given the lack of fundamentals for forming an independent state. Furthermore, this Palestinian state should bear the brunt of securing the Israeli entity, subduing any Palestinian resistance against the Israeli project and arming itself with the necessary means for undertaking this mission.

This Palestinian state would be geographically isolated from its Arab neighbours, surrounded by Israel from all sides, its airspace and general defence sinking under Israeli supervision. It would be economically linked to the state of Israel, thus rendering this nascent state incapable of independence at the public service and economic levels. It would further have terminate national ties with almost one half of its dispersed population through a mechanism of compensation to be paid to Palestinian refugees around the world in return for their nationalization in the countries of their settlement, or in any other countries of the world and according to a pre-planned distribution to be endorsed by Israel. All ties to the Palestinians of 1948, who number some 1.2 million individuals, are also to be broken. These would become part of the so-called 'State of Israel'. The Madrid Conference of 1991 laid the foundations for the results described above, considering that the achievement of lasting peace in the Middle East is a function of the consent by all Arab nations to multilateral peace negotiations, which would result in the normalization of relations with Israel and which would resolve the issues of security, water, trade and the like on the basis of Israel's projection into the Arab world's very tissues. This was planned to occur at a time when the Palestinian cause would be placed on a slow backburner, eventually forcing the Palestinian Authority to make available those future requirements of the Israeli entity, all the while bearing responsibility for lax implementation of obligations, a one-way responsibility not reciprocated by Israel. This was to legitimize the Israeli entity on both the Palestinian and Arab levels, rendering it independent, owner of all the necessary constituents for a legitimate state given the signature of the land's rightful owners on such concession. The Palestinian cause would thus fade away forever. Numbers provide a clearer and more truthful picture of reality:

Palestine, from the river to the sea, extends to over 27,027 square kilometres.

Land confiscated by Israel during the 1948 occupation amounts to 20,770 square kilometres, or 77 per cent of Palestinian territories in which 6.5 million inhabitants live today, of which 1.2 million are Palestinians.

The West Bank alone represents 5,879 square kilometres. Two

million Palestinians live therein. Israel has set up around 200 settlements dispersed in the various West Bank areas, in which 180,000 settlers live today.

The Gaza Strip is a 378-square-kilometre piece of land in which 1.2 million Palestinians live. Israel has set up 20 settlements therein, providing home for some 8,000 settlers.

The total number of Palestinians living under occupation comes to 4.4 million individuals. A similar number of Palestinians is dispersed across the world.

The total number of Israelis in occupied Palestine is 5.5 million, out of a total of 13 million Jews worldwide.

As such, maintaining the West Bank settlements and guaranteeing their security would leave the Palestinians with only half of the West Bank and Gaza Strip lands agreed upon – 3,128.5 square kilometres representing 11.5 per cent or approximately one-ninth of total Palestinian land.

A gradual process of annexation was launched in 1948, at which time the Israelis represented only one third of Palestine's inhabitants. The partition plan issued through UN Resolution 181 back then provided Israel with over 54 per cent of Palestinian land. This has now developed into 88.5 per cent if the settlements in the West Bank and Gaza Strip are accounted for. Such a takeover makes any allegedly sought Palestinian state incapable of survival, especially if we were to take note that the highest population density in the world is actually in the Gaza Strip, where the number of Palestinian inhabitants per square kilometre is 4,762 given that one-third of the strip is under Israeli occupation by way of Jewish settlements.

Would a compromise of this nature bear any potential for Palestinian existence? Would it suffice for the Israelis, or would the rest of the Arab world still be a target of Israeli avarice? Would the surrender of Palestinian land guarantee true peace for these people living dispersed across the world and under siege in but a part of their rightful nation?

Compromise falsely and belligerently hoists the banner of peace, and its repercussions would not stop at any particular limit, for its chapters would only continue to demolish the Palestinian and Arab realities, subsequently targeting Islam. Should US hegemony continue as it is at present, and should international acquiescence to Israeli requisites and Middle Eastern aspirations that do not require further analysis persist without hindrance, Israel would not stop at controlling it all.

The Promise of Victory

Regarding the religious obligation, Jerusalem is the birthplace of the Prophets, and the land on which Prophet Muhammad (PBUH) trod:

> Glory to [Allah] Who did take His servant for journey by night from the Sacred Mosque to the Farthest Mosque whose precincts We did bless in order that We might show him some of Our signs: for He is the one who heareth and seeth [all things].[1]

It is not permissible to squander the land of Muslims or that which is sanctified. Rising to their defence and liberation is a natural obligation for which all Muslims are liable. As Imam Khomeini declared:

---

1. Surah no. 17, *al-Israa*, verse 1.

The extortionist government of Israel, through its tendentious plans for Islamic nations and Muslims, represents a great danger. It is feared that confrontation may become impossible should Muslims show lassitude. Given that the danger is directed at the very essence of Islam, it is the duty of all Muslims, and specifically of Islamic states, to take the initiative for the obliteration of this pond of decay with all possible means, and not to decline the *mujahideen* any assistance towards this end.[1]

Such danger has persisted and continues to manifest in destruction throughout our entire region, not to mention in the pain we have suffered as a result. We have been promised victory, for in God Almighty's words:

> *And We decreed for the Children of Israel in the scripture: Ye verily will work corruption in the earth twice, and ye will become great tyrants. So when the time for the first of the two came, We roused against you slaves of Ours of great might who ravaged [your] country, and it was a threat performed. Then We gave you once again your turn against them, and We aided you with wealth and children and made you more in soldiery. If ye do good, ye do good for your own souls, and if ye do evil, it is for them [in like manner]. So, when the time for the second [of the judgments] came [We roused against you others of Our slaves] to ravage you, and to enter the Temple even as they entered it the first time, and to lay waste all that they conquered with an utter wasting. It may be that*

---

1. *Imam Khomeini speaking of the Palestinian Cause*, published by the Institution for Organizing and Publishing the Remnants of Imam Khomeini, p. 110. (Quoted from *al-Nour* newspaper, issue of September 28, 1968.)

> *your Lord will have mercy on you, but if ye repeat [the*
> *crime] We shall repeat [the punishment], and We have*
> *appointed hell a dungeon for the disbelievers.*[1]

The role of those who persevere and resist in and around the Dome of the Rock in Jerusalem is mentioned in the accounts of the Prophet (PBUH):

> One sect of my people shall uphold their religion, conquer their enemy, and will never be harmed by any assailant except that which befalls them of distress and hardship, and they will remain as such until God's order comes unto them.

When asked where this party is, the Prophet (PBUH) said: 'In Beit-ul Maqdis (Jerusalem) and under its wings.'[2] Tradition also speaks of the appearance of the Twelfth Imam, Imam al-Mahdi (PBUH), who will work to purify Jerusalem. Accounts quoted from the Prophet (PBUH) state:

> A man of my people treading on my path and tradition shall emerge. God shall bestow heavenly grace on him, and the land shall offer its benediction. He will disseminate justice on the land that would by then be a haven for tyranny. He works for seven years on this nation. He reaches Beit-ul Maqdis [Jerusalem].[3]

Therefore, there is no separation between the religious duty of liberating Palestine and the Godly promise of victory. Both

---

1. Surah no.17, *al-Israa*, verses 4–8.
2. Al-Haithami; *Mujamma' al-Zawa'ed.*, vol. 7, p. 288.
3. Sheikh Ali al-Kourani, *Sayings of Imam al-Mahdi*, vol. 1, p. 134.

represent sufficient motive for resistance and *jihad* and for refuting the current reality despite the challenges and perils.

Returning to the political aspect, we observe through close inspection of the steps that led to the creation of this extortionist Zionist entity over a decade and of the level of its expansionist aspirations that we, as an existence, shall cease or fall under Zionist colonialism that would make of us followers living on the crumbs of their feasts, our fate subjugated to their control. Such would be a meaningless life of repression. It is also the course of reality that we observe through the unfolding of events on the political scene. Acquiescence to Israel's occupation would, under any banner, lead to complete surrender and the defeat of our nation.

The solution is represented by the *Intifadah* and resistance – expressions of refusal to the Israeli project, representations of the *jihad* condition and of legitimate denial. Following the path of resistance is not confined to particular methods, frequency or timing of operations. What is important is persistence, as much as determined by those concerned given circumstances, capabilities and capacity to inflict the highest number of casualties on this enemy with the least human loss among the ranks of the *mujahideen*. Resistance operations aim at exhausting the enemy, which is a cumulative process without immediate results but with traces and repercussions that may lead to a slow or sometimes sudden change.

Priority should be awarded to resistance activity; thus the need for continuous mobilization and cultivation of younger generations. Resistance should become a national and Islamic concern, a course that overpowers those who sway from it, the foundation block for a society of forbearance that prides itself on its achievements and sacrifices, strengthening such resistance further and responding to it.

This is the only available solution that carries any potential for the successful realization of objectives. It provides the Palestinian people with a choice and with some possible confidence against the definitively harmful course of compromise.

Results of the Palestinian Armed Struggle

Were it not for armed struggle, the national Palestinian identity would have vanished. In spite of fifty-three years of occupation, the only factor that has served to preserve the existence of a Palestinian cause is armed struggle. Otherwise, all Israeli efforts would have concentrated on integrating the Palestinians within the lands annexed by Israel in 1948, providing them with Israeli nationalities in preparation for other measures that would cancel the demand for a free Palestine. Armed resistance, on the other hand, served to keep the conflict open, and kept the banner of 'liberating Palestine' hoisted. This is what kept alive the cause in the hearts and minds of Palestinians across all the Occupied Territories, and is also a factor upsetting Arab conscience and contributing to placing the Palestinian cause on the agenda of international concerns.

Gandhi and Mandela's models for struggle are not applicable here, for circumstances in Palestine are completely different and Israel is not the least affected by such modes of retaliation. On the contrary, Israel is ready to usurp this type of action by encouraging groups of Israelis to demonstrate and march with the

Palestinians under a banner of 'peace', and this without changing the fact of occupation one bit.

Throwing stones, demonstrations and boycotting of Israeli products might be beneficial but are limited in extent. They are appropriate and constructive contributions, but do not achieve results on their own. The *Intifadah* crystallized further when it shifted to armed resistance. Only then did the Israelis actually feel its dangers and efficacy, for prior to this development tens of Palestinians would be killed without any consequence at once. Israel accounts for every single lost human soul, considering the security of Israeli individuals to be a pivotal and central objective. Such security can only be confronted through armed resistance, with all other modes being only supportive, of partial effect, and insufficient to substitute for such resistance.

Experience has clearly demonstrated that *jihad* leads to mobilization across the nation, that the blood of martyrs affects youth, raising their sense of responsibility, and that from the sacrifice of every martyr new readiness is born to a new group of *mujahideen*, exponentially so. Blood becomes a trusteeship borne by its bearer until the time of delivery, and is accompanied by the Godly promise of reward:

> *Allah hath bought from the believers their lives and their wealth because the Garden will be theirs: they shall fight in the way of Allah and shall slay and be slain. It is a promise which is binding on Him in the Torah and the Gospels and the Qur'an. Who fulfilleth His covenant better than Allah? Rejoice then in your bargain that ye have made, for that is the supreme triumph.*[1]

---

1. Surah no. 113, *al-Tauba*, verse 111.

One should therefore not halt the struggle based on Israel's aggressive reactions, for these are only part of the expansionist plan. In all cases, the Palestinians face two possibilities:

First, confrontation may succeed at forcing Israel to study its steps and ease the aggressiveness of its measures out of concern that intense aggression may breed reciprocal retaliation.

Second, Israel may be left to escalate its aggression in a manner that would only breed hostility and result in the natural mobilization of all neutral, fearful or watchful groups, as well as of those who foster compromise. Such mass affiliation to the ranks of the Resistance would provide it with new recruits who would not have contributed to *jihad* were it not for Israel's aggressive provocations.

The question of the effectiveness of such resistance and its possibilities for success is only a temporary one, emerging in intermittent phases. It is important to seize the opportunity and overtake this argument, for those who are dedicated to compromise will eventually be faced with Israel's exhausting requisites, which are unconvincing. As such, they would resort to resistance as being the only option for reinstating control. It is important to emphasize practical resistance as opposed to theoretical discussions about such resistance. This does not negate the fact that some groups are completely opposed to resistance whatever its results and as such, it is required that persuasive and forceful mobilization environments be created in order to deter such groups from proliferating tameness and acquiescence among the people. The undercurrents should bear deeper and more effectively, attempting to keep the resistance fire burning. The importance of resistance is in its persistence whatever the circumstances and throughout all phases of local, regional, international and Israeli pressure.

The Palestinians need a source of strength in their self-defence and quest for nationhood and for the future. Military power is out of question given the Israeli barrier, as is political pressure given the presence of US obstacles. Further, the Palestinians are at the very least incapable of deterring Israeli zeal for further targets except through possession of some sort of power. This much-needed power is one that cannot be held under siege, resisted or neutralized: it is the power of martyrdom. The Israeli menaces with death those who fear death, but is impotent in the face of those who are ready for mortality. Resistance is what has kept the Palestinian cause alive and exposed Israel's true colours.

Security is the Pillar of Israel's Existence

Security and final insistence on compromise represent two fundamental requirements for the Zionist entity to close the chapter of confrontations and establish itself indefinitely.

Security cannot be realized through aggression, imprisonment, imposition of adverse living conditions or the destruction of homes ... Such pressure might serve to deter the Palestinian *Intifadah* and to impede resistance operations, but whatever the Israelis' power or capability of occupation, there will always be a need for a regrouping of efforts and manpower in order to achieve their security. These dense and costly efforts have been to no avail. Hurting the Israelis is therefore a function of cracking their security and dealing them consecutive blows, thereby bringing down one of its basic foundations. Concentrating on inflicting pain on Israel serves to demonstrate to all occupiers that stable living is a far-fetched and difficult objective. It weakens the economy and perplexes the government, distorts its calculations and ruptures its plans. It instigates an internal Israeli discussion about the future of the state, enfeebles the influx of immigrants into Palestine and prompts some to actually leave.

To confuse the Israeli security front, the *Intifadah* does not require massive capabilities. Belief in the Lord and the will for martyrdom, turn humble military means into operative and effectual power. Although a coherent organizational setup is helpful to resistance activity, it is not a requirement, as groups drawn from various towns and villages can, through decentralized functioning and without any sharing of resources, undertake operations that can harm the occupational power.

Secrecy while training, gathering information or executing operations, is a continuous need. Such secrecy is not limited to warding off enemy eyes, but also to averting the eyes of enemy collaborators. Care should also be taken not to share plans with friends or next of kin, for these may, unintentionally and in all good faith, spread sensitive information that may be harmful to resistance members. It is beneficial for combatants to openly display their routine daily activities such as attending educational institutions or going to work, thus securing a cover for their *jihad* and preserving the element of surprise. Throwing stones is an act of zeal and ardour undertaken by young men who are completely exposed to the enemy, while resistance operations require covert and calculated planning within a very tight, closed circle concealed from the public eye. We should distinguish between the public *jihad* mobilization of individuals and the publicizing of actual practical resistance steps, for the first is beneficial and the second is harmful. Secrecy requires patience and discipline until such time as victory or martyrdom is achieved, and the publicizing of actions should be timed so as to render any enemy reaction ineffectual.

Practically, the *Intifadah* has been transformed into an armed resistance that is different from its initial form of a stone uprising. In its resistance formula, the *Intifadah* has become more effective and of a deeper consequence, for it is now capable of puncturing Israeli security and inflicting heavy losses.

Facing difficulties in the security arena, the Israelis are in need of Palestinian assistance. Their efforts thus focus on the creation of a Palestinian Authority with a trained and equipped military structure operating with the aim of deterring any resistance activity against Israel. The Authority's ability to understand the Palestinian mentality is definitely better than that of the Israeli government, for it enjoys freedom of movement and understands the societal fabric. Further, intra-Palestinian clashes only serve to weaken the resistance and reassure Israel. Thus, charging the Authority with the question of Israeli safety is, to the Israelis, a necessary step for the achievement of security, that which cannot bear up in the face of resistance and its willpower.

We therefore come to realize the extent of the Israeli focus on security measures and requirements. Peace discussions witnessed through many an international conference and resulting in many resolutions were really discussions about Israeli security. Any Israeli step forward is preceded by a toll of security requisites. The Oslo Agreement was built on custodianship of Israeli security, while both the Mitchell and Tenet reports clearly brought to the surface what requisites are thought to achieve security for the Israelis.

The Palestinian Authority is concerned, irrespective of whether it participates in resistance activity or not, for it cannot help defend that very power that is annexing the future of Palestine. As such, where resistance fighters face the hardship of being hunted down by their very own, accurate planning should be implemented beforehand in order to refrain from any clashes and maintain cooperation with those who embrace *jihad* aspirations. The basic principle that should govern all activity is that of keeping the flame of resistance burning and in all circumstances, while placing Israeli security within the targeting sphere.

There is no need to fear this picture, which should be a source of pride. Resistance is a noble and honourable act, legitimized by heavenly revelations and by the laws of circumstance. It is defence in the face of aggression and not an initiative. It is a reaction to the crimes of invasion, occupation, massacres and eviction. It is a human expression of justice, freedom of choice and aspirations for independence, a model for confronting oppression and for opening the doors of life to the subjugated. And when it aims to hit the aggressor right in the heart of the security issue, its results would only be limited to this: security.

Targeting Israeli Civilians

Dealing blows to Israeli security does, however, affect Israeli citizens, which poses two issues: the one questioning the purity of legitimate resistance actions, and the other having repercussions in the sphere of international support for the Palestinian cause. Conclusions in this context would be true if perceived partially. A comprehensive view would definitely change the impression, for the Israeli military has been in the process of killing both combatants and civilians in their homes or places of work and using any means ranging from air force to implanted bombs, sniping and assault. Such is considered to be an effective method for impeding resistance activity. Israeli settlers are armed, and their record of killing Palestinian civilians under the banner of self-defence or retaliation has gone unnoticed and unchecked. Palestinians also face a high degree of racism.

How should the Palestinians react in self-defence? There is no alternative to resistance activity that targets first and foremost the Israeli military. But where these members of the military alienate themselves from the battle domain and seek refuge in villages and towns behind a shield of civilians, and when Israeli settlers continue to murder and aggress, thus turning the Israeli civilian population into a form of military, then the target becomes this society of militants. In addition, one should consider the inability of resistance to hit its target of direct aggressors without affecting those civilians around them, noting that there is no other way of deterring the Israeli military from going too far in its assault of Palestinian civilians unless those very military members feel the extent of damage that could befall their own homes or families as a reaction to their targeting of civilians. If the Israeli military, with all its might, does not limit its confrontations to resistance combatants, then depriving the resistance of acts of reciprocity would simply deny it the ability to exert pressure, or achieve balance in this domain of horror, thus weakening its effectiveness in confronting occupation.

Necessity does not compromise the legitimacy of this act. The opinion of world nations and the international community cannot accommodate the righteousness of the Palestinian cause, and thus the question of legitimacy cannot be tarnished as a result. Rather, it is based on the notion that Israel is oppressed and has every right to retaliate and do as it pleases. Palestinians are asked to endure and are charged when they undertake defensive action. The banner of protecting civilians is raised only in the face of Palestinians – a demonstration of international bias, of taking any Palestinian success under siege.

The Israelis, on the other hand, are not subjected to such pressure. They enjoy the freedom of choosing from any number of measures, irrespective of the crime's viciousness, and seize the opportunity needed to fulfil their objectives as deemed fit. It is only a right of the Palestinians to work in self-defence and bring about a balance that could avert danger to Palestinian civilians.

Zionist history swarms with violations of the simplest of human rights. Upon mere mention of the state of Israel, the dark images of twentieth-century history are evoked, and the mind fills with images of massacres, occupation, eviction and aggression that have filled horizons and have been recorded through media, with modern history books bearing witness. The titles of such massacres are only witness to the landmarks implanted on the path of annexing Palestine, and important historical milestones are identified by the names of these massacres:[1] Jerusalem, Haifa, Samiramis, al-Ramlah, etc ...

---

1. The Arab Committee for Supporting the Islamic Resistance in Lebanon issued (through its *Resistance Newsletter* published in Egypt) the following account of Israeli massacres (see the May 15, 2002 issue):

Prior to the 1948 calamity, 62 massacres were committed against the Palestinian people, with a toll of 3,000 dead and about 10,000 wounded. Of these are the well-known Haifa Massacre of July 9, 1938 where two car bombs were blasted, leading to the death of 12 Palestinians and wounding 52; the Jerusalem Massacre of July 13, 1938, committed in a market where 10 Palestinians fell dead and 31 were wounded; the Balad El-Sheikh Massacre of December 31,

All the targets were civilians, men, women and children, and all the massacres were part of the Israeli domination plan drawn for the territories before 1948. Zionist gangs executed these massacres under the cover and custodianship of the British government. The Israeli military was later to openly execute them through organized plans targeting civilians and through providing cover for the actions of settlers. This is only proof that the Zionist project, with all its power, is incapable of achieving its targets except through massacres. Successive Israeli governments have walked the same track, while the international community only lent its silence, refraining from any practical or even theoretical step that should condemn or deter such crimes.

Focus on targeting Israeli security hits the enemy where it hurts and treads on a path that is incomparable to the massacres initiated by Zionists, for it is an act of self-defence, a reactionary stroke. The voices raised in condemnation of Palestinians are only a form of suspicious support for Zionist aggression, for when such condemnation is only directed towards Palestinians it

---

1947 where 60 were martyred and hundreds wounded; the Samiramis Hotel Massacre, executed by the Hagana gang, killing 19 and wounding 20; the Arab Saraya Massacre, whereby a car bomb was planted near the Yafa clock tower, killing 70 and wounding tens of civilians; the Sa'sa Massacre of February 14, 1948, where 60 were martyred and tens were injured, the majority children; the al-Ramla Massacre of January 15, 1948, led by Yitzhak Rabin and David Ben-Gurion of the Irgun gang, where tens were killed; the Haifa-Yafa Train Massacre of March 31, 1948 where 40 people were killed and 60 wounded at the hands of the Stern gang; the Deir Yassine Massacre of April 9, 1948 where 254 were murdered, including 25 pregnant women and 52 children below 10 years of age, and hundreds were wounded.

Massacres continued after 1948. These included the Kfar Kassem Massacre of October 29, 1956 where 49 were martyred and tens wounded; the Khan Younes Massacre of November 3, 1956, where 500 were killed and hundreds wounded.

serves to provide the necessary political cover for the occupation's expansionist feat.

In the context of targeting Israeli security, quick results are not a requirement. A rock disintegrates long after being continuously subjected to small drops of water. This is true even more where the model is a Zionist one that is quite aware of its deeds, and that carries characteristics of cowardice that force it to seek refuge behind foreign powers given its own feeble motives and weak essence. In God Almighty's words:

> *They will not fight against you in a body save in fortified villages or from behind walls. Their adversity among themselves is very great. Ye think of them as a whole, whereas their hearts are diverse. That is because they are a folk who have no sense.*[1]

Such continuous threat to Israel's security weakens it and disperses its powers, revealing to the large nations of the world the difficulty of its continued existence. International reactions to martyrdom attacks, especially from the US, have revealed the bitterness and extent of success achieved through these attacks. Should such resistance activity continue, the world would be made aware of a new reality and would be compelled to review in due course those biased international resolutions. At the least, this activity might freeze further support of Israeli requisites. Despite international bias in favour of Israel over a whole century, possible future changes on the international scene should be taken into consideration. All empires that have ruled throughout history have one day ceased to exist, and the fall of the USSR is but one contemporary signal

---

1. Surah no. 101, *al-Hashr*, verse 14.

of the universal order whereby nations rise and prosper then decline and collapse.

Signature Draws Israel's Boundaries

The second pillar of Israel's existence is represented by the subscription to the boundaries it seeks for itself, through Palestinian submission and signature on an agreement that would condense the Palestinian state into a small portion of its territory. Such signature would relieve Israel of the banner of occupation; for the rightful owners of the land would have themselves abandoned it.

Israel seeks to enforce this subscription in the context of an international hegemony, as administered by the US, attempting to crush all future possibilities of reinstating the Palestinian people's rights, and offering general, vague promises to them while promising Israel a detailed and specific schedule of commitments to be achieved through a pre-specified execution mechanism. We can read this conclusion through the vision of President George W. Bush on the Middle East,[1] which was unfortunately perceived by Arabs and Palestinians to be moderate and acceptable when compared with the extremism of Israeli Prime Minister Sharon. This speech became an alternative to all previous efforts in the quest for compromise. Below is an overview of some of its key points:

1. Acceptable Palestinian leadership is that which expresses the convictions and politics of the US and commits to the

---

1. Office of the Press Secretary, June 24, 2002. White House speech by President George W. Bush on Palestinian leadership.

establishment of organizations and institutions that foster this direction. Leadership will undergo a testing phase, the ultimate reward of which would be the creation of a temporary Palestinian state that would last only inasmuch as a US-Israeli blessing would permit. After depriving it of all reasons for power or rebuttal, this state would represent the end of the tunnel for the Palestinian cause. In the words of President Bush:

'And when the Palestinian people have new leaders, new institutions and new security arrangements with their neighbours, the United States of America will support the creation of a Palestinian state whose borders and certain aspects of its sovereignty will be provisional until resolved as part of a final settlement in the Middle East.' There is thus no role for the people in this choice of leadership, as the result is already premeditated. Either the people choose that which is acceptable to the US or the US refuses the choice under the pretext that leadership is not befitting of the people, for 'Peace requires a new and different Palestinian leadership'.

2. The condition for creating a Palestinian state is the fulfilment of a particular mission: that of annihilating the resistant *Intifadah* through a persistent war that aims to entirely uproot the movement. All civil defence and security forces of the Palestinian state would be subjected to international supervision in such a way that their very creation and functions would be dedicated to the protection of the Israeli entity's stability, while their structural design would

be outlined so that subjugation and control are ensured. In the same speech Bush says:

> 'And the United States will not support the establishment of a Palestinian state until its leaders engage in a sustained fight against the terrorists and dismantle their infrastructure. This will require an externally supervised effort to rebuild and reform the Palestinian security services. The security system must have clear lines of authority and accountability and a unified chain of command.'

3. Should security measures succeed in impeding the *Intifadah*, the direct reward would be withdrawal of the Israeli forces into pre-*Intifadah* areas. As such, all political steps would be postponed while the Palestinian Authority would be continuously monitored under the banner of Israeli security and in a manner according to US-Israeli blessing:

   'As we make progress towards security, Israeli forces need to withdraw fully to positions they held prior to September 28, 2000.'

4. Occupation ends following a compromise resulting in the creation of a Palestinian state. Negotiations to this end would take place between the Israelis, who possess all means of exerting pressure, and the Palestinians, who have been deprived of everything. As such, Israeli propositions would be non-negotiable dictations founded on a Palestinian recognition of secure Israeli borders and taking into account the necessary equipment needed for the Palestinians to carry out this role:

'This means that the Israeli occupation that began in 1967 will be ended through a settlement negotiated between the parties, based on UN Resolutions 242 and 338, with Israeli withdrawal to secure and recognized borders.'

Here we notice the clause 'Israeli occupation that began in 1967 will be ended', indicating that no occupation had taken place before then and limiting the conflict to those lands annexed in 1967.

5. 'With intensive effort by all, this agreement could be reached within three years from now.' The allegedly sought solution that was stated in Oslo thus evaporated. The Oslo Agreement had specified five years from the date of Gaza-Jericho First, and these ended in 1998 only to start again by way of a three-year promise, the ultimate aim of which is perhaps the possibility of achieving some form of agreement without any sure abidance by the suggested time-frame. Moreover, the aforementioned conditions, which could be used for forcible exaction, make of this time limit a vague and unbinding promise.

Can such tactics and alleged promises lead anywhere, especially given the recurring requirements to enforce Israel's conditions, which do not stop at a limit and that only seem to increase over time? Did the international community ever oblige Israel to abide by its signed promises? Did Israel ever abide by a schedule of events? And did Israel, throughout its various signed agreements, provide any clear milestones and specific measures of progress, as the Palestinian Authority was obliged to do?

Subscription to temporary promises, banking on practical

manoeuvring, and reliance on implementation details for the evaluation of agreements or the mistakes therein are measures that would embroil the Palestinian position in further waivers and lead to a compromise that leaves the Palestinian people bereft. Betting on hawks and doves inside the Israeli entity is also unrealistic, for the Labour Party, which did increase the number of settlements and embark upon major battles, is now part of the coalition government. Even where the Likud and the Labour parties are gulfs apart in terms of tactics or viewpoints, the objective that both wish to attain for the Israeli entity is that of entrenched establishment. This conviction provides sufficient reason for confrontation.

What would the Israelis be left with should the Palestinians refuse to respond? What would be the result if all Palestinian groups and the bountiful Palestinian people reorganized their efforts in this struggle? The Israeli's confusion was clear when all groups in the domain of battle came together within the frame of a resistant *Intifadah*: Hamas joined forces with Islamic *jihad*, Fatah, the National Front for the Liberation of Palestine, and other groups and sects representing all citizens without exception.

Palestinian leadership is called upon to benefit from such regrouping and societal support for the resistance of occupation. This would provide a certain immunity in the face of exerted pressure and a sufficient justification for refuting the submission sought by Israel. Instead of seeking a solution that is marketable to society, the responsibility for which would be borne by a Palestinian leadership that would eventually be accused of conspiracy where such solution failed to fulfil the least of Palestinian requirements, it would be best for leadership to use civilian pressure as an excuse, a force that cannot be spurned, and eventually a ticket during negotiations. All would be mobilized and the ball would be in the Israeli court.

The worst that could happen is an Israeli determination to alienate, besiege or threaten those members of Palestinian leadership. Resistance only flourishes with such acts of enemy vengeance, gaining in popularity and denying the counter-party any possibility of breaking united societal willpower. Should those leaders become martyred, then such would be the will of God Almighty, for only He specifies the timing of fate. Martyrdom is written in the glorious book of the nation, and if the leadership survived, it would mark a great achievement. When all societal forces move in this direction, the current that marks such zeal and enthusiasm would be transformed into an immunity that forbids opportunists and the heedless from leading the march.

Israeli leaders resort to the will of the people and hide behind it at any pressure interval, and do so despite their military power and political influence. Americans negotiate with the Arabs over the necessity of assisting the Israeli government in its endeavours given the public pressure that Israel faces internally. This was clearly demonstrated throughout the Barak years when the late Syrian President Hafez al-Assad was asked to renounce and waive certain rights in order for Barak to be able to market the agreement with Syria internally.[1] Given all of the above, it is only suitable for Palestinian and Arab leaders not to challenge and oppose their very own, or bear the brunt of historical renunciations that are at the least submissive and inequitable. It is befitting of these leaders to transform the force of their people

---

1. The Syrian president naturally refused to respond to such manoeuvres, and the Barak version of compromise was never achieved with Syria.

into a shield of immunity, steadfastness and the achievement of rights. The Palestinian people have manifested high skill and distinguished *jihad*; they are qualified support for those who are faithful among their leaders and should work hand in hand with these in confronting challenges.

Political management of the conflict must come out of the tunnel that demands answers to such recurring Israeli requisites as: the surrender of Israeli tourism minister Rechavam Ze'evi's killers,[1] providing Israelis with tips on martyrdom operations before they are actually undertaken; charging the Palestinian Authority with the responsibility for any operations against Israel; the condemnation of martyrdom operations; detaining *mujahideen* combatants; undertaking internal reform within the Palestinian Authority; and so on. These demands place a cordon of accountability and interrogation around Palestinian leaders. Given all of the above, a reciprocal form of interrogation is now needed and Palestinian requirements should now surface: the eviction of Israelis from all occupied Palestinian territories; the handing over of those responsible for murdering Palestinian children; recognition of the right to resist given the fact of occupation; releasing Palestinians held in Israeli prisons; holding Israel responsible for the economic hardships and starvation suffered by the Palestinian people; and so on.

The Palestinian Authority should not hastily provide guarantees to Israel, as the latter openly declares its vision of a unified Jerusalem under Israeli management and speaks of maximum withdrawals from the West Bank that do not exceed 42 per cent of this Palestinian land. This should not be taken to mean that negotiations

---

1. Ze'evi was assassinated by a group affiliated with the Popular Front for the Liberation of Palestine.

should be restricted to restoration of the 1967 annexed lands; nor should it mean acquiescence to the surrender of one hand-span of Palestinian soil. It is but a guide to the minimum politics of negotiation that should leave the door open for developments and for a variety of future options.

Where resistance continues to raze Israeli security, and the Israeli entity fails to achieve a signature that legitimizes its existence and delineates its borders, the chances of reinstating Palestinian land are still be present.

Postponing the Discussion on Liberation Borders

A predicament is posed by the existing divergence of opinion amongst the various Palestinian groups, who do not concur on the nature of these rights. Some believe in total liberation of all Palestinian soil, from the river to the sea, while others settle for boundaries that do not exceed what was allocated after the June 4, 1967 occupation in accordance with UN Resolution 242. Such a dilemma would surface if discussions were to occur between these groups. Postponing the debate, and concentrating on congruent work amongst all parties in the face of Israeli assaults that violate all rights, would render those who acquiesce to partial liberation unsatisfied with the political course of negotiations and would set on track a phase of cooperation within the framework of *jihad* against Israel, for *jihad* is the only weapon available to all parties. If and when Israel bows and accepts the minimum requirements, the second difficult phase emerges – that which requires elaborate discussion to prevent internal Palestinian strife. While the hope for liberation would persist, the time is appropriate for the discussion of the issues posed, unless there is a frightening Palestinian climbdown from the acceptable minimum – then those doing so would not be able to defend their position given all the sacrifices made by the Palestinian people. The Palestinian Authority bears the responsibility for acting within a margin that protects those elements of strength without inviting the predicament into its midst.

Doubtless, the circumstances surrounding Hizbullah's experience in Lebanon are different from those of the Palestinian *Intifadah*. It is inappropriate to haphazardly apply one experience in another context. However, common denominators are generally and sometimes specifically present.

Just as Hizbullah has benefited from the experience of the Palestinian resistance and its history of struggle with Israel, so have the Palestinian people found in Hizbullah's political and mobilization rallying, tactics and approach to domain activity an inspiration and new hope for liberation.

Broad banners are a sufficient source of such inspiration. The Party possesses limited military power and an organization with a restricted number of members. But through belief and the priorities of resistance and martyrdom, Hizbullah succeeded in liberating the larger part of South Lebanon and the Western Bekaa on May 24, 2000, following an eighteen-year struggle with a military force reputed as being invincible and that enjoying intense hegemonic support. This was a light at the end of the Palestinian tunnel, a hope that liberation might be achieved by treading the path of resistance and martyrdom. What happened in Lebanon can be repeated in Palestine.

Similarity mainly lies in the nature of the enemy and the extent of international support for Israel, the existence of occupation and the viciousness of its aggression, all against the preparedness of youth for *jihad*, the conviction of the populace in supporting the uprising, and the despondency of reaching any advancement through negotiations.

But the Palestinian reality is more difficult than that faced by Lebanon, for Palestinian land is the primary centre of occupation. As such, Palestinian resistance is considered a strategic change station, for its achievements bear repercussions on the entire region.

The Responsibility of Arabs and Muslims

Arabs and Muslims are responsible for providing Jerusalem and the rest of Palestine with support and assistance. This is true both due to the religious commandment of defending the sanctified and refusing its occupation and oppression, and as a result of sure interest in refuting the aggressive Israeli establishment and its expansionist aspirations.

In Imam Khamenei's words:

> Today, Muslim nations and populations, and especially those of the Arab world, carry a huge responsibility. The duty of governments is dangerous and heavy, but that of the populace, especially religious clerics, political figures and educated individuals, as well as remaining key constituents, is not any lighter. This responsibility is

encapsulated in the provision of assistance, the raising
of morale and the fostering of jihad.[1]

What is required is the consecration of the Palestinian struggle as
a central cause for the entire nation of Islam, thereby mobilizing
and amassing all financial, media, cultural, political and military
potential for the achievement of this aim. Each country would
then contribute practical steps, programmes and appropriate
methods of assistance based on its own circumstances, the
position of supporters in the national and social context, and their
actual or future potential capabilities. Maximum effort should
be exerted to ensure that direct support of the cause remains a
priority. No Arab or Muslim group has any excuse for negligence
or for leaving the Palestinian people to suffer on their own.

Regimes are not exempt from this responsibility, but their
contribution is perhaps best achieved by refraining from
interference, for on the other side are international regimes
that take it upon themselves to nourish and sponsor the Israeli
requisites. It is not possible to bet on Arab concurrence, especially
given the present state of the Arab world. The Arabs' mutual
adoption of the Palestinian cause would not represent a surrogate
for liberation. In spite of this, factions and societal groups
should at least exert the minimum effort towards persuading
their national regimes to support the Palestinian cause. The least
that can be achieved is an adoption of the cause as a reflection
of public concern, which would provide the proper context
for hesitant countries that may wish to hide behind the will of
the people.

---

1. Imam Khamenei's speech at the opening of the international conference on
   Imam Khomeini and support for the Palestinian cause, Tehran, June 2–3,
   2002.

Broad rules and principles are not sufficient to discuss support for the central cause. Many details bearing on the level of seriousness and the extent of concern should be brought into the discussion. No party should be denied the appropriate means of support, which, if grouped, would represent an important asset contributing to victory. Our aspirations should not be too unrealistic, for those who live in the heart of the conflict are the ones who endure its true force. Public work would, however, fulfil a supportive function. The demonstrations that stormed the Arab world in support of Palestine would reveal the extent to which this cause is alive and present in society's sentiment and conscience, and serve to draw the attention of the international public to the depth of the conflict in our region. Further, financial support would fill a gap should it reach the right groups. Media coverage can shed light on the oppression suffered by the Palestinians, and is an eye-opener for the world. Military support, provided through appropriate methods, plays a role in propping up resistance. No one knows how things will eventually develop, and the role to be played by the region is yet unspecified. However, careful planning and preparation are needed outside the traditional declared circles in order to undertake whatever is necessary to support the Palestinian cause at the appropriate time.

FIVE

Issues and Stance

Participation in State Institutions

Participation in Parliamentary Elections[1]

Following the introduction of internal stability in Lebanon after public institutions resumed their work on rehabilitation and reorganization, and as part of the Taif Accord's repercussions, it was decided that Lebanese parliamentary elections would resume in 1992 – twenty years[2] after the last round. This issue represented the most prominent practical objective at the level of internal Lebanese policy.

Parliamentary representation of Hizbullah was not a clear choice for the faction at the time, a decision that called for deep internal debate. As such, Council suggested that the mechanism for ultimate decision-making should go through a twelve-

---

1. This discussion of Hizbullah's participation in Lebanese parliamentary elections is presented here and not in Chapter Three ('Key Milestones in the History of Hizbullah'), although such participation is indeed a key achievement. It is discussed separately here given the necessity of elaborating on the wide debate that took place both inside and outside of the Party over the issue, and given the relation of this topic to subsequent ones. This should facilitate the reader's comprehensive understanding of cause and effect between the various issues.
2. The last round of elections took place in April 1972. Thereafter, parliamentary elections were not possible throughout the war years (1975–1992).

member delegation grouping the most prominent Hizbullah representatives, inclusive of Council members. Debates focused on the following issues:

1. What is the extent of the legitimacy of taking seats in a Parliament based on a confessional political system that does not represent Hizbullah's view of an ideal system?

2. Where the legitimacy issue is solved, would participation be considered a form of acquiescence to the political system's reality, including the responsibility of adopting and defending such a system, and abandoning the Islamic vision?

3. What are the costs and benefits of participation, and are there any such drawbacks or advantages that could be considered to outweigh sure and clear benefits?

4. Would participation lead to a re-organization of priorities of the type that would result in abandoning the cause of the resistance in favour of taking part in the internal political game?

Many a concentrated debate was held to these ends, and the various central unit supervisors presented their opinions, which were later compiled by the assigned delegation. What follows is a summary of the results.

The delegation could not respond to the first question of legitimacy, as it fell within the domain of the Jurist-Theologian and was therefore an issue for religious representatives to discuss. This is so given the opinion of some that representation in a non-Islamic system does not conform with overall Islamic philosophy, as the obligations cast by religious commandment clearly call for the creation of an Islamic nation and an Islamic ruling system, and duties should remain outside any interim systems whatever their nature.

Others proposed the possibility of representation by individuals[1] as opposed to an all-encompassing faction representation. Concern was over granting legitimacy to a non-Islamic order and thereby extending its existence. By doing so, Muslims would have contributed to what might impede or postpone the eventual replacement of such an order. But this is a theoretical discussion based on many assumptions and generalizations that does not take into account circumstantial and national differences or what constitutes the basis for interests or detriments, although it clearly fixes those essential principles. Awarding priority to interests at the expense of principles is not permissible, but consideration of interests within the scope of preserving the principles is acceptable.

The delegation resorted to continuing the discussion of the last three issues in order for all facts to be compiled and presented to the Jurist-Theologian, who would ultimately define the doctrinal legitimacy and manner of dealing with the existing regime in Lebanon, especially in relation to parliamentary elections.

Participation in parliamentary elections is an expression of sharing in an existing political structure, Parliament being one of the regime's pillars. It does not, however, represent a commitment to preserving the structure as is, or require defence of the system's

---

1. An example would be the participation of al-Muhaqiq al-Karaki as an Islamic *sheikh* in the Safavid Dynasty. See p. 32 of the introduction of *Jame' al-Maqasid*, issued by The Institution of the Prophet's Kin.

deficiencies and blemishes. A position in Parliament denotes a representation of a certain group of people and allows the parliamentarian to maintain his viewpoints and defend them, enjoying a freedom of acceptance or refusal and the capability of making his position clear based on his background. Of the issues open for discussion is the very structure of the system to which the participant appertains. Suggestions for change could always be made, and influence on proposed legislation remained a sure possibility.

As such, Parliament is a form of representation where the banner of absolute allegiance to the system is not applicable. There is a sufficiently wide margin for operation and expression irrespective of whether the appropriate results would actually be achieved or not. It suffices for one to be able to defend his or her position in order to avoid entrapment within a particular political structure. Besides, would opposition operating from outside the system use an approach that differs from the statement of opinion, objection or the proposing of alternatives? This was notwithstanding the fact that outsiders would lack the systems and influential means for achieving their targets. So, parliamentary participation would be an instrument for achieving change, as an official path that has a wider reach.

In addition, there are sizeable advantages to such participation, the most prominent of which are:

1. Parliament is a political podium from which the concerns and issues of the Resistance could be voiced. Discussion of ways to maintain and support the Resistance is possible from that standpoint. The creation of an atmosphere conducive

to drawing public attention to the voice of the Resistance could be achieved through public representation.

2. Through parliamentary discussions, influence on the budget allocations of the various ministries becomes possible, and thus the concerns of the people – be they social, developmental, health-oriented or pertaining to living standards – as well as the concerns of the deprived regions, could be voiced.

3. *A priori* knowledge of legislation that is still under preparation also becomes possible, allowing for the study and formulation of opinion on the matter as well as the suggestion of amendments. This serves to alleviate the surprise of being suddenly bound by legislative realities that cannot be discussed after their official adoption.

4. Another interest is presented through a network of potential political relations. Representatives of Lebanon's various sects and districts become part of such a network, and direct discussions are possible with all parties on any number of issues. This can promote close relations and understanding, eliminate false barriers and erroneous perceptions, and achieve a result that fosters discussion and acceptance of the other.

5. Recognition by one of the main institutions of the Lebanese government of Party parliamentarians, who represent a particular segment of the public, blends the Resistance into those officially and publicly recognized bodies.

6. Of interest also is the presentation of an Islamic point of view that should be present alongside other proposed viewpoints.

These favourable arguments do not negate the existence of some drawbacks, as for instance the difficulty of achieving accurate public representation given the limit on the number of representatives allowed in Parliament. As such, parliamentary presence is more of a political representation than a public one. In addition, there is the issue of the passage of legislation that may not conform to Islamic doctrine or *Shari'a* principles despite opposition by the Party's parliamentarians. Another negative aspect has to do with the brunt of responsibility that is borne by the parliamentarian for execution of individuals' and regional requisites for public services, at a time when Parliament is the legislative as opposed to the executive body of government. However, the sum of pros outweighs the cons and makes interest in parliamentary representation a worthy concern.

Priorities are decided at the Party political level. Given that resisting Israeli occupation takes precedence over all other priorities, and given that parliamentary representation was not pre-conditioned on any issues that would affect the fact of resistance, there is no need for concern that such participation would have a negative bearing on resistance activity, for the Party's decision to take part in parliamentary elections was declared and clearly linked to the persistence of resistance activity, and voters were aware of this programme at the time of the elections. As such, elections should be perceived as a form of support for the Resistance and not the contrary.

Some public powers and leading figures had a false impression that the magnetism of internal politics would pave the way for a reconsideration of the priority awarded to resistance activity. Such an impression is linked to the perception of these individuals that political life represents the ultimate of all aspirations. This differs from the Party's view which is inclined to the integration of political work with resistance activity without any conflict between the two. Rather, such a combination is thought to be complementary, as the internal concerns and plights of the people are carried to the national level while the interests of the state and the *umma* (the nation of Islam) in liberation from Israeli occupation is only strengthened through the persistence and empowerment of resistance.

Based on the above, the delegation's vote was ten out of twelve in favour of parliamentary participation as not only an interest but also a necessity. This was harmonious with Hizbullah's vision for conveying the concerns of the people and their interests up to the national political level, and not in conflict with the priority of *jihad* for liberation. It also served to realize a number of good political outcomes, to provide a nascent Islamic faction with a new experience, and to mark an important step forward in terms of interaction with others. But such participation could not be set apart from the particularity of the Lebanese domain, the nature of elections therein, or the admissible level of freedom of choice. The outcome of these issues may be entirely different in other countries where different circumstances prevail. In all cases, discussion centred on participation in Lebanese parliamentary elections from the standpoint of belief in Islam, and the results were positive.

After presentation of the delegation's findings, the question of legitimacy was sought and guidance was requested from the

Jurist-Theologian Imam Khamenei, who was supportive and granted his permission. The issue of participation was resolved and the project entered the Party's plan of action. On July 3, 1992, Secretary General al-Sayyed Nasrallah held a press conference declaring Hizbullah's decision to participate in Lebanese parliamentary elections, which were to take place in Bekaa on August 23, 1992.

Results of Participation in Parliamentary Elections

The time-span between adoption of the participation decision and the first phase of that election round did not exceed fifty days. This was the first public election in which the Party was participating, and the lack of knowledge or experience in this regard manifested itself. The Party's supporters were not accustomed to this type of work, which requires rallying and mobilization efforts before and on the day of elections, and for the support of a public relations network to aid in the building of coalitions, which bears on election results.

Broad policy guidelines were drawn, and working plans had already been determined prior to the announcement of the actual participation decision. Council then distributed the various follow-up roles. The Secretary General supervised the overall political direction and the various associations to be formed. The Deputy Secretary General was in charge of the central committee for field administration of elections across all Lebanese districts, and recommended coalitions; executive decisions were presented to the Council for consideration.

The level of voter turnout was remarkable. Hizbullah had

created the largest single organized campaign operation in Lebanon, grouping Party members, supporters and admirers. It was not limited to the religiously devout only, but drew all those believers in the viewpoints and actions of Hizbullah even where they were far from being religiously committed. It was evidence of the scope of public support for the Party and of the extent to which people were ready and prepared to engage in fatiguing voluntary work in order to participate in Hizbullah activities and strengthen the Party's position. Party supporters were present at every ballot, distinguished not only by their dress code and active presence, but also by the extent to which they conformed to ballot rules while remaining in constant contact with their supervisors through telecommunications. Hizbullah represented a model for election campaigning, later imitated by many.

Hizbullah presented a comprehensive political and social programme,[1] diverging from the standard campaigns that had focused on publicizing candidates' pictures and reputations without concentrating on any particular plan or programme. With this, Hizbullah took the step towards providing priority of the programme over the person, a step that may have left a mark on Lebanese political life.

Hizbullah succeeded in achieving a varied representation at the regional level where it was present: the Bekaa, South Lebanon, Beirut and its southern suburbs. The Party established the Allegiance to the Resistance coalition comprising twelve Members of Parliament: eight of the Shi'ite sect, two Sunnis, one Roman Catholic and one Maronite Christian.[2] This was a new model of

---

1. See the Appendix on the Election Programme at the end of this book.
2. These twelve MPs were from a total 128 parliamentarians. Eight represented the Bekaa district: al-Sayyed Ibrahim Amine al-Sayyed; Sheikh Ali Taha; Sheikh Khodor Tleis; Hajj Muhammad Yaghi; Rabia Keyrouz (Maronite);

an Islamic movement: a coalition of parliamentarians pertaining to a variety of sects, an exuberant interrelation of powers whose visions coincide with Hizbullah's to a certain extent but who do not comply with the religious and behavioural modes of conduct required of Hizbullah members, all while conforming to the political guidance of the Party.

Evaluation of the participation in three rounds of elections over the years 1992, 1996 and 2000 demonstrates that the above analysis accurately conforms to reality. For Hizbullah's parliamentarians have blended with the Lebanese fabric, which enabled them to reach out to the various groups in record time. They have entered the political reality from within, and revealed the Party's other face. Their active participation in the discussion of proposed legislation led to the labelling of the Allegiance to the Resistance as the most important coalition for the studying of parliamentary plans and proposals. The coalition's members participate in all parliamentary committees and have contributed a number of budgetary measures in favour of deprived areas. Official recognition of the Party's proper representation of the public has been achieved, a fact which enraged the US administration and Israel. As per diplomatic sources, the Party's resistance arm was fortified as a result of such representation and the 'terrorism' smear attached to it was only weakened.

A number of drawbacks were recorded. Coalitions during the 1996 campaign imposed unconvincing candidate lists or inappropriate representation, which led to Hizbullah's loss of

---

Saoud Roufael (Catholic); Dr Ibrahim Bayan (Sunni); and Dr Mounir al-Hujeiri (Sunni). Two represented the South: Hajj Muhammad Raad and Hajj Muhammad Fneish; while Hajj Muhammad Burjawi represented Beirut and Hajj Ali Ammar represented the Baabda province of Beirut's southern suburbs.

the Beirut and southern suburbs seats, for the Party had refused to respond to the imposed arrangements. Hizbullah also did not achieve the necessary number of representatives for other areas.[1] The situation improved in the following elections (2000),[2] where priority for the continuation of resistance activity served to avert any internal conflicts or to distract from core concerns. Thus, attention was paid to avoiding any political discord that could have repercussions on the network of key relationships, whether with Amal or other important figures or groups, or that could have a bearing on the relationship with Syria.

Lebanese election law changed between one round and another, and was tailored to the needs of some key leaders, as well as confessional and regional calculations. As such, Beirut was once a single electoral district and then split into three separate constituencies, while the Bekaa shifted from being three districts to one and then to two. The electoral law did not stabilize, altering with every round.

Hizbullah considered the smaller electoral district that traditionally covers Lebanon's provinces to be unrepresentative of the population given the potential power that money could muster for buying votes in these small provinces, and given also the dominance of family allegiance whereby choice is determined based on a candidate who is next of kin; or yet the supremacy of the sectarian factor that is usually characteristic of any one

---

1. Nine members of the Allegiance to the Resistance were elected – of which five were in Bekaa, including one Sunni and one Maronite – while four represented the South.
2. Twelve members of the Allegiance to the Resistance entered Parliament: five represented the Bekaa, including two Sunnis; five represented the South, with one Maronite member in addition to one representative of Beirut and another of Baabda.

province. With these setbacks prevailing, qualified candidates who are truly concerned with their regions' plights could not be elected without consideration of the sect and family to which they belong. The election domain thus turned into a ranch, a trading house for capitalists.

Hizbullah thus called for an Intermediate Constituency grouping more than one province at a time[1] and based on majority. This was proposed to be the best among all previously proposed options, these being:

1. The Small Constituency;

2. The Provincial Constituency, where it is customary for the political make-up of candidate lists to rule over that which results from public choice;

3. The Unified Electoral District, whereby the whole country would be considered as one constituency in which all political powers dissolve, leaving the configuration of the candidate list to whoever possesses leadership and power. With such a formation, proper representation becomes impossible; candidacy would closer resemble appointment as determined by the efforts of political and influential figures, thus impeding the election process by keeping only the façade of elections.

---

1. There are twenty-five provinces in Lebanon in addition to the governor-ship of Beirut. As such, the Small Constituency would refer to twenty-five electoral districts with the exception of Beirut, while the Provincial Constitu-ency would represent four electoral districts. The proposed Intermediate Constituency groups several provinces in one governorship under one electoral district, thereby shrinking the number of electoral districts usually observed under the Provincial Constituency formula.

An election law based on majority rule within a unified electoral district for the whole country is considered to be the ideal solution, for all powers would then be allowed their right of representation as based on the number of supporters they could muster at the national level. No party would be denied such right due to the dispersion of voters across more than one region or to the relative influence of coalitions that usually determine the fate of elections. Further, a parliamentarian would be elected to represent the whole of Lebanon, which makes him or her more responsive to this wider national constituency – even if particular efforts are devoted to the region with which he identifies. Moreover, should the recommendations of election-laws expert Abdo Saad[1] be adopted, there would be no fear of losing on numbers, or of one sect voting for the representatives of another. Saad's plan in this regard is the most outstanding so far, and has been presented as the basis for a promising discussion in preparation for proper treatment of the issue. The plan distributes the number of parliamentarians among their sects as previously defined, and ensures appropriate suffrage to all factions and powers as per their presence in their domain and the level of national support they receive. With these we are freed of legislation that is formulated to suit individuals, and the direction of elections would stabilize according to the best possible national interplay of powers.

Hizbullah parliamentarians have responded to many individual concerns. They have provided many regional services, especially in the Bekaa area where the balance of parliamentary representation was in favour of the Allegiance to the Resistance coalition. Other

---

1. See Abdo Saad's election plan in *As-Safir* of June 6, 1997. Further amendments to the plan undertaken by the project's author himself were published in the issue of March 30, 1999. The plan contains an implementation mechanism as well.

officials could not sideline these achievements, some of them required arduous follow-up and extensive political pressure.

However, services beyond those funded by the government budget (which were expended in their proper accounts) as well as personal services for individuals seeking appointments to government jobs were very limited. These require ministerial approvals of the type that calls for exploitation of an individual's position as a member of the executive corps in favour of a few MPs with whom an exchange of services or political or election support would be agreed.

Many instances of ministerial assistance to parliamentarians had as a final aim the strengthening of public support. Hizbullah did not take part in such exchanges out of concern for its credibility and regard amongst the people. The Party provided voluntary services in the form of financial support or donations, thus filling the gap created by the regime's usual approach in resolving social-service issues.

From the start, Hizbullah did not consider representation in Parliament as constituting the Party's ultimate dream that would lead to the shores of peace and achieve its objectives. This assembly is but one force of influence, not the ultimate one. Some aims may be achieved through it, but not all. As such, some coalitions might succeed and so would the plans and legislative proposals that go with them; while other alliances might fail, affecting the projects they foster.

Entering the Executive Government

The complications involved in forming part of the executive government are different from those of parliamentary participation.

Executive government is just that – an executive body linked to overall policies at the political, social and economic levels. Individuals in government are charged with implementation and defence of any of such policies, even where they stand at odds with it. As such, all ministers bear responsibility for government actions, which renders Hizbullah's acceptance of working from within the government a factor of the availability of the appropriate conditions that are in harmony with the Party's beliefs. A ministerial position is not an achievement without responsibilities, but bears repercussions that affect the overall direction. Care must therefore be exercised before rushing into this track in order for choice to be rational and beneficial.

Those who support participation in the executive government have their justifications:

1. The political course that leads to participation in parliamentary elections has a continuum represented by entry into government, without which performance would be lacking and the Party would not be able to capitalize on its efforts.

2. The political structure in Lebanon accommodates entry into any of the successive governments, irrespective of their performance or overall direction, for participation is an expression of compromise and of concord of interests. Further, it is possible for any group represented in government to distinguish itself to a certain extent and set itself apart from full responsibility for all government action.

3. Participation would represent a practical model for the

Party's ministers that could be followed by others, thus enriching the governmental experience. Further, these members of government would have a say in the executive decisions affecting the nation as a whole.

4. A minister would provide regional and individual services that would lead to further support for the Party at the public social level. The presence of a Party member in a ministerial position would be beneficial given the authoritative possibilities available and would make the exchange of services with other ministers possible.

Opponents to governmental participation have an answer to each of the above justifications, and harbour points of view characterized by stringent conditions making the entry into government an exception based on overriding positive factors. These validate their opinion as such:

1. Contrary to the track adopted by the various officials and figures of power in the country, Hizbullah did not launch its political *jihad* vision and its plan of action with the final objective of reaching the pinnacle of government participation given the present sectarian formula prevailing in Lebanon. Hizbullah's objectives were clearly outlined as being primarily resistance against the Israeli enemy for the sake of liberating occupied land and the presentation of an Islamic model of political work that is in line with the *Shari'a*, serving the people, properly representing them and working in their interests, inasmuch as these goals do not conflict with the Resistance and the aforementioned

Islamic political experience. As such, it would be impossible to adopt a single political mechanism unless it concurred with the achievement of the objectives. Where participation conflicts with these objectives, the motive for seeking a ministerial position drops, the resulting losses being far less significant than losing track of the ultimate objective.

2. No matter how much Hizbullah set itself apart, the Party would still be responsible for the repercussions of government action through its ministers. Thus, if the Lebanese government opted for the track of negotiations with Israel within a context of compromise spanning the whole region, Hizbullah would have to opt out, for acceptance of the course and actual participation in it would seriously conflict with the Party's policy of confronting Israel. On another level, if the government's adopted economic policy were judged unable to achieve the necessary growth, subjecting the country to dire living conditions, then it would not be possible to follow suit and accept the social consequences.

   Furthermore, if the policy of partitioning and partaking requires the presence of unqualified figures or of inadequate performance within the government corps, then all would have to bear responsibility at a time when one or two Party ministers might not have sufficient authority or influence to execute change in a manner befitting of societal aspirations and of the trust of the populace in the course – that course which has adopted an Islamic vision and which refuses to provide a distorted or false image in exchange for a few limited services.

3. Change from within and distinguished performance are issues open for discussion. The possibility of introducing change might not be present at all in certain situations, especially where the government is formed of twenty or thirty ministers with the Party represented by one or two. In this case, majority is not sufficiently influential for the introduction of change. Further, given the effective presence of a partitioning policy among the three heads of Lebanon's power troika (the president of the republic, the prime minister and the president of Parliament), a certain mechanism presides over the course and decisions of the Council of Ministers. As such, the Council is converted into an executive framework for preset policies that ministers can only marginally comment on without any assurance that such comments will be of any consequence. At best, these would just be points of view that could be dissipated through voting whereby the sum of all ministers would finally bear the responsibility for a decision.

How can individuality flourish in such circumstances, where individual conduct goes unnoted and where the issues and requests raised are larger than any individual minister can achieve? How can it surface amidst an environment necessitating acquiescence to certain partitioning or appointment schemes that do not meet the appropriate requisites and only form part of the necessity of cooperating with others, whereby the uncooperative minister would be considered responsible for objecting, instigating clashes or impeding progress – which would eventually lead to struggle or leaving the post? The scenario and the reaction of others to such developments cannot be predicted.

The Lebanese system has a certain particularity in the manner of choosing a government. The president and the country's sectarian distribution receive priority over the contents of the cabinet's programme, the programme being more of a formality that is not construed as a working document to which the cabinet is accountable. Entry into government is thus primarily a function of suitability, while the expectation that objectives will be achieved and that results will be positive cannot be supported beforehand by evidence or precedence.

The above refers essentially to non-participation in the executive government. Participation would be an exception to be undertaken only where convincing rationales are provided for the issues discussed, where the unambiguous possibility of achieving objectives is present, or where sure interest supersedes all other problems. In order for the verdict not to be a pre-judgement or a definitive unswerving stance that is only concurrent with the Party's overall course, the discussion of membership in the Council of Ministers would be posed on every round of its formation where a review of facts, advantages and drawbacks is undertaken. Such discussion would be considered worthier than a definitive *a priori* answer.

Hizbullah discussed the cabinet's programme and the issue of participation every time a prime minister was charged with forming a government. Hizbullah's standpoint since 1992, and still today, has been one of abstention from participation in any of the successive governments that have since then been formed either by Prime Ministers Rafik al-Hariri, Salim al-Hoss. Although the Party was in favour of charging al-Hoss with the post of prime minister following evaluation of his convictions and personality, the Party abstained from the vote of confidence for the al-Hoss cabinet and also denied such a vote of confidence to all the others. This was either due to issues within the cabinet's programme or to rejection of the expected political course or performance of the government.

The Party is in accordance with its analysis and overall vision. The course of action adopted by successive governments has proved an inability to close those administrative reform gaps that have accompanied every administration. The same is true of economic policy, the submission of the cabinet to its president's vision and the apparent political confusion in terms of internal follow-up, in addition to the issue of partitioning that presents itself and that never fails to create internal tensions and impediments. For these reasons, the Party took the standpoint of objective opposition, that which comments on the government's performance, treating one subject at a time, with positive results including praise and the adoption of viewpoints and negative ones including refusal and criticism.

As such, the Party criticized the political performance of Prime Minister al-Hariri during his first government of 1992, at which time he had expected to resolve the Palestinian issue by the spring and had built his political standpoints around this expectation. The Party further disapproved of his performance at the level of the economy, which is based on regional political change and which has subjected the country to excessive debt. The Party was later to speak well of the government and of its prime minister when the latter stood in support of the Resistance. This oscillation also characterized the Party's relationship with President Elias al-Hrawi, with whom the Party was at odds over his views on the Resistance, his refusal of religious education in schools and his proposal of civil marriage legislation. President al-Hrawi was later praised for his support of the Resistance. It was largely due to such support that President Emile Lahhoud has been in harmony with Hizbullah. The president's backing of the Party, and his defence and strong adoption of the Resistance and its plans instigated discussions of a possible coalition between the president and Hizbullah. The same was also said of Prime Minister Salim al-Hoss, given his positive views supportive of the Resistance.

The Party's standpoint on participation in successive executive governments does not mean that any offers have actually been made to it to participate. In some instances, steadfast US efforts were exerted to forbid the naming of any Hizbullah members in the cabinet while in others the prime minister was of the opinion that co-existence with the Party within one cabinet was beyond his capabilities. But on the two instances when the proposition came close to realization, the Party expressed its unwillingness to participate given the above reasons, and did so both directly and indirectly.

Entry into a governmental set-up is different from parliamentary elections. As such, when Hizbullah took the decision to join Parliament as a body representing the people and as a legislative order whereby the responsibility of stating opinion could be exercised without bearing the brunt of implementation, the decision to participate in the 1996 and 2000 elections did not require further discussion. Follow-up in terms of candidacy, executive mechanisms and routine details was a natural consequence. The course of executive government participation, on the other hand, requires a stop at every station in order for the discussion of participation to take place and for the proper facts and convincing evidence warranting a ministerial post to be available should it be proposed.

Functions and Services

The decision to participate in parliamentary elections also meant a natural acceptance of partaking in municipality elections,[1] for the latter not only represents the root of the former but is also more relevant to the provision of direct public services at the level of smaller entities: the village and the individual. Further, functions within the government's institutions differ from those within executive government, since implementation at the level of the municipality is bound by individual discretion according to the function in question. Some functions, such as management of the Casino du Liban or preparation for events such as the Miss Lebanon pageant, concerts, dancing revelries and so on, are considered sinful and are therefore prohibited. These are unlikely to be assumed in light of Islamic ideology. However, other functions pertaining to education, administration and so on are not problematic *per se*, and it is the right of every citizen to apply for and assume these positions based on merit.

Here lies the problem. Employment in Lebanon is subjected to a preset system of allocation and favouritism, not based on qualifications and merit. Sectarianism enters the formula to award some positions to one sect over another, taking into account the necessity of achieving the desired ratio of Muslims to Christians, and making the average acceptable score different for every sect. This denies the qualified from attaining their deserved positions, and burdens public administration with incompetent personnel. Individuals selected for public service employment

---

1. The first post-war municipality elections took place on May 24, 1998, thirty-five years after the last round (1963).

enjoy a particular sectarian-and-favouritism combination, or are blessed with positions for which no one is allowed to compete.

As such, being part of the executive governmental body assists in securing a certain portion of the lot that is the subject of allocation. Non-participation, as is the case with the Party, exposes those Hizbullah supporters to the most stringent of conditions when applying to the public service corps. This represents a major imbalance in the sectarian system, one that turns the state into a farm and splits citizens between supporters and opponents. The system that should be in place is one where only some specific positions are subjected to the government's political vision, while other public service functions are left to the public and awarded based on merit. This paves the way for true reform that rises on the shoulders of the qualified. Otherwise, the Lebanese government would always fail in the provision of appropriate public services to its citizens.

Administrative employment has transformed into political appointment, and Hizbullah simply refused to follow the trend of securing employment or public service benefits for the Party's supporters at the expense of political concessions that are not in agreement with the Party's religious and political beliefs. Frequent talk of the 'Lebanonization' of Hizbullah or of the Party's immersion in Lebanon's internal political life is only one other form of enticing abandonment of Party principles, of the priority awarded to resistance activity and confrontation with Israel. Such talk is directed at inducing the disarmament of Hizbullah and the surrender of its reasons for power. It is directed against the Party's rejection of a political compromise that is found to be inequitable to the Palestinian cause and to the detriment of the region.

Although positive towards the Resistance, the Lebanese political administration attempts to alienate it from internal political and public-service gains. This issue intersects with the natural competition among Shi'ite officials over posts available to the sect. Furthermore, international interests – especially the US's – add to the pressure exerted on the Party to substitute its resistance plan for public posts, services and financial support.

Upon the formation of the first al-Hariri government in 1992, these reservations were reciprocal. The Party perceived the prime minister's plan as a danger linked to political compromise, to a promise of a spring that would end resistance activity and pave the way for Lebanon's bilateral negotiations with Israel, with all the requisites that entails. The prime minister saw Hizbullah as an impediment to his plans and an opponent to his policies, considering the Party's existence to be a temporary inevitability and thus not needed in the realm of relationships. As such, the relationship began with tension between the two, and such a stance was openly declared.

With time, and with the obstruction of the political compromise process, both parties agreed to the necessity of bridging the gap with a relationship, for Hizbullah was represented in the government through its parliamentarians, who needed a form of dialogue with the cabinet while the latter needed their opinions on proposed legislation. Furthermore, the changing regional horizon made of Lebanon's political situation a particular and distinctive reality that assumed a bilateral political and practical benefit between the government and the Party. Convinced that mutual tension would come to no avail, preference was awarded to judgement through facts instead of building on apprehensions and suspicion. A new phase thus started between the two. Hizbullah's stance was based on a number of fixed premises: opposition and subsequently no votes of confidence for the government, despite the necessity for communication with the prime minister and cabinet ministers; and subsequently open declaration of issues on which the Party and the cabinet diverged, accompanied by explanations and validations, without reaching the point of conflict or rupture of relations. This change in approach was practically demonstrated at a time when the prime minister was expressing reciprocal accommodation.

Such change did not translate into facilitation of public service employment for the Party's supporters, nor did it mean better regional services, for these are factors of sectarian interests and partitioning or allotment frameworks practised amongst government officials. Given that Hizbullah has opted for working within the political mechanisms prevailing in the country and using them as channels for expressing acceptance, dissent, demands and disagreement, the Party has done whatever is necessary to allow for attending to the plights of the people based on the following two tenets:

1. Issues pertaining to public service and employment should not conflict with the priority concern for resistance activity. Should demands and political escalation lead to conflicts that distract attention from, impede or hinder the gathering of the populace around the Resistance and *jihad*, demands would be declined or submission would be the option, in protection of the Resistance and its interests.

2. Demands should achieve the desired targets, succeed

at recording a certain stance or work towards achieving cooperation with other groups in order to create circumstances conducive to the population's interests. However, where demands are transformed into internal bickering, trailing behind one or another group, or to a political step that recommends one faction or group over another without consideration of the people's interests, it is best to suffice with expressing a specific and candid stance and drop the pursuit of a dead-end matter dedicated to the strife of others.

Given the authoritative control of the government on labour and student unions as well as other such movements whose idols and representatives are clearly part of the regime, union activity that is free of political influence has become extinct – a situation bred within a framework of oscillating power between government officials. Such activist groups are thus bound by a margin of manoeuvre that is delineated by way of intra-governmental compromise, the paradox being that the government is itself responsible for impeding the activities of groups, squandering their effectiveness as independent movements and laying obstacles in the path of their activists. These facts result from agreements reached in the *coulisses* between various officials, to which key government members are witness and manage during times of conflict. As such, activist movements now progress through minefields. Recurring divides within the labour union, deliberate disintegration of syndicate and union alliances at major turns, and the eventual halt of union activities all bear witness to this effect. Such confusion within the activist domain, when viewed in tandem with the two tenets of Hizbullah's participation in government, reveals the reasoning behind the Party's stance, which was at times conservative and sometimes daring, earning the Party a reputation for extremism at the internal political level.

Blaming the Party for negligence on the internal front is unwarranted, as revealed through live evidence of Hizbullah's opposition to a real estate company's plans for uprooting 50,000 citizens from the Ouzai area, working to replace it with the Elyssar plan. Hizbullah opposed the establishment of a wholesale grocery market in the midst of the Ghobeiri residential area, resulting in the abandonment of the government plan. The Party insistently called for the set-up of the Baalbeck-Hermel Development Council and for an independent administrative governorship in that area, but only reached deadlock with the officials concerned.

Hizbullah advocated for teachers and labourers; brought forward the concerns of Middle East Airlines employees to avert their dismissal; worked to end the circulation of polluting diesel-powered vehicles while seeking an equitable solution for their owners and drivers; held two important conferences on the development of the Baalbeck-Hermel area and the liberated South, presenting two studies to the government (to no avail); and followed up on many public and private plights. When the Party rushed to the defence of Middle East Airlines employees, it was criticized; and when it stood against the erection of a bridge in the midst of Ouzai, a project detrimental to the area and which did not conform to the Elyssar plan, the Party was slandered. Lebanese political life is accustomed to this mode of interaction and vilification which leads to conflict, the status quo usually reinstated thereafter. Hizbullah's vision and approach differ markedly from this scenario, but such is the price of involvement in the political arena, a price the Party has attempted to keep at a minimum.

Perception of this resistance party that has turned to internal concerns arouses a peculiar discussion of Hizbullah's nature. This transformation was a source of confusion to many who had solely associated Hizbullah with the confrontation of Israeli occupation and its repercussions and with the achievement of a successful liberation. The Party is a resistance and a politicized body, a liberator and a servant of the people, one working in the political, cultural, social, educational, parliamentarian and other spheres. It is therefore a Party concerned with the plights of people at all levels, just as Islam draws the path for man at all levels.

True, the Party's concerns may tilt to one side over another given the circumstances. Lebanon's previous conditions did not allow for proper parliamentary elections, and as such Hizbullah was not concerned with parliamentary functions. Today, circumstances are so conducive, and Hizbullah has therefore entered the parliamentary turf with those convictions it holds dear, a move that contributed to the support and completion of those convictions. The Party's preparedness and level of response to the first round of parliamentary elections (1992) gave the impression that Hizbullah had changed its course and altered its priority concerns. But the declaration was clear at the time: parliamentary work would not affect the quest for *jihad*; it was, rather, complementary to and supportive of *jihad*.

Involvement in Parliament is complementary to Hizbullah's various roles. Experience bore out this declaration. Hizbullah's parliamentarians were effective in their endeavours, while the Resistance pursued its *jihad* mission also with success and efficacy. Work was therefore complementary within the Party's framework, the Party standing for religious beliefs, *jihad*, politics, culture and more.

It would be erroneous for Hizbullah to follow a one-track approach and neglect other practical functions, for then it would lose its Islamic particularity, which translates into a comprehensiveness of direction. There is a great difference between refusing to participate in an area and not being able to. It is justifiable not to undergo the parliamentary experience when objective hurdles make it impossible, or when a study of the givens and preparation for such an experience do not promise success. However, refusing the experience for the sake of restricting the Party's work to a set of cultural issues is an isolation of the Islamic practice from its other life aspects and an abandonment of the terrain to all other powers. Further, such action would only paint a partial impression of Islam's contribution to society, leading to negative repercussions.

Islam and Sectarianism

The Muslim-Christian Dialogue

The Lebanese milieu was surprised to see a Hizbullah delegation represented by the late parliamentarian Sheikh Khodor Tleis and Hizbullah Political Assembly member Nawaf al-Moussawi visiting Bkirke, the seat of the Christian Maronite Patriarch Mar Nasrallah Boutros Sfeir. This took place on December 1, 1992, with print media headlines and articles of the following day clearly demonstrating their astonishment. Two reasons were behind such surprise.

First, this was an unprecedented move for Hizbullah, which had never worked on such a relationship before, and which was besieged by a number of false claims and accusations concerning the Party's perception of Christians and its stance towards them. Second, this visit came following a long period of frozen relationships between the predominantly Muslim areas of West Beirut and the Maronite Patriarchal representation, which was largely due to political conflicts and the unstable relationships between Hizbullah and the emerging post-Taif Lebanese government. How could Hizbullah take the initiative for such a meeting within these circumstances?

Party leadership took this decision as part of an overall vision to open communication channels with all except those harbouring connections with Israel, as for instance the Lebanese Forces militia. It is well known that the nature of the relationship with the Maronite Patriarchy falls within the scope of Muslim-Christian dialogue and political ties with existing powers in the terrain. Achieving oneness between these two powers is not the aim; rather it is the identification of common denominators that assist in the realm of mutually significant issues and ensure amicable resolution of existing conflicts, notwithstanding of course the preservation by each party of its religious beliefs, particularities and overall visions, except for those visions that are prone to change.

Hizbullah decided that the meeting should be open and above-board, not of a traditional courtesy nature. Each party was to present all issues and speak out on all sources of agreement and conflict in order for a clear relationship to be founded. Parliamentarian Tleis summarized the issues discussed through a post-meeting declaration:

The meeting was fruitful. It was sufficiently clear and open for all parties to remain at ease. It was cited that detachment gives rise to estrangement while closeness is a source of cordiality [...] We have discussed many national and regional issues throughout the meeting, and discussion was deep, clear and candid. We have asked His Grace the Patriarch to request the Vatican and the Pope to open dialogue between Israel and the Vatican, pronouncing our concerns with respect to this issue. We also talked about the Muslim-Christian dialogue and general openness in Lebanon, assuring the Patriarch that we are dialogue seekers [...] We have also stressed that this Resistance which is defending our nation and country and which has successfully deterred the enemy from further expansionist occupation requires the support of all Lebanese individuals [...] We have also emphasized our view that cultural, political and religious freedoms in Lebanon are sanctified issues that should not be tampered with.[1]

As an expression of the continued relationship with Hizbullah, a Patriarchal envoy led by the Patriarch's assistant Roland Abou Jaoudeh visited Secretary General Nasrallah on January 22, 1993, whereby it was declared that this was a reciprocal visit to that initiated by the Party. Other meetings ensued and were either held directly with the Patriarch or through the joint committee created for that purpose. The relationship passed through phases of successive or intermittent communication, depending on circumstances and political stance, but preserved the original intended pace for permanence. His Grace the Patriarch expressed his respect for the Party despite divergence of opinion on a

---

1. *Al-'Ahd*, no. 441.

number of issues, stating that: 'unlike other political powers which say what they do not do, Hizbullah's words are not any different from its deeds.'

The notion of Christian apprehension of Muslims and Muslim feelings of inequitable treatment due to the politics of Maronite sectarianism are both responsible for many wars which befell Lebanon, the latest of which was the 1975 Lebanese civil war lasting fifteen years. Religious and political dialogue is of paramount importance. Religious dialogue is needed only at the general level, for discussion of theological beliefs is a sensitive area to explore, a turf charged with *a priori* barricading behind fixed convictions. It is thus important for dialogue to predominate and for a political relationship based on respect and equitable treatment of all citizens, on the fostering of peaceful coexistence with dialogue as the basic tenet, and on holding fast to the principle that Lebanon is for all and not for one or another division.

Hizbullah's relationships were not limited to one Christian wing. Many visits were made and relationships founded with all other Christian religious leaders, be they Orthodox, Catholic, Armenian, Assyrian or others. Further, relationships with Christian political leaderships were also initiated, Hizbullah always asserting its interest for associating with all wings and working towards whatever achieves a life of partnership among the Lebanese people in their one country. Just as it is unsuitable to deal with all Muslims as one entity with a single approach and prospectus, it is also inappropriate to consider all Christians as having one frame of mind and a single approach. It is also important to delineate the difference between political and religious dialogue, for each has its turf and its constituents. The requirements are for a political dialogue that transcends those unsolved religious obstacles, and for common objectives towards a unified nation to rest as a basis for all programmes and plans of cooperation between the concerned parties.

This approach was not free of problems, for sectarianism is quick to mingle with whatever is religious, turning into forms of tribal intolerance that are as far as could be from religion. Had the matter been confined to divine messages, relationships would have been smoother and results much better, for such divine doctrines have many commonalities. Moreover, many a religious banner has been hoisted in the name of Muslims and Christians that are as far as could be from practical religious implementation in both private and public life. This only serves to show that the ordeal originates from sectarianism and does not have roots in the divine messages.

In spite of this, it is important to transcend the sectarian hurdles in favour of cooperation, of the search for that which assembles and does not disperse, for whatever brings opinions together and does not alienate. It is important to do so even when the exertion is significant. Lebanon needs to be a stable abode for all Lebanese, where outsiders should not be allowed to interfere either on land or in the manner of living. Lebanon's particularity as a nation of various sects is an issue of paramount importance, and dialogue should be fostered to organize differences in lieu of submitting to the scams and desires of others.

Sectarianism versus Devoutness

The French and British mandates over Arab lands led to a partitioning of this region into smaller states that are not naturally split either geographically or ethnically, or even in terms of language. The area's customs, families and traditions very much intersect. Partitioning was based on the plans that both colonialist powers had laid out in order to safeguard their dominion and the interests of the parties that cooperated with them. Lebanon thus came under direct French custody given the country's Christian particularity.

Lebanon attained independence in 1943, and formed as one nation with several religious sects – eighteen altogether. A sectarian regime was formed whereby power was distributed among the various wings either by way of constitutional law or through common practice. A fifteen-year Lebanese war ensued, conducted in the name of Muslim-Christian sectarianism, hoisting banners of Christian apprehension in predominantly Muslim surroundings, the need to safeguard and develop internally acquired gains, and a Muslim feeling of inequitable treatment given a weak role in government disproportionate to the number of Muslims in Lebanon. There was also a regional banner linked to the Palestinian problem and its repercussions. What followed fifteen years thereon was the Taif Accord, which translated into a constitution abating the effect of prevalent norms and practices and transforming them into constitutional law as, for instance, was the case with troika distribution of power among three sects. Change also increased the cabinet's authority and shifted the distribution of parliamentary seats from a ratio of five to six between Muslims and Christians to a one-to-one distribution. The Taif Accord was the bridge towards ending the rebellion of Major General Michel Aoun and towards a new beginning for Lebanon marked by the organization of constitutional institutions, the launch of parliamentary elections, the unification of leadership for the Lebanese army, and the tearing down of obstacles between the various regions. The essence of the regime remained sectarian, however, and implementation was still subject to sectarian balance.

Within such a context, Hizbullah was formed in 1982 as a party adopting Islam as its fundamental creed and doctrine, viewing religion as a divine set of guidelines that encompass all heavenly-sent missions, all of which have been completely included in Islam, and calling for the implementation of such a doctrine in people's daily lives. Whoever abides by Islamic principles in both public and private life, at the level of religious belief and actual implementation, is considered a devout believer. It is thus not sufficient for one to be born Muslim or to have a Muslim parent in order for the banners of belief and abidance to be hoisted, for actual expression comes through visions, forms of worship and practical behaviour. The Holy Qur'an distinguishes between mere affiliation with Islam and actual belief:

> *The wandering Arabs say: 'We believe.' Say [unto them, O Muhammad]: 'Ye believe not, but rather say, "We submit", for the faith hath not yet entered into your hearts.'*[1]

Affiliation is compelled upon one at the time of birth, while belief is voluntary and based on free will. As such, affiliation and belief concur in a believer and do not do so in one who is Muslim simply for being born or registered as such. The call for abidance entails a call for both belief and devoutness.

Sectarianism, on the other hand, represents the association of individuals with a particular sect due to birth as such and therefore being partial to that sect for the mere fact of belonging

---

1. Surah no. 106, *al-Hujurat*, verse 14.

to it. This is akin to familial, tribal or regional fanaticism, the difference being in the title and the number of those involved. Given that the sectarian regime in Lebanon has fostered such faith-based affiliations and awarded every sect a number of privileges and gains, it is no wonder that the political, union, election, developmental, cultural and media turfs in Lebanon have all been affected by such an environment, and that many an aspect of such movements has been affected by confessional adherence. The pride of a Muslim's affiliation to the Muslim group thus no longer means abidance by *Shari'a* or doctrinal principles. The same is true for Christians, or rather for all sub-groups in Lebanon's Christian and Muslim worlds.

Candidacy for a parliamentary position bears a sectarian title, just as assuming a governmental position means benefiting from the portion assigned to a particular sect. Distribution of development projects across Lebanon takes into account the power balance among sects in those regions, and the appointment of key first-row governmental positions is closely associated with the population's sectarian distribution. As such, affiliation to and defence of sectarianism have become a norm. This, of course, was dragged into the political arena as the reason behind certain amicable or discordant political relations, for alliances and divergences based on internal sectarian or regional calculations affected the overall environment and created an atmosphere of constant disagreement and antagonism on many details – and behind the veil of sectarian interests lies private interest.

There is a fundamental difference between religious devoutness and sectarianism; the first is a form of compliance while the second denotes intolerance. Devoutness does not engulf all those pertaining to a particular sect; it is restricted to those few or many who practically comply with fundamental religious principles. Whoever labels devoutness as sectarianism, and does so for the mere fact that the religiously devout are Muslims, is on a false track. Hizbullah is therefore neither a sectarian party nor a party for a particular sect. It is a Muslim party founded on the system and order of the Prophet (PBUH) and His family of disciples, bearing a comprehensive vision, and grouping in its ranks all those who believe in its ideology and discipline irrespective of their sectarian affiliation at birth.

Some may call for following Christianity, which may represent a manifestation of missions rival to that of Islam. People once again fall captive to sectarianism, thus making the distinction between religion and sectarianism meaningless. This is an inadmissible predicament, since Christianity calls for worshipping and obeying God Almighty and for commitment to the Ten Commandments. Christianity is therefore an open call to avoid wrongdoing, to establish ethical education, and to abstain from the pleasures of life in this world in return for the gifts of the hereafter. This, in general, does not contradict Islam's call for worship, good ethics and straightness in life. However, the additional commitments in Islam derive from its comprehensiveness at the level of the social order. They also derive from the form of government and are not limited to behavioural guidance of the individual. As such, the Islamic system concurs with Christianity on many aspects pertaining to guidance of the individual. Nevertheless, a distinction exists in terms of the scope and comprehensiveness of the two religions, as we can deduce from the Divine Islamic message.

Hence, there is no reason to narrow the scope of our adherence to religion or refuse diversity and change, as the Islamic direction is not aimed at contradicting Christianity but rather at completing it.

Adherence to religion raises a virtuous citizen whose behaviour is reflected in his approach to society, for he is required to be reliable; impartial; honest; sincere; a working contributor to society whose religion deters him from committing the prohibited due to a strong faith in God Almighty's wakeful supervision, judgment and the Day of Resurrection. Whatever the effect of personal discipline or societal restrictions, nothing is more successful in shaping an individual's behaviour than religious faith. Hizbullah's achievements in the realm of Resistance against Israeli occupation, the provision of social services and the safeguarding of public interests through internal involvement in political life are but fruits of such faith. These should not be measured against a few religious slogans that were hoisted by some groups and which lack such meaning and such level of religious ethic. When the Lebanese Forces raised the cross as a slogan and focused on the sectarian dimension to gather supporters, they were not expressing the religious commitment that Christianity calls for.

The religious, *jihad*, political and social behaviour adopted by Hizbullah has offered a rich experience for twenty years now, which has contributed a new and influential meaning to Lebanese life through its presentation of a model that is applicable to the surroundings at least in some aspects. As such, religious devoutness can transcend the sectarian trap and remain a suggested path parallel to others. Let competition be over the fundamental principles such as our perspective of the universe, man and life. Let it not be a fanaticism countering other prevailing sectarian fanaticisms.

Consequently, the call for including religious topics as part of school education derives from the effect that religion has on breeding useful behaviour in life, as the problem never had its source in adherence to religion but rather in the lack of devoutness and in the efforts exerted towards exploiting religion. Should religious education form part of the sectarian game, and should we seek a common ground that would satisfy all sects, a cancellation of the integrated religious approach as it is presently perceived by those who believe in it would ensue, and a new sect would be created, which would deprive the doctrines of their roots and flatten them in such a way that drains their ability to be useful and effective in the cultivation of the individual.

It is very easy to be labelled partisan or sectarian in a country like Lebanon. The accusation provides a shortcut for some in their quest to neutralize an opponent. However, this is only ideological repression and a confiscation of liberties, especially since general political conduct usually reveals the essence of any proposal and uncovers true motives. Religious individuals prove their stance and thesis, while sectarians are denounced through their very sectarianism, especially where the weighing scale is built on principles and not parochialism.

It is also easy to launch slogans calling for the alienation of religion from the spectacle of life under the pretext of handling the sectarian problem in Lebanon. But reality proves that although many of the factional positions and powers hoist non-religious and secular banners, they are, at the same time, deeply rooted in sectarianism, a fact that is only evidenced through practical political behaviour. As such, who possesses the authority to distinguish between that which is religious and that which is sectarian? Who has the right to authorize public action and forbid it to sectarian movements? And why are the non-religious allowed, using weak arguments void of any solution for the existing sectarian reality, to freely express their ideas and convictions while the religious are not permitted to present their arguments?

One member of Parliament did put forward an idea for a legislative proposal that would annul the sectarianism of Lebanese factions. He saw in this an introduction to founding a Lebanese political life to replace the traditional sectarian distribution. By doing so, he plunged himself right in the midst of the sectarianism issue, for when the condition for abandoning party sectarianism is based on the percentage distribution of sectarian leaders, and where the number of members from a certain sect does not exceed a certain percentage, then the faith-based system applied in the state's institutions would have found its practical interpretation in the actual structure of the Lebanese parties. The presence of parties would thus be a presence of sectarian balance and not a contribution to Lebanese political life. Through this proposal, the problem of sectarianism would only be transferred from the level of the public political framework to the foundations of party infrastructure, making of confessional distribution an actual given in every Lebanese institution.

Moreover, who can give the legal cover for a secular party to operate in Lebanon while a religious party is denied such right under the pretext of confessional quandary? Freedom cannot be divided, and it is the right of all to express their views and beliefs on condition that force and subjugation are not used to impose such views. If secular parties are certain of the validity of their thesis, of their suitability to ameliorate political life, these parties should demonstrate practical proof in the field instead of seeking shelter behind laws needed to overcome the political obstacles of membership. We must dispose of the principle of provisional freedom that is applicable to one ideological set at the expense of another, for it is principle that we are concerned about and not the form behind which such ideas hide.[1]

Annulling political sectarianism is considered to be an optimal and sound prelude for alleviating the burdens of the system in Lebanon. It paves the way for the gradual dismissal of the obstacles causing inequality amongst citizens and leading to differences in the rights and obligations of one sect over another. It would also contribute to annulling sectarianism at the level of the civil service, which is currently based on distribution of the state's gains as shares. It should treat the mismanagement problem in order to reinstate the natural role of qualifications, and achieve equitable rights and obligations amongst citizens.

Moreover, we need not fear for the sects, since suitable laws that safeguard freedom of religion and worship can indeed be enacted. As for qualifications, they can be found in all sects, and if calculations were based on citizenship, the problem would no longer exist for the rule would apply to all. The lesson is in playing the part for the sake of the country instead of allowing the interests of certain groups to rip it apart. A calm and objective

1. Western democracies have often failed the test of freedom of expression, as when some students wearing headscarves were denied enrolment in French and German public schools under the pretext that such dress is a demonstration of religious ceremony that challenges the traditions of Western society. This was done despite the knowledge that this dress code is a part of faith and not a form of competition for a slogan. They also failed to recognize the freedom of the other when they stood up to the Islamic movements in Algeria and some other countries, discrediting their elections under the pretext of an impending Islamic danger. As a result, a lot of suffering has come about in these countries which persists today.

study, supported by evidence, launched through dialogue, and based on identification of those risks inherent in the details as opposed to generalizations and misgivings, should accomplish a suitable project with a proprietary mechanism, however long it takes. Haste is not called for, while negligence only worsens this sectarian system that is unable to put forth appropriate solutions to our issues, and which bears inside it factors for its own collapse and the weakness of its citizens' solidarity.

There is no connection between annulling political sectarianism and the personal status law. This law organizes social relations between a couple and their children in the context of marriage, divorce, inheritance and general matters pertaining to couples. In Islam, this is divine law, not a special jurisprudence that can be changed or replaced. For what God Almighty legalizes cannot be considered prohibited by anyone, and what God Almighty prohibits cannot be legalized by anyone. It was mentioned in the Prophetic tradition: 'What Prophet Muhammad (PBUH) permitted will remain permissible until Judgment Day, and what he forbade will remain forbidden until Judgment Day'.[1]

The personal status law has no effect on the public political system. Some secularists seek its cancellation in order to break one of the basic tenets of religious commitment, one that has become entrenched in general customs even amongst the non-religious and has become the basis for protecting against a drift outside the circle of religion. Some Christian wings use the question of the personal status law as a margin for manoeuvre, for they are

---

1. As told by Imam al-Sadek (PBUH), quoted from al-Hurr al-Aamili in *Important Chapters in the Principles of the Twelve Infallible Imams*, vol. 1/643.

well aware of Muslims' adherence to it on the basis of legitimacy. They pose it as a medium of exchange: an untouched personal status law in return for unbothered political sectarianism and retaining the basic foundations of the sectarian system.

Civil Marriage

Former Lebanese President Elias al-Hrawi adopted a bill related to the personal status law and to optional civil marriage,[1] meaning for it to become a law applicable in Lebanese courts alongside those personal status laws applied by both Muslims and Christians. Motives were entirely in the realm of addressing a civil matter: the lack of such a law drives some Lebanese couples abroad so they can get married in accordance with the civil laws prevailing in some foreign countries.

This reality obliges our competent national civil courts to apply those foreign laws under which marriage contracts were signed. However, this is to the detriment of the principle of Lebanese sovereignty in the field of legislation. Besides, it imposes financial burdens on citizens. Some Lebanese people – protected by the freedom of choosing one's creed – change their sect within the same religion and sometimes entirely change their religion in a bid to disavow the consequences of marriage within the framework of the governing sectarian law. This also does wrong to legal and social stability. Hence, the motives ended up considering that 'the state is responsible for providing an atmosphere that contributes to the fostering of a national blend', which means that this bill is considered the necessary pillar for the practical cancellation of sectarianism.

---

1. The full text of this bill was published in *as-Safir*, February 6, 1998.

A defect already exists in allowing a marriage contract to be signed outside Lebanon. As we shall later prove, the same consequences prevail at the civil marriage level as those prevailing in Lebanon. Given a sectarian framework, disowning the outcome of a marriage will always occur, for civil marriage law is only optional and a couple might choose not to apply it, a matter which renders the above-mentioned motives void. A comparison between civil marriage and legitimate Islamic marriage will clarify the negative social effects resulting from civil marriage and show the objective reasons behind refusing it.

Civil marriage is a contract concluded between a male and a female, entailing rights and obligations; it bears aspects that cover the span of their marriage life and that comprehensively cover the elements of personal status. In other words, civil marriage is not merely a contract signed in front of a civil judge. Those who choose civil marriage do so for the conditions and effects it entails, not because of its relative ease of achievement.

Islamic marriage is also a contract signed between a male and a female and on which legitimate rights and obligations are imposed. It is accomplished through an affirmative answer from both sides. It is practically easier than a civil marriage; the presence of a clerk during the signing of the marriage contract is only to ensure validity, and the attendance of two witnesses[1] at the court is merely for legal registration. However, the guidelines governing a religious marriage differ from those of a civil marriage.

A number of steps and effects apply to religious marriage, and could be either formalities or fundamentals. They are interpreted

---

1. According to the Jaafari faith, the marriage contract is accomplished and considered true without the attendance of two witnesses, while the presence of two witnesses is obligatory according to the Sunnis.

as the foundation principles, rights and obligations. The contract, for instance, requires a specific oral phrase. It cannot be made valid by merely saying 'I want you to be my wife [or husband]', or if it is accomplished so as to show acceptance of the two parties. Rather, the marriage is founded on the wife's positive answer with these particular words: 'I marry you upon a dower worth ...'; the man should accept by saying: 'I accept.'

Choosing an Islamic marriage translates into acceptance of all the Islamic laws applicable to the organization of personal status. Moreover, a couple need not obtain legal consent, for the contract is in itself that consent. The couple can also add a number of conditions that are permissible under Islam and that do not contradict with permanent principles.

The contract requires the couple to be committed to their legitimate rights and obligations. Guardianship in running the family is borne by the husband, and it is he who should spend on his wife and children even where the woman is wealthy. The wife is not obliged to spend while living in her husband's house; it is a matter of choice. Should irreconcilable differences occur between a couple where divorce is deemed to be the only solution, the latter would only be effective and true where the husband states to his wife, with or without mentioning her name, the words 'You are divorced.' Wording is essential, or else the divorce is not effective. The divorce procedure also requires the presence of two just witnesses.[1]

A religious marriage contract also includes inheritance obligations. If the husband dies without children, his wife inherits one quarter of his wealth; where there is at least one child, the wife inherits one-eighth of her husband's wealth. If the deceased

---

1. According to the Jaafari faith.

husband has many children, a male's share of an inheritance is equivalent to that of two females.

If divorce occurs, a mother has the right to foster her son for two years, and her daughter for seven years, after which it is up to the man to foster and cultivate the children. Expenditure is a responsibility to be borne by the man throughout the period of custody. These details and many others are considered legal responsibilities of Islamic marriage.

The rules of civil marriage are different, although some concur with those of religious marriage. They also differ from one country to another and from one law to another. Differences between the two forms of marriage can be understood from the bill proposed by President al-Hrawi.

According to Article 20 of the proposed bill: 'The wife has to contribute to home expenditure if she possesses money', meaning if she is rich or is generating an income. She is therefore considered a partner to her husband in spending. However, Islamic rules consider expenditure to be a duty of the husband; the wife should not spend at all. Where the wife shares with her husband the burdens of the family, such an act would be voluntary, not a duty, and he cannot force her to spend. According to this article, however, she is obliged to do so.

Another difference is detected in Article 34 of the proposed civil marriage law: 'The wife is forbidden to remarry before 300 days have passed after breaking the marriage.' In Islam the so-called *iddat* or period of waiting is three menstruation cycles, or three months, while in the case of the husband's death the wife can remarry after four months and ten days. The proposed bill made the waiting period ten months, and this, we believe, is unfair to the woman, for it is a long period that is not linked to determining whether the wife had been pregnant or not prior to divorce or to her husband's death. Such a long waiting period has no justification and should be discretionary.

Article 73 differs fundamentally from Islamic doctrine. It is concerned with adoption: 'Adoption is a juridical contract that establishes rights of legitimate foster sons and daughters with their foster parents.' This means that the adopted child becomes a legitimate child and enjoys all rights accordingly. In Islam, however, an adopted child cannot be a legitimate child.

According to civil law, if a married couple adopts a boy and later gives birth to a girl, she will naturally be deemed his sister. Article 83 states that 'new prohibitions that hinder marriage arise between the parents and their relatives on the one hand and the adopted child on another.' This means that the adopted child cannot marry his foster sister, and she must act as a sister does towards her brother. However, under Islam, she is not his sister and he may marry her, and as such she will behave towards him not as a brother but as an outsider.

Under civil marriage, the adopted child has full rights; if either parent dies, the adopted child is entitled to an inheritance alongside his foster brothers and sisters and under the same conditions. Under Islam, the adopted child is denied inheritance. This is how rights are mixed up and lost, for what is allowed in *Shari'a* or Islamic law is prohibited in civil marriage and vice versa.

The Holy Qur'an contains verses forbidding adoption:

> *Allah hath not assigned unto any man two hearts within his body, nor hath He made your wives whom ye declare [to be] your mothers, nor hath He made those whom ye claim [to be] your sons. This is but a saying of your*

mouths. But Allah sayeth the truth and He soweth the way. Proclaim their real parentage. That will be more equitable in the sight of Allah. And if ye know not their fathers, then [they are] your brethren in the faith, and your clients.[1]

These are verses that flatly prohibit us to consider the adopted child as an actual legitimate child, as in doing so we would be pursuing proscribed acts of pre-Islam.

The rules of civil marriage are different from those of legitimate Islamic marriage, and there is no possibility of harmonizing the two systems. The wording is sufficiently different between the two to warrant expectations of further difficulties upon implementation.

Mixed Marriage

Islamic law permits a man to marry a woman who adheres to another revealed religion (Christianity or Judaism). Some scholars are, however, very reserved in this regard, and tend to forbid this matter. Nevertheless, other scholars permit it and consider marriage between a Muslim man and a Christian or Jewish woman to be a forthright legitimate matter. But the basic problem which all Muslims, Sunni and Shi'ite , unanimously agree upon, is that a Muslim woman cannot marry a Christian or Jewish man, the act being labelled as a sin and the marriage considered void from the Islamic point of view. The relationship is seen as mere adultery. However, civil marriage law sees this relationship as a natural one, for the civil code is simply bound by a different set of rules.

---

1. Surah no. 33, *al-Ahzab*, verses 4–5.

The true wisdom behind such a constraint was revealed through many a discussion. A Christian or Jewish man does not originally recognize Islam as a divine religion – speaking here from a sheer religious point of view and not from a political standpoint. Further, this matter does not refer to the social relations that Islam fosters, encourages and respects. A Christian or Jewish man does not recognize the Prophet Muhammad (PBUH). Although every person bears responsibility towards his religion, when a marriage is established with a man who does not recognize his wife's Prophet, it is almost certain that he will not maintain her religion, nor will he leave her with the choice to abide by her faith. All restraints would be removed, and there would be no guarantee that the wife would keep to her convictions and her religion if she so wishes. However, when a Muslim man marries a Christian or Jewish woman, the latter can always maintain her religion, for Islam recognizes the prophets Moses and Jesus (PBUT). The problem is thus no longer such, and the marriage can be appropriately conducted.

A sound solution for our Lebanese society requires examination of the real problems in lieu of creating new ones. The number of Lebanese people with mixed-marriage problems is low, and as such does not warrant the enactment of laws for a small portion of society the effects of which on family unity (or disunion, for that matter) will be substantial. This subject is not related to religious adherence, whether to Islam or to Christianity, but rather to convictions. Problematic circumstances may result from marriages where a couple rarely shares the same opinions. Such marriages usually do not last long, eventually ending in divorce.

Islam prohibits mixed marriage between a Muslim woman and

a Christian or Jewish man, mainly being due to harmony being the foundation on which all marriages should be built in order to ensure internal stability for children, and because safeguarding the well-being of marital life is a prerequisite for preserving the interests of the marriage.

Some may change their religion in order to get married, considering their conviction in the other as being more important than their religious belief. This would be an entirely personal matter; such people have sought a solution to their problems in line with their beliefs and ability to commit. They thus bear the load of those legal responsibilities and duties that such a decision entails, and in doing so do not tamper with social balance. However, we do not advocate a change in religion for the sake of a marriage based on fervour and passion.

The educational repercussions of the proposed civil marriage law are a threat to family structure and unity. Should it be an obligatory form of marriage (as opposed to being optional), its effects on family disintegration would be wider and more precarious.

The proposed bill for optional civil marriage in Lebanon is a step towards secularizing the personal status law and distancing religion from the arena of daily life. The great majority of Lebanese people do not support it as a solution.[1] Legitimate Islamic marriage has always protected the family, serving to spare society those crises faced for instance by the West, where civil laws governing marital relations have resulted in millions

---

1. An opinion poll carried out by *As-Safir* newspaper in 1998 revealed that 69.5 per cent of the population opposed optional civil marriage. Percentages across religions differed: 88 per cent of Sunnis opposed, as did 81 per cent of the Shi'is, 42 per cent of Maronites, 36 per cent of Orthodox, 52 per cent of Catholics and 57 per cent of Druze.

of children living at orphanages. Although efforts to organize these orphanages and to create near-family atmospheres therein are numerous, these homes are still a source of many personality complexes. The solution lies in strict laws protecting the family entity from disintegration, legal confusion, of the intertwinement of rights with obligations.

One problem plaguing Lebanon is the penetration of sectarianism into every aspect of a citizen's life. Sectarianism is used as a legitimate key for political and social promotion, an introduction to fanaticism that may doom the country or foster partitioning and public corruption. Sectarianism also creates imbalances in the political compass of some groups. The Taif Accord called for forming a national board to terminate political sectarianism,[1] and the first step in this direction should call for practices that do not single people out on the basis of their religious identity, but which award every individual equal rights and obligations before the law. This is the minimum solution for a harmonious regime able to accommodate a variety of sects.

Islamic Movements and the Question of Unity

The spread of Islam intensified in the lands where it originated during the last two decades of the twentieth century. It accompanied the effects of the Islamic revolution in Iran that urged the adoption of the Islamic option. In addition, the prevailing frustrations that followed the failure of partisan and factional experiences, all harbouring various ideological lines from

---

1. Paragraph 2 (g) of the Lebanese National Accord, published by the Lebanese National Assembly in 1989.

the extreme right to the extreme left, fostered Islam as an option. The rise of Islam was also accompanied by the Soviet Union's failure to protect the Communist project – the inspiring symbol for communist movements. Islam rose, too, as imperialist Western democracies failed in their disguise behind shining slogans and exposed their true intentions. Finally, Islam grew after nationalist movements, so popular in the Arab world, failed to market their ideologies and tap popular emotions.

Attempts to uproot Islamic conduct, fervour, and adherence to specific customs and traditions went in vain. Bitter experiences invoked the latent longing for identification with one's natural origins and for return to Islam. Extensive Islamic activity proliferated throughout the region.

The various emerging Islamic movements – or the old movements that returned with renewed vitality or spirit – did not share the same principles or working mechanisms, and at times differed markedly. Some considered their counterparts infidels and apostates, while others considered all Islamic movements – except themselves – to be unbelievers.

It is impossible to evaluate those Islamic movements as representations of the Islamic trend or vision. In all fairness, they should be distinguished from each other, evaluated separately or as a group where common ideological ground exists for such evaluation. Islamists themselves denounce the attitudes of some Islamic movements, and at times proclaim these to have deviated from Islam's true representation in a major way. It would be malicious of politicians or researchers to perceive all Islamic movements as one entity. They aim to profit from the mistakes or deviations of some Islamic movements in order to harm others, which falls back on their *a priori* perception of Islam and their refusal of its ideology.

Perceiving all Islamic movements as one entity is the easiest way to topple them all on the basis of apparent similarity.

The Algerian experience, for instance, was bitter and complicated, and had inauspicious consequences. Some of those Islamists who inappropriately engage in armed conflict bear the responsibility for the outcome, as do the regime's officials, for they nurtured hostility against the Islamists and falsely accused them of carrying out certain actions, publicizing these in many French, British and US reports. Further, local and international circumstances had led to the abolition of municipality elections in Algeria, and the people's expression of choice through parliamentary elections – the results of which were in favour of the Islamists – was denied under the pretext that the Islamists would pose a threat in an oil-producing country and the largest country in North Africa.

The Algerian experience is not a good representation of all Islamist experience. Some Islamists in Algeria do not support armed violence against the regime, and reject this approach. They disagree with other Islamic wings, but their voices either go unheard or are not allowed to rise in the first place. As such, no other voice remains but that of the extremists, which justifies the strike against Algeria's Islamic movement with all its moderate and extremist branches. Hence, the Algerian experience is specific only to that country.

Under the leadership of Imam Khomeini, Iran laid the foundations for an Islamic state based on popular choice and without the need to resort to a military coup or to foreign intervention. In spite of all the oppositions that the new revolution faced, the experience was successful. Both East and West fought against it through the Iran-Iraq war that was imposed on the Islamic Republic for eight years, which had as a major aim the toppling of the new Islamic revolution. Iran's experience was a success and continued to present a model of an Islamic state that is in line with the modern era. Iran chose an electoral voting system that confirmed the choice of the people; it made available the opportunity for wide internal dialogue and for a representation of diversity, all while maintaining the laws of the sacred *Shari'a* on which basis state systems and constitutions were codified.

Iran's revolution is a contemporary one. It ushered in the modern era's new developments from the Islamic standpoint and vision, and drew the interest of many who were concerned with Islam as a model to be studied and an example to be followed. In view of its power and capability to withstand challenges, it instigated debate in the West. The case in point was the extent to which Iran could draw and attract a vast section of the Islamic world.

Therefore, we cannot introduce the experience of Algeria as a unique, representative example of the approach used by Islamic movements. In fact, no single experience can be presented as one that symbolizes all. The experience of each of Iran, Algeria, Afghanistan and others are distinct. The name of Islam may not be linked to violence, killing and massacres; the religion is a representation of tolerance, virtuousness, humanity and free choice at its best. Islamic movements that commit mistakes in their approach are the only parties responsible for such mistakes, for Islam's teachings are very clear. As Commander of the Faithful Imam Ali (PBUH) put it: 'God's religion is not identified through men but through the marvel of right. Know what right is and you will come to know its adherents'.[1]

Many of the concepts being considered today as pertaining to Western regimes are identical to those previously introduced and spelled out by Islam: human rights, freedom of choice, respect of beliefs, and so on. These form the basic fundamentals of Islamic law. Whereas the Western world has taken heed of these categories and applies them throughout Western countries as would befit particular interests, Islam has called for these principles to be a foundation for all humanitarian practice: *We sent thee not save as a mercy for the peoples.*[2]

Islam considered man as the pivotal axis of all *Shari'a* laws. Man represents the central point and the value of essence amongst all of life's creatures:

> *Verily We have honoured the children of Adam. We carry them on the land and the sea, and have made provision of good things for them, and have preferred them above many of those whom We created, with a marked preferment.*[3]

Man is the successor of God Almighty on earth, for as is mentioned in the verses, God Almighty said to the angels: *I am about to place a viceroy in Earth.*[4] This viceroy was meant to be an exemplary human who is committed to the divine teachings, to those established humanitarian rights that the infallible Imam Zein al-Aabideen (PBUH) has described in his *Message of Rights* that included fifty privileges in different fields.

---

1. Sheikh al-Mufid, *al-Amali*, p. 5.
2. Surah no. 21, *al-Anbiya'*, verse 107.
3. Surah no. 17, *al-Isra'*, verse 70.
4. Surah no. 2, *al-Baqara*, verse 30.

Islam also gave man the freedom of choice, as faith is a question of belief that requires an individual's voluntary, unforced conviction. It is only through such freedom that values, rights and obligations can rest on firm bases. Even if people differ in their adherences or commitments to the revealed religions, they are respected for their acts of worship, whether performed in a mosque or a church. It is not within anyone's rights to interfere and force change or modification of faith, for such is the freedom of belief that every individual has a right to enjoy.

Moderation and Extremism

Western, and particularly US, attempts to accuse Islamic movements of fundamentalism, extremism and terrorism are aimed at paving the way for taking ideological control of the Islamic world. This aim is brought forward in a way that is conducive to the targets of political, economic and military dominion. It was from this seed that the attributes 'moderation' and 'extremism' were born. The US and the West generally brand some regimes as 'moderate' for the mere fact that they suffice themselves with Islamic slogans and acquiesce to a framework of extreme subordination to hegemony. Moreover, Islamic movements are considered extremist merely where their visions and interests are in confrontation with international hegemony. Clear definitions are now required to classify both types of movements and regimes. Thus, if the term 'moderation' were an expression of a pure and honest Islamic notion that invites people to Islam through wisdom and good sermons, if it signifies adherence to Islamic principles and ethics and to refusing tyranny and for a call to legitimate self-defence and rejection of occupation, then Hizbullah would be considered moderate. Whatever contradicts these characteristics is viewed as extremism, including distorting the reputation of Islam; uncivil behaviour; oppressing others; and killing the innocent. This delineation applies to Islamic movements and to every party or faction in the world that behaves inhumanely.

Labelling resistance movements that struggle against occupation in Lebanon and Palestine as 'extremist' simply because they fight Israeli occupation is merely a political standpoint and not a depiction of the essential nature of such movements. Such a political description is of no significance for it falls within the realm of conflicting interests and diverging values. This is what imperialist regimes have made us accustomed to, and here let us pause to consider: who appointed these regimes as guardians or arbitrators with a right to award people, movements and regimes certificates of good political and ideological conduct? Do they have a right to speak of moderation and extremism, when they themselves stand accused of colonialism, imperialism and the subjugation of people?

Hizbullah made great strides in terms of liberating the larger part of occupied Lebanon. The Party enjoyed tremendous public support and the esteemed backing of political authorities, religious figures and factional powers. Hizbullah was further committed to restraint during the various liberation phases, to refraining from any acts of vengeance, despite its power and the standing that the Party enjoyed. Nevertheless, this Party could not evade the smearing labels chosen by US-Israeli politics: 'extremism' and 'terrorism', labels lacking in the simplest logical and realistic evidences. But then again, this is only befitting of the hegemony and domination approach expressed time and again through the US-Israeli standpoint. It is another attempt to impose those policies drafted for Lebanon and the region.

General defence of Islamic movements does not exempt them from the obligation to review their objectives and approach, to evaluate their experience at the level of the people and of their countries' regimes. Sufficient openness and dialogue should be made possible among these movements in order for those bright experiences to simmer through. Dialogue needs to be conducted not against a background of assimilation and accommodation but rather with a spirit for improvement, correction of mistakes and achieving advancement in order to reach contemporary aspirations.

A difficulty is posed when conducting such a dialogue. Many Islamic movements bound themselves to fanatic restrictions and particularities that promote party and sectarian zeal and stifle effective cooperation. However, it is required from these movements to make at least the smallest of steps in the direction of dialogue; they should make use of any window of opportunity for constructive collaboration, for this would eventually be reflected on the nation of Islam, which longs for the Islamic view. Our nation should recognize its true enemies rather than confronting fabricated illusory foes that are drawn to represent other Islamic movements. Falling prey to such confusion benefits only the enemy, who thrives on our internal differences and on intolerable extremism.

It is obvious that acquaintance between Islamic movements is very weak, even where these movements are similar; perhaps knowledge of the other does not even exist or is limited to superficial and passing communication. Yet, there are many issues that require understanding and assistance: benefiting from successful experiences; exchanging advice on public affairs; and agreement on common causes that affect the whole nation, the most notable being the Palestinian cause, and many other issues.

The question is not linked to the sensitivity of regimes in different countries, for a margin of particularity remains and should remain. The suggestion is not for Islamic movements to share their particularities, for such sharing of strategies is not appropriate. Rather, the aim is to arouse concern about the common public causes at the level of the nation of Islam. This is necessary, and should be achieved within boundaries that are harmonious with the capability and particularity of each country and as is deemed fit by the Islamic movement in each country.

Spreading the Hizbullah Experience

Some have put forth the idea of spreading the Hizbullah experience of Lebanon to other countries through the establishment of Party branches within a centralized framework. Council examined this idea and in a short time concluded with a refusal, the main reasons being the following:

1. The responsibility for taking action and the mechanisms for such action are bound to the population of each country. Those interested should bear the responsibility of establishing an appropriate Islamic party, since national particularities differ and drawing delicate similarities is not possible. If initiators in one country aspire to benefit from a practice carried out in another, they can always gather the relevant information and become acquainted with what may enable

them to establish their own party, drawing on those inspiring goals and experiences that may enrich their movement.

2. Other Islamic movements and parties may already exist in these countries, which could instigate some sensitivity towards a new party with a foreign administration. Further, establishment might appear as an attempt to take advantage of Hizbullah's history in order to marginalize the role of other existing local parties, which may also create inter-party disputes in the operational field and therefore undermine the possibility of achieving practical results. In addition, the regime of a particular country may become sensitive towards an 'imported' party and target it, hindering its progression.

3. Individuals establishing this party would be in the phase of development, and their level of performance and popularity would not portray those achievements realized in Lebanon following a long history of work and struggle. As such, a false and incomplete impression may be given, which would charge the original party (Hizbullah) with certain responsibilities that are not rightfully warranted.

It is natural for many to be drawn to the notion of transmitting the successful experience of Hizbullah to another country. This may seem a relatively easy endeavour. However, many objective obstacles exist, and consideration of what is safer and more suitable under the current circumstances of the Islamic world make it more plausible for each country to have its own party, commanded and based from within, which could build appropriate relations with other parties as part of its programme and movement. This should serve the introduction of the Islamic project better, as adherence would be generated from within in the form of local support.

Objectors to this formula may find that the universality of Islam does not accept such division. What they neglect to consider is that universality in thought, conduct and general objectives is not at odds with pursuing suitability of implementation for every time and place. Such attention to appropriateness helps achieve the desired effective presentation for the Islamic project, in lieu of a canned, limited vision of Islam that is imposed irrespective of changes and special circumstances. In addition, Islam has a margin of freedom for organizational procedures and for the particularity of performance in a manner that maintains the firm principles of the religion untouched. Furthermore, since the goal is not related to expanding the leadership or organization of a certain party but to achieving objectives, these lines or parties should choose what is appropriate for them. The problem can be resolved, too, by settling for the centralism of the Jurist-Theologian, who lays down the general rules for the nation of Islam. As such all other implementation details would be left to each different country.

Communication between the Islamic parties in different countries can be established in a manner that is conducive to all. Whether through regular meetings, conferences or bilateral contacts, ideas and advice can be exchanged and the experience of each party can be brought forward for others to benefit from.

Unity of Coordination and Practical Unity

Achieving Islamic unity between the Sunnis and Shi'is in different countries and at all levels is one of Hizbullah's fundamental goals. This message is evidenced in God Almighty's words: *And hold fast, all of you together, to the cable of Allah, and do not separate.*[1] Yet unity does not mean the complete annulment of religious, factional or regional particularities for the sake of achieving unison in ideology and approach. In fact, the mere adoption of this grand title or goal does not annul the justifications for diversity in the interpretation and understanding of Islam, the approach adopted or the leaders selected.

For many centuries, differences have existed among scholars on the interpretation of doctrinal principles. Methods and priorities were drawn according to differences in experience, horizons of awareness, and educational and applied backgrounds. It is therefore inappropriate to ponder the goal in an unrealistic or subjective manner. Distinction exists within the one faith, among the Islamic movements within one country, and between the scholars of one region. There is no harm in maintaining diversity as long as it remains within the circle of free choice that is based on individual or group convictions and that does not transcend to the realm of conflict, fighting and accusations of blasphemy. This is especially true given the impossibility of annulling diversity, as this is human nature and a result of many objective, personal, educational and environmental factors.

By unity we mean the search for common ground at the practical level, that which assembles and leads to cooperation, coordination and unification of efforts within the public sphere of

---

1. Surah no. 3, *al-'Imran*, verse 103.

common issues. A united force of Muslims must come together in the face of threats and challenges. Such common causes and goals can be specified, as can the practical mechanisms of cooperation be drawn according to the degree of each side's ability, levels of conviction and particular characteristics. Cooperation should open new horizons that were not obvious before, and should create a cordial environment among the various wings.

Unity is not limited to determining the framework of cooperation and coordination. In some cases, it can be achieved through an initiative that any one side may take following conviction or a comprehensive vision that is not restricted to direct private concerns, but goes beyond to include concerns of the Islamic world. The initiative would then be voluntary, not as a result of demand or prior coordination, but rather as part of the normal duty of bearing public concern and of an awareness of the impact that any specific movement or action may have on all. This a practical form of unity. Both combine to achieve the common goal.

What is happening today in Palestine, for instance, is a cause of concern for all Muslims although the direct impact is far greater on Palestinians. The marked rally of support that we see in favour of Israel indicates the level of significance that the dominating powers award, despite their diverging interests, to establishing the Zionist entity at the expense of the Palestinian people, not forgetting of course those goals which stretch beyond Palestine to the entire Middle East region.

Since Palestine and Jerusalem represent the worthiest cause, the support of which is unquestionably legitimate, it is our duty to gather our capacities and divergent wings in order to support it with all possible means. And here lies the importance of unity. It calls in part for the coordination of efforts and resources through meetings and discussions to delineate methods of support, the composition of a unified standpoint and identification of essential ideas. Taking into consideration the circumstances of participants, their potential, the extent of their interests and priorities, is of importance. This 'unity of coordination' requires direct contact between the various wings, whether intense or intermittent. Another form of unity is demonstrated through expression of a political position, a personal or subjective step derived from convictions and priorities without coordinating with others, but in line with whatever serves the Palestinian cause. This is what we call 'practical unity'.

Hizbullah launched its field confrontational activity against Israel through an Islamic Resistance built around the priority and principle of expelling Israeli occupation. Many achievements realized in Lebanon were reflected on the Palestinian reality. Hizbullah also expressed its belief in liberating all parts of Palestine, and undertook political, operational and mobilization measures towards this goal, thus meeting with the *Intifadah* within the framework of practical unity. Many coordination meetings were held with various Palestinian factions, as many as bilateral or group meetings could be. Results were manifested in terms of support and cooperation using whatever methods and potentials could be mustered and in accordance with objective and appropriate circumstances.

What has been mentioned about the Palestinian cause applies to all the other legitimate causes with a practical difference that hinges on the extent of their importance and the availability of means for cooperation. The rush of superpower hegemony into our countries to loot our wealth and deprive us of will and independence requires us to forge a unity by which we arm ourselves. The challenge is to confront the unification of dominant powers around the US in support of its expansionist and dominating projects.

By objecting to US foreign policy in the region and the attacks on Iraq, Libya and Afghanistan, decrying the exploitation of oil wells and the domination of the strategic spots in the region, Hizbullah would be practically united with opponents of US policy. In addition, when it does not submit to the threats that aim at changing Party policies and positions on many issues, Hizbullah would also be expressing unity with opponents of US policy. Moreover, when the Party cooperates with other sides to boycott American goods, issue positions, and carry out common public activities, it would be expressing unity of coordination with these wings.

It is quite apparent that the circle of unity is wide. With some, unity can be realized owing to one form of expression, while with others it may require many other forms. It can produce immediate results in some cases, and offer a modest contribution in others. Unity is sometimes limited to the theoretical, but it can also accumulate useful practical results.

The benefits of unity are countless. So there is no need to waste effort interpreting its dimensions. Its field stretches widely for those who want to take steps towards it, so it is pointless to narrow its scope and complicate the explanation of its expressions. There is no excuse for any side to unilaterally assume charge of the nation's affairs, or to be isolated from the general course, for every side is bound to need others at some critical point, and may not find them.

Nevertheless, this does not hinder conducting a calm and

constructive dialogue to work out those cultural, political, theoretical and practical differences. In addition, dialogue should be restricted to attaining benefits – not to evoking sensitivities and discord. It should deal with subjects that are considered priorities and which might bear the possibility of bringing different opinions closer or modifying them. Dialogue should also be conducted between individuals who accept it irrespective of where it may lead. Whether it leads to solutions or to a further deepening of differences, it should not cease to represent a continuum of cooperation and communication, without turning into a scorecard for futility.

We should not be apprehensive of dialogue or its results. We must be brave enough to follow through in its course, take into consideration the conditions stated above, and break the deceptive rigidity of 'always being right', thus unleashing the mind for a wider reach of open legitimate choices.

Kidnapping Foreigners

The Lebanese state lost its central authority during the war years of 1975–90. At one point, it was divided into two administrations (between 1988 and 1990), and authority was distributed amongst factional, militia and partisan powers across the different regions. Many groups with their own agendas developed. Despite the foundation of the Joint Forces within a framework of a national movement in the so-called West Beirut region where the Muslims and the PLO were based, and despite the launch of the Lebanese Forces in East Beirut where Christians, the Liberal Party, the Guardians of the Cedar and other similar groups were, the performance of any group or party inside any one of the two regions did not necessarily express the commitment of all others to it. Deeds and actions were charged to only one wing or militia, others not sharing in the liability. A partial or complete uncovering of an act was at times insignificant to many factions. Given numerous centres of power, the complicated relations between the factions and authorities, and the lack of one central reference point, many events took place as a natural consequence of a troubled region in which all the colours of the political spectrum and of military and security presence could be found. Such events included kidnapping, the very approach to which revealed many issues:

1. A series of kidnappings extended throughout the Lebanese civil war, from beginning to end. Among the earliest incidents was that of June 1975, when Colonel Ernest Morgan, head of planning at the US military aid mission, was kidnapped. Then followed the abduction of three French guards at the French embassy in West Beirut (July 1976); three Irish soldiers from the Irish battalion in South Lebanon (December 1988); and, in August of 1991, the Frenchman Jérome Liro. In a January 1989 report titled 'The Price of War', the Lebanese daily newspaper *Al-'Amal* mentioned that more than seventy-five kidnapping incidents had already taken place,[1] the toll being more than 100 captives from different nationalities.

---

1. *Al-'Amal* reported in its January 22, 1989 issue that the number of kidnappings had reached seventy-five, with a total of ninety-eight detainees. The names and nationalities of the kidnapped (including those mentioned above) were detailed as well as the dates and outcomes of operations (released, killed, or exchanged). Abductors' names were also mentioned. As for Liro, he was

2. Nationalities targeted in these operations included American; French; Soviet; Italian; British; Swiss; Irish; Dutch; Spanish; Norwegian; Swedish; German; Belgian; Iranian; Indian; Cypriot; Jordanian; Kuwaiti; Libyan; and Saudi.[1] Such great diversity was due to the variety of factions that carried out these operations, and the motives and reasons behind the abductions.

3. The hostage-takers varied between individuals and organizations. Actions were at times individually planned, but for the most part politically organized. Kidnappers sometimes declared responsibility through issued statements in which their purposes were stated, but at times remained unknown:

   a) The abduction of International Red Cross Commissioner Stephan Jackme in Sidon in an operation carried out by the brother of resistance fighter Nehme Sharif Hachem of the Lebanese National Resistance. Occupation forces in the town of Zrariyeh had detained Hachem in March 1985, and later denied his detention. His brother resorted to this act in order to draw public attention, both local and international, and that of the Red Cross in particular, to the fate of his kidnapped brother.[2] The Red Cross commissioner was released a few days after his abduction.

---

mentioned in the *As-Safir* newspaper on August 9, 1991, after *al-'Amal's* survey.

1. Ibid.
2. *As-Safir*, August 22, 1985.

b) The Organization of Socialist Revolutionary Work claimed responsibility for kidnapping the American colonel Ernest Morgan[1] and maintained its readiness to release him in return for food, clothing, and construction materials for the Maslakh-Quarantina quarter in the Eastern region of Beirut.

c) The Armed Revolutionary Factions in Lebanon abducted the president of the French Cultural Centre in Tripoli, Gilles Sydney Berol, demanding in return the release of Abdul Kader Saadi, who was detained in France.[2]

d) Islamic Jihad claimed responsibility for the kidnapping of a number of Americans, French and British. This organization is considered to have undertaken the greatest proportion of kidnapping activity. It justified its acts in a long statement handed over to British journalist John McCarthy after he was released. The statement was addressed to the Secretary General of the United Nations at the time, Javier Perez de Cuellar, and was later distributed inside the UN headquarters in Geneva. It read, in part:

> The issue of detainees and prisoners in the world is one of the outcomes of our confrontation with the powers of hegemony, which America leads as the mother of all corruption along with its germ Israel [...] As such, the issue of detainees is the reaction of Muslim freedom fighters to those practices. It is also an effort to release our *mujahideen* (freedom fighters) who are in prison.

---

1. *Al-'Amal*, op. cit.
2. Ibid.

> And this kind of reaction will continue as long as we
> are facing the same deeds, and because we believe in the
> necessity of work to release our freedom fighters from
> the prisons of occupied Palestine and Europe, and to
> solve the problem of those we hold in our prisons.[1]

The organization expressed its objection to the policies
adopted by America, Britain, and France, and to the support
of Israel.

e) The Organization of Revolutionary Justice claimed
responsibility for kidnapping four French journalists to
'send a warning to the French government and prompt
all French people to contemplate [the situation] in
order to put an end to all the French interference
in Lebanon, and to stop any military or political
intervention within the Lebanese domain.'[2]

f) The Organization of the Oppressed in the World
kidnapped four Lebanese Jews, and declared its readiness
to swap them for detainees of the al-Khiam prison[3] in
South Lebanon, which was under the supervision of the
Antoine Lahd group, agents of Israel.

g) The Islamic Jihad for the Liberation of Palestine outlined
its policies in its first statement, declaring responsibility
for kidnapping four Americans. The aim was to 'to open
the road to *jihad* against the basic enemy of the Islamic
people, especially the oppressed Palestinian people'. The
statement also mentioned that 'the abductees work on

---

1. *An-Nahar*, August 13, 1991.
2. *An-Nahar*, March 3, 1986.
3. *An-Nahar*, November 18, 1985.

executing American conspiracies under the cover of teaching at Beirut University.'[1]

h) The Lebanese Forces, an offshoot of the Phalange Movement, kidnapped four Iranian diplomats,[2] including the chief advisor at the embassy of the Islamic Republic. The incident took place at the Barbara checkpoint on the coastal road between Beirut and Tripoli. Nothing more has ever been revealed about the fate of these individuals.

i) The Islamic Liberation Organization – Khaled bin Walid Forces, Beirut Section claimed responsibility for abducting four Soviets and stipulated in its statement that 'the flagrant assault against the Muslim Tripoli should be ended' in order for them to be released. The abductees were released almost one month later.

Other organizations also claimed responsibility for kidnapping, such as the Organization of the Mujahideen for Freedom, which kidnapped two Germans in order to release Muhammad Ali Hmadeh, who was detained in Germany. The Organization of Militant Revolutionary Cells claimed responsibility for kidnapping the second secretary of the South Korean embassy in Lebanon.[3] And so it continued.

It is apparent from these acts and from the statements issued by local dailies that the kidnappings were reactionary expressions

1. *An-Nahar*, January 29, 1987.

2. *Al-'Amal*, op. cit.

3. Ibid.

against international parties such as the US, Britain or France, a form of objection to their policies and a means for exerting pressure on them. They were also bargaining chips for detainees held in some foreign states; for exerting pressure for the release of prisoners held by Israel and inside al-Khiam prison; for achieving local demands; or for expressing objection to the role of one administration or another inside Lebanon. These operations were conducted secretly given the factions' lack of equality with their targets, and as a form of pressure used to persuade the targeted side to offer concessions or to give in to demands.

It is also apparent that some of these active groups had adopted an Islamic approach, as expressed in their statements. However, their Islamic commitment does not mean that Hizbullah is responsible for them or for their acts. The actions of our Party are declared, and its line of conduct is very clear. Its resistance activity is openly acknowledged and its leadership is known. Regardless of the Party's opinion of kidnapping, and of the debate over the reasons that led to such acts or which calls for dealing with them, Hizbullah has never been involved in or responsible for any of these incidents. The Party expressed its position frequently, and revealed its point of view concerning this question in the following detailed statement:

> It is no longer useful for the US administration to resort to accusing Hizbullah on the subject of foreign detainees, or to disguise the actual reasons behind this issue. Everyone already knows the sides that claimed responsibility for these incidents. Everyone already knows the reasons behind this question of kidnapping. The US administration supported this

form of detention via its custodianship and backing of Zionist crimes against our oppressed people in Palestine, South Lebanon and the Golan. America also encouraged such actions by backing its allies' practices in Lebanon: the fate of thousands of Muslims abducted by the so-called 'Yarze Army' during the administration of Amine al-Gemayyel is still unknown. Furthermore, the fate of the Iranian diplomats who were kidnapped by the Lebanese Forces is still vague. The US administration bears responsibility for all these practices and actions. Moreover, the method of detaining civilians, kidnapping innocent people and perpetrating massacres against them is a method that the Zionist entity was founded upon and which it is still pursuing. The abduction of Sheikh Abdul-Karim Obeid from his very home is a blatant example of such Zionist methods for which the US administration provides cover and support, and furnishes with all the means for killing and criminality.

Hizbullah has always maintained that it is free of any responsibility for abducting foreigners in Lebanon. In addition, it holds the US administration responsible for the persistence of this issue. Hence, Hizbullah invites the US public, mass media and international organizations to assume responsibility and to pressure the US administration to work towards a peaceful conclusion to this issue. This should be realized through releasing the Lebanese, Palestinian and Iranian hostages from Israeli and Israeli-collaborator prisons, as well as from the prisons of US allies in the region. The US administration would be held responsible for any complication in this regard, for the ball is in its court especially now that efforts have been made by the Islamic Republic of Iran and Syria to release the abducted Americans as a step on the road to ending the predicament. Furthermore, the media should take heed of the Lebanese, Palestinian and Iranian detainees as much as it awards attention to foreign detainees. It should condemn the support extended by the US administration and its allies to the Zionists, the 'Yarze Army' and the 'Lebanese Forces'.[1]

In all cases, this file was closed at the end of 1991, when the last foreign hostage in Lebanon was released. It was one of the byproducts of the Lebanese war, and all its justifications and repercussions have thus ended, except for the unknown fate of the four Iranian diplomats, and the Lebanese and Palestinian prisoners still detained in Israeli prisons.

The US administration's insistence on opening the file, after shutting it for ten years, is merely aimed at accusing Hizbullah, pressuring and blackmailing the Party in order to draw commitments from it concerning Israel. However, the US administration is not equipped with any evidence to support its political and illicit charge, and will therefore reach no conclusion in this regard.

---

1. *Ad-Diyar*, May 4, 1990; *al-'Ahd*, no. 306, vol. 6.

SIX

Regional and International Relations

The Relationship with Iran

Under the leadership of Imam Khomeini, Iran's Islamic Revolution of February 11, 1979 reverberated as an earthquake across the region, affecting the map of alliances and the extent of hegemony as well as the very interests of external powers. Iran's stature shifted from being America's military base in the region; a source of concern for the Soviet Union; the policeman of the Gulf area; and the sword at the neck of the Arabs there in order to protect the Zionist entity at the times of the Shah, to one of an Islamic regime rejecting America's hegemony; supporting the rights of the Palestinian people; aspiring to cooperation with its Arab neighbours; and distinct from both East and West through the ideological and political particularities of its leader, Imam Khomeini.

During the first few days of victory, the Israeli embassy in Iran closed down, later to become the Embassy of Palestine. Student groups broke into the US embassy, uncovering its schemes and secret intelligence role and neutralizing its capability to exploit the nation. The emerging Islamic state opened the doors of cooperation to the international community of states, organizations, parties and various other world forces of influence. Several conferences were held on Islamic unity, the Palestinian cause, and the role of group and Friday prayer *imams* as well as other topics with the purpose of fostering awareness, exchanging opinion and cooperation.

In Lebanon, religious scholars and Islamic groups detected a source of hope and support in the nascent Iranian state. Upon its foundation, Hizbullah saw a possibility for achieving its goals and aspirations through the backing and reinforcement expressed by the Islamic Republic of Iran. This was manifested through the dispatch of the Islamic Revolutionary Guard to Lebanon in the wake of the Israeli invasion with a mission to train and recruit Lebanese youth willing to combat Israel. Iranian aid was offered time and again in support of Lebanon's steadfastness, and as a contribution to existing social needs.

The relationship between Hizbullah and Iran was forged through the Party's efforts to make use of this innovative experience in the region and to secure a champion for the cause of confronting Israeli occupation. Rapidly and confidently, the relationship developed, its positive aspects accruing from the first instance. Many reasons lay behind this success, the most important being:

1. Both Iran and Hizbullah believe in the jurisdiction of the Jurist-Theologian, and that Imam Khomeini was himself that leader – the embodiment of this jurisdiction in our times. Iran and the Party thus met within one framework of international leadership legitimacy.

2. Iran's choice of an Islamic republican system of government coincided with the Islamic principles held by Hizbullah. Harmony at the general guideline or theoretical level was thus present, although the detailed application of these

guidelines was subordinate to the particular characteristics of each country in question.

3. Political concord also existed on the issue of Iran's absolute rejection of superpower hegemony, the safeguarding of independence, and support for all the liberation movements – especially those aimed at resisting Israeli occupation. Such was the view held by Hizbullah, with a priority awarded to the confrontation of Israeli occupation and whatever that entails in terms of opposing powers or projects of domination.

Iran represents a vivid manifestation of Islam's applicability, one that every Muslim adherent should observe and contemplate. It altered the widespread, gloomy picture of Islam that was the result of ignorant errors and enemy conspiracy. It provided a case in point for popular elections, street opposition and steadfastness that resulted in overthrowing the Shah and in achieving this change without a military coup or outside support. It provided the example for instituting a system of free choice of representatives, the election of Sayyed Muhammad Khatami as president being only one such recent example. Iran's experience also manifested success through its attention to freedoms, respect for opinion divergence, women's rights and the management of state institutions.

On the other hand, Hizbullah stands for a pioneering experience in resistance, one that won the admiration of Iran, at both popular and state levels, for it represents a portion of the hopes that the oppressed peoples of this world pin on each other when facing immense, successive challenges.

It is only natural that views and principles overlap with interests in these types of relations, irrespective of whether the relation is between two states or between a state and a party. It is also natural for every side to achieve its aims from the relationship without conflict when the basis is one of independence in the work arena and individual accountability. Perhaps the impression in such a case is that the weaker side is consecrated to the stronger, given that the sphere of interests of the more powerful may encompass those of the weaker. There is some truth therein, where the stronger party exercises direct administration and the weaker one only executes. It is not, however, possible where the aims of both are realized through independent action.

When Hizbullah liberated South Lebanon and the Western Bekaa with the effective help of Iran, it achieved its declared goals for which martyrs contributed their sacrifices. Through this, Iran realized its vision of rejecting occupation and supporting *mujahideen* freedom fighters. These are recorded gains for both Hizbullah and Lebanon, as well as for Iran; they are also marked rewards for Syria, the Palestinian *Intifadah* and for every person who believes in resistance and liberation. By the same token, these are losses for Israel and its collaborators, for the US and for everyone extending support to Israeli occupation.

Iran's foreign policy has thus far been characterized by adherence to core broad principles, and has held constant throughout the change of Iranian presidents starting from Imam Khamenei during his presidency, on to the election of Sheikh Ali Akbar Hashemi Rafsanjani and finally with the election of al-Sayyed Khatami. Such consistency is a direct function of the plans traced by Jurist-Theologian Imam Khomeini and held later by Imam Khamenei. Supporting the rights of the Lebanese and

Palestinian people and backing any resistance against occupation are established principles of Iranian policy. Moreover, these are issues with which the Iranian people – whether ordinary citizens, religious scholars, intellectual, social public figures or any of the various political powers – have concurred.

Hence, all bets placed on the collapse of Iran-Hizbullah relations failed; the notion that the relationship would be affected by differences amongst the two main powers inside Iran did not correspond to reality. Divergence between Iran's conservatives and reformists includes different views on state administration, state construction and economic, social, cultural and legal policies. It does not embrace perspectives on resistance, the support of which the two parties agree to.

The Party is not connected to events taking place inside Iran, for these are considered to be internal concerns linked to the choices and convictions of the Iranian people and their representatives. Moreover, Hizbullah is not a protégé of either political current inside Iran; instead, it has fostered sound relations with both, and with their representatives. The Party's scope of work and interest requires appropriate groundwork, not indulgence or interference in the affairs of others. Furthermore, the relationship between Hizbullah and Iran does not mean in any way that their experiences are similar or that they share common denominators. Instead, it is a genuine collaboration on common convictions and on the requirements of the relationship, a candid, transparent and declared relation that has realized great practical benefits for Lebanon.

The concentrated campaign launched by the Western and especially American media, and directed by Israel and the circles of hegemony against this relationship between Iran and

Hizbullah, is but part of a colonialist policy aimed at disbanding the various field forces, dividing to conquer. This contrasts with the common practice where countries of the world work towards forging alliances and building strength through collaboration all while maintaining their own convictions and serving their own interests.

In Lebanon, when all parties sought to extend the bridge of relations with states and powers of the world in accordance with their own vision and interests, the US, France, Israel, Egypt, Libya, Saudi Arabia and the former Soviet Union all took part in such ties. Each party had its justification for its version of relations with Lebanon irrespective of whether it finally transformed into a form of conspiracy or remained limited to soliciting support. Moreover, such is the genre of relations amongst states, relations that may emanate from similar principles but that later transform into either leader-follower scenarios or to genuine cooperation. This picture varies according to a state's stature, convictions, capabilities and regime.

Since the world is treading the path of globalization traced by US domination – the exclusive pole of power in the world – and since submission generally characterizes countries across the globe, it follows that the states or movements that harbour aspirations contradicting those of the US are naturally accused, pressured and subjected to image distortion. This is only part of the plan aimed at foiling the possibilities of unity and weakening the abilities of feeble groups to muster strength through a pooling of potentials.

It is in this light that we come to understand the importance and necessity of the relationships between Hizbullah and Iran, Hizbullah and Syria, Lebanon and Syria, the Palestinian resistance and Syria and between Syria and Iran. Moreover, the significance of any relations amongst the Arabs themselves could be understood, as are relations with Iran or any power supporting Arab rights in this region. For such relations represent real support for all cooperating parties, are not affected by concentrated hostile campaigns founded on weakening the power of unity, and succeed as long as we continue to work on forging closer ties and solidifying cooperation.

Arabian Gulf states have come to realize the importance of relations with Iran and have understood Iran's true intentions for cooperation in order to safeguard the region's resources from the grip of foreigners. These states have also grasped that the Iraq-Iran War, which for eight years threatened the emerging state and exhausted the region's wealth exorbitantly, was not in the interests of any country in the region. Rather, it rendered a great service to both the US and Israel. Syria alone realized the importance of relations with Iran early on, and worked towards fortifying and developing them. Others discovered the depth of the Syrian vision only later.

The Relationship with Syria

The late Syrian President Hafez al-Assad set out with an ideological, historical and strategic perspective on the conflict with Israel. In cooperation with the Soviet Union, he worked on building military clout to achieve balance against Israel's surging armament. It was he who, in 1973, prompted Egypt to enter the October war, and who spoke at length to his visitors on the region's history, the distinguishing characteristics of its peoples and the need to restore Arab rights. Throughout the Assad years, Syria adopted a political course that called for holding the fort against Israel's projects, promoting Arab solidarity to face all pressures, supporting resistance against occupation and cooperating with all allies towards this end.

Syria acted to turn Lebanon into a source of strength for it, as opposed to a weak flank that its foes could seek to exploit. Lebanon's geography and sectarian diversity, as well as the nation's political distinctiveness both in the past and currently, are factors that made it a field for disputes and the settling of accounts. When conflict flared between the National Movement – with its Muslim majority and PLO support – and the Christian political stronghold, a sharp sectarian re-organization ensued that was repudiated by the large, influential countries of the world. Christians sought Syria's help in order to restore the sectarian balance, and hence Syrian forces entered Lebanon to halt the sectarian bloodshed and any subsequent division along political lines.

Nonetheless, the Lebanese front, with its basic military squads represented by the Christian Lebanese Forces, abandoned the alliance with Syria and turned to Israel for military training and armament, subsequently facilitating the Israeli invasion of 1982 which tightened the bridle around Beirut and led to thousands of causalities among Syrian ranks. Protected by Israeli tanks, this movement brought its leader Bashir al-Gemayyel to the presidency and took hold of the Lebanese army. As such, Lebanon awoke to watch more than a third of its territory come under occupation, a service rendered to Israeli politics. Syria's position in the region was weakened; it was painfully stabbed by an Arab state that was assumed to be in solidarity with it as opposed to espousing Israeli occupation.

Under these circumstances, Iran declared its support for Syria and its readiness to carry out the order of Imam Khomeini and dispatch its Islamic Revolutionary Guard to stand by Lebanon in its confrontation with occupation. President al-Assad agreed to this, and the Guard passed via Syria into Lebanon to train the youth who were to form Hizbullah – priority being the defiance of the Israeli occupation.

The relationship between Hizbullah and Syria was initially restricted to coordination on security issues, facilitating the movement of activists and their arms and handling any emerging problems, and did not extend to a political relationship. On the one hand, the Party was interested in the act of resistance and those circumstances that would facilitate it and did not lend attention to the development of political ties. On the other hand, Syria dealt with the Party as a resistance movement and not as an integrated political representative body.

While each side recognized the importance of the other, it was perhaps the lack of direct political dialogue that perpetuated some mutual obscurity when perceiving the other. Had Syria not been a champion and supporter of the Resistance, objection by internal political currents – and especially by those in authority whose view of the Resistance was not one of complete support – would have exhausted Syria. Furthermore, had Hizbullah's resolve not been as staunch, Israel would have never been entrapped or expelled from Lebanon, an achievement that was of great benefit and bearing to Syria's position.

It was within this context that Syrian forces entered Beirut on February 24, 1987, with the aim of putting an end to raging inter-party strife in the city, in which Hizbullah took no part. In the midst of a tense atmosphere, a Syrian army force infiltrated a building on Fathalla Street where a number of Hizbullah members stayed and committed a massacre resulting in twenty-seven martyrs for the Party. An impasse ensued, yet Hizbullah restrained its members from taking any reactive measures lest they become embroiled in strife and turmoil. Whatever the magnitude of the event, adopting a pragmatic approach aimed at treatment of the causes and elimination of any reasons for tension, distrust or misleading estimations was the key. Normalization of relationships was achieved after a while, although sorrow over the event persists.

The June 1988 clashes between Amal and Hizbullah prompted a decision by Syrian forces to infiltrate Beirut's southern suburbs under the banner of separating the fighting parties and re-establishing security. Hizbullah had many concerns, the main one being a possible siding of Syrian troops with Amal. Hizbullah's leadership requested a meeting with President al-Assad in order to obtain direct, official guarantees on the issue. And so it was: the Syrian president reassured Hizbullah leaders that its deployment of forces in Beirut's southern suburbs was only for security reasons without any biased intentions.

The meeting also represented a suitable opportunity for an ideological and political discussion, the first of its kind at this level between Hizbullah's leadership and Syria. Several political meetings followed, within the framework of the quartet committee set up to treat the repercussions of Amal-Hizbullah incidents (the committee members being Syria, Iran, Amal and Hizbullah). Bilateral meetings also took place between Hizbullah and Syrian foreign minister Farouk al-Shara', laying the foundations for continuous political discussion over common issues primarily related to the conflict with Israel. Several meetings were also held with the late Major Basil al-Assad, Vice President Abdul Halim Khadam and Major General Ghazi Kenaan.

The relationship with Syria developed tremendously towards the end of Amal-Hizbullah clashes. On many occasions, through press interviews and various public statements, Syria expressed its appreciation of Hizbullah and its *jihad* struggle, and declared its support for the choice of resistance without reservation. President al-Assad defended the right to resistance and distinguished it from terrorism, maintaining that Syria openly stood in support of such resistance in both Lebanon and Palestine in spite of all pressures exerted, especially by the US, to isolate Hizbullah.

Both the US and Israel expected a change in Syrian policy after the death of President al-Assad. In contrast, Syria's new President Bashar al-Assad continued to pursue the same policy track, and has further accentuated his interest in both the Lebanese and Palestinian resistance, considering both to be legitimate rights, and defending their plight in the face of Zionist discrimination at the most important of international forums through open declarations for the whole world to hear.

For its part, Hizbullah expressed appreciation of and esteem for Syria's standpoint while maintaining adherence to the option of a strategic and supportive relationship. Syria had played the pivotal role in drafting the Taif Accord, and had entered Lebanon only as requested by the Lebanese government. Through its presence and exercise of authority, Syria brought an end to Lebanon's civil war; worked on restoring state institutions; supported the Lebanese army; resolutely backed the Resistance; and ended the state of affairs whereby some Lebanese groups could acquire strength by allying with Israel. Syrian presence in Lebanon was therefore a source of protection from Israeli influence and control, and was not only meant to be a pivot in Syria's conflict with the Israelis.

It is only natural that Hizbullah's views concur with those of Syria, for no one is safe from Israel's ambitions – those that stretch beyond Palestine to engulf the entire region. As such, should the active powers of the region fail to unite and target Israel at its weakest, no one would be spared disaster. Hizbullah has never denied that its relationship with Syria is based on a computation of the interests of the Resistance. Syria is the only Arab state that has unwaveringly supported the Resistance, and has helped achieve Lebanon's great liberation.

Hizbullah's activity was characterized by far-reaching independence, even if this is not a familiar mode of relations between parties and states. However, the Party's clear political views and its faultless practical performance, in addition to its skilful follow-up to rally support for its resistance, were sources of reassurance to Syrian leadership that harmony does exist between the Party's course and the Syrian vision. A high-ranking Syrian political official once said in this context: 'If we actually sit and think together, we would not agree as much as is manifested through practical action.'

Some might perceive the level of Hizbullah's identification with both Syria and Iran as unusual. However, the Party recognized that the presence of a number of factors created sufficient ground for benefiting from the support of these two countries, these factors being: Hizbullah's need for active supportive power; its belief in the significance of both Iranian and Syrian support; the existence of strategic Syrian-Iranian relations since the Islamic Revolution's victory, which have not ceased and have only strengthened since then; mutual appreciation by both countries of each other's stature, goals and roles; and cooperation insofar as internal confidentiality is respected. Hizbullah thus benefited while guarding its own freedom of choice and individuality.

Hizbullah's relationship with Syria therefore rests on the Party's strong ideological and political principles. Furthermore, the Party's interest in maintaining efficient Lebanese-Syrian relations emanates from a geopolitical equation that has placed Lebanon, weak all through its history, within political, regional and international spheres. While Lebanon's alternatives are limited, they are of direct bearing on neighbouring states, and Lebanon itself is directly influenced by these states.

At this historical milestone, Lebanon faces one of two alternatives: a Syrian versus an Israeli alliance, two mutually exclusive choices. Lebanon's adopted political choice bears significant repercussions on the region's future and acceptance of one alliance implies denial of the other. Immediately after the Israeli invasion, Israel's effects on those alternatives available to the Lebanese state prompted Lebanon to make its final choice of alliance. This was further called for following the Taif Accord during which time the extent of Syrian influence was felt and both the local and regional repercussions of this relationship were revealed.

We do not consider the relationship with Syria to be either mandatory or accidental, but rather the cornerstone for facing major regional obligations. Furthermore, this relationship has not stood at the limits of concept or interest, but has rather translated into a lengthy experience of grave and complicated circumstances. The relationship with Syria has so far proven its utility and necessity.

Relationship with the other Arab Regimes

The difficulties faced by Arab regimes do not emanate from popular demands, whatever their extent, but from the onerous burden of an international system dominated by a single pole which aims to redraw the regional map according to its own interests and to the requirements of Israel. No Arab regime is exempt from falling prey to this scenario; all face hard and painful obligations, and all are transformed into executive tools of conflict with their own people. US hegemony only safeguards the authority of leaders that comply with US interests, and given its strong international position, the US is capable of fastening any accusation to any entity of choice, launching slogans deemed sufficiently attractive to carry out a series of procedures aimed at toppling regimes, whether these regimes actually stand culpable as accused or not.

Arab regimes need to adopt a series of changes aimed at achieving reconciliation with their peoples. This is a prerequisite for facing foreign challenges which are no longer restricted in form to military occupation but have rather taken more contemporary facets, such as the offer of protection that entails the set-up of military bases; international resolutions that dedicate state resources to the interests of greater powers; mercantile strategy dictating prices and production volumes as per US and other Western interests; and so-called 'world peace', that which delivers solutions at the expense of land and other legitimate rights.

Such change calls for impartiality, equitable treatment and sensitivity to civilian needs. As Commander of the Faithful Ali bin Abi Taleb said:

> Let the things you like most be those which are moderate in the question of right, more general in the

question of justice, and more representative of people's needs. For the discontent of the common people ills the satisfaction of the prominent, and the discontent of the prominent is forgiven through the contentment of the common people.[1]

Change is needed to grant people the right of expression, of convening, of inquisition and of political and social activity. Change requires re-thinking the structure of regimes, the updating of laws and the revival of economies. Realization of such change breeds an internal vitality that helps fortify countries against outside risks. It calls for objective treatment of issues. Otherwise, regimes would continue to defend leaders from their own suppressed populations who continue to harbour and contemplate confrontational feelings.

Active social forces are therefore required to work diligently and contribute to positive transformation through political means, away from armed conflict, for the use of arms against one's own propagates turmoil, and armed conflict against regimes only transforms countries into battlefields where every side oversteps the rules in order to safeguard its own existence.

No one profits in these wars. Algeria under the military repression of the ruling authority and through the Islamic movements' resort to weapons is quite different from the Algeria of today, although the path of change was lengthy. In Bahrain, the reinstatement of relations between the ruling body and the opposition without any resort to armed struggle produced a positive and active atmosphere, albeit one that is still nascent. As

---

1. Imam Ali bin Abi Taleb, *Nahj al-Balagha*, from the recommendation of Imam Ali (PBUH) to the leader of al-Ashter upon the latter's appointment as ruler of Egypt, book no. 53.

such, efforts should be directed towards rallying the people and encouraging popular action, for this is a strong asset irrespective of direction, and is an influential means of creating natural and gradual change – a legitimate pivot for any side to count on.

Any political direction falls short of proving itself without popular support. Egypt's experience after the Camp David Accord is sufficient proof: its late President Anwar Sadat signed the peace treaty with Israel and agreed to the normalization of relations; but street opposition to such normalization has aborted all practical procedures adopted towards this end since 1979. No one has the capability of bypassing street opposition.

Hizbullah's relationship with most Arab regimes[1] did not exceed the scope of normal communication, although the effectiveness of such communication varied according to the administration in question. Hizbullah has no relations with certain regimes whose very nature and underlying stature or political stance are fundamentally at odds with the Party's chosen principles, the main priority of which is represented by the confrontation of Israel. As such, where Hizbullah harbours certain criticism, especially on key issues or at key milestones, such disapproval is manifested openly without resort to clash or dispute. The Party commends those who demonstrate the appropriate stance in key situations without prejudice and in line with their viewpoints, observing and upholding any contribution that Arab regimes offer in the context of the conflict with Israel.

In its approach, Hizbullah aims at encouraging all means of integrating support for resistance. This reflects on the type of

---

1. Syria excluded, as the separate treatment of the subject on relationships with Syria has revealed.

relations forged with others and the nature of Party interests. Disparity amongst visions is a function of divergent priorities. Accordingly, the Party invites everybody to adopt the priority of resistance. Whoever takes up the slogan of liberating Arab regimes as a prerequisite for liberating Palestine is on an erroneous track and is only complicating the task of liberation. For the worthier cause is that of liberating Palestine, based on which the Arab regimes and their peoples should become free of this nightmare that overshadows and plagues all adopted policies in our region.

Relations with the US

Following the end of the First World War and the fall of the Ottoman Empire, the Arab and Islamic world was divided into smaller entities shared by the victorious nations, at the head of which were France and Britain. The region was therefore categorized as a political and economic supplement to those greater powers. This was established as part of a cultural vision that ruled out the capacity of Islam to lead and worked hard to alienate it from the intricacies of practical daily life, replacing it with slogans of modernity, democracy and human rights, all of which emerged more clearly after the Second World War. The world was divided between two poles of international influence, the US leading the capitalist West that upheld said slogans, and the USSR leading the socialist camp that worked with a historical determinism to supplant world belief systems and implant the then widespread communist ideology.

In spite of socialism's attraction for intellectuals and youth over three decades (the 1950s to the 1970s), and notwithstanding the hopes it carried for freedom from capitalist hegemony, equality and fairness for the proletariat, and the power of rule for the community as opposed to the individual, it nevertheless toppled with the fall of the Soviet Union during the second half of the 1980s, bringing these hopes to an end and further empowering capitalism's cultural prerogatives, essentially devised by the US. The US had already exercised control over much of the region, the bulk of which was affiliated with Western policy due either to bilateral interests or to the categorization of communism as a form of atheism. Hence, America became the one influential power beyond dispute, and gradually removed France and Britain from their colonialist status, imposing its policies overall. The US staged wars and undertook measures primarily suitable to US interests, continuously working to subjugate international organizations and satellite states that adhered to such interests.

The US's ceiling of prerogatives when dealing with other states was drawn on the basis of securing US national interests and those of the American taxpayer without accounting for any moral, religious, human or political checks that might hinder the execution of such interests, even where this meant human loss in the order of thousands or hundreds of thousands (as was the case in both Nagasaki and Hiroshima).

As for the cultural banners of freedom, democracy, equality, human rights and the supremacy of law, these are internal American slogans often used in the context of extortion against states, organizations or individuals. They are used vehemently where they coincide with US interests, or are simply tools of pressure employed towards other ends such as control over natural, human or political resources. They may also be totally ignored where the targeted parties finally submit to US policy.

From here, the problem plaguing any relationship or dialogue with the US rests with the political supremacy of this single world power. Inequality characterizes all phases of the relationship, from approach to dialogue to vision, to the *de facto* priority of US interests over any other upon the contemplation of solutions, and finally to the lack of any tendency for compromise by either interlocutor. It is essentially the supremacy of US interests that interrupts the channels of dialogue and neutralizes their effects beforehand.

Since its establishment in 1982, Hizbullah has observed contemporary US foreign policy and positions as being ultimately geared towards supporting the existence and foundations of the Israeli entity, furnishing it with justifications for financial, military or political power, and awarding high consideration to its intermediate and long-term requirements for goal achievement. This, of course, has been coupled with US hostility towards any movements that denounce or resist Israeli occupation and its repercussions.

The US categorized the Islamic Resistance in Lebanon as a form of terrorism,[1] working on many occasions to rouse Lebanese public opinion against it. The US also instigated internal strife in Lebanon in an attempt to strike and distract the Resistance. It supported and covered for two wide-ranging Israeli aggressions, in July 1993 and April 1996, both aimed at dismantling the Resistance and its structure. It exerted pressure on Lebanese authorities to take action against the Resistance, and launched a wave of

---

1. 'Terrorism' is the common word employed to refer to any contradiction of US policy.

statements and threats at all levels of the US administration, calling for, at the least, the crippling of the Resistance's capability to confront Israel, and at the most, termination of the Party's existence – taking Hizbullah out of Lebanese life. US action then focused on ensuring Israeli security at a time when major parts of Lebanon remained under occupation. In essence, the US aimed to ensure that the occupied zone in Lebanon constituted the vital political margin of manoeuvre for any security guarantees or political agreements to be signed with Syria or Lebanon.

As such, the former US Assistant Secretary of State Richard Murphy proposed handing over the responsibility for security in South Lebanon to Amal in 1987 – which was a pretext for invalidating any resistance presence and for creating fertile ground for internal strife or burdening Amal with a complicated responsibility. In all cases, Israel would be the sole beneficiary. Amal did not entertain this suggestion, and the scenario never saw the light.

Then came the notion of charging the Lebanese army with the responsibility of security in South Lebanon following the failure of the 1993 aggression and in the wake of Yasser Arafat's signature of the Oslo Agreement. Voices were raised as to the great dangers that awaited South Lebanon should the army not take charge of safeguarding the people. In reality, such measures were only a statement of obligation granted to Israel that all resistance activity should be halted. They were but a recipe for clash between the army and the Resistance. Many Lebanese officials were swept in the direction of army deployment, but Lebanese-Syrian talks, and awareness of the threats posed by this proposal, led to its failure – depriving both Israel and the US of any action against Lebanon, Lebanon's interests or the Resistance.

Subsequently, having exhausted its presence in Jezzine through its militia of collaborators, Israel attempted to exploit its withdrawal from the area and its suburbs by way of a 'Jezzine First' scenario. The US propagated the concept, declaring it an accomplishment calling for a price on the Lebanese side in the form of security and political cooperation, or else the situation in the South would only collapse. The US predicted that the traces of the previous occupation period were bound to prompt Muslim-Christian strife or the settlement of accounts between the Resistance and the inhabitants of Jezzine. By contrast, the Resistance passed the test, and not one incident disrupting the liberation process was recorded. The official Lebanese stance was to overcome all potential negative aspects of the new situation, and security forces were deployed to ensure citizens' safety. All this was achieved without any guarantees or security commitments by Lebanon in favour of the enemy, including no pledges that operations from within the liberated region would not be launched.

The epitome of American bias was revealed in the year 2000 during the very liberation process, where the US worked hard to exchange Israel's escape from Lebanon as a result of continuous resistance strikes for a political and security agreement through which the front with Lebanon would finally be closed but all aspects of occupation would remain. The US propagated the notion that Israel had actually implemented UN Resolution 425 in accordance with international law and then introduced, with assistance from the United Nations, the notion of the Blue Line as an alternative to Lebanon's internationally recognized borders. The US further pressured Lebanon to deploy the Lebanese army in the South and commit to preventing attacks against Israel. In this manner, the US did not spare any efforts to realize Israel's demands, lay obstacles for the Resistance and prepare for an eventual strike against it.

US interference further trespassed into the most delicate details of Lebanese political life, the aim always being that of beleaguering Hizbullah. This was clearly manifested during the first parliamentary elections of 1992, when the Party's plans for a coalition of activists in the Bekaa was rebuffed by one leading parliamentary personality who cited pressure by the US as the reason. The US was using all its influence to ensure that the Party's representation was limited to one deputy only. In fact, the US aimed at preventing Hizbullah's participation in parliamentary elections altogether – participation that would only legitimize the representation of popular forces in the governmental entity. Hence, the highest possible ceiling was for one deputy only, and no more were to be tolerated.[1]

The US also expressed its aspiration for a Lebanese state that provided the necessary social services for its citizens, particularly those in the southern parts of the country. Hizbullah's influence and magnetism through its provision of services was to be sidelined. The US also promulgated the notion that Hizbullah should be dealt with as a terrorist organization, and actually made contact with some internal Lebanese entities to instigate aggression against the Party, citing the US's justification for not

---

1. No coalition was formed then and the Party entered the election campaign in the Bekaa. Hizbullah won an entire and completely open list of eight seats for the Allegiance to the Resistance coalition out of a possible ten. During a Hizbullah leadership meeting with the late Major Basil al-Assad the latter congratulated the Party, contentedly saying: 'You now have officially recognized parliamentary representation. America's pretext for accusing you of terrorism is now void, for the people's choice has spoken in your favour.'

assisting Lebanon as being primarily linked to the presence of Hizbullah. The US even sought to confiscate Party funds and did not spare any opportunity for media broadcasting to perpetuate accusations against the Party through the US ambassador in Lebanon or other officials in the US. All attempts were made, and means exploited, to distort the image of and exert pressure on Hizbullah.

What has been mentioned above represents only a handful of examples of US aggression against Hizbullah, let alone the generally oppressive US policy pursued against the peoples of the region. US hostility has manifested through words and actions alike, and has encompassed all aspects and phases of the Party's presence. This stands in contrast with Hizbullah's beliefs and actual conduct, both being in harmony with Islam's principles and with the cause of legitimate resistance against Israeli occupation. Hizbullah's stance has therefore been clearly at odds with US policies for the Middle East. As such, the Party considered calls for meeting and dialogue as communicated through some US Congress officials to be futile, and refused the approach in spite of frequent requests conveyed through both Lebanese and non-Lebanese officials and especially those brought forward through the various US delegations visiting Lebanon after liberation.

Hizbullah's stance is clear: the Party is well aware of US motives in the region, permanent intentions that are not a function of any changing conditions and that are not subject to modification; the US does not take any detailed step or perform any action whatsoever unless this directly feeds the pre-drawn policy of supporting Israel; furthermore, the US realizes the fundamental quality of Hizbullah's principles, as clearly manifested through resistance, sacrifice and social action undertaken to defend and liberate the land. As such, the encounter between the Party and the US administration would not add anything new to the acquaintance of each side with the other's views, and would not alter the stance on either side.

If this is the case, why, then, has the US sought to meet with Hizbullah through various members of the US Congress? This is but a repercussion of post-liberation developments, which established Hizbullah as an active and powerful presence whose role and influence cannot be sidelined. The US aims to exercise pressure via such direct encounters, and achieving some exchange of political gains offered indirectly through European mediators. Generous aid for the liberated South, and for underprivileged regions falling within the sphere of Hizbullah's influence, was offered through these mediators, the condition being that the Party abandon its resistance role, settle for the gains of liberation and turn attention to internal political activity. In this context, the US ambassador to Lebanon Vincent Battle inquired in June 2002 about the possibility of allocating some internal gains to the Party in an attempt to distract interest from resistance activity.

Hizbullah refused to meet with the Americans for several reasons. Of these we note only the most important:

1. When a Party that has sacrificed and struggled for legitimate rights meets with those who have not spared any effort to support aggression against such rights and against the peoples of the region, especially those in Lebanon and Palestine, such an encounter would only be equivalent to providing the aggressor – the US – with a certificate of good conduct.

2. The encounter would fall within the realm of the general style of US foreign policy, which is openly pragmatic and flexible in terms of general titles and vague promises, but which in essence does not bear any practical interpretation contradicting the permanent bias in favour of Israel. As such, Hizbullah does not wish to render the US a service by succumbing to its approach.

3. Hizbullah has nothing to add to its already declared, clear and well known positions. Furthermore, it does not expect any change in the US position. The encounter would therefore be inconsequential, and might confuse public opinion over possibilities and events that are really baseless. It is therefore futile to deceive public opinion given the apparent clarity of the situation.

Since the US bears responsibility for its pursued foreign policies, it is essential to distinguish between its administration and its affiliates on the one hand and the American citizen, intellectual or journalist on the other. Hizbullah does not have any reservations about meeting with non-US officials or individuals outside the public sphere, and would do so whether the aim was simply dialogue, media declaration or any other purpose falling beyond the scope of realizing benefit for the US.

Even though Hizbullah considered that the US administration maintained an unfair policy towards it, and supported Israel's aggression and occupation of Lebanon and elsewhere in the region, the party's stance had always been on the political level, exposing the US political mistakes in the Middle East.

Following the events of September 11, 2001, Hizbullah issued a communiqué denouncing the attacks, which read:

> Does the US administration really plan to strike back at the perpetrators of the recent attacks and their sponsors, or does it want to take advantage of these tragic events to widen its hegemony over the world and pursue even more deeply its unfair policies, which have degenerated to this level of hatred amongst the peoples of the world and many of its governments?
>
> ... We feel sorry for the killing of innocent people in any part of the world and our Lebanese compatriots, who were victims of the Zionist massacres in Cana and other places – which the US administration refused to condemn at the time, at a meeting of the UN Security Council – know best the pain and sorrow of those who lose loved ones in tragic events.[1]

Although the US administration acknowledged the wide popular support of Hizbullah in Lebanon, along with its clear stance focusing on resistance to the occupation, it still insisted on smearing it as a terrorist group. This only reveals the total US bias with regard to Israeli aggression, massacres, destruction of homes and terrorizing of civilians in occupied Palestine.

Relations with the European West

With the advent of a unilateral world power as represented by the US, European influence has steadily declined over the past

---

1. Various newspapers, including the Lebanese daily *al-Anwar* and the Saudi daily *al-Sharq al-Awsat*, September 17, 2001.

two decades. Meanwhile, the US pole expended every effort to tighten its grip on the world within a context of political and economic globalization that interferes with nations' and regions' private concerns, and that eventually places all within the sphere of US private interests.

Europeans, and especially the French and British, attempted to benefit from their former colonialism of the Middle East by maintaining roles therein. The French exaggerated their capability for drawing the future of Lebanon, clearly manifested starting from the repercussions of the 1982 Israeli invasion where French troops participated in the multinational peacekeeping forces deployed in Lebanon in 1983, and ending with their support of General Michel Aoun prior to the latter's demise. France failed to back Aoun's plans of 1990, and came to realize the extent to which the US had mastered the rules of the political game, expelling all other interested states from it, and forging regional relationships on the basis of common interests with countries in the domain. France thus acquiesced to playing the rear man behind the leading US policy, and did so in spite of differences on certain issues where the ambitious French need for distinction was apparent. This role proved ineffectual in confronting US plans for the region or US determination in executing such plans.

The British, on the other hand, chose to become the absolute addendum to US policy while attempting to expose some theoretical differences. Since full and obvious US support for Israel fulfilled all of the latter's requirements, no practical assistance could be offered by the UK. It focused on bridging relationships with particular channels in the region, perhaps hoping that these contributions would gain some advantage within the limited role that Britain conceded for itself. In the meantime, the US seized the throne of world leadership.

As for the rest of Europe, the choice was made for a European Union (EU) that speaks for all on issues of the Middle East. The EU's direct presence was not politically or practically effective in the region, but this did not hinder its embassies and channels from communication, seeking acquaintance and gathering knowledge and participation in a number of limited activities.

From this standpoint, Hizbullah's relationship with Europe became possible given that no instances of direct aggression from the European side could be detected. Furthermore, a common interest in dialogue and communication was openly manifested at both ends, despite prior knowledge of substantial disparities in points of view.

Considerable improvement of relations between Hizbullah and Europe could be observed following the 1996 Israeli aggression against Lebanon. Bilateral meetings and visits were not limited to exchanges of opinion but translated into practical albeit limited cooperation with a number of embassies on some general issues. These encounters were publicly announced, as was the case with the visit of European Ambassadors, of whom we note the French and British ambassadors, to the Hizbullah Secretary General. Visits were not restricted to local embassy members, and many special envoys arriving from their countries of origin were received. At the top of these envoys' priorities was communication with Hizbullah.

The pace of relations with Europe differs across countries. With some, meetings are regular, dialogue is continuous and follow-up is permanent. With others, encounters were limited to acquaintance, awareness as to standpoint, or discussion of particular issues. As for relations with institutions, social organizations and the like, these are still nascent and quite weak. Perhaps official relations are more effective in terms of diluting European apprehension and enticing further European interest in developing ties.

Hizbullah perceives the ambitious role that Europe has chosen to adopt as a catalyst for tempering the US's overindulgence and power monopoly. It bears benefit inasmuch as it represents a differentiated Western role, one that takes into account part of the needs and particularities of the Arab and Palestinian reality. It does not entail any imaginary hopes, but rather provides an opportunity for benefit should it happen to bear any fruit in spite of the disappointing classification of Hamas and Islamic Jihad on Europe's list of terrorist organizations, and notwithstanding the weak support for human rights manifested towards the Jenin massacres and aggressions that continue to be suffered inside Palestine. Even if the European stance were limited to one nascent voice that accommodated Europe's interests in the region and that took into account the antagonistic attitude adopted by the region's people against US policy, it would still be a beneficial step promising growth through time.

Europeans, on the other hand, perceive this relationship as a relief from the responsibility of fully backing the US in its unswerving support of Israel – an attempt to draw a path differentiated from the prevalent US norm. They have also discovered the extent of public sympathy for the Resistance and discerned that ignoring this rejoinder between the Resistance, the general public and the ruling authority is ultimately without merit. Europe came to realize that Hizbullah's active presence in Lebanese life and the regional repercussions of its existence place the Party in a position where dialogue becomes worthwhile, especially given the Party's openness to all currents and entities, its reception of discussion and dialogue, and its willingness to cooperate on issues of common ground.

Both parties realize that the steps in this relationship are carefully calculated, that the fundamental political stance of each end is a given throughout the development of the relationship, and that events shall affect its gradual growth. Hizbullah supported the role that France assumed in its participation in the 1996 April Accord committee, and the Party's positive messages in this regard were accurately perceived on the French side. Similarly, Germany's proposal to effect an exchange of detainees in Israeli prisons for Israeli soldiers held by Hizbullah was positively adopted by the Party. The British ambassador to Lebanon was also well received following his request for a meeting, despite the Party's caution with regard to the general British stance. Such attitudes were not one-sided, for there is an apparent reciprocity in interest to take steps in this direction. Relationships are a matter of mutual exchange, and each end perceives them based on its own convictions, calculations and interests.

Western hegemony had previously predominated over the region, working on Westernization as a replacement for the prevalent Islamic proposition. A rooted Islamic infrastructure that blends with instinctive native thought, coupled with a failed attempt at marketing Western thought due to discovery of the regional colonization and exploitation intentions inherent therein, combined with the success of the Islamic Revolution in Iran and a general resurrection of Islamic movements, are all factors that came into play to uncover differences and widen the gap between Muslims and the West.

Irrespective of this, dialogue channels should remain open with the West without any prejudices about the complications or pace of results and without any exaggerated hopes or illusions, while taking into consideration the caveats surrounding such dialogue, the most important of which are:

1. Islam calls upon us to provide space for constructive dialogue, to listen to others, their proofs and arguments: *Say: Bring your proof [of what ye state] if ye are truthful.*[1] As such, dialogue forms an integral part of a wise call towards God – *Call unto the way of thy Lord with wisdom and fair exhortation*[2] – and a frame for calm and logical exchange: *... and reason with them in the better way.*[3] The exchange of knowledge is founded on logic that does not assume *a priori* negation of the other, but rather calls for discourse that exhausts all proofs and attestations.

2. A preliminary difficulty informs dialogue with the West, which concerns finding the common stage for launching such dialogue. While it is in our interest to adopt an ideological approach that discusses founding principles, it is in Western interests to promote such interchange from the standpoint of political and power influence. Each group departs from distinct ideological givens, attempts an amalgamation of supportive events to prove the rationale behind such givens, and approaches dialogue with the aim of winning ground as opposed to bridging gaps. The

---

1. Surah no. 2, *al-Baqara*, verse 111.
2. Surah no. 16, *al-Nahl*, verse 125.
3. Surah no. 16, *al-Nahl*, verse 125.

futility of this approach is but an obvious conclusion. It is therefore imperative for both participants to distinguish and separate the ideological from the political, and to protect the discussion from those equivocal assumptions of what applicable results could be.

3. Consolidation of the general guidelines adopted by the two currents, Islam and the West, should serve to unveil the extent of common ground regarding what concerns the spread of justice for the common good. In contrast, interpretation of these guidelines is where divergence of opinion lies, especially in view of the clear differences that ensue at the practical level and that are a function of ideological backgrounds and principles.

4. The West is accustomed to exporting principles and terminologies. It therefore deals with dialogue as a formality that conceals an interest in subjugation. In spite of this, the discussion channel is possible, and so is bringing forth objective reasoning to prove the difficulty of imposing the Western programme. Dialogue is hampered when condescension or suggestions of inferiority come into play. Only a sense of equality can lead to positive outcomes.

5. Various Islamic movements and organizations, acting together as one and with shared responsibility, would launch a campaign of generalizations in the wake of such dialogue, and may well highlight the issue of accountability for implementing any agreed results. It is therefore important to disentangle responsibility from such group sharing, and

to clearly pinpoint the direction of dialogue as perceived by Hizbullah's specific vision without bearing the brunt for others' actions. Similarly, it is not possible to perceive the West as a single mass. As such, let dialogue observe whatever differences amongst Western nations exist, no matter how small and irrespective of whether Western ideological principles are common and easily identifiable.

6. It is imperative to avoid a complete abstraction of ideology from political and practical performance, even if the frame of discussion requires debate in order to identify differences and common ground.

We thus conclude that the process of dialogue is a slow, long-term and complicated one, but is nevertheless a minimum requirement for the sake of trying all avenues possible in order to clarify one's position and listen to that of others. It is beneficial to extend the scope of dialogue and enlarge its reach to encompass all segments of Western society, in order to circumvent those filters that avoid its proper reach to the general public or to cultured members of society. The truth of what we are should be revealed.

Dialogue should replace the notion of a 'clash of civilizations', for it is the more righteous and appropriate path. There is no need to presuppose its results and burden it with presumed failure. By the same token, it is not wise to depend on such dialogue for influential and significant achievements, for we are speaking of the methodology and conduct between East and West, not laying the foundations for any confident or pessimistic outcomes. When dialogue is the ultimate aim, an aperture is opened in the rigid wall, and whatever approach is adopted will eventually be bound to discussion as an ultimate end, just as the attitude of the conversing parties will be shaped and practical results with a bearing on whole nations and their peoples would be clarified. Such debate is not limited to nations, or to party powers with nations, but rather reaches cultured and political segments and the public at large with the hope that should one channel fail, another will continue.

The US is directing matters towards eventual conflict within the context of its declared stance: 'You are either with us or against us.' Dialogue places the US in awkward situations, forcing it to engage in discussions of fundamentals that it cannot keep at bay. Superiority naturally characterizes the US approach due to sheer US power, which enables this nation to impose its opinions and interests. The essence lies in the aftermath of this US approach: clash may result with the oppression of the weaker by the powerful, but breeds hatred and enmity, and harbours explosive factors for building up tension and leading to wars.

Communicating with Public Opinion

Addressing the international public is of benefit irrespective of the hurdles inherent in actually convincing it. Two principal difficulties pose themselves in this context. First, there is the vast number of erroneous assumptions about Islam and Muslims, which have become givens dictating international opinion. Second, the role of a media sympathetic to the Zionists and directed by the agencies of hegemonic powers has well served the purpose of spreading misgivings and misinformation that work to shape public opinion by way of gripping scenarios and persuasive image technologies.

We notice how the US went out of its way to impede the broadcast of any Usama bin Laden's speeches on US media channels and especially on CNN, categorizing these broadcasts as a danger to national security, and further persuaded European nations to follow suit. This is a clear example of dictating what should and should not be broadcast. Israeli media also shapes information in a manner similar to military censorship, the aim being management of overall public opinion especially when the issue concerns *jihad*, Resistance and *Intifadah* operations. On separate occasions, Israel interfered to object to BBC and CNN broadcasts, and restricted the transmission of the latter's programmes inside the Zionist entity until the manner of handling Zionist issues was amended. It is not difficult to observe the apparent bias of Western media in favour of the Zionist course. Similarly, such terms as 'fundamentalism', 'terrorism', 'danger to democracy' and 'respect for human rights and fundamental freedoms' are used as pressure-tactic keywords that aim to propagate the policies of powers of hegemony within a political, cultural and media framework drawing on all sources of influence to shape public opinion against the Islamic movement.

In spite of it all, addressing international public opinion is of high importance, irrespective of whether the benefits are expectedly meagre. However, we should not fall prey to the obsession of losing public opinion should it fail to respond to the logic of our platform or to objectively distinguish the reality of events. Where certain individuals or groups could be attracted to all or part of our convictions, this would be considered a valuable step towards penetrating the wall of deception. Our strategies should take public opinion into consideration, and should address it with the language, style and proof befitting its level of culture and awareness. Events are abundant and developments occur in haste; the mistakes of the powerful coupled with the oppression of the weak all conspire with the element of time to shed some light on the real picture.

We should also not forget regional public opinion, on which we should focus attention and for which we should provide facts, and to the benefit of which we should dissect and clarify the overall picture in order to prevent the imported view of events from predominating. In this context, general slogans and guidelines are insufficient: we should delve into details and provide proof, support our credibility and share our cause, encourage public opinion to live the responsibility of contributing to an effective and influential force in the quest against an imposed view of the world as presented by the circles of international hegemony.

It is our duty to choose to the best of our abilities and means in the race with the powers of hegemony and the measures they employ. The live pictures presented by the Resistance through video recordings of *jihad* operations[1] and their subsequent airing on television had their effect on both our audience and that of the enemy, providing our public with an incentive for support and trust while spreading fear amongst the ranks of the Israeli military and uncovering its pretences of power. These recordings proved

---

1. War coverage by the Resistance entered the field for the first time in 1986, with footage of the invasion of the occupied Sujud fort at the top of the Jabal Safi hill in Iqlim al-Tuffah, and subsequently conveying the liberation of this post in all operational details. Following the first television broadcast of this operation, the camera became an essential element in all resistance operations. Hizbullah inaugurated its radio station, Al-Nour, in 1988, and its TV station, al-Manar, in 1990.

to international public opinion the firmness of our stance and the eagerness for martyrdom in the name of freeing the land. A wide debate about events in the region was spurred as a result.

The United Nations Security Council

It is no longer a secret that the international law upon which the United Nations General Assembly and Security Council were founded diverges markedly from the practical performance of the five permanent members of the Council, those with the right of veto and which benefit from this right, altering the principles of international law and interpreting it in what befits their interests. At the pinnacle of these is the US, which has used its veto time and again in apparent domination of the Security Council, exploiting it whenever possible and overriding it whenever there is sufficient cause or interest to do so.

The importance of having an international forum for resolving international disputes is not a debatable question, for international issues need a coordinator at such a level should peace predominate in the world. However, replacing principles and laws with power and authority, favouring the interests of the north over the south, monopolizing international management of the human economy and devising solutions that are to the detriment of populations at large, especially to the oppressed peoples of the world, have transformed the Security Council into a sword at the neck of the poorer nations, one borne by the dominating powers of supremacy, raising the banner of 'international will' in the face of principles, rights, values and moralities.

'International will' is the flat retort when questioning the objective, legal and human rationale behind Israel's occupation of Palestinian land and the reasons behind absolute US support for the establishment of the Israeli state. Discussion cannot reverse events, and all nations must accede to this will as a permanent given. Discussion then moves on to the details of this status quo.

Who, then, can redeem abrogated human rights? Who is it who can respect the will of the people, restore justice and support the subjugated against their oppressor? The powerful nations excel at playing the game of turning the Security Council into a referee with double standards, an entity biased towards the favoured, harsh on the disadvantaged. UN Security Council resolutions operate in one of two dimensions: one manifests a unified binding character to which the entire world is held accountable; the other has an inconclusive temperament, leaving sufficient room for those affected by the decision to buy time, lean on the resolution and perhaps later replace it as they deem fit.

An international resolution is therefore binding when it is issued to discipline Iraq, Libya, Iran or Afghanistan. It would, in such a situation, call for a callous international offensive in the Gulf, as was the case against Iraq.[1] As for UN Resolutions 242 of 1967 and 338 of 1973, both calling for Israeli withdrawal from Palestine, as well as Resolution 425 calling for Israeli withdrawal from Lebanon, these fall within the circle of optional Israeli implementation, unhampered by any form of pressure, completely in line with Zionist interests and receiving clear international support as led by the US.

Reconsideration of the rights of certain countries to use

---

1. Reference is made here to the second Gulf War, following Iraq's invasion and occupation of Kuwait on August 1, 1990; a US-led war was launched on January 16, 1991 on the basis of a United Nations Security Council resolution.

the power of veto is therefore due, as is substitution of this decision-making mechanism with another that serves to reinstate international justice. It is a prerequisite for restoring the United Nations' true role. Observation reveals that issues brought forth for General Assembly voting differ markedly in terms of result from what the UN Security Council decides through its five-member, authoritative forum. (Assembly decisions do not have binding power, nor are they supported by implementation measures.) The Assembly's declaration of Israel as a discriminatory nation is but witness to the infringements that the UN Security Council commits in its support of Israel, turning a blind eye to Israel's crimes against humanity in general and the Palestinian people in particular.

It has been proven that the world revolves around interests, with no room for principles. As such, rights must be maintained at all costs, and those who wish to exercise their rights should draw on all financial and moral support to defend them, remaining patient in the face of the difficulties they are bound to encounter. For divine laws prevail throughout all eras, and tyranny will be conquered no matter how many battles are lost. The world is a changing place. After one carries out their duties, wisely and properly preparing ground for encounter, hope remains great when one trusts in God.

SEVEN

Hizbullah's Future

Presence and Influence

As Hizbullah stepped into the scene of events through resistance activity, its verbal communications were initially geared towards the priority of military confrontation with Israel. In only a short while, Hizbullah succeeded in establishing a distinguished presence through atypical *jihad* operations at a time when political life was moribund in Lebanon given long years of civil strife.[1] International attention and Israeli focus turned towards the growth of this resistance movement and to its declared and open emergence in early 1985. A deluge of accusations of 'fundamentalism' and 'terrorism' poured onto the Party, and the Western media – as directed by intelligence bureaus – repainted the Party's steadfast and combative character as intolerable. A series of foreign and local declarations and analyses were broadcast referring to districts being controlled by Hizbullah and sealed from the outside world, where a new way of life, very different from the one the people were used to, was in practice; Hizbullah was also accused of a callousness that could not leave

---

1. Since the Party's establishment in 1982, and until the demise of General Aoun in 1990, Beirut and its suburbs were split between east and west. Internal armed conflict predominated. At the same time, Hizbullah's operations against Israeli occupation in the South and Western Bekaa also drew focus.

room for any sort of relationships, and a harshness demonstrated during confrontations with the Israeli army and its collaborators. Hizbullah's image was thus discernible only through military presence and activity, until it became evident to the majority of analysts as well as ordinary people that its presence was linked solely to resistance activity, not further, and that the Party was incapable of maintaining a presence without the fact of resistance. It was inherently assumed that Hizbullah would fall prey to any reconciliation in the region, and that the Party's existence was temporary, pertaining only to the exceptional phase of struggle with Israel.

The impression that Hizbullah was solely interested in resistance activity was also adopted by a good number of the Party's founding members, mainly on account of the circumstances surrounding its formation, the necessities of mobilization in the war against Israeli occupation and the Lebanese reality then prevalent. Substantial cultural, educational and practical effort was needed within circles of support in order to prepare for the Party's decision to take part in the 1992 parliamentary elections. General public outreach was required, as well as responses to recurring press questions and detailed clarifications regarding the initiation of contact or forging of relationships with various constituents and public figures.

The fieldwork undertaken within various communities and syndicates, as well as through election campaigns and Parliament, served, together with Hizbullah's speeches and addresses, to gradually unveil the Party's wide-ranging views, its perceptions of politics, and its various interests. These attributes are typical of any local political party in any country, the distinction being

Hizbullah's objectives and the particularity of resistance activity in Lebanon.

For Hizbullah is Islamic before being a resistance party, and its ideological commitment is what spurs it to refuse occupation and combat Israel. The Party follows a comprehensive life programme, its duties not being limited to one charge over another – although *jihad* receives ultimate priority. Hizbullah's stature and social commitment were realized through strong belief in such a programme, representing solutions for real issues. The Party achieved some of these solutions through occupational resistance – a successful experience marked by distinguished performance that rested on individual, group, social, political and military efforts, and that bore fruit through liberation on May 24, 2000, with an impact on the masses of supporters who continue to rally around Hizbullah's leadership.

On such a basis, the Party is no longer a concept presented for discussion, a programme that needs to win conviction. It has now transformed into a reality entrenched at the core of national events. The Party's membership was not limited to *jihad* or military groups, but expanded into the social, political and cultural fabric of the general population. It did not stop at the limits of Hizbullah partisans, but became a widespread movement drawing men, women and children and transcending confessional or district boundaries. If continuity is a function of a well-designed theoretical framework and programme, while the practical course is linked to popular outreach, then the existence of both of these assets to the Party should provide it with foundations for steadfast continuance. What, then, could hinder such progress after the Party has passed several vital tests,[1]

_____

1. These include the Amal-Hizbullah ordeal, the July 1993 Israeli aggression,

which many wagered to be the beginning of the end? Hizbullah has emerged stronger, and laid foundations for further presence and further influence.

As for recurrent US and Israeli threats, these are only pressure tactics imposed on the Party and its supporters – elements of psychological warfare, which if successful would provide desired results without any resort to action. However, this type of warfare fails when waged against an organization grounded in ideological principles, one that knows well the nature of its objectives and the prices to be paid in their pursuit. Such threats translated on many an occasion into massive assaults, aggression that could very well recur. But this is only part of the confrontation process, although the methods employed do not guarantee results for the belligerent, which could fall prey to its own trap. Despite all the tools of aggression it employed, Israel was forced to withdraw from much of occupied Lebanon. No one expects the toll of any further aggression to be modest, and additional sacrifices must be made. However, the rewards of determination are worthier. Moreover, as US and Israeli policies are based on forcefully imposing the facts and conditions of occupation, we are left with but two alternatives: surrender versus confrontation.

Hizbullah has made significant strides with respect to people's perceptions of the Party, and has enlarged its scope of regional and international relations. Significant change can be felt in terms of Western conduct *vis-à-vis* Hizbullah, this being a direct result of wise Party management, declarations and choices of relationships. However, one should not depend much on these indications or the extent of their permanence – despite their positive qualities underlining the Party's relative importance, and notwithstanding

the April 1996 Israeli aggression, and the May 2000 liberation victory.

the contrast between the now-perceived reality and the tainted picture of Hizbullah propagated in its early beginnings.

Two Pressure Alternatives

As the offensive launched against Hizbullah is great, the question of the Party's continuity will impose itself. Where Israeli aggression fails to eliminate Hizbullah's existence, developments in the region may lead to circumstances that present either or both of the following situations:

1. *The provocation of internal strife with the Lebanese army or with other local forces, which would call for political measures by the Lebanese government to eliminate the existence of the Party as a resistance movement.* Such an occurrence would not be presented as a transient problem. Rather, in order for desired results to be secured, the issue would emerge as a political stance that gradually introduces sufficient reasons for strife and eventually leads to the desired conflict. It would be impossible for this process to succeed, for the political standpoints of the Lebanese army and of influential local forces are in complete harmony with and support of resistance. Political alliances within Lebanon have been woven based on the stance that each of the local forces has taken against Israel. Such circumstances granted resistance activity a priority in terms of adoption and significance.

    Espousal of resistance as a priority is an issue closely linked to regional circumstances. The Syrian position, for instance, does not tolerate any events bearing the seeds of a clash with the Resistance movement in Lebanon. Add to this the mode of conduct adopted by the Resistance when dealing with internal issues, consideration for the local forces operating on Lebanese territory, and avoidance of any interference with state issues of security, and we come to understand the reasons for internal reassurance with respect to Hizbullah. There is no sufficient reason for any local constituents to contemplate confrontation with Hizbullah, as discord does not fulfil the objectives of these constituents and only renders service to Lebanon's foes.

2. *Exerting pressure on Syria to abandon its support of Hizbullah.* Given that Syria is the constituent that provides the political cover and catalyst for Hizbullah's continuity, lifting such cover would expose the Party, isolate it and render the Resistance vulnerable when attacked.

Chances of this probability coming to pass are also weak, owing to various factors: the calmly and gradually growing strategic relationship between Syria and Hizbullah; the numerous common viewpoints on regional developments; the credibility accruing to Hizbullah since the first invasion and until liberation; the concrete bilateral need for maintaining mutual cooperation in the face of challenges; and the seriousness of Syria's position with respect to Israeli occupation.

However grave and complicated the circumstances, options remain open for cooperation between Syria and Hizbullah, where all obstacles and dangers can be transcended with a high level of understanding and with the least damage. Under President Hafez al-Assad, Syria alone bore the brunt of defending the rights of both Lebanon and Palestine to resist occupation and refused to equate resistance with terrorism. President Bashar al-Assad refused any tarnishing of the Resistance and of its sound objectives, declaring his adherence to the options chosen by this movement without reservations. Such acts do not represent transient backing or even a mere declaration that rights need to be observed. Resistance has transformed into an integral part of permanent Syrian beliefs and politics, and this is sufficient assurance of continued support.

The Persistence of Resistance

The Resistance emerged as a reaction to Israeli occupation, which started in Palestine and stretched to other Arab regions. Therefore, as long as Israeli occupation continues to exist, resistance will persist, for resistance emanates from a fundamental belief in eliminating occupation and does not represent a temporary or haphazard condition. Since the repercussions of occupation have stretched to engulf the occupation of land, terrorizing of the region, displacement of the Palestinians, infringements on regional airspace and appropriation of the water resources of neighbouring countries such as Lebanon, then defiance of such occupation must continue. It must do so according to various methods according to the nature and geography of circumstances, the aim being to deprive Israel of the opportunity to achieve its goals while making use of the regional and international political realities to the best extent possible.

Diplomats and journalists have frequently posed the question:

what would become of Hizbullah if Lebanese land was completely liberated, and all captives and detainees were finally freed? Both Israel and the US look forward to an answer in order for their plans and programmes to be drawn accordingly. Hizbullah insists on not providing an answer to this question, for the issues are intertwined, and developments bring forth much change and many surprises. To every future possibility there is a different detailed answer, and as possibilities are numerous, so is the number of possible answers to this question. When a reply of any sort serves to fulfil an Israeli need, then it is better left unsaid. It is useless for Hizbullah to bind itself to any *a priori* positions that would later be subject to inquisition. Add to this the complexities and interplay amongst various developments on the Palestinian, Syrian and Lebanese fronts, and Israel's possible actions in the region; then the need for preparedness becomes paramount over the provision of any untimely statements.

Further, it is neither possible to delineate a unique channel for resistance operations, nor to limit their margin of manoeuvre to pre-specified methods. It is wiser to keep all choices and possibilities open. Planning future results and drawing alternative plans for their achievement might only expose such plans to enemy eyes. It is best to beleaguer the enemy and cause it to worry over what surprises may be in store.

It is unprecedented for the Israeli occupiers to adhere to any specific future decision. The Israelis are known to keep all options open until the last moment, to benefit from manoeuvring and juggling to the highest extent possible. The surface area and boundaries of Palestine are thus subject to negotiation, as is the nature of the Palestinian state. Similarly, the time needed to reach a conclusion to the Palestinian situation is directly linked to assurances with respect to Israeli security. Steps are taken one at a time, and the next step is determined only after complete achievement of the previous one. What, then, prompts us to conduct our planning any differently? Why should we not keep all of our options and avenues open?

Some pose the concern that such a train of thought by the Resistance is bound to trap Lebanon in a cycle of confrontation for a long period to come. These concerns are unfounded if measured against the core reasons for confrontation: aggression against Lebanon was initiated by Israel under the banner of assuring Israel's security, and has stretched over twenty-two years, during which Lebanon was lured time and again into a political accord that would provide the Israeli entity with its much-sought security guarantees. Occupational avarice did not cease with Israel's defeat and withdrawal in May 2000. Israel's lack of action in this regard is only a result of fear and concern about the level of preparedness or possible reactions of the Resistance. This situation only accentuates Lebanon's need to maintain this potential power for confronting possible dangers.

Furthermore, the repercussions of occupation are still felt by Lebanon in the form of the presence of refugees, continuous infringements on Lebanon's airspace and territorial waters, Israeli occupational presence in the Shebaa Farms, the retention of detainees in Israeli prisons, and continuous attempts to deny Lebanon the use of its own natural water resources. Irrespective of how Israel attempts, compulsively, to deal with some of these issues, it shall continue to represent a threat to Lebanon.

Lebanon and Palestine

Let us not forget our responsibility of supporting the Palestinian people, the association between the Palestinian cause and our own daily realities and how the Palestinian issue reflects on Lebanon and the entire region. This makes belief in liberation a unified, common cause. The manner of support is tied to many political and geographic factors.

The basic foundation for confronting imminent Israeli danger could be stated as follows: the Israeli entity represents a grave peril to Palestine and to the entire region, one that should be countered, confronted and resisted. All means should be employed in facing this hazard and every confrontational phase will be shaped by its needs and prevalent circumstances. The basis is to refuse the legitimacy of occupation and to adopt the persistence of resistance as a core pillar. There is no need to speak of any future steps. For every event there is discourse.

Does this mean that the Lebanese front will open for providing assistance to the Palestinian interior? This is a future question subject to the aforementioned treatment of future questions, the answer to which would only serve the purposes of Israel. No one can guarantee the extent of Israel's future aggression or the fronts that could open to battle or close, for this issue is not limited to a decision by the Resistance but is rather linked to a variety of regional developments that could open doors to all possibilities. Haste is unnecessary; the bottom line is to fortify and prepare for confrontation without falling prey to the intimidation of recurring menace, for such a menace is of a much lesser impact than the difficult and dangerous results of succumbing to Zionist pressures and demands.

Hizbullah believes in the duty of completely liberating all occupied Palestinian and other Arab lands, considering that the implantation of the Zionist entity in the region is illegitimate – a cancerous gland the existence of which is only a prelude to dominion over the entire region. The interests of the powers of hegemony and their support for this entity of extortion do not justify the subjugation of our entire region to the pre-planned occupational project. It is therefore not only a necessity but a legal, moral and human duty to do one's utmost for the sake of liberation. If the imposition of occupation should come by the power of armament and international support, then the defeat of the occupation should come through resistance and the pooling of all liberating forces in the region.

The road is not yet paved and results are not imminent, but hopes should remain high and efforts exerted for their fulfilment. All those pursuing the goal of liberation should seek cooperation, reinforcement and resistance of occupation.

Assuming that a reconciliation is achieved and new contours are drawn for Palestine and the region, Hizbullah would never sign in its favour, for such a settlement would only bind its adopters while leaving the state of Palestinian reality unchanged. Palestine is for the original Palestinians. But how would such a refusal be interpreted? This is a function of circumstances, and when refusal is itself the objective, preparation for its repercussions follows naturally. There is no need to hastily presume alternatives in this direction.

Hizbullah takes into consideration the objective circumstances surrounding it and includes them in its calculation of practical measures. However, the Party does not succumb to these circumstances, nor surrenders to their pressures. Hizbullah preserves well its beliefs and fundamental principles, and no interim tactics can affect these or present a sufficient price for their abandonment. The Party attempts to make best use of political circumstances in the quest for empowering the Resistance. The Resistance is not isolated from the environment in which it operates, but does not form part of any political deals or compromise scenarios that may serve to topple it or legitimize the fact of occupation. There is no alternative but to seek liberation, irrespective of time or difficulties. Of fundamental importance is trust in God, in oneself, in righteousness and patience – both during sacrifice and while anticipating results.

Future Expectations

When speaking of the future, it is imperative to evaluate the present, that which is the source of success or failure, continuity or abatement, growth or evanescence. The indicators need to support the future possibilities that present themselves.

Should we return to the founding systematic approach, we would find it in the Islamic programme – which has maintained a strong and effective course for over 1,400 years since its introduction – on the basis of which Hizbullah's path was launched clearly and steadfastly. Since affiliation is by default connected to a doctrinal and ideological upbringing of the individual as well as on Islamic conduct, and given that mobilization and edification form integral parts of the Party's course, doctrinal fundamentalism has thus raised a group that is closely attached to the Islamic approach, that which carries a self-sufficient potential for sustenance. Such a foundation was not limited to partisans, but included segments of society varied in age, activity and social status, as various a group as could be found.

Hizbullah did not seek to be a centripetal force that draws people irrespective of the Islamic programme. In fact, a strong mark recorded in favour of the Party was its success in being so effective in drawing recruits, delegating responsibilities, networking among groups, achieving a practical experience in the field of *jihad* – all interpretations of sound Islamic substance. This is what fortifies the Party's coherence and endurance in the face of challenge.

As the Party naturally developed, from weakness through to strength, minority to abundance and seclusion to cooperation, each of the various phases was actually founded on a strong structure despite the speed of growth, which is due most to the level of sacrifice and above all to God's support of His believing worshippers. A strong and well-founded structure cannot crumble through intimidation or hegemonic imposition.

Moreover, the people's need for a leader, the Party's achievements through raising issues and through successful practical experience, the dawn of hope it brought to a painfully depressed region taking the path of subdued surrender to Israel: all promise continuity for Hizbullah.

To clarify further, any danger to Hizbullah or to other similarly active forces mainly emanates from offensive decisions by the US and Israel. As for Israel's experience of imposing its boundaries and security requirements, this has failed to bear fruit despite fifty-four years of occupational presence in Palestine. The US experience, similar to that of Israel in terms of method and approach, is on a thorny track. The US was initially faced with a regional wave of hatred and was incapable of employing its authority for manoeuvring the tools of conflict. It was later uncovered in a direct terrorist act of hegemony. This is the US's hour of crisis, the beginnings of its demise.

While the US's objective of geopolitical change in the region was executed through a direct aggression on Iraq, the ensemble of Palestine, Lebanon and Syria form part of Israel's aggression targets, Israel poised to benefit from the repercussions of US aggression to fulfil its own projects.

But as Israel has failed to sustain itself unaided, the US therefore took on a supportive and offensive role. This book has already discussed Israel's inability to achieve stability; let us now discuss the US's overall plans to dominate the region, including the crippling of Hizbullah, without resort to possible Israeli action (now impeded) or a far-fetched but nevertheless possible US action.

The US is capable of spreading ruin and destruction in the region, of extorting the region's resources and attacking its regimes, parties and people. But this is only the power of the occupier, the colonizer, not an eternal stable power. On the other hand, our ability to integrate potential and resist is permanent and exponential. Our legitimate right is in itself a source of power, and our logic is sound. We are resolute about continuing on this course.

It would be erroneous to limit our thoughts to the present point in time or to the nature of circumstances surrounding us. Alongside the issue of Hizbullah's future, there is also the question concerning the future of the US, Israel, the region and the world in its entirety. Factors of change, pressure and political circumstances do not affect one entity only, and the indicators for success or failure are subject to principles that are applicable to all. Believers are distinguished by trust and confidence in God Almighty's support, a supplementary power that enables them to benefit from the consequences of belief, that which the aggressor does not enjoy.

Let us then free our spirits from the impression that our enemy is insurmountable, for there is a point of weakness to every foe and it is our duty to determine that point and lend it concentrated focus. Let us take on the duty of exerting every effort to preserve our independence and our principles. Let us realize that victory starts from within, and if we believe in God's victory, then it will surely come: *And We desired to show favour unto those who were oppressed on the earth, and to make them examples and to make them the inheritors.*[1] If we are confident that our actions but pave the way for Imam al-Mahdi's emergence[2] – he who will bring evenhandedness and justice after the reign of tyranny and despotism – then the future is quite promising. On God let the believers rely.

---

1. Surah no. 28, *al-Qasas*, verse no. 5.
2. All divine religions concur on the emergence of a saviour at the end of time. To Muslims, he is Imam al-Mahdi (PBUH). While Sunni Muslims consider that the Imam will be born a few years before the end of time, Shi'is believe he has been alive for a long time, but that people are not aware of his presence. He is the twelfth of the Infallible Imams, Muhammad bin al-Hassan, whose bloodline reaches up to Imam al-Hussein (PBUT). Born in 255 AH, Imam al-Mahdi will appear at the right time to rule with justice.

Hizbullah's 1992 Election Programme

In the Name of God, the Merciful, the Compassionate

Those who, if We give them power in the land, establish worship and pay the poor due and enjoin kindness and forbid iniquity. And with Allah rests the outcome of events.[1]

Feeling responsibility towards our oppressed people in Lebanon, their significant and critical needs and ignored living requirements;

And in light of a conscientious and profound reading of the country's deteriorating situation, the magnitude of international developments, their effect on the local scene and the necessity for directly confronting those conspiracies that are being woven to target our people, their lands, rights and dignities;

And based on an actual diagnosis of the scale of potential dangers, the opportunities possible for Islamists to assume an essential role in sidestepping those dangerous glides, and supporting the track chosen by the Islamic project and cordoning its steps;

And in harmony with the religious doctrines that guide us and serve as our reference and manual;

---

1. Surah no. 22, *al-Hajj*, verse 41.

And in appreciation of the necessity for an honest expression of our people's aspirations, pains, hopes and ambitions;

And in response to Hizbullah's attained credibility, the people's appreciation of Hizbullah's enormous sacrifices, of its quest for serving public interest and its strict adherence to principles;

We have resolved, trusting in God, to take part in the election process based on a comprehensive political programme for the achievement of which our candidates will expend every effort, calling our people to support such programme and follow up on its implementation.

To our dear noble Lebanese, our dear oppressed,

In this sensitive and dangerous phase of our wounded country's history, and amidst massive international changes that have stormed through states, toppled regimes and changed the face of politics and alliances, and at a time when the Zionist enemy still perches over a dear part of our land in South Lebanon and the Western Bekaa, painting the most horrible of assault and exploitation pictures, all while the project of hegemony as led by the US continues to bet on subduing Lebanon and the region, on achieving recognition of the Zionist entity, and on normalizing relations with it while diluting the identity of the region's civilizations and linking the fate of the people to the wheels of Western economies and industries, with all that entails in terms of confiscation of wealth, imposition of regimes and execution of programmes;

Under such circumstances, Lebanon prepares for its first parliamentary elections in twenty years, and the Lebanese people face a significant historical responsibility that has a bearing on every effort to determine the country's future political reality, be that at the level of the new order's structure or with respect to its roles, relations or functioning.

If such parliamentary elections are assumed to contribute to a new order whereby political sectarianism is rebutted and the foundations for a government representing the will of the Lebanese people are set, then Hizbullah's decision to participate in these elections alongside Party supporters and friends would, as always, rest on its permanent political and fundamental principles, those which the Party has continuously stood by and proved time and again through the blood of its martyrs, sacrifices of its freedom fighters, pains of its captives, detainees and wounded and grief of the oppressed and martyrs' families. The Party's best leaders and freedom fighters have made many a sacrifice to uphold these principles – the pinnacle being that offered by the leader of the Resistance, leading martyr al-Sayyed Abbas al-Moussawi, along with his wife and child, as well as Sheikh Ragheb Harb and Sheikh Abdel Karim Obeid, and many other heroes who have joined the train of martyrs and resistance fighters – expelling Zionist occupation on many occasions, imposing its defeat and unconditional retreat for the first time in the history of struggle against this enemy, redeeming the hope of victory to the nation, reinstating self-confidence, and providing Lebanon the breathing space to solve its dilemmas away from any direct tampering by the Zionist enemy.

These fundamentals have become an integral part of our people's mindset, turning into a daily *jihad* and political track that rests on two pivotal objectives:

1. To liberate Lebanon from Zionist occupation and from being an addendum to the powers of hegemony;

2. To abolish political sectarianism.

Hizbullah has thus far played a central role in achieving major strides on both counts. It is now imperative to cooperate with other devoted parties in order to complete the necessary steps towards the achievement of full liberation, the forging of internal peace on the basis of political concord that is furthest as could be from abominable sectarian biases or narrow confessional discriminations, and the cessation of any destructive warfare while objectively and responsibly dealing with its causes and repercussions, in such a way that no one is being deprived and no one is granted special privileges.

By launching this election campaign, Hizbullah is attempting to raise the level of political work in Lebanon either by espousing candidacy based on a programme that honestly and seriously treats the issues of the people, or through the Party's choice of candidates that has been furthest from being conditioned to narrow, sectarianism, that which has always nurtured divisions amongst our people. Hizbullah is bringing the contest to a higher level through its responsible adoption and continuous monitoring of the interests and issues of the people, as epitomized through giving credence to all things said, maintaining devotion in all actions or follow-ups undertaken and utmost concern for the rights of citizens, their support, defence of their land and safeguard of their pride and dignity.

Hizbullah's candidates harbour no ambitions to compete for power, nor to seek personal gain, but rather for abiding by a divine ordinance in front of God to whom belongs all might and majesty, in order to safeguard the land and ensure the interests of the faithful, and achieve those objectives for which the martyrs and freedom fighters have departed this life.

From this standpoint, Hizbullah's candidates will work seriously and diligently both inside and outside the Lebanese Parliament in order to achieve the following set of objectives:

At the General Political Level

First: Resistance

The protection of Lebanon, of its unity and cultural affinity with its Islamic and Arab vicinity, requires of us to adopt the path of resistance against Zionist occupation until all occupied soil is liberated. Such dedication is serious, especially after it has been proven that resistance activity is capable of collapsing the invaders' plans for imposing a political reality that is to the detriment of Lebanon and the Lebanese, and after it has been clarified that resistance is the only available choice for blocking enemy plans to forcibly exact concessions and resignations. Further, resistance is a natural prerequisite for liberation of the land, safeguard of its unity and that of its people.

This choice requires us to work towards the following:

1. Adherence to the choice itself, bearing responsibility for resistance fighters, facilitating their *jihad* paths and endeavours and ensuring formal, political and national adoption of their cause.

2. Putting in place the proper programmes for guiding recruits and efforts towards the goal of defending our people, creating a society of resistance and endurance at all levels, especially in South Lebanon and Western Bekaa.

3. Contribution of the government, represented by all its institutions and especially the military body in the quest for liberation and defence of the land and people.

4. Awarding serious and practical attention to the Occupied Zone, and undertaking the necessary and appropriate measures towards foiling the current Zionist project for achieving normalization of relations.

5. Urging the state to award attention to the welfare of families who have lost their head of household either to Israeli prisons or as a result of Israeli aggression, or where the head of household has been permanently incapacitated.

6. Attention to the plight of Lebanese detainees imprisoned by the Zionist enemy and its collaborators, and undertaking serious steps to achieve their freedom.

7. Rejection and condemnation of all efforts towards forming an accord with the Zionist entity that has been fundamentally erected on the basis of aggression and confiscation of other people's lands; consistently thwarting any efforts towards the normalization of relations with this entity.

Second: Abolition of Political Sectarianism

Political sectarianism is one of Lebanon's deep-seated ailments, responsible for the corrupt nature of Lebanon's current regime and for all the pains and political, cultural, social, security and developmental misfortunes that have plagued the country. It is the malignant point of entry for all powers of hegemony to voraciously tamper with Lebanon's destiny and the future of its people. One of the first goals for any Hizbullah candidate will be to expend every effort in collaboration with all loyalists in the quest to abolish such political sectarianism during the first constitutional government of this intended Parliament.

Third: The Electoral Law

Hizbullah calls for amendment of the electoral law in a manner that allows the Lebanese people to select their representatives from amongst the widest possible electoral base. This should be achieved through:

1. Considering the whole of Lebanon as one electoral district;
2. Consenting to a minimum age of eighteen years for the voting constituent.

Fourth: Political and Communication Freedoms

1. Guaranteeing freedom of creed and religious expression; respect for the sanctity of all divine religions;

2. Enactment of laws guaranteeing the freedom of political work;
3. Organization of media according to a framework that takes into account respect for public morals and general civility;
4. Respecting the rights of private media institutions to work independently, subject to the above constraint and without custodianship by the state or its representatives.

Fifth: Nationality

1. Enactment of a modern law awarding Lebanese nationality that transcends sectarian conditions and political favouritism and nationalizes those who deserve it, without discrimination or any sectarian or confessional extortion;
2. Awarding nationality to the Wadi Khaled Arabs and to refugees from the Seven Villages.

Sixth: The Displaced

1. Ensuring the complete return of all displaced;
2. Finding solutions for the displaced from the Occupied Zone;
3. Creating a comprehensive development plan for all areas where displaced persons currently reside.

Administrative, Social and Educational Levels

This programme urges the reform of the educational,

administrative, social and developmental infrastructure in Lebanon, in addition to stressing a number of persistent issues at these levels that require the collaboration of all powers for their resolution:

First: The Administrative Level

1. Abolition of employment based on sectarian or confessional grounds;
2. Adoption of qualifications as the basis for employee selection, as opposed to nepotism;
3. Training public administration employees regularly as per the requirements of technological advancement;
4. Empowering officials responsible for public administration auditing.

Second: The Development Level

1. Protection of local production and development of national resources through supporting both the industrial and agricultural sectors;
2. Opening export markets for these two sectors;
3. Developing infrastructure in oppressed regions and improving transportation, telecommunications, water and electricity utilities in these areas;
4. Subsidizing animal farming, fisheries and artisans;
5. Creation of job opportunities for all Lebanese people and protection of the labour force;
6. Rationalization of agricultural production, and the

institution of necessary centres, cooperatives and technical laboratories for the benefit of the sector;

7. Development of low-income regions; raising them to the level of the more prosperous Lebanese areas, following which balanced regional development should be pursued.

Third: The Educational and Cultural Level

1. Improving the state of public education at all levels and in all segments, especially as relates to vocational and technical education;

2. Making education obligatory at least up until the intermediate school level;

3. Supporting the Lebanese University and especially the schools of practical or applied studies;

4. Awarding special attention to distinguished students and encouraging research within the Lebanese University;

5. Rewriting the national history curriculum based on an objective syllabus, and taking into account the standards of Lebanon's cultural affiliation with its Islamic and Arab surroundings;

6. Safeguarding and encouraging religious education;

7. Reactivation of teaching schools for all teaching levels;

8. Improvement of the economic, educational and functional situation of public school teachers;

9. Translation of teaching programmes into Arabic.

Fourth: The Social Level

1. Enactment of laws concerning health and social-security

benefits and covering all Lebanese individuals, including the needs of free professionals, day labourers and the old-aged;

2. Reform of all institutions concerned with offering social or health services;

3. Building government hospitals and health centres across Lebanon.

Based on this programme, Hizbullah joins the Lebanese Parliament, taking it upon itself to represent the concerns of the oppressed in Lebanon, praying to God Almighty to accept this endeavour and support it as He sanctions, and hoping that victory, dignity and advancement will come to pass at the hands of Hizbullah's sons, loyalists and freedom fighters; God is all-hearing, all responsive.

Peace be upon you, God's grace and His blessings.

References

Religious References

Ali, Yusuf, *The Meaning of the Holy Quran*, Amana Books, 1998.

The Torah, Beirut, Dar al-Sharq, 1983.

bin Abi Taleb, Imam Ali, *Nahj al-Balagha*, Beirut, Dar al-Adwaa', 1986.

al-Aamili, al-Sheikh Muhammad bin Hassan al-Hurr, *Wasael al-Shi'a*, Beirut, Ahl el Bayt li Hia al-Turath, 1993.

Basha, Habib, et al, *Christian Teachings for the Catholic Church*, Lebanon, Police Library, 1999.

al-Haithami, Noureddine, *Mujamma' al-Zawa'ed*, Beirut, Dar al-Kutb al-Ilmiah, 1988.

ibn Hanbal, al-Imam Ahmad, *Musnad Ahmad*, Beirut, Dar Sader.

al-Hindi, Ala'eddine Ali al-Muttaqi, *Kanz al-Amaal*, Beirut, al-Risala, 1989.

al-Karki, al-Muhaqqiq al-Sheikh Ali bin al-Hussein. *Jame' al-Maqasid*, Qum, Ahl el Bayt Est., 1991.

Khamenei, Dar al-Imam Ali al-Husseini, *Ajjwibat al-Istiftaat*. Beirut, Dar al-Haq, 1995.

Khomeini, Dar al-Imam Ruhullah, *Tahrir al-Wasilah*, Beirut, Dar al-Ta'aruf, 1981.

al-Mufid, al-Sheikh Muhammad bin Muhammad bin al-Numan, *al-Amali*, Qum, Islamic Press, 1983.

Pickthall, M. M., *The Meaning of the Glorious Quran*, Amana Books, 1996.

Qassem, Naim, *Ashura, Madad (un) wa Hayat*, Beirut, Dar al-Hadi, 2002.

al-Rayshhary, Dar al-Sheikh Muhammadi, *Mizan Dar al-Hikmah*, Beirut, al-Dar al-Islamiah, 1985.

al-Sadr, al-Sayyed Muhammad Baqr, *Khilafat Dar al-Insan wa Shahadat Dar al-Anbiya'*, Beirut, Dar al-Ta'aruf, 1979.

al-Suddouk, Dar al-Sheikh Muhammad bin Ali Dar al-Qummi, *al-Khisal*, Qum.

al-Suddouk, Dar al-Sheikh Muhammad bin Ali Dar al-Qummi, *al-Amali*, Qum, al-Bi'tha, 1997.

al-Tabarsi, al-Sheikh Ahmad bin Ali, *al-Ihtijaj*, Najaf, Dar al-Nu'man, 1966.

al-Tabatabai, al-Allama Muhammad Hussein, *al-Mizan fi Tafseer al-Qur'an*, Beirut, al-A'lami, 1971.

Wehbe, Malek, *al-Faqih wal Sulta wal Umma*, Beirut, al-Dar al-Islamia, 2000.

Cultural, Political and Media Sources

Abu Subeih, Omran, *Daleel al-Mustawtanat al-Israelia fil Aradi al-Arabia al-Muhtallah* (The Guide to Israeli Settlements in Occupied Arab Lands), Amman, Dar al-Jaleel, 1991.

Ayed, Khalid, *al-Isti'mar al-Istitani lil Manatek al-Arabia al-Muhtallah Khilal 'Ahd al-Likud* (The Colonialist Settlements on Arab Occupied Lands During the Likud Years), Nicosia, The Institute for Palestinian Studies, 1986.

The Forum of Islamic Scholars (Tajammu' al-ulamaa' almuslimeen), *The April 17, 1983 Accord*, Beirut, Centre for Islamic Unity (Markaz al-wihda al-islamia), 1988.

Jaber, Munther Mahmoud, *al-Shareet al-Lubnani al-Muhtall* (Lebanon's Occupied Zone). Beirut, Institute for Palestinian Studies, 1999.

Hizbullah Central Media Unit, 'The Open Letter', Beirut, 1985.

Hizbullah Central Media Unit, *Amirat al-Thakira* (Biography of Martyr Scholar Abbas al-Moussawi), Beirut, 1993.

Hizbullah Central Media Unit, *Sijill al-Nour*, Beirut, 1998.

Hizbullah Central Media Unit, 'Hizbullah's Annual Record (1997)', Beirut, 2000.

Hizbullah Central Media Unit, *Safahat izz fi Kitab al-Umma*, Beirut, 1993–2000.

Hizbullah Central Media Unit, *Malaff al-Istitan fil Daffa al-Gharbiya*, Beirut, al-Hudhud.

Hizbullah Central Media Unit, *Mukawamat Watan was Iradat Shaab*, The Lebanese Brigade for the Confrontation of Israeli Occupation.

Hizbullah Central Media Unit, *Malhamat al-Majad* (Ballad of Glory). War media coverage by the Islamic Resistance.

Hussein, al-Sayyed Adnan, *al-Ihtilal al-Israeli fi Lubnan* (The Israeli Occupation of Lebanon), Beirut, Centre for Strategic Studies and Research, 1998.

al-Kayyali, Abdel Wahhab (et al), *Mawsouat al-Siyasa* (The Political Encyclopedia), Beirut, Arab Institute for Studies and Publications, 1994.

Khalil, Hussein, *al-Mufawadat al-Arabia al-Israelia* (Arab-Israeli Negotiations). Beirut, Bisan for Publishing and Distribution, 1993.

Khomeini, al-Imam Ruhullah, *al-Qadiyya al-Falastinia fi Kalam al-Imam al-Khomeini* (Speeches on the Palestinian cause), Tehran, Institution for Organizing and Spreading the Tradition of Imam Khomeini, 1995.

Khomeini, al-Imam Ruhullah, *Manhajiyat al-Thawra al-Islamiah* (The Islamic Revolution's Order), Tehran, Institution for Organizing and Spreading the Tradition of Imam Khomeini, 1996.

Khomeini, al-Imam Ruhullah, *al-Imam fi Muwajahat al-Suhyunia*, Tehran, Media Centre for the Fifth Commemoration of Victory, 1983.

Markaz al-Arabi lil Ma'alumat, *An-Nasr al-Mokhaddab*, published by *as-Safir*, Lebanon, 1st edn, 2006.

al-Sadr, al-Sayyed Muhammad Baqr, *Iqtisaduna* (Our Economy), Beirut, Dar al-Kitab al Lubnani, 1977.

Qassem, Naim, *Mujtama' al-Muqawama*, Dar al-Ma'arif al-Hikmiya, Beirut, 2nd edn, 2008.

Internet

The Official Site for the Palestinian Authority, www.sis.gov.ps

The National Palestinian Information Centre, www.pinic.org.ps

The Israeli Information Centre for Human Rights, Beitslim, www.btslem.org

Jihad al-Binaa, www.gihadbinaa.org

www.dirasat.net

http://www.domino.un.org/unispal.nsf

www.babil.info

Press Releases and Media Publications

The Social Martyrs' Institute, 'Continuous Giving to Preserve Custody', Lebanon.

The Islamic Health Organization, *Wa Tastamirr fi Khidmatikum* (And Continues to Serve You), Lebanon, 2002.

Imdad – The Islamic Philanthropic Committee, *al-Imdad* (Assistance), Lebanon, 1998.

Organization for the Wounded, *al-Jarha* (The Wounded), Lebanon, 2001.

The Consultative Centre for Studies and Documentation, *Harb al-Sa'at al-thalatha fi ansarya* (The Three-Hour War of Ansarya), Beirut, 1998.

The Consultative Centre for Studies and Documentation, *al-Harb al-Thamina fi Nissan 1996* (The Eighth War of April 1996), Beirut, 1996.

The Arab Committee for the Support of the Islamic Resistance, issue no. 7, Cairo, 2002.

The Palestinian Encyclopedia Committee, *Encyclopedia of Palestine – Special Studies*, vol. 1, 'Geographic Studies', Beirut, The Palestinian Encyclopedia Committee, 1990.

'The National Lebanese Accord', The National Lebanese Assembly, 1989.

Musalha, Noureddine, *Israel al-Kubra wal Filistinioun, Siyasat al-Tawassou', 1997–2000* (Greater Israel and the Palestinians, the Expansion Strategy 1997–2000), Beirut, Institute for Palestinian Studies, 2001.

Mustapha, Amine, *al-'Alakat al-Amerikia al-Sahyouniya* (American-Zionist Relations), Beirut, Dar al-Waseela, 1993.

Palestinian National Liberation Movement (Fatah); Nicholas Ziade (ed.), *Diary of Jerusalem*, 1981.

Heiberg, Marianne (et al), *Palestinian Society in Gaza, the West Bank and Arab Jerusalem, A Survey of Living Conditions*, Beirut, Institute for Palestinian Studies, 1994.

The Lebanese Ministry of Information, *South Lebanon, 1948–86, Facts and Numbers*, Beirut, Ministry Publications Unit, 1986.

Newspapers

Al-'Ahd (renamed *al-Intiqad*), vols 1–15; published by Hizbullah.

Al-Anwar (Lebanon)

Al-Hayat (pan-Arab)

Al-Immar wal-Iktissad (Lebanon)

As-Safir (Lebanon).

Al-Sharq (Lebanon)

Al-Sharq al-Awsat (pan-Arab)

Al-Mustaqbal (Lebanon)

An-Nahar (Lebanon).

Al-'Amal (Lebanon).

Ad-Diyar (Lebanon).

Al-Kifah al-Arabi (Lebanon).

Davar (Israel).

Other Sources

Hizbullah internal sources and resistance fighters.

The library and sources at the Consultative Centre for Studies and Documentation, Beirut.

Index

Subheadings are in page number order.